The Great Movie Series

EDITOR-IN-CHIEF:

James Robert Parish

ASSOCIATE EDITOR:

Florence Solomon

CONTRIBUTING EDITORS:

John Robert Cocchi

T. Allan Taylor

Richard Traubner

The Great Movie Series

SOUTH BRUNSWICK AND NEW YORK:
A. S. BARNES AND COMPANY

LONDON: THOMAS YOSELOFF LTD

© 1971 by A. S. Barnes and Co., Inc.
Library of Congress Catalogue Card Number: 78-146771

A. S. Barnes and Co., Inc.
Cranbury, New Jersey 08512

Thomas Yoseloff Ltd
108 New Bond Street
London W1Y OQX, England

ISBN 0-498-07847-7
Printed in the United States of America

to Kay Francis

Kay Francis (1905–1968)

CONTENTS

Abbreviations Utilized in the Book

AA: Allied Artists
Col.: Columbia
FC: Film Classics
MGM: Metro-Goldwyn-Mayer
Mon.: Monogram
PRC: Producers Releasing Corporation
Par.: Paramount

RKO: RKO Radio
Rep.: Republic
20th: Twentieth Century-Fox
UA: United Artists
Univ.: Universal
WB: Warner Bros.

ACKNOWLEDGMENTS

ALLIED ARTISTS (Al Steen)

ALAN G. BARBOUR

DeWITT BODEEN

LORAINE BURDICK

JANE DANZIGER

MRS. R. F. HASTINGS

KEN D. JONES

DOUG McCLELLAND

ALVIN H. MARILL

NORMAN MILLER

MOVIE POSTER SERVICE (Bob Smith)

DON SHAY

CHARLES SMITH

MRS. PETER SMITH

TWENTIETH CENTURY-FOX (Jay Remer)

UNITED ARTISTS (Mike Hutner)

and special thanks to Paul Myers and his staff for their cooperation at the Theatre Collection, Lincoln Center Library for the Performing Arts, New York City.

INTRODUCTION

One of the most consistently overlooked aspects of cinema history has been the series film, the staple product of most major Hollywood studios during the 1930s and 1940s. What *Marcus Welby, M.D., Ironsides,* and *Here's Lucy* are to contemporary television watchers, so *Dr. Christian, Ellery Queen* and *Blondie* were to the faithful throng of movie-goers of decades ago—or even of today with the *James Bond* theatrical film series. The series films hold a unique attraction for American audiences, who have always doted culturally on any commodity that comes in clusters—whether movies with continuing characters and situations, the collected works of W. Somerset Maugham, the ever-living presence of *As The World Turns,* or Kelloggs' Variety Pak. Thus it is no wonder that most television markets in America constantly feature *Sherlock Holmes Theatre, East Side Comedies* ("The Bowery Boys"), *Charlie Chan Theatre,* etc. It is reassuring for audiences to have a recurring group of familiar performers going through their paces in well-explored plot routines in expected genres. As Snoopy might say: "Happiness is having a Tom Conway *Falcon* film to watch every Sunday night."

Mention the term *film series* and most people are likely to confuse the format with *serials* (action chapter plays which conclude each 13- to 20-minute episode with a hopefully rousing anticlimax, e.g. *Daredevils of the Red Circle* [1939], *Don Winslow of the Coast Guard* [1943]; or with *sequels* (a self contained film that spawns continuation follow-up films, dealing with an established set of characters in a carry-over progression of events, e.g. *Four Daughters* [1938] to *Four Wives* [1939] to *Four Mothers* [1941], *The Robe* [1953] to *Demetrius and the Gladiators* [1954], *Planet of the Apes* [1968] to *Beneath the Planet of the Apes* [1970]). In contrast, a pure-breed *series* is built on a basic set of characters, governed by a particular backlog of events, which control, but do not hinder, the future tide of their happenings. Thus *Boston Blackie* will always be an ex-crook turned alleged good guy, he will usually have his pal Runt around, and will generally be harassed by Inspector Farraday; but unlike a true sequel film, an individual entry in the series may change its locales and supplementary cast of characters at will, with just the lead series' figures and their characterizations remaining constant.

When the Depression hit full swing in the early 1930s, and Hollywood needed more gimmicks than bank night to lure viewers back into the theaters, the double-bill feature films became standard practice in the United States. This situation led the studios down many paths to satisfy their quota agreements with exhibitors. One of the easiest solutions was to prepare a basic property, which if it caught the public's fancy, could be churned out in rehash form in the guise of a series. And the studio system was ripe for such a practice—with contract players in abundance, newly signed actors needing a safe, obscure testing ground (it is amazing how many series films went unreviewed by critics in most major cities!), staff producers/writers/directors working by the year rather than by the individual picture; it was a marvelous way to utilize overworked house talent and keep the exhibitor well stocked with product for showing. And most series films were so inexpensive to produce—a change of background could be accomplished by merely using the trusty rear projection screen, and pronto Charlie Chan or The Saint would be in a new city or country—and less discriminating audiences of the day did not mind very much, if at all.

Series films have encompassed all genres of movies: slapstick farce, *Blondie;* detective stories, *Philo Vance;* westerns, *Hopalong Cassidy;* jungle adventure, *Tarzan;* domestic comedy, *Andy Hardy;* hospital drama, *Dr. Kildare;* super spy yarns, *Matt Helm,* or animal fare, *Francis, the Talking Mule.* Since the series films were geared for the action-family-matinee film trade, few of the properties were focused on female stars: *Maisie, Blondie,* and *Ma and Pa Kettle* were the exceptions to the rule of feeding the audiences with plenty of he-man action, adventure, and slapstick.

The quality of theatrical film series varied considerably: Columbia Pictures, the prolific home of the mini-budgeted series, ground out a vast number of such properties, as cheaply and quickly as possible . . . and *Ellery Queen, Boston Blackie,* and *Blondie* showed the rush. In contrast, a studio such as MGM could hastily yet efficiently mass-produce a series, and the result would be entirely different, e.g. *Maisie, The Thin Man* or *Dr. Kildare.* The MGM Tarzan films were generally carefully produced entries with great effort and expense put into the finished product. Despite the differences in quality, the patina of each series seemed to work for the property, building a peculiar yet effective flavor. One could hardly imagine a lavishly-turned-out *Bowery Boys* film to be fun, or trying to enjoy a *James Bond* epic denuded of Ken Adams's set decoration, John Barry's music, or John Stears's special effects.

Seeing the canon of a film series in retrospect is always educational viewing, to check the progress of fledgling actors making their initial bids for cinema stardom (such as Lana Turner in *Andy Hardy,* Lloyd Bridges in *Boston Blackie,* or Clint Eastwood in *Francis the Talking Mule*) or observing established cinema stars in the twilight of their careers: e.g. Warner Baxter in *The Crime Doctor* or Warren William in *The Lone Wolf.* Because of their general low-budget quality, very rarely did certain calibers of performers ever play in series films: young stage actors turning to Hollywood in the late 1920s and early 1930s, such as James Cagney, Kay Francis, Fredric March, and Joan Blondell, never were required to appear in series, although Miss Blondell came the closest at Warner Bros. with the visually exciting *Gold Diggers* films.

Big name specialty players from vaudeville and radio who invaded Hollywood in the early 1930s, like Ed Wynn, Kate Smith, and Ethel Merman, were not put into series movies, although with the sad results of their odd cinema careers, they might have done better in such a showcase. (Lesser show business personalities did make the series route in the late 1930s and 1940s; among them were country and western singers like the Jim Wakely Trio in *Hopalong Cassidy* or magician John Calvert in *The Falcon.*

It was always easy to trace the studio's and the public's reception to a given film series. If the lead actor could easily be replaced (i.e. William Gargan for Ralph Bellamy in *Ellery Queen* in contrast to substitute Johnny Weissmullers and Maureen O'Sullivans in *Tarzan*) , then it was clearly a property easily dispensable with by all concerned. As soon as the series dropped the lead character's name from the film's title, then it was a safe assumption that the public (and the exhibitors) was tiring of the property and needed to be coaxed (misled?) into seeing further installments—e.g., *Blondie,* which in 1943 suddenly tagged its biannual installments *It's A Great Life* and *Footlight Glamour,* or *Dr. Kildare* (which properly should have been titled *Dr. Gillespie*) ended its series with three disguised entries: *Three Men In White, Between Two Women,* and *Dark Delusion.* And another sure key that a series's demise was imminent would be the sell-off of a property from one studio to another—e.g., *The Falcon* going from RKO to Film Classics, or the general decline of *Tarzan* after its departure from the MGM stable.

The most enduring theatrical film series to date has been Tarzan—still as active today as when it made its cinema debut in 1918. The most prolific series property has been *Hopalong Cassidy,* in which William Boyd appeared in all of the 66 productions. In contrast was the short-lived but very profitable *Matt Helm,* which had Dean Martin on the move for only four installments.

As financial conditions spurred the factory mass production of series in the 1930s and 1940s, so the general public acceptance of television in the late 1940s caused havoc in Hollywood and saw the eventual end of the double-bill system at most cinemas. And as the *Matt Helm* series did prove and *James Bond* is now undergoing, it is increasingly financially difficult to better a previous series entry, without exorbitant costs erasing all possible profit margins. To whet the more discriminating filmgoer's taste is far more troublesome than it was

25 years ago. Thus, the film series in America has almost disappeared, and moved over to the video media for another stand. (In England, where costs have not yet hit the American high, and the public is more indulgent of just-plain-entertainment, the late 1950s and 1960s saw the advent of the *Carry On*, *Miss Marple*, and *Doctor At* series.

In presenting within this book a representative grouping of American-made sound film series (which are or will be shown on television—not to mention art house reissue) , many intriguing properties had to be put aside: e.g. *The Three Mesquiteers*, *Joe Palooka*, *Mexican Spitfire*, *The Jones Family*, *Henry Aldrich*, *The Cisco Kid*, *Scattergood Baines*, *Dick Tracy*, *Rusty*, *The Whistler*, *Bulldog Drummond*, *The Higgens Family*, etc.— perhaps a sequel to this series volume will remedy that.

James Robert Parish
Brooklyn Heights, N.Y.

The Great Movie Series

ANDY HARDY

In 1937, MGM, then under the aegis of studio mogul Louis B. Mayer, filmed an unpretentious domestic comedy *A Family Affair* based on the Broadway play *Skidding* (1928) by Aurania Rouveyrol. The pleasant enough black and white programmer revolved around Judge James Hardy (Lionel Barrymore), his wife (Spring Byington), Aunt Milly (Sarah Haden), and the three Hardy children (Julie Haydon, Mickey Rooney, and Cecilia Parker). The storyline, with marked similarities to Eugene O'Neill's *Ah! Wilderness,* dealt with the idyllic trials and tribulations of a normal middle-class American family living in Carvel, a small midwestern town. With widespread audience acceptance, Mayer promptly decided to turn the one-shot film into a new series. In the next two decades, sixteen additional "Hardy Family" segments were churned out, bringing $25 million profit to Metro. Most of the entries were efficiently spewn forth by George B. Seitz's economy unit. The films served as an excellent training ground for such studio starlets as Judy Garland, Kathryn Grayson, Lana Turner, Donna Reed and Esther Williams. (Between the nominal end of the *Andy Hardy* films in 1946 and the property's finale in 1958 with *Andy Hardy Comes Home* a radio series appeared with Mickey Rooney and Lewis Stone recreating their film roles.)

Andy Hardy films were geared to have strong but restrained humor, set in a sensible and warm atmosphere. Slapstick and wisecracks were carefully avoided in the homey series. Judge Hardy's success with his children was due to his ability to be a guide, philosopher, and friend. In his heart to heart, fireside talks, he moralized without being intolerably sentimental or sententious. His children presented willing subjects for his wisdom: Marian was characterized as impressionable, eager for all the social climbing and material benefits so much a part of American society. Andy with his attractive-ugly face, unmodulated voice, filled with awkward gestures, and bubbling with excitement over trifles was the ideal 1930s and 1940s young man of the family. At times, Andy could be swelled with self pride, condescending and swaggering, but eventually he would come to grips with himself. Mrs. Hardy was seen as consistently loyal and faithful, always placid and the complete mother. Aunt Milly, the slightly sad spinster, was filled with good-natured helpfulness, and just a twinge of busybodyness. The teamwork of the repertory group among the Hardy clan was hard to beat.

Starring as wholesome, engaging, youthful Andy Hardy (whose favorite words were: "gosh," "gee," and "swell") Mickey Rooney rose to being MGM's top star in the early 1940s, and became a leading boxoffice favorite. Rooney (Joe Yule, Jr.) was born September 23, 1920, in Brooklyn, the son of vaudeville performing parents. He made his official stage debut at fifteen months. At age four he made his first film, *Not to be Trusted*, playing a midget, and his initial feature was *Orchids and Ermine* (1927). By the late 1920s he had migrated to Hollywood and had landed the lead role in the Mickey McGuire short subjects (which lasted through 86 episodes). After freelancing in assorted minor roles at a variety of Hollywood studios, he became an MGM player in 1934 (having made his first sound feature at that studio in 1932 —*Emma*) with such roles as *Manhattan Melo-*

drama (1934) and *Ah! Wilderness* (1935) to his credit. He was usually cast as the male star as a child. As Puck in *A Midsummer Night's Dream* (1935) he rose to prominence, with other noteworthy parts in *Captains Courageous* (1937), *Young Tom Edison* (1940), *Babes on Broadway* (1941), *Human Comedy* (1943), *National Velvet* (1944), showing his versatility as a straight actor or a dancer-singer-musician. After World War II, in which he served in the armed forces, the $150,000 a year actor, finished out his MGM contract, and then began freelancing again, in such films as *The Big Wheel* (1949) and *Off Limits* (1953). By the mid-1950s, he was no longer in popular demand and was reduced to a leading character actor, appearing in *The Bridges at Toko-Ri* (1954), and *Francis in the Haunted House* (1956). For his role in *The Bold and the Brave* (1956) he was nominated for a best supporting actor Oscar. In the 1960s, he was seen in *Private Lives of Adam and Eve* (1960), *Breakfast at Tiffany's* (1961), *Requiem for a Heavyweight* (1962), *The Extraordinary Seaman* (1968), *The Comic* (1969) and *The Cockeyed Cowboys of Calico County* (1970) his 112th feature to date. Besides appearing in his own television series and guest-starring on variety programs, he has made a number of striking stabs at dramatics, his most famous role in *The Comedian* (1957). The 5'3" actor has been married seven times: to Ava Gardner, Betty Jane Rase, Martha Vickers, Elaine Mahnken, Barbara Thomasen, Margaret Lane, and Carolyn Hockett, and he has six children. Rooney recently toured the United States in such stock shows as *George M* and plays the nightclub circuit.

A Family Affair revolved around Judge Hardy's efforts to be reelected to office, while opposing a new public works program in Carvel. As the family and town arbiter, he found time to clarify the facts behind his older daughter's separation from her husband, which threatened to cause a minor scandal. After this entry, MGM recast some of the major roles in the Hardy family. Lewis Stone and Fay Holden became Judge and Mrs. Hardy, and one of the two daughters Judy (Julie Haydon) disappeared from the storyline. They along with Rooney, Sara Haden (save for two episodes in which Betty Ross Clarke was Aunt Milly Forrest), Ann Rutherford (as high minded, ever loyal girl friend Polly Benedict), George Breakston (as Andy's friend Beezy) comprised the *Andy Hardy* repertory group.

In *You're Only Young Once* the family goes to Santa Catalina for a vacation. Both Marian, age 19, and Andy, age 16, fall in love, and it is up to Judge Hardy to retrieve the kids from their summer romance—which he does in a restrained, tactful manner. An epilogue to the film suggested that other domestic problems would be cropping up that he, Judge Hardy, would have to contend with in forthcoming years. *Judge Hardy's Children* revolves around the family's stay in Washington, D.C., where the Judge is serving as chairman of a special committee. Marian's head is turned by the rich social life, and Andy succumbs to the charms of a young French girl. Once again, it is up to the good Judge to salvage the situation.

Love Finds Andy Hardy shows America's favorite youth at the vacillating age of prime adolescence. He is in love with two girls at once, and a third, Betsy Booth (Judy Garland), helps him out. The first-rate script balances the humor of Andy's lovelorn courtships with a bit of mild drama when Mrs. Hardy's mother has a serious illness. (Garland sings, "Meet the Beat of My Heart," "It Never Rains but It Pours," and "In Between"). *Out West with the Hardy's"* is set into motion when the Judge's rancher friend has water rights problems, and the Judge takes his family along when he goes there to solve the legal dispute. Before the climax, Andy learns humility and some common sense, and Marian fortunately falls out of love with her cowboy idol.

The Hardys Ride High finds the middle-class family suddenly legatees to a large fortune, and they take possession of a palatial mansion. The plot is built around the way the family reacts to their new social status. A particularly good moment of pathos is Aunt Milly's realization that a new casual acquaintance does not want to marry her. *Andy Hardy Gets Spring Fever* has Andy falling in love with his high school dramatics teacher, and suffering all the agonies of first love. He writes a play which is presented by his classmates, with Andy in the lead role. It takes all the Judge's wisdom plus the teacher's cooperation to bring Andy down to earth again. *Judge Hardy and Son* focuses on the Judge's attempt to help an elderly couple in need of financial assistance. In the midst of the Hardys' involvement with these people, Mrs. Hardy is stricken with pneumonia. By the finale, the Hardys have achieved a better perspective on life.

In *Andy Hardy Meets Debutante*, Andy falls in love with the photo of a New York society girl.

When the Judge makes a business trip to Manhattan, Andy tags along. Besides pursuing his romantic interest, Andy tries to crash society's 400. Once again Betsy Booth aids her platonic love. The badly disillusioned Andy gets a man-to-man talk from the Judge on democracy and all ends well. (Garland sings "I'm Nobody's Baby" and "Alone.") *Andy Hardy's Private Secretary* finds Andy, now about to graduate from Carvel High, too big for his boots. As the school big shot, he makes poor girl Kathryn Land (Kathryn Grayson) his secretary to handle data on his extracurricular high school activities. Andy flunks his English examination and almost fails to graduate, before he has a rude awakening to the facts of life. (Grayson sings "Lucia" and Strauss's "Voices of Spring.")

Life Begins for Andy Hardy has Andy, now graduated from high school, and wanting to earn his own living, despite the Judge's request that he go to college. Andy moves to New York for a month to see if he can make good. He works at a stock broker's office, falls for the telephone operator there, and only after Betsy Booth and the Judge intervene, does Andy realize he knows nothing and that he had better go to college. (Garland recorded four songs for the film, but none were used.) *The Courtship of Andy Hardy* gets underway when the Judge, who is handling a local marital separation case, asks Andy to help the client's daughter Melodie (Donna Reed) become more socially popular at school. Andy is a bit patronizing in his assistance, until Melodie falls in love with Andy and he becomes a transformed person.

Andy Hardy's Double Life has the 18-year-old youth off to college, where he discovers that girls take him seriously. Due to financial and academic jams, he has his first big split with his father. *Andy Hardy's Blonde Trouble* revolves around Andy's romantic attachments in college, and his troublesome friendship with bubbling twins Lee and Lyn Walker (Lee and Lyn Wilde), which eventually leads him into a bad scrape with the Dean (Herbert Marshall). The Judge arrives just in time for a campus visit and sets things straight. *Love Laughs at Andy Hardy* has Andy, returned from World War II, going back to Wainwright College as the perennial freshman, involved in juvenile anguish over a mistaken romance.

Andy Hardy Comes Home shows the adult Andy, now a top executive at a leading California aircraft company, returning to Carvel with his wife and children, hoping to scout for a missile factory site for his employers. He becomes embroiled with the town council and folk, until matters are reconciled and the now grateful community asks him to run for the Judgeship, once held by his late father. (Montage sequences were utilized from *Love Finds Andy Hardy* and *Andy Hardy's Double Life*.)

Contemporary audiences would be hard put to accept the ultra good, apple pie virtues of Judge Hardy and family. The unsophisticated, naive Andy is enough to try most people's patience, accentuated by the unerring wisdom of Judge Hardy and the incredible patience of his saintly wife. The failure of the MGM scripters to deal with the then contemporary social problems and realities was amazing. Not until the fifteenth episode in 1946 was there any real mention of World War II (done mostly as a concession to the well publicized fact that Rooney had been away from Hollywood for three years serving in the Army). As with the other established film series, once the characteristics of the main players became firmly entrenched, their reactions to any set of events was all too predictable, and the situations became too often the mixture as before.

Despite the Metro screenwriters shipping the Hardys frequently outside of Carvel's town limits to other destinations (the West, New York, Washington, D.C., and Wainwright College), the folksy homeside influence was always there. At the slightest infraction of social norms, Judge Hardy would be ready with his fatherly talks, and Andy, gulping in silent confusion and realization of his errors, would be a reformed boy-man. The fact that the 20-year-old-plus Rooney was portraying a teenager bothered audiences little, until *Love Laughs at Andy Hardy*, when the camera unerringly showed that Rooney was no longer a youth in body, let alone in heart. Nevertheless, filmgoing audiences of the day were extremely taken with the *Andy Hardy* format, its stock company of players, and the whole never-never land of Carvel, U.S.A.

Lionel Barrymore, Rooney, Julie Haydon, Cecelia Parker, Spring Byington, Sara Haden, Eric Linden. (A Family Affair)

Rooney and Lana Turner. (Love Finds Andy Hardy)

Rooney, Parker, Gordon Jones, Virginia Weidler.
(Out West with the Hardys)

Truman Bradley and Rooney. **(The Hardys Ride High)**

Rooney, Ann Rutherford, Stone, Fay Holden, Sara Haden, Cecelia Parker. (Judge Hardy and Son)

Rooney and Ann Rutherford. (. . . Gets Spring Fever)

Lewis Stone, Cecelia Parker, Fay Holden, Sara Haden,
Mickey Rooney, Judy Garland. (Andy Hardy Meets
Debutante)

*Sara Haden, Stone, Fay Holden, Rooney, Cecelia
Parker* (. . . Meets Debutante)

Rooney and Stone (. . . Meets Debutante)

Judy Garland and Rooney. (Life Begins for . . .)

Rooney and Stone (. . .'s Private Secretary)

*Parker, Rooney, Sara Haden, Fay Holden, Stone.
(The Courtship of . . .)*

*Esther Williams, Rooney, Ann Rutherford. (. . .'s
Double Life)*

Bonita Granville, Rooney, Lee Wilde. (. . .'s Blonde Trouble)

Rooney and Bonita Granville. (Love Laughs at . . .)

ANDY HARDY
A FAMILY AFFAIR (MGM, 1937) 69 M.

Producer, Lucien Hubbard, Samuel Marx; director, George B. Seitz; author, Aurania Rouverol; screenplay, Kay Van Riper; camera, Lester White; editor, George Boemler.

Judge Hardy	Lionel Barrymore
Mrs. Hardy	Spring Byington
Marian Hardy	Cecilia Parker
Andy Hardy	Mickey Rooney
Joan Hardy	Julie Haydon
Wayne Trenton	Eric Linden
Frank Redmond	Charley Grapewin
Bill Martin	Allen Vincent
Aunt Milly	Sara Haden
Polly	Margaret Marquis
Hoyt Wells	Selmer Jackson
Oscar Stubbins	Harlan Briggs

YOU'RE ONLY YOUNG ONCE (MGM, 1938) 78 M.

Director, George B. Seitz; author, Aurania Rouverol; screenplay, Kay Van Riper; camera, Lester White; editor, Adrienne Fazan.

Judge Hardy	Lewis Stone
Andy Hardy	Mickey Rooney
Marian Hardy	Cecilia Parker
Mrs. Hardy	Fay Holden
Frank Redmond	Frank Craven
Polly Benedict	Ann Rutherford
Jerry Lane	Eleanor Lynn
Bill Rand	Ted Pearson
Aunt Milly	Sara Haden
Hoyt Wells	Selmer Jackson
Captain Swenson	Charles Judels
Sheriff	Oscar O'Shea

JUDGE HARDY'S CHILDREN (MGM, 1938) 78 M.

Director, George B. Seitz; screenplay, Kay Van Riper; camera, Lester White; editor, Ben Lewis.

Judge Hardy	Lewis Stone
Andy Hardy	Mickey Rooney
Marian Hardy	Cecilia Parker
Mrs. Hardy	Fay Holden
Polly Benedict	Ann Rutherford
Aunt Milly	Betsy Ross Clarke
Wayne Trenton	Robert Whitney
Margaret Bee	Ruth Hussey
Steve Prentiss	Leonard Penn
Suzanne Cortot	Jacqueline Laurent
Miss Budge	Janet Beecher
Radio Announcer	Boyd Crawford
J. O. Harper	Don Douglas
Peniwill	Edward Earle

LOVE FINDS ANDY HARDY (MGM, 1938) 90 M.

Director, George B. Seitz; screenplay, William Ludwig; camera, Lester White; editor, Ben Lewis.

Judge Hardy	Lewis Stone
Andy Hardy	Mickey Rooney
Betsy Booth	Judy Garland
Marian Hardy	Cecilia Parker
Mrs. Hardy	Fay Holden
Polly Benedict	Ann Rutherford
Aunt Milly	Betsy Ross Clarke
Cynthia Potter	Lana Turner
Augusta	Marie Blake
Dennis Hunt	Don Castle
Jimmy MacMahon	Gene Reynolds
Mrs. Tompkins	Mary Howard
Bill Collector	Frank Darien
Beezy	George Breakston

OUT WEST WITH THE HARDYS (MGM, 1938) 90 M.

Director, George B. Seitz; screenplay, Kay Van Riper, Agnes Christine Johnston, William Ludwig; camera, Lester White; editor, Ben Lewis.

Judge Hardy	Lewis Stone
Andy Hardy	Mickey Rooney
Marian Hardy	Cecilia Parker
Polly Benedict	Ann Rutherford
Mrs. Hardy	Fay Holden
Aunt Milly	Sara Haden
Dennis Hunt	Don Castle
Jake Holt	Virginia Weidler
Ray Holt	Gordon Jones
Bill Northcote	Ralph Morgan
Dora Northcote	Nana Bryant
H. R. Bruxton	Thurston Hall
Aldrich Brown	Tom Neal

THE HARDYS RIDE HIGH (MGM, 1939) 81 M.

Director, George B. Seitz; screenplay, Kay Van Riper, Agnes C. Johnson, William Ludwig; camera, John Seitz; editor, Ben Lewis.

Judge Hardy	Lewis Stone
Andy Hardy	Mickey Rooney
Marian Hardy	Cecilia Parker
Polly Benedict	Ann Rutherford
Emily Hardy	Fay Holden
Aunt Milly Forrest	Sara Haden
Dennis Hunt	Don Castle
Phillip Westcott	John King
Consuela McNish	Virginia Grey
Terry B. Archer	Minor Watson
Dobbs	Halliwell Hobbes
Jonas	George Irving
Saleswoman (Miss Booth)	Aileen Pringle

ANDY HARDY GETS SPRING FEVER (MGM, 1939) 85 M.

Director, W. S. Van Dyke II; screenplay, Kay Van Riper; camera, Lester White; editor, Ben Lewis.

Judge Hardy	Lewis Stone
Andy Hardy	Mickey Rooney

Marian Hardy	Cecilia Parker
Polly Benedict	Ann Rutherford
Mrs. Hardy	Fay Holden
Aunt Milly	Sara Haden
Rose Meredith	Helen Gilbert
Stickin' Plaster	
(Harmon Higginbotham, Jr.)	Terry Kilburn
Beezy	George Breakston
Sidney Miller	Sidney Miller
Tommy	Charles Peck
James Willet	Stanley Andrews
Mark Hansen	Byron Foulger
Lt. Charles Copley	Robert Kent
Member of Audience	Maurice Costello

JUDGE HARDY AND SON (MGM, 1939) 90 M.

Director, George B. Seitz; screenplay, Carey Wilson; art director, Cedric Gibbons; music, David Snell; camera, Lester White; editor, Ben Lewis.

Judge Hardy	Lewis Stone
Andy Hardy	Mickey Rooney
Marian Hardy	Cecilia Parker
Polly Benedict	Ann Rutherford
Mrs. Hardy	Fay Holden
Aunt Milly	Sara Haden
Mrs. Volduzzi	Maria Ouspenskaya
Euphrasia Clark	June Preisser
Elvie Norton	Martha O'Driscoll
Mrs. Norton	Leona Maricle
Clarabelle Lee	Margaret Early
Mr. Volduzzi	Egon Brecher
Nurse Trowbridge	Edna Holland
Interne	Jack Mulhall

ANDY HARDY MEETS DEBUTANTE (MGM, 1940) 89 M.

Director, George B. Seitz; screenplay, Annalee Whitmore, Thomas Seller; camera, Sidney Wagner, Charles Lawton; editor, Harold F. Kress.

Andy Hardy	Mickey Rooney
Judge Hardy	Lewis Stone
Mrs. Hardy	Fay Holden
Marian Hardy	Cecilia Parker
Betsy Booth	Judy Garland
Aunt Milly	Sara Haden
Polly Benedict	Ann Rutherford
Aldrich Brown	Tom Neal
Daphne Fowler	Diana Lewis
Beezy	George Breakston
Mr. Carrillo	Cy Kendall
Underwood	George Lessey
Mr. Benedict	Addison Richards

ANDY HARDY'S PRIVATE SECRETARY (MGM, 1941) 101 M.

Director, George B. Seitz; screenplay, Jane Murfin, Harry Ruskin; camera, Lester White; editor, Elmo Vernon.

Andy Hardy	Mickey Rooney

Judge Hardy	Lewis Stone
Mrs. Hardy	Fay Holden
Steven Land	Ian Hunter
Aunt Milly	Sara Haden
Polly Benedict	Ann Rutherford
Kathryn Land	Kathryn Grayson
Harry Land	Todd Karns
Mr. Davis	John Dilson
George Benedict	Addison Richards
Beezy	George Breakston
Clarabelle Lee	Margaret Early
Jimmy MacMahon	Gene Reynolds
Mr. Harper	Donald Douglas

LIFE BEGINS FOR ANDY HARDY (MGM, 1941) 100 M.

Director, George B. Seitz; screenplay, Agnes Christine Johnson; art director, Cedric Gibbons; music director, Georgie Stoll; camera, Lester White; editor, Elmo Vernon.

Andy Hardy	Mickey Rooney
Judge Hardy	Lewis Stone
Betsy Booth	Judy Garland
Mrs. Hardy	Fay Holden
Polly Benedict	Ann Rutherford
Aunt Milly	Sara Haden
Jennitt Hicks	Patricia Dane
Jimmy Frobisher	Ray McDonald
Beezy	George Breakston
Dr. Waggoner	Pierre Watkin
Dr. Gallagher	Ralph Byrd
Dr. Storfen	Purnell Pratt

THE COURTSHIP OF ANDY HARDY (MGM, 1942) 93 M.

Director, George B. Seitz; screenplay, Agnes Christine Johnson; camera, Lester White; editor, Elmo Vernon.

Andy Hardy	Mickey Rooney
Judge Hardy	Lewis Stone
Mrs. Emily Hardy	Fay Holden
Marian Hardy	Cecilia Parker
Polly Benedict	Ann Rutherford
Aunt Milly	Sara Haden
Melodie Nesbit	Donna Reed
Jeff Willis	William Lundigan
Janet Nesbit	Frieda Inescort
Clarence O. Nesbit	Harvey Stephens
Beezy	George Breakston
Harry Land	Todd Karns
Red	Frank Coghlan, Jr.

ANDY HARDY'S DOUBLE LIFE (MGM, 1942) 92 M.

Director, George B. Seitz; screenplay, Agnes Christine Johnson; music, Daniele Amifhteartrof; art director, Cedric Gibbons; camera, John Mescal, George Folsey; editor, Gene Ruggiero.

Andy Hardy	Mickey Rooney

Judge James Hardy	Lewis Stone
Mrs. Emily Hardy	Fay Holden
Marian Hardy	Cecilia Parker
Polly Benedict	Ann Rutherford
Aunt Milly	Sara Haden
Sheila Brooks	Esther Williams
Jeff Willis	William Lundigan
Wainwright College Girl	Susan Peters
Botsy	Robert Pittard
Stedman's Attorney	Arthur Space
Lincoln's Attorney	Howard Hickman
Red	Frank Coghlan, Jr.
Prentiss	Mantan Moreland
Tooky	Bobby Blake

ANDY HARDY'S BLONDE TROUBLE (MGM, 1944) 107 M.

Director, George B. Seitz; screenplay, Harry Ruskin, William Ludwig, Agnes Christine Johnson; music, David Snell; art director, Cedric Gibbons; camera, Lester White; editor, George White.

Judge James Hardy	Lewis Stone
Andrew Hardy	Mickey Rooney
Mrs. Emily Hardy	Fay Holden
Aunt Milly	Sara Haden
Kay Wilson	Bonita Granville
Katy Henderson	Jean Porter
Dr. Lee	Keye Luke
Dr. M. J. Standish	Herbert Marshall
Lee Walker	Lee Wilde
Lyn Walker	Lyn Wilde
Mrs. Townsend	Marta Linden
Spud	Jackie Moran
Mark	Tommy Dix

LOVE LAUGHS AT ANDY HARDY (MGM, 1946) 94 M.

Producer, Robert Sisk; director, Willis Goldbeck; screenplay, Harry Ruskin, Willis Ludwig; art director, Cedric Gibbons; camera, Robert Plenck; editor, Irvine Warburton.

Andrew Hardy	Mickey Rooney
Judge Hardy	Lewis Stone
Aunt Milly	Sara Haden
Kay Wilson	Bonita Granville
June Blair	Lina Romay
Mrs. Hardy	Fay Holden
Coffy Smith	Dorothy Ford
Mr. Benedict	Addison Richards
Duke	Hal Hackett
Dane Kitteredge	Richard Simmons
Haberdashery Proprietor	Clinton Sundberg
Miss Geeves	Geraldine Wall
Tommy Gilchrest	Charles Peck
Telegraph Clerk	Lucien Littlefield
Freshman	John Walsh

ANDY HARDY COMES HOME (MGM, 1958) 80 M.

Producer, Red Doff; director, Howard Koch; camera, William W. Spencer, Harold E. Wellman; screenplay, Edward Everett Hutshing, Robert Morris Donley; art director, William A. Horning, Urie McCleary; music, Van Alexander; editor, John B. Rogers.

Andy Hardy	Mickey Rooney
Jane Hardy	Patricia Breslin
Mother Hardy	Fay Holden
Marian Hardy	Cecilia Parker
Aunt Milly	Sara Haden
Beezy Anderson	Joey Forman
Doc	Jerry Colonna
Thomas Chandler	Vaughn Taylor
Mayor Benson	Frank Ferguson
Jack Bailey	William Leslie
Councilman Warren	Tom Duggan
Sally Anderson	Jeanne Baird
Cricket	Gina Gillespie
Chuck	Jimmy Bates
Andy, Jr.	Teddy Rooney
Jimmy	Johnny Weissmuller, Jr.
Betty Wilson	Pat Cawley

BLONDIE

Columbia Pictures made a wise choice when it selected Bernard Murat ("Chic") Young's long running comic strip *Blondie* (which had been a King Features Syndicate property since 1930 and is still published daily and Sunday in 1600 newspapers globally) as the basis of a projected modestly budgeted film series. Between 1938 and 1950, the studio turned out 28 under-ninety-minutes black and white episodes in the hectic life of scatter-brained Dagwood Bumstead, his more intelligent and sensible wife Blondie, their two children, Baby Dumpling and Cookie, and the smartest member of their family, their dog Daisy. (On radio, the *Blondie* series was heard from 1939–1951, featuring Arthur Lake as Dagwood, Penny Singleton, Alice White, Patricia Van Cleve, and Ann Rutherford as Blondie, Leone Ledorix, Larry Simms, Jeffrey Silver, and Tommy Cook as Alexander (Baby Dumpling), Marlene Ames, Joan Rae, and Norma Jean Wilson as Cookie, and Hanley Stafford as J. C. Dithers. Each program began with the famous "Uh-uh-uh-don't touch that dial! It's time for B-l-o-n-d-i-e!" On television, *Blondie* was seen from January–December, 1954, and for a four-month retry in 1958; with Pamela Britton in the title role, costarring with Arthur Lake. A new *Blondie* series had a shortlived network airing during the 1968–1969 video season, featuring Will Hutchins and Patricia Hartley.)

The essence of *Blondie* was that the typical American male is a boob at heart, and is constantly mucking things up due to his overzealous, over-inflated ego drive. Only through the patience and intelligence of a wise and understanding wife does life run smoothly for such as Dagwood Bumstead.

This philosophy was carried over into the film series, which made a living caricature out of the cartoon strip, but still retained enough semblance of humanity to be acceptable by audiences. Whether Dagwood is rushing out of the house after a feverish effort to down his breakfast, and knocks over the ever present mailman (played with fortitude by Irving Bacon, later by Eddie Acuff and Dick Wessel), or raiding the refrigerator at nighttime to prepare a triple decker fantasy sandwich, he is the prototype of the sappy underdog. And what made the series so believable was that Blondie accepted her husband as normal, and never was unduly upset by his gross stupidities or ridiculous carryings-on—after all, she in her own way was typical of American housewives: overspending at department stores, trying all sorts of schemes to bolster her husband's professional standing, and getting into a variety of scrapes in her efforts to supplement her household budget.

Penny Singleton was born Mariana Dorothy McNulty in Philadelphia. Her father was a newspaperman and her uncle was a former Postmaster General. As a child, her showbusiness experience consisted largely of singing illustrated songs at film theatres, and doing occasional mimic routines. After attending Columbia University, she returned to the theatre, appearing as a songstress and acrobat on Broadway in such musicals as *Good News* (1928), *Follow Through* (1929), *Hey Nonny, Noony* (1932). Then in the mid 1930s came Warner Bros. and MGM film contracts, with insignificant roles, usually as the other woman. Her one good part in this period was in *After the Thin Man* (1936) as a nightclub singer. In 1937, she married Dr. Lawrence Singleton (a dentist), had her book of verse published, and dyed her brunette hair blonde in order to get the *Blondie* title role when actress Shirley Deane withdrew from the part due to illness. In 1941, she married Bob Sparks, who produced several of the *Blondie* entries. Once into the series, she found it difficult to obtain other acting roles. She did appear in *Go West Young Lady* (1941) with Glenn Ford, *Swing Your Partner* (1943) with Louise Fazenda, and *Young Widow* (1946) with Jane Russell. After *Blondie* ended, she returned to the nightclub circuit. In the 1960s, she became active with the American Guild of Variety Artists, serving two terms as its president, and is now its executive vice president. She led the Radio City Music Hall Rockettes during their 27-day walkout in Manhattan in 1966. A few years ago, she made national headlines when she sued the AGVA over alleged intra-guild corruption, and they counter-sued.

Arthur Lake (nee Silverlake) was born in 1905 in Corbin, Kentucky. His father and uncle did an aerial act and were known as the "Flying Silverlakes." Lake's mother was stage actress Edith Goodwin. When the family switched from circus work to the vaudeville circuit, Lake and his sister joined the act. The group toured the south, billed as "Family Affair." Lake first appeared in motion pictures in "Jack and The Beanstalk" (1917). During the 1920s, he had an on-again, off-again Hollywood career ranging from westerns to light comedies, his most impressive role being in *Skinner's Dress Suit* (1925). During slack periods in the cinema, he played in vaudeville. Lake's initial sound feature was *Air Circus* (1929). During the 1930s, he appeared in such features as *Silver Streak* (1934), *Orchids to You* (1935) and *Topper* (1937). Once Lake was into the *Blondie* series, he became so typed by the dim-witted character he played that only rarely did he have the opportunity to appear in non-"Blondie" roles, such as *Sailor's Holiday* (1944), *The Ghost That Walks Alone* (1944) and *Three Is a Family* (1944). In the early 1950s, he did a short-lived teleseries, *Meet the Family,* with his actress wife, Patricia Van Cleve (who had played Blondie on radio during its last five years on the air). The Lakes now reside in Santa Monica, California, and have two grown children.

The initial "Blondie" film set the pace for the series, showing the two-pronged emphasis that would remain for all 28 entries. One thread of each entry would concern Dagwood's effort to obtain an office raise, usually dependent on his completing to perfection a designing project before a competing firm could outbid J. S. Dithers's architecture building firm.

(Jonathan Hale played Dithers for eighteen entries—then Dagwood's employer became George Radcliffe, enacted by Jerome Cowan). The soon standardized format called for Dagwood to be fired in the course of his bungling, the Bumsteads' valiant efforts to help Dagwood get reinstated by wooing an important, recalcitrant client to the Dithers' fold, and the eventual peacemaking between boss and employee. And no task was too small or absurd for Dagwood. In *Blondie Has Servant Trouble* Dithers orders his worker and Blondie to take up residence in a supposedly haunted house on the Patterson estate so that he can end the rumors that are hurting real estate values in the housing project. Nor is any plan of the Bumstead household sacred, when Dagwood's boss has a whim that must be pacified. In *Blondie's Secret* Radcliffe wants Dagwood to postpone his vacation, and hires someone to steal the Bumstead's suitcases, leading to a run-in with a counterfeiting gang. The final entry, *Beware of Blondie,* finds Dagwood temporarily in charge of J. C. Dithers's firm (Edward Earle assumed the Dithers role for this episode) and becoming innocently involved with a beautiful client who is out to defraud the company. Dagwood, never much of an executive, is hard put to stay on an even keel in his moment of office power.

The other avenue of plot in the series focused on the Bumstead household. For the initial ten entries, the family consisted of Blondie, Dagwood and Baby Dumpling (Larry Simms), along with the precocious mutt Daisy. To show how smart Baby Dumpling is, the youth's good friend Alvin Fuddle (Danny Mummert) is always in attendance, offering the needed contrast to point up Baby Dumpling's virtues (two or three steps behind Alvin is his ever loving mother, Mrs. Fuddle, accurately portrayed by Fay Helm). In *Blondie Brings Up Baby* the young Bumstead starts his school career; in *Blondie Goes to College,* the son —now known as Alexander—goes off to military academy, and *Blondie Hits the Jackpot* finds Alexander now shaving and having his first romance. *Blondie's Blessed Event* sees the birth of Cookie (Marjorie Kent), a sweet addition to the household, who never disappoints her proud parents.

Several *Blondie* chapters revolve around the almost human Daisy, who like the Bumstead children remains stolidly imperturbable midst the helter skelter chaos of home life. In *Blondie on a Budget* a major scene focuses on Daisy getting tipsy; *Blondie in Society* has Daisy competing with Chin-Up, a great dane, who takes first prize in a local dog show; in *It's a Great Life* Dagwood misunderstands his boss's request to purchase a certain house, and instead buys Reggie the horse, leading to canine jealousy and Bumstead's entry in a chic fox hunt. *Life with Blondie* shows Daisy being selected pin-up pooch by the Navy, and once becoming a famous dog model, being kidnapped by an underworld gang.

The ups and downs of the Blondie–Dagwood romance play a certain share in the series's entries. Blondie can get jealous of Dagwood, as she does in *Blondie* when she misunderstands his pursuit of an important client; in *Blondie's Lucky Day*, Dagwood hires an ex-WAC to work in the Dithers firm and Blondie is not happy about the situation; in *Blondie's Anniversary* she finds a watch which she believes is a gift for her, and when it is not, her dependable good humor departs. *Blondie on a Budget* has Dagwood's ex-chorine old flame showing up, causing domestic fireworks.

Not all of the action takes place at the Bumstead house: *Blondie Takes a Vacation* finds them at a resort helping the owner; *Blondie Goes Latin* has the Bumsteads joining Dithers on a cruise to South America (this entry allows Blondie to do a musical number); *Blondie Goes to College* finds the duo at Lehigh University catching up on their education; *Blondie's Hero* has Dagwood accidentally signing up for the Army reserve and being caught in basic training (much of the action was filmed at O.R.C. Training Center, Fort MacArthur, California).

Once in a while there were topical moments in the *Blondie* series. In *Blondie for Victory*, she is working for the Housewives of America; and in *Blondie Hits the Jackpot*, the smart blonde wins a radio contest (a media craze popular in the late 1940s).

For a low-budget series, *Blondie* occasionally surprised its viewers (especially when seen in reissue or on television) at the number of supporting players in the casts who went on to film stardom. *Blondie on a Budget* has Rita Hayworth as Joan Forrester the gold-digging dancer; Glenn Ford appears as Charlie in *Blondie Plays Cupid*, the youth Blondie is trying to match up with Millie (Luana Walters); Tito Guizar turns up as Don Rodriguez in *Blondie Goes Latin* supplying a musical comedy flavor to that entry; Larry Parks portrays college jock Rusty Bryant in *Blondie Goes to College;* Hans Conried is an ascorbic author in *Blondie's Blessed Event;* veteran character comic Hugh Herbert portrays an eccentric millionaire in *It's a Great Life,* in which Blondie goes into the cookie-making business to earn extra money; James Craig is seen briefly in a bit part in *Blondie Meets the Boss.*

After the initial fourteen "Blondie" entries, Columbia Pictures lost interest in the series, feeling that boxoffice appeal had died from the property (an obvious indication of this fact is that entries numbers thirteen and fourteen do not mention "Blondie" in the title, hoping instead to gain new disguised appeal from the double-bill entry.) However, in late 1943 when *Blondie*'s two or three entries per year schedule stopped, audiences wrote into the studio with such zest, that the property was reactivated and continued onward until 1950, when it virtually creeked to a halt. By then, the plodding, transparent stories held no surprises and age had creeped up on Penny Singleton and Arthur Lake, removing the freshness of young middle age from their performances.

Penny Singleton, Simms, Daisy, Lake.

Penny Singleton and Arthur Lake. (Blondie)

Lake, Simms, Penny Singleton. (. . . Plays Cupid)

Second left: Kirby Grant, Ruth Terry; right: Harry Barris, Lake. Other musicians are Red Stanley, Bill Morgan, Louis Wood. (. . . Goes Latin)

Lake, Penny Singleton, Simms. (. . . In Society)

Penny Singleton, Esther Dale, Lake. (. . . Goes to College)

*Lake, Penny Singleton and Sylvia Field (next to Miss
Singleton). (. . . For Victory)*

Marjorie Weaver, Lake, Penny Singleton. (Leave it to . . .)

Penny Singleton and Lake. (. . .'s Lucky Day)

Lake, Penny Singleton. (. . .'s Holiday)

Lake, Penny Singleton, Anita Louise, Rice, Jerome Cowan. (. . .'s Big Moment)

Larry Simms, Marjorie Kent, Penny Singleton, Lake. (. . .'s Anniversary)

Penny Singleton and Lake. (. . .'s Secret)

Penny Singleton and Lake. (Beware of . . .)

Penny Singleton, Alan Dinehart III, Lake. (. . .'s Big Deal)

Penny Singleton and Lake with Jack Rice and Joseph Crehan. (. . .'s Secret)

BLONDIE

BLONDIE (Col., 1938) 69 M.

Associate producer, Robert Sparks; director, Frank R. Strayer; screenplay, Richard Flournoy; art director, Lionel Banks; musical director, Morris Stoloff; camera, Henry Freulich; editor, Gene Havelick.

Blondie	Penny Singleton
Dagwood	Arthur Lake
Baby Dumpling	Larry Simms
C. P. Hazlip	Gene Lockhart
Elsie Hazlip	Ann Doran
J. C. Dithers	Jonathan Hale
Chester Franey	Gordon Oliver
Mr. Hicks	Stanley Andrews
Alvin	Danny Mummert
Mrs. Miller	Kathleen Lockhart
Dorothy	Dorothy Moore
Mrs. Fuddle	Fay Helm
Nelson	Richard Fiske
Daisy	Himself
Mailman	Irving Bacon
Judge	Ian Wolfe

BLONDIE MEETS THE BOSS (Col., 1939) 58 M.

Producer, Robert Sparks; director, Frank R. Strayer; screenplay, Richard Flournoy; story, Kay Van Riper, Richard Flournoy; camera, Henry Freulich.

Blondie	Penny Singleton
Dagwood	Arthur Lake
Baby Dumpling	Larry Simms
Dot	Dorothy Moore
Dithers	Jonathan Hale
Marvin	Don Beddoe
Francine	Linda Winters
Alvin	Danny Mummert
Ollie	Stanley Brown
Freddie	Joel Dean
Nelson	Richard Fiske
Betty Lou	Inez Courtney
Mailman #1	Irving Bacon
Bit Man	James Craig
Bit Man	Robert Sterling

BLONDIE TAKES A VACATION (Col., 1939) 61 M.

Producer, Robert Sparks; director, Frank Strayer; screenplay, Richard Flournoy; story, Karen De Wolf, Robert Chapin, Richard Flournoy; camera, Henry Freulich; editor, Viola Lawrence.

Blondie	Penny Singleton
Dagwood	Arthur Lake
Baby Dumpling	Larry Simms
Daisy	Himself
Alvin Fuddle	Danny Mummert
Jonathan Gillis	Donald Meek
Harvey Morton	Donald MacBride
Matthew Dickerson	Thomas W. Ross

Mrs. Dickerson	Elizabeth Dunne
John Larkin	Robert Wilcox
Holden	Harlan Briggs
Mailman	Irving Bacon
Creditor	Milt Kibbee

BLONDIE BRINGS UP BABY (Col., 1939) 67 M.

Producer, Robert Sparks; director, Frank R. Strayer; screenplay, Gladys Lehman, Richard Flournoy; story, Robert Chapin, Karen De Wolf, Richard Flournoy; art director, Lionel Banks; music director, M. W. Stoloff; camera, Henry Freulich; editor, Otto Meyer.

Blondie	Penny Singleton
Dagwood	Arthur Lake
Baby Dumpling	Larry Simms
Daisy	Himself
Alvin Fuddle	Danny Mummert
J. C. Dithers	Jonathan Hale
Abner Cartwright	Robert Middlemass
Book Agent	Olin Howland
Mrs. Fuddle	Fay Helm
Melinda Mason	Peggy Ann Garner
Mason	Roy Gordon
Miss White	Grace Stafford
School Principal	Helen Jerome Eddy
Mailman	Irving Bacon
Salesman	Robert Sterling
Chauffeur	Bruce Bennett
Police Judge	Ian Wolfe

BLONDIE ON A BUDGET (Col., 1940) 73 M.

Producer, Robert Sparks; director, Frank R. Strayer; screenplay, Richard Flournoy; story, Charles M. Brown; camera, Henry Freulich; editor, Gene Havlick.

Blondie	Penny Singleton
Dagwood	Arthur Lake
Baby Dumpling	Larry Simms
Daisy	Himself
Joan Forrester	Rita Hayworth
Alvin Fuddle	Danny Mummert
Marvin Williams	Don Beddoe
Mr. Fuddle	John Qualen
Mrs. Fuddle	Fay Helm
Mailman	Irving Bacon
Brice	Thurston Hall
Theatre Manager	William Brisbane
Bartender	Ralph Peters

BLONDIE HAS SERVANT TROUBLE (Col., 1940) 70 M.

Producer, Robert Sparks; director, Frank R. Strayer; screenplay, Richard Flournoy; story, Albert Duffy; camera, Henry Freulich; editor, Gene Havlick.

Blondie	Penny Singleton
Dagwood	Arthur Lake
Baby Dumpling	Larry Simms

Daisy	Himself
Alvin Fuddle	Danny Mummert
J. C. Dithers	Jonathan Hale
Eric Vaughn	Arthur Hohl
Anna Vaughn	Esther Dale
Mailman	Irving Bacon
Horatio Jones	Ray Turner
Morgan	Walter Soderling
Mrs. Fuddle	Fay Helm
Taxi Driver	Murray Alper
Photographer	Eddie Laughton

BLONDIE PLAYS CUPID (Col., 1940) 68 M.

Producer, Robert Sparks; director, Frank R. Strayer; screenplay, Richard Flournoy, Karen De Wolf; story, Karen De Wolf, Charles M. Brown; camera, Henry Freulich; editor, Gene Mildord.

Blondie	Penny Singleton
Dagwood	Arthur Lake
Baby Dumpling	Larry Simms
Daisy	Himself
J. C. Dithers	Jonathan Hale
Alvin Fuddle	Danny Mummert
Mailman	Irving Bacon
Charlie	Glenn Ford
Millie	Luana Walters
Tucker	Will Wright
Uncle Abner	Spencer Charters
Aunt Hannah	Leona Roberts
Saunders	Tommy Dixon
Newsboy	Rex Moore

BLONDIE GOES LATIN (Col., 1941) 69 M.

Producer, Robert Sparks; director, Frank R. Strayer; screenplay, Richard Flournoy, Karen De Wolf; story, Quinn Martin; music director, Morris Stoloff; camera, Henry Freulich.

Blondie	Penny Singleton
Dagwood	Arthur Lake
Baby Dumpling	Larry Simms
Daisy	Himself
Lovey Nelson	Ruth Terry
Don Rodriguez	Tito Guizar
J. C. Dithers	Jonathan Hale
Alvin Fuddle	Danny Mummert
Mailman	Irving Bacon
Little Girl	Janet Burston
Hal Trent	Kirby Grant
Captain	Joseph King
Cab Driver	Eddie Acuff
Musician	Harry Barris

BLONDIE IN SOCIETY (Col., 1941) 77 M.

Producer, Robert Sparks; director, Frank R. Strayer; screenplay, Karen De Wolf; story, Eleanore Griffin; art director, Lionel Banks; music director, M. W. Stoloff; camera, Henry Freulich; editor, Charles Nelson.

Blondie	Penny Singleton
Dagwood	Arthur Lake
Baby Dumpling	Larry Simms
Daisy	Himself
J. C. Dithers	Jonathan Hale
Alvin Fuddle	Danny Mummert
Waldo Pincus	William Frawley
Doctor	Edgar Kennedy
Cliff Peters	Chick Chandler
Mailman	Irving Bacon
Announcer	Bill Goodwin
Carpenter	Garry Owen
Saunders	Tommy Dixon
and	

Robert Mitchell's Boys Choir

BLONDIE GOES TO COLLEGE (Col., 1942) 74 M.

Producer, Robert Sparks; director, Frank R. Strayer; screenplay, Lou Breslow; story, Warren Wilson, Clyde Bruckman; camera, Henry Freulich; music director, M. W. Stoloff; editor, Otto Meyer.

Blondie	Penny Singleton
Dagwood	Arthur Lake
Baby Dumpling	Larry Simms
Daisy	Himself
Laura Wadsworth	Janet Blair
J. C. Dithers	Jonathan Hale
Alvin Fuddle	Danny Mummert
Rusty Bryant	Larry Parks
Babs Connelly	Adele Mara
Ben Dixon	Lloyd Bridges
"Mouse" Gifford	Sidney Melton
J. J. Wadsworth	Andrew Tombes
Mrs. Dill	Esther Dale
Announcer	Bill Goodwin

BLONDIE'S BLESSED EVENT (Col., 1942) 69 M.

Producer, Robert Sparks; director, Frank R. Strayer; screenplay, Connie Leo, Karen De Wolf, Richard Flournoy; camera, Henry Freulich; editor, Charles Nelson.

Blondie	Penny Singleton
Dagwood	Arthur Lake
Baby Dumpling	Larry Simms
Cookie	Norma Jean Wayne
Daisy	Himself
J. C. Dithers	Jonathan Hale
Alvin Fuddle	Danny Mummert
George Wickley	Hans Conried
Ollie	Stanley Brown
Mr. Crumb	Irving Bacon
Sarah Miller	Mary Wickes
William Lawrence	Paul Harvey
Little Girl	Dorothy Ann Seese
Interne Bit	Arthur O'Connell
Waiter	Don Barclay

BLONDIE FOR VICTORY (Col., 1942) 70 M.

Producer, Robert Sparks; director, Frank R. Strayer;

screenplay, Karen De Wolf, Connie Lee; story, Fay Kanin; camera, Henry Freulich; editor, Al Clark.

Blondie	Penny Singleton
Dagwood	Arthur Lake
Baby Dumpling	Larry Simms
Daisy	Himself
Cookie	Majelle White
Herschel Smith	Stuart Erwin
J. C. Dithers	Jonathan Hale
Alvin Fuddle	Danny Mummert
Sergeant	Edward Gargan
Miss Clabber	Renie Riano
Mr. Crumb	Irving Bacon
Mr. Green	Harrison Greene
Hoarder	Charles Wagenheim
Mrs. Williams	Sylvia Field
Mrs. Jones	Georgia Backus

IT'S A GREAT LIFE (Col., 1943) 75 M.

Producer-director, Frank R. Strayer; screenplay, Connie Lee, Karen De Wolf; camera, L. W. O'Connell; art director, Lionel Banks; editor, Al Clark.

Blondie	Penny Singleton
Dagwood	Arthur Lake
Alexander	Larry Simms
Timothy Brewster	Hugh Herbert
J. C. Dithers	Jonathan Hale
Alvin Fuddle	Danny Mummert
Collender Martin	Alan Dinehart
Bromley	Douglas Leavitt
Mailman	Irving Bacon
Cookie	Marjorie Ann Mutchie
Daisy	Himself
Reggie	Himself
Piano Tuner	Si Jenks
Salesman	Ray Walker
Bit Boy	Dickie Dillon

FOOTLIGHT GLAMOUR (Col., 1943) 70 M.

Producer-director, Frank R. Strayer; screenplay, Karen De Wolf, Connie Lee; camera, Philip Tannura; art director, Lionel Banks; editor, Richard Fantl.

Blondie	Penny Singleton
Dagwood	Arthur Lake
Alexander	Larry Simms
Vicki Wheeler	Ann Savage
J. C. Dithers	Jonathan Hale
Mr. Crumb	Irving Bacon
Cookie	Marjorie Ann Mutchie
Alvin Fuddle	Danny Mummert
Randolph Wheeler	Thurston Hall
Mrs. Dithers	Grace Hayle
Jerry Grant	Rafael Storm
Daisy	Himself
Father	James Flavin
Mr. Clark	Arthur Loft

LEAVE IT TO BLONDIE (Col., 1945) 72 M.

Producer, Burt Kelly; director, Abby Berlin; screenplay, Connie Lee; camera, Franz F. Planer; art director, Perry Smith; editor, Al Clark.

Blondie	Penny Singleton
Dagwood	Arthur Lake
Alexander	Larry Simms
Rita Rogers	Marjorie Weaver
J. C. Dithers	Jonathan Hale
Eddie Baxter	Chick Chandler
Alvin	Danny Mummert
Cookie	Marjorie Ann Mutchie
Mrs. Meredith	Eula Morgan
Mr. Fuddle	Arthur Space
Mailman	Eddie Acuff
Henry	Fred Graff
Ollie	Jack Rice
Magda	Maude Eburne
Daisy	Herself
Mary	Anne Loos
Secretary	Marilyn Johnson

LIFE WITH BLONDIE (Col., 1945) 70 M.

Producer, Burt Kelly; director, Abby Berlin; screenplay, Connie Lee; camera, L. W. O'Connell; music director, Mischa Bakaleinskoff; editor, Jerome Thoms.

Blondie	Penny Singleton
Dagwood	Arthur Lake
Alexander	Larry Simms
Cookie	Marjorie Kent
Dithers	Jonathan Hale
Glassby	Ernest Truex
Pete	Marc Lawrence
Hazel	Veda Ann Borg
Ollie	Jack Rice
Tommy	Bobby Larson
Blackie	Doug Fowley
Cassidy	George Tyne
Dogcatcher	Edward Gargan
Rutledge	Francis Pierlot
Anthony	Ray Walker
Postman	Eddie Acuff
2nd Policeman	Robert Ryan
Driver	Steve Benton

BLONDIE KNOWS BEST (Col., 1946) 69 M.

Producer, Burt Kelly; director, Abby Berlin; screenplay, Edward Bernds, Al Martin; camera, Philip Tannura; music director, Mischa Bakaleinikoff; editor, Aaron Stell.

Blondie	Penny Singleton
Dagwood	Arthur Lake
Baby Dumpling	Larry Simms
Cookie	Marjorie Kent
Dr. Schnidt	Steven Geray
J. C. Dithers	Jonathan Hale
Jim Gray	Shemp Howard

Charles Peabody	Jerome Cowan
Alvin Fuddle	Danny Mummert
Dr. Titus	Ludwig Donath
Conroy	Arthur Loft
David Armstrong	Edwin Cooper
Ollie	Jack Rice
Mary	Alyn Lockwood
Gloria Evans	Carol Hughes
Ruth Evans	Kay Mallory

BLONDIE'S LUCKY DAY (Col., 1946) 69 M.

Producer, Burt Kelly; director, Abby Berlin; screenplay, Connie Lee; camera, L. W. O'Connell; music director, Mischa Bakaleinikoff; editor, Aaron Stell.

Blondie	Penny Singleton
Dagwood	Arthur Lake
Alexander	Larry Simms
Cookie	Marjorie Kent
Johnny	Robert Stanton
Mary Jane	Angelyn Orr
Dithers	Jonathan Hale
Mr. Butler	Paul Harvey
Ollie	Jack Rice
Tommy	Bobby Larson
Mayor	Charles Arnt
Mailman	Frank Jenks
Salesman	Frank Orth

BLONDIE'S BIG MOMENT (Col., 1947) 69 M.

Producer, Burt Kelly; director, Abby Berlin; screenplay, Connie Lee; camera, Allen Siegler; music director, Mischa Bakaleinikoff; art director, George Brooks; editor, Jerome Thoms.

Blondie	Penny Singleton
Dagwood	Arthur Lake
Alexander	Larry Simms
Cookie	Marjorie Kent
Miss Gray	Anita Louise
George M. Radcliffe	Jerome Cowan
Alvin Fuddle	Danny Mummert
Ollie	Jack Rice
Mr. Greenleaf	Jack Davis
Slugger	Johnny Granath
Mr. Little	Hal K. Dawson
Mailman	Eddie Acuff
Mary	Alyn Lockwood
Pete	Robert De Haven
Joe	Robert Stevens
Theodore Payson	Douglas Wood
Daisy	Herself
Bus Driver	Dick Wessel

BLONDIE'S HOLIDAY (Col., 1947) 67 M.

Producer, Burt Kelly; director, Abby Berlin; screenplay, Constance Lee; camera, Vincent Farrar; music director, Carter DeHaven, Jr.; editor, Jerome Thomas.

Blondie	Penny Singleton
Dagwood	Arthur Lake
Alexander	Larry Simms
Cookie	Marjorie Kent
George Radcliffe	Jerome Cowan
Samuel Breckenridge	Grant Mitchell
Pete Brody	Sid Tomack
Mrs. Breckenridge	Mary Young
Paul Madison	Jeff York
Alvin Fuddle	Bobby Larson
Cynthia Thompson	Jody Gilbert
Ollie	Jack Rice
Mary	Allyn Lockwood
Postman	Eddie Acuff
Mike	Tim Ryan
Bea Mason	Anne Nagel
Tom Henley	Rodney Bell

BLONDIE IN THE DOUGH (Col., 1947) 69 M.

Director, Abby Berlin; screenplay, Arthur Marx, Jack Henley; story, Arthur Marx; music director, Mischa Bakaleinikoff; camera, Vincent Farrar; editor, Henry Batista.

Blondie	Penny Singleton
Dagwood	Arthur Lake
Alexander	Larry Simms
Cookie	Marjorie Kent
George Radcliffe	Jerome Cowan
Llewellyn Simmons	Hugh Herbert
J. T. Thorpe	Clarence Kolb
Alvin	Danny Mummert
Robert Dixon	William Forrest
Mailman	Eddie Acuff
Ollie	Norman Phillips
Baxter	Kernan Cripps
Quinn	Fred Sears
Daisy	Herself
1st Board Member	Boyd Davis
Mrs. Thorpe	Mary Emery

BLONDIE'S ANNIVERSARY (Col., 1947) 67 M.

Director, Abby Berlin; screenplay Jack Henley; camera, Vincent Farrar; art director, George Brooks; music director, Mischa Bakaleinikoff; editor, Al Clark.

Blondie	Penny Singleton
Dagwood	Arthur Lake
Alexander	Larry Simms
Cookie	Marjorie Kent
Gloria Stafford	Adele Jergens
George Radcliffe	Jerome Cowan
Samuel Breckenridge	Grant Mitchell
Sharkey	William Frawley
Burley	Edmund MacDonald
Dalton	Fred Sears
Ollie	Jack Rice
Mary	Alyn Lockwood
Carter	Frank Wilcox
Mailman	Eddie Acuff
Bit	Al Zeidman
Parker	Larry Steers

BLONDIE'S SECRET (Col., 1948) 68 M.

Director, Edward Bernds; screenplay, Jack Henley; camera, Vincent Farrar; art director, George Brooks; music director, Mischa Bakaleinikoff; editor, Al Clark.

Blondie	Penny Singleton
Dagwood	Arthur Lake
Alexander	Larry Simms
Cookie	Marjorie Kent
Radcliffe	Jerome Cowan
George Whiteside	Thurston Hall
Ollie	Jack Rice
Alvin	Danny Mummert
Dog Pound Attendant	Frank Orth
Mary	Alyn Lockwood
Mailman	Eddie Acuff
Larry	Murray Alper
Chips	William "Bill" Phillips
Mona	Greta Granstedt
Ken Marcy	Grandon Rhodes
Daisy	Herself
Nurse	Paula Raymond
Big Man	Allen Mathews
Sergeant	Joseph Crehan

BLONDIE'S REWARD (Col., 1948) 67 M.

Director, Abby Berlin; screenplay, Edward Bernds; camera, Vincent Farrar; art director, George Brooks; music director, Mischa Bakaleinikoff; editor, Al Clark.

Blondie	Penny Singleton
Dagwood	Arthur Lake
Alexander	Larry Simms
Cookie	Marjorie Kent
George Radcliffe	Jerome Cowan
Alice Dickson	Gay Nelson
Ted Scott	Ross Ford
Alvin	Danny Mummert
John Dickson	Paul Harvey
Ed Vance	Frank Jenks
Bill Cooper	Chick Chandler
Ollie	Jack Rice
Postman	Eddie Acuff
Mary	Alyn Lockwood
Officer Carney	Frank Sully
Cluett Day	Myron Healey
Leroy Blodgett	Chester Clute
Ad Lib Bit	Bob Manning

BLONDIE'S BIG DEAL (Col., 1949) 67 M.

Producer, Ted Richmond; director, Edward Bernds; story-screenplay, Lucile Watson Henley; camera, Vincent Farrar; art director, Perry Smith; music director, Mischa Bakaleinikoff; editor, Henry Batista.

Blondie	Penny Singleton
Dagwood	Arthur Lake
Alexander	Larry Simms
Cookie	Marjorie Kent
Radcliffe	Jerome Cowan

Norma	Collette Lyons
Dillon	Wilton Graff
Slack	Ray Walker
Forsythe	Stanley Andrews
Rollo	Alan Dinehart, III
Mailman	Eddie Acuff
Ollie	Jack Rice
Mayor	Chester Clute
Fire Chief	George Lloyd
Mary	Alyn Lockwood
Alvin	Danny Mummert
Daisy	Herself
Boy	Teddy Wells
Girard	Ronnie Ralph
Marvin	David Sandell

BLONDIE HITS THE JACKPOT (Col., 1949) 66 M.

Producer, Ted Richmond; director, Edward Bernds; story-screenplay, Jack Henley; camera, Vincent Farrar; art director, Perry Smith; music director, Mischa Bakaleinikoff; editor, Henry Batista.

Blondie	Penny Singleton
Dagwood	Arthur Lake
Alexander	Larry Simms
Cookie	Marjorie Kent
Radcliffe	Jerome Cowan
J. B. Hutchins	Lloyd Corrigan
Louise Hutchins	Ann Carter
Restaurant Proprietor	George Humbert
Luke	David Sharpe
Alvin	Danny Mummert
Brophy	James Flavin
Mailman	Dick Wessel
Gus	Ray Teal
Mary	Alyn Lockwood
Daisy	Herself

BLONDIE'S HERO (Col., 1950) 67 M.

Producer, Ted Richmond; director, Edward Bernds; story-screenplay, Jack Henley; camera, Vincent Farrar; art director, Perry Smith; music director, Mischa Bakaleinikoff; editor, Henry Batista.

Blondie	Penny Singleton
Dagwood	Arthur Lake
Alexander	Larry Simms
Cookie	Marjorie Kent
Marty Greer	William Frawley
Alvin	Danny Mummert
Sergeant Gateson	Joe Sawyer
Danny Gateson	Teddy Infuhr
Mary Reynolds	Alyn Lockwood
Mae	Iris Adrian
Tim Saunders	Frank Jenks
Mailman	Dick Wessel
Corp. Biff Touhey	Jimmy Lloyd
J. Collins	Robert Emmett Keane
Richard Rogers	Edward Earle

Mrs. Rogers	Mary Newton	Dagwood	Arthur Lake
Recruiting Sergeant	Pat Flaherty	Alexander	Larry Simms
Fruit Salesman	Ted Mapes	Cookie	Marjorie Kent
Captain Masters	Frank Wilcox	Toby Clifton	Adele Jergens
Mike McClusky	Frank Sully	Mailman	Dick Wessel
Daisy	Herself	Ollie	Jack Rice
		Mary	Alyn Lockwood
		Herb Woodley	Emory Parnell
		Harriet Woodley	Isabel Withers
		Alvin	Danny Mummert
		Adolph	Douglas Fowley
		Samuel P. Dutton	William E. Greene
		Daisy	Herself
		Dithers	Edward Earle

BEWARE OF BLONDIE (Col., 1950) 66 M.

Producer, Milton Feldman; Director, Edward Bernds; story-screenplay by Jack Henley; camera, Henry Freulich, Vincent Farrar; art director, Perry Smith; music director, Mischa Bakaleinikoff; editor, Henry Batista.

Blondie	Penny Singleton

BOMBA

With the continued popularity of *Tarzan* at the movie boxoffice in the late 1940s, it was natural that film producers would seek similar jungle formats to toss at the public. About the same time that Columbia Pictures began their low-budget *Jungle Jim* series with ex-Tarzan star Johnny Weissmuller in the lead, fledgling producer Walter Mirisch (who went on to found The Mirisch Film Company) pounced on another perennially popular series of juvenile adventure books, "Bomba, the Jungle Boy," created by Roy Rockwood in the 1920s. To portray the prince of the jungle, Mirisch contracted another *Tarzan* alumnus, John Sheffield then 18 years old and professionally idle since outgrowing the Boy role in *Tarzan* two years earlier.

Sheffield was born April 11, 1931, in Pasadena, California. His father, Reginald Sheffield, was a British screen, stage, and radio actor, noted for playing the original movie David Copperfield in 1913. As a young child, Sheffield was very sickly, requiring a rigid exercise schedule, which proved fortuitous for his career in later years. He made his acting debut at the age of seven in Paul Osborn's play *On Borrowed Time* starring Victor Moore. Then came Sheffield's screen test for the *Tarzan* series in 1939 and his debut in *Tarzan Finds a Son*. Between making *Tarzan* films, his last being *Tarzan and the Huntress* (1947), he had featured roles in *Little Orvie* (1940) with Ernest Truex; *Lucky Cisco Kid* (1940) with Duncan Renaldo, and *Million Dollar Baby* (1941) with Priscilla Lane.

At 5' 11½", the blue eyed, brown-haired youth with a British accent was the perfect physical choice for the wholesome Bomba, the well-bred articulate jungle ruler, who could swing his 190 pounds lithely through the trees, battle rampaging animals, or quash rebellious natives. The benign Bomba was equally adept at politely courting the assorted mild heroines who crossed his jungle path.

To film the *Bomba* series, Mirisch negotiated with Allied Artists (soon to be the successor to Monogram Pictures and the distributor of the popular kiddie matinee fare, *The Bowery Boys*). At the Allied Artists studios, the most economy-minded of all the major film factories, veteran serial-action director Ford Beebe was assigned to handle the "Bomba" films. To utilize footage from *Africa Speaks* (1930) a documentary-travel film, the locale of the *Bomba* stories was changed from South America to Africa. Beebe was able to salvage enough vintage stock shots from *Africa Speaks* to splice into the continuity of the entire dozen *Bomba* series—an amazing feat in itself! All the black and white *Bomba* entries were under eighty minutes. After their theatrical release, the *Bomba* films showed up in edited versions on television as a syndicated package entry.

Bolstering the meager production values of the soundstage jungle atmosphere, Allied Artists eventually built a special swimming lake tank to capture some underwater footage of Sheffield in action, material that was reused throughout the series. The undemanding scripts were peopled with the least expensive actors available; only occasionally did a striking personality turn up in *Bomba* pictures; such as ex-child star Peggy Ann Garner who was the heroine in *Bomba, the Jungle Boy*.

Smoki Whitfield appeared as the faithful native Eli (or sometimes as Jonas, Hadji). Among the animal helpers who joined Bomba in his romps was Kimba the chimp.

The simplistic plotlines for the series were usually thinly veiled excuses to splice in chanced-upon jungle animal and action footage. In the debut film, *Bomba, the Jungle Boy,* George Harland (Onslow Stevens) and his daughter Pat (Peggy Ann Garner) are photographers touring the African veldt for pictures of wild animals. They encounter Bomba, who later rescues the girl from local opposition. In *Panther Island,* a newly arrived agriculturist on the Island encounters difficulties with the natives who superstitiously believe that the black killer panther on the prowl is really a devil reincarnated. For the climax, Bomba battles the animal in its cave haunt. *The Lost Volcano* finds Bomba rescuing the small son of a zoologist who has been kidnapped by two jungle guides in the hopes that the youth can lead them to the treasure buried in the cave near the reactivated volcano. *The Hidden City* episode concerns Bomba's efforts to assist Leah (Sue England), a jungle orphan ignorant of her own past identity. She is being exploited in a power play by the villainous ruler of the Hidden City. Bomba is forced to attack the guarded fortress and engages in a life and death struggle with the ominous ruler.

The Lion Hunters has two corrupt animal hunters, Forbes and Martin (Morris Ankrum, Douglas Kennedy), trapping lions in the territory of the Masai, who revere the animals as sacred. In a savage combat, an enraged lion attacks the villains, allowing Bomba to free the entrapped heroine Jean (Ann Todd). *The Elephant Stampede,* the hokiest but the best of the series, details the conflict between two crooks who are illegally killing elephants to obtain ivory. After murdering their guide, the villains capture Bomba who calls upon his pachyderm friends for help; they rescue him, with the culprits (John Kellogg, Myron Healey) confronted by a potentially untimely end.

African Treasure switches back to the hidden wealth motif, with an unscrupulous geologist team really being diamond smugglers. With the help of his animal friends, Bomba captures the thieves and frees Lita (Laurette Luez), the entrapped heroine.

The Jungle Girl details Bomba's efforts to trace the skeletons of his unknown parents, revealing that a ruthless native chief had them killed. After the chief's daughter Boru (Suzette Harbin) dies in a jungle fire, the native lord is brought to justice by the everpresent Bomba. This entry is particularly weak in the acting realm. *Safari Drums* resorts to the tired premise of the jungle prince being joined by his animal friends in corralling a greedy guide who murdered and robbed a noted geologist. *Golden Idol* revolves around a priceless statue which is stolen from the Watusi tribe by an Arab chieftain. Bomba relies on the talking drums to send for help, with the villain being trounced by Bomba in an underwater finale. More discriminating viewers wondered at the strange customs of the African tribe in this entry, whose chief had a harem and which, according to the story, was situated "near the Tanganyika border."

Bomba serves as a guide again in *Killer Leopard* when he leads film star Linda Winters (Beverly Garland) through the brush to find her long-lost husband, who left home when his embezzling activities became too obvious. Winters (Donald Murphy) proves to be currently involved in diamond smuggling, Bomba and he fight, Bomba and the ferocious leopard battle, with justice triumphing all around.

In the concluding series entry, *Lord of the Jungle,* Bomba arranges for the destruction of the fierce rogue leader of an elephant herd in order to protect the other elephants from extermination by a trio of unsavory government hunters.

With this twelfth *Bomba* film, the series had exhausted its basic formula about the jungle youth, not to mention its scant supply of African decor, stock footage, and pseudo-native atmosphere. The then 24-year-old Sheffield retired from acting, invested his earnings from this film series in real estate in Santa Monica and Malibu, and enrolled as a pre-medical student at U.C.L.A. Sheffield, a much heavier, balding married man with two sons, presently lives in Malibu, managing his real estate holdings.

In late 1970, Allied Artists reactivated interest in the *Bomba* series with producer Barry Lawrence preparing a new edition with a modern-day setting.

Johnny Sheffield.

Sheffield.

Sheffield with Peggy Ann Garner. (Bomba the Jungle Boy)

Sheffield and Lita Baron (. . . on Panther Island)

Grandon Rhodes, Marjorie Lord, Elena Verdugo, Donald Woods. (Lost Volcano)

Sheffield, Martin Wilkins, John Kellogg, Myron Healey. (Elephant Stampede)

Sheffield, Leon Belasco, Sue England, Damian O'Flynn, Smoki Whitfield. (The Hidden City)

Sheffield. (African Treasure)

Sheffield. (. . . and Jungle Girl)

Sheffield, Rick Vallen (middle). (The Golden Idol)

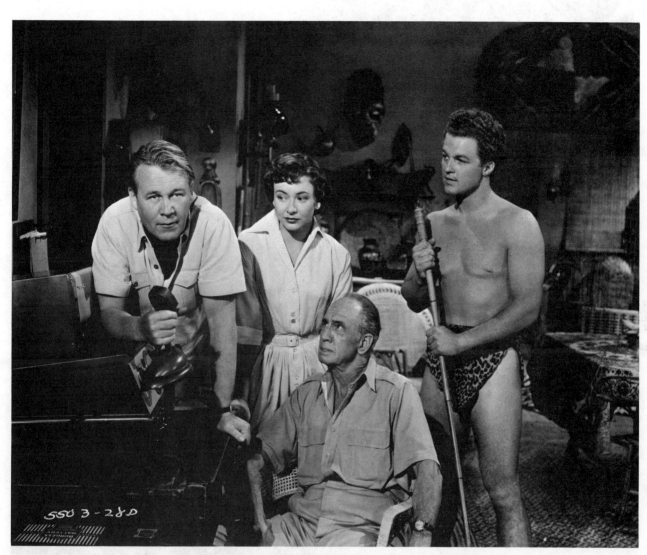

*Wayne Morris, Nancy Hale, Leonard Mudie (seated),
Sheffield.* (Lord of the Jungle)

Rory Mallinson, Beverly Garland, Russ Conway, Sheffield, Donald Murphy, Barry Bernard (on the ground). **(Killer Leopard)**

Nancy Hale, Sheffield. **(Lord of the Jungle)**

BOMBA

BOMBA, THE JUNGLE BOY (Mon., 1949) 70 M.

Producer, Walter Mirisch; director, Ford Beebe; screenplay, Jack DeWitt; camera, William Sickner; editor, Otho Lovering, Roy Livingston.

Bomba	Johnny Sheffield
Pat Harland	Peggy Ann Garner
George Harland	Onslow Stevens
Andy Barnes	Charles Irwin
Eli	Smoki Whitfield
Mufti	Martin Wilkins

BOMBA ON PANTHER ISLAND (Mon., 1949) 76 M.

Producer, Walter Mirisch; director, Ford Beebe; author, Roy Rockwood; screenplay, Ford Beebe; music director, Edward Kay; camera, William Sickner; editor, Richard Heermance.

Bomba	Johnny Sheffield
Judy Maitland	Allene Roberts
Losani	Lita Baron
Andy Barnes	Charles Irwin
Robert Maitland	Henry Lewis
Eli	Smoki Whitfield

THE LOST VOLCANO (Mon., 1950) 67 M.

Producer, Walter Mirisch; director, Ford Beebe; screenplay, Jack DeWitt; art director, Dave Milton; music director, Ozzie Caswell; camera, Marcel Le Picard; editor, Richard Heermance.

Bomba	Johnny Sheffield
Paul Gordon	Donald Woods
Ruth Gordon	Marjorie Lord
Barton	John Ridgely
Daniel	Robert Lewis
Nona	Elena Verdugo
David	Tommy Ivo
Higgins	Don Harvey
Charles Langley	Grandon Rhodes

BOMBA AND THE HIDDEN CITY (Mon., 1950) 71 M.

Producer, Walter Mirisch; director, Ford Beebe; screenplay, Carroll Young; music director, Ozzie Caswell; camera, William Sickner; editor, Roy Livingston.

Bomba	Johnny Sheffield
Leah	Sue England
Hassan	Paul Guilfoyle
Hadji	Smoki Whitfield
Dennis Johnson	Damian O'Flynn
Raschid	Leon Belasco
Abdullah	Charles La Torre

THE LION HUNTERS (Mon., 1951) 75 M.

Producer, Walter Mirisch; director-screenplay, Ford Beebe; music director, Martin Skiles; camera, William Sickner; editor, Otho Lovering.

Bomba	Johnny Sheffield
Forbes	Morris Ankrum
Jean	Ann Todd
Martin	Douglas Kennedy
Jonas	Smoki Whitfield
Lohu	Robert Davis

BOMBA AND THE ELEPHANT STAMPEDE (Mon., 1951) 71 M.

Producer, Walter Mirisch; director-screenplay, Ford Beebe; art director, Dave Milton; camera, William Sickner.

Bomba	Johnny Sheffield
Lola	Donna Martell
Miss Banks	Edith Evanson
Chief Nagalia	Martin Wilkins
Bob Warren	John Kellogg
Joe Collins	Myron Healey
Andy Barnes	Leonard Mudie
Mark Phillips	Guy Kinsford
Malako	James Adamson
Native	Max Thrower
Native	James Payne

AFRICAN TREASURE (Mon., 1952) 70 M.

Producer, Walter Mirisch; director, Ford Beebe; author, Roy Rockwood; screenplay, Ford Beebe; music director, Raoul Kraushaar; art director, Martin Obzina; camera, Harry Neumann; editor, Bruce Schoengarth.

Bomba	Johnny Sheffield
Lita	Laurette Luez
Greg	Arthur Space
Pedro	Martin Garralaga
Hardy	Lane Bradford
Barnes	Leonard Mudie
Gilroy	Lyle Talbot
Eli	Robert "Smoki" Whitfield
Tolu	James Adamson
Water Bearer	Jack Williams
Timid Native	Wesley Bly
Native Slave	Sugar Foot Anderson
Native Mail Boy	Woodrow Wilson Strode

BOMBA AND THE JUNGLE GIRL (Mon., 1952 70 M.

Producer, Walter Mirisch; director-screenplay, Ford Beebe; art director, Dave Milton; camera, Harry Neumann.

Bomba	Johnny Sheffield
Linda	Karen Sharpe
Ward	Walter Sande

Boru	Suzette Harbin
Gamboso	Martin Wilkins
Kokoli	Morris Buchanan
Barnes	Leonard Mudie
Boru's Lt.	Don Blackman
Constable	Bruce Carruther
Messenger	Jack Clisby
Linasi	Amanda Randolph
Kaje	Roy Glenn
Bearer	Bill Walker

SAFARI DRUMS (AA, 1953) 71 M.

Producer-director, Ford Beebe; author Roy Rockwood; screenplay, Ford Beebe; art director, David Milton; camera, Harry Neumann; editor, Walter Hannemann.

Bomba	Johnny Sheffield
Peggy	Barbara Bestar
Conrad	Emory Parnell
Steve	Paul Marion
Brad Morton	Douglas Kennedy
Barnes	Leonard Mudie
Eli	Robert Whitfield
Sumbo	James Adamson
Collins	Carleton Young
Murphy	Rory Mallinson
Native	Jack Williams

THE GOLDEN IDOL (AA, 1954) 71 M.

Producer-director, Ford Beebe; author, Roy Rockwood; screenplay, Ford Beebe; art director, David Milton; camera, Harry Neumann; editor, John Fuller.

Bomba	Johnny Sheffield
Karen Marsh	Anne Kimbell
Joe Hawkins	Lane Bradford
Ali Ben Mamoud	Paul Guilfoyle
Barnes	Leonard Mudie
Eli	Smoki Whitfield

Gomo	Roy Glenn
Abdullah	Rick Vallin
Ezekial	James Adamson

KILLER LEOPARD (AA, 1954) 70 M.

Producer, Ford Beebe; director, Ford Beebe, Edward Morey, Jr.; screenplay, Ford Beebe; art director, David Milton; camera, Harry Neumann.

Bomba	Johnny Sheffield
Maitland	Russ Conway
Jonas	Bill Walker
Conji	Milton Wood
Charlie Pulham	Barry Bernard
Fred Winters	Donald Murphy
Linda Winters	Beverly Garland
Eli	Smoki Whitfield
Deevers	Rory Mallinson
Comm. Barnes	Leonard Mudie
Saunders	Harry Cording
Policeman	Guy Kingsford
Daniel	Roy Glenn

LORD OF THE JUNGLE (AA, 1955) 69 M.

Producer-director-screenplay, Ford Beebe; art director, David Milton; music director, Marlin Skiles; camera, Harry Neumann; editor, Neil Brunnenkant.

Bomba	Johnny Sheffield
Jeff Woods	Wayne Morris
Mona Andrews	Nancy Hale
Paul Gavin	Paul Picerni
Kenny Balou	William Phipps
Eli	Smoki Whitfield
Comm. Andy Barnes	Leonard Mudie
Elisha	James Adamson
Pilot	Harry Lauter
Molu	Joel Fluellen
Molu's Wife	Juanita Moore

BOSTON BLACKIE

Concurrent with its other low-budget detective series, Columbia Pictures began its *Boston Blackie* series in 1941 and mass-produced thirteen installments over the next eight years, starring Chester Morris in the title role of the former jewel thief and con artist turned good guy. More so than the other contemporary sleuthing series, *Boston Blackie* relied on humorous moments to carry the routine crime solving picture, rather than as relief effect from the detective melodrama. Based on Jack Boyle's *c.* 1910 book, the Boston Blackie character first appeared in films in *Boston Blackie's Little Pal* (1918) and had been utilized in several motion pictures before Columbia revived the property. The early Columbia *Boston Blackies* were directed by such expert craftsmen as Robert Florey and Edward Dmytryk, which gave the black and white entries snappier pacing and livelier action than the later installments. (On radio, *Boston Blackie* began as a summer replacement for *Amos 'N Andy* and had Chester Morris in the title role, later replaced by Richard Kollmar; Lesley Woods and Jan Miner were Mary the helpful heroine; Inspector Farraday was played by Maurice Tarplin, Richard Lane, and then Frank Orth; and Tony Barrett was heard as Shorty. On television, a *Boston Blackie* series began in 1951, lasting for 58 half-hour episodes, with Kent Taylor as the sleuth, Lois Collier as Mary, and Frank Orth as Inspector Farraday.)

It was fortuitous for both Columbia Pictures and Chester Morris that the studio selected the veteran powerhouse actor for the Blackie role. Morris gave the characterization a snappiness and pep, albeit on a low intellectual level, so sadly missing from *The Crime Doctor* and *The Lone Wolf* films. The format of the *Blackie* thrillers always had wise-cracking, girl-chasing Blackie in dutch with the law, and usually harassed by Inspector Farraday (Richard Lane), head of the homicide squad, who suspected that the one-time crook was up to his old bag of tricks again. Blackie, the underworld's best pal and its severest deterrent was surrounded by amiable but dull witted Runt (George E. Stone) his faithful crony on all his capers, and often by Arthur Manleder (Lloyd Corrigan), a wealthy playboy who was always willing to help—however incompetently—his pal Blackie. As with most of Columbia's economy series, the backgrounds and sets were all backlot studio, with most unpretentiously furbished sets (often shabby and garish), peopled by such Columbia contract players as Lloyd Bridges, Harriet Hilliard, Dorothy Malone, Ann Savage, Nina Foch, Larry Parks, Iris Adrian, and Jeff Donnell. If Lynn Merrick turned up in two *Blackie* adventures as different heroines, no one seemed to mind.

Chester Morris (John Chester Brooks Morris) was born in New York City on February 16, 1901, the son of actors. (His brothers Gordon and Adrian and his sister Wilhelmina were also in show business.) After graduating from the New York School of Fine Arts in 1916, he joined the Westchester Players. He made his Broadway debut in *The Copperhead* in 1918, and thereafter was frequently seen in New York productions and touring shows, such as *Thunder* (1921) and *Crime* (1927). He made his film debut in *Alibi* (1929) for which he was Oscar nominated. Other pre-

Blackie credits included: *The Big House* (1930), *Blondie Johnson* (1933), *The Three Godfathers* (1936), *Five Came Back* (1939), and *No Hands On the Clock* (1941). During World War II, Morris made several U.S.O. tours, and in 1949 he traveled with *Detective Story*. In the 1950s, he was seen in road companies of *View From the Bridge* and *Advise and Consent*. His last film role in the decreasing cinema market was as the fight manager in *The Great White Hope* (1970). Morris married Suzanne Kilborn in 1927; they had a son and a daughter. They were divorced in 1938; in 1940, Morris married Lillian Barker. He died of an overdose of barbiturates on September 11, 1970, in New Hope, Pennsylvania. He was appearing at the time at the Bucks County Playhouse in *The Caine Mutiny Court Martial*.

Meet . . . has ex-crook Blackie and Runt encountering Marilyn Howard (Constance Worth) on an ocean liner docking in Manhattan. When a murder occurs, Blackie trails her to Coney Island, and becomes enmeshed with a spy ring operating there. *Confessions of . . .* centers on a man killed at an art auction, with Blackie being accused of the crime by the police. Before the climax, he has broken up an art racket operating in Gotham. *Alias . . .* finds Blackie arranging a Christmas show at the state prison. After his performance of magical feats, convict Joe Trilby (Larry Parks) manages to escape, determined to hunt down the man who framed him. In an action-full finale, Blackie locates the missing convict and the criminal duo responsible for Joe's sentence. This entry proves again that all the lucky breaks go to Boston Blackie and the police never have a chance.

. . . Goes Hollywood is set into motion when Blackie receives an S.O.S. from a California friend to take $60,000 from his apartment and bring it to Hollywood. The police catch Blackie at his pal's safe, but allow him to go to California so they can follow him and perhaps discover the whereabouts of the lost Monterey diamond. *After Midnight With . . .* deals with Ed Barney (Walter Baldwin) who is released from prison, and tells his daughter Betty (Ann Savage) that he has hidden some diamonds in a safety deposit box. Betty tells her acquaintance Blackie about the secreted merchandise. Once again, just as he is about to retrieve the gems for Betty, the police arrive on the spot and arrest him for Barney's murder. Blackie escapes and trails Joe Herschel (Cy Kendall) who runs a nightclub, and who has kidnapped Betty, to find out where the gems are. Before the finish, Herschel and his double-dealing gang battle it out, and a well-paced car chase ensues.

One Mysterious Night has the gambit of Blackie being called in by the police to help recover the Blue Star of the Nile diamond, which has been stolen at a war relief exhibit. In this entry, Blackie even carries a police badge! Involved in the adventure are Dorothy Anderson (Janis Carter), a super-enterprising girl reporter; with Paul Martens (William Wright) and Matt Healy (Robert Williams) as gem thieves. . . . *Booked on Suspicion* has Blackie posing as an auctioneer to help a friend. Blackie accidentally sells a bogus Charles Dickens first edition volume, which leads to murder and his implication in the homicide. Lynn Merrick as Gloria Mannard is the unfriendly feminine interest in the caper.

In *. . .'s Rendezvous,* James Cook (Steve Cochran), a homicidal maniac escapes from prison, and goes on a revengeful killing spree, murdering his dance hall girlfriend, and a hotel maid. He holds Sally Brown (Nina Foch) hostage, before Blackie can lead the police to the rescue. *A Close Call for . . .* pulls all the tried-and-true tricks of the mystery-detective formula, with an extra dose of comedy as the loudmouth Blackie is framed on a murder charge. Gerry Peyton (Lynn Merrick) is the menace—albeit unconvincing—in the tame adventure. *The Phantom Thief* finds Blackie caught again at the scene of two killings, tied into sinister seances and a rash of ghostly apparitions. Aided by his funny henchman Runt, Blackie tricks the guilty blackmailer-murderer into making a confession.

. . . and the Law has Blackie again performing magic tricks (Morris was quite proficient at the sleight of hand art) at a women's penitentiary variety show, which inadvertently gives one of the inmates a chance to escape and take revenge on her former magician partner. Because he is implicated, Blackie must solve the mystery, which he does via a recording machine, catching the murderer's confession. *Trapped by . . .* shows Blackie posing as a guard at wealthy Mrs. Carter's (Sarah Selby) party. Then a private detective assigned to the case is killed in a suspicious car crash. When Mrs. Carter's ultra-expensive pearl necklace is heisted, Blackie is the obvious suspect and he must crack the riddle to demonstrate his innocence.

. . .'s Chinese Venture comes into play when Blackie and the Runt are seen leaving a Chinese laudry, whose proprietor is found dead. Breezy Blackie and Runt must catch the real murderer running loose in Chinatown.

Rochelle Hudson, Chester Morris, Charles Wagenheim, Richard Lane, Bill Lally. (Meet Boston Blackie)

(Alias . . .)

Walter Sande, Richard Lane, Morris, Lloyd Corrigan,
Constance Worth. (. . . Goes Hollywood)

George E. Stone, Morris, Don Barclay. (After Mid-
night With . . .)

Morris, Lynn Merrick. (Booked on Suspicion)

Trudy Marshall, Morris, Constance Dowling. (. . . And The Law)

Nina Foch, Morris. (. . .'s Rendezvous)

Patricia White (later Patricia Barry), George E. Stone, Morris, June Vincent. (Trapped by . . .)

Frank Sully, Benson Fong, Philip Ahn, Lane, Morris,
Charles Arnt, Joan Westbury, Sid Tomack. (. . .'s
Chinese Venture)

BOSTON BLACKIE

MEET BOSTON BLACKIE (Col., 1941) 58 M.

Producer, Ralph Cohn; director, Robert Florey; author-screenplay, Jay Dratler; camera, Franz F. Planer; editor, James Sweeney.

Boston Blackie	Chester Morris
Cecelia Bradley	Rochelle Hudson
Inspector Farraday	Richard Lane
The Runt	Charles Wagenheim
Marilyn Howard	Constance Worth
Monk	Jack O'Malley
Georgie	George Magrill
Mechanical Man	Michael Rand
Freak Show Barker	Eddie Laughton
Freak Show Doorman	John Tyrrell
Dart Game Barker	Harry Anderson
Blind Man	Byron Foulger

CONFESSIONS OF BOSTON BLACKIE (Col., 1941) 65 M.

Producer, William Berke; director, Edward Dmytryk; author, Paul Yawitz, Jay Dratler; screenplay, Paul Yawitz; camera, Philip Tanura; editor, Gene Milford.

Boston Blackie	Chester Morris
Diane Parrish	Harriet Hilliard
Inspector Farraday	Richard Lane
The Runt	George E. Stone
Arthur Manleder	Lloyd Corrigan
Mona	Joan Woodbury
Detective Mathews	Walter Sande
Buchanan	Ralph Theadore
Caulder	Kenneth MacDonald
Eric Allison	Walter Soderling
Ice Cream Man	Billy Benedict
Cop	Mike Pat Donovan
Motor Cop	Jack Clifford
Express Man	Eddie Laughton
Taxi Driver	Jack O'Malley

ALIAS BOSTON BLACKIE (Col., 1942) 67 M.

Director, Lew Landers; screenplay, Paul Yawitz; camera, Phil Tannura; editor, Richard Fantl.

Boston Blackie	Chester Morris
Eve Sanders	Adele Mara
Inspector Farraday	Richard Lane
The Runt	George E. Stone
Arthur Manleder	Lloyd Corrigan
Detective Mathews	Walter Sande
Joe Trilby	Larry Parks
Roggi McKay	George McKay
Jumbo Madigan	Cy Kendall
Steve Caveroni	Paul Fix
Warden	Ben Taggart
Bus Driver	Lloyd Bridges
Doorman	Ernie Adams
Police Sergeant	Edmund Cobb

Bell Hop	Sidney Miller
Cop	Bud Geary
Johnson	Duke York

BOSTON BLACKIE GOES HOLLYWOOD (Col., 1942) 68 M.

Producer, Wallace MacDonald; director, Michael Gordon; screenplay, Paul Yawitz; music director, Morris Stoloff; camera, Henry Freulich; editor, Arthur Seid.

Boston Blackie	Chester Morris
The Runt	George E. Stone
Inspector Farraday	Richard Lane
Whipper	Forrest Tucker
Slick Barton	William Wright
Arthur Manleder	Lloyd Corrigan
Steve	John Tyrrell
Sergeant Mathews	Walter Sande
Gloria Lane	Constance Worth
Stewardess	Shirley Patterson
Sergeant	Ralph Dunn
Cab Driver #3	Charles Sullivan
Cab Driver #4	Al Herman
Tenant	Jessie Arnold
Hotel Manager	Cy Ring

AFTER MIDNIGHT WITH BOSTON BLACKIE (Col., 1943) 64 M.

Producer, Sam White; director, Lew Landers; author, Aubrey Wisberg; screenplay, Howard J. Green; art director, Lionel Banks; music director, M. W. Stoloff; camera, L. W. O'Connell; editor, Richard Fautl.

Boston Blackie	Chester Morris
The Runt	George E. Stone
Inspector Farraday	Richard Lane
Joe Herschel	Cy Kendall
Marty Beck	George McKay
Sammy Walsh	Al Hill
Sergeant Mathews	Walter Sande
Betty Barnaby	Ann Savage
Diamond Ed. Barnaby	Walter Baldwin
Dixie Rose Blossom	Jan Buckingham
Arthur Manleder	Lloyd Corrigan
Justice of Peace Potts	Dick Elliott
Cigar Clerk	Don Barclay
Fence	John Harmon

ONE MYSTERIOUS NIGHT (Col., 1944) 61 M.

Producer, Ted Richmond; director, Oscar Boetticher, Jr.; screenplay, Paul Yawitz; art director, Lionel Banks, George Brooks; music director, M. Bakaleinikoff; camera, L. W. O'Connell, editor, Al Clark.

Boston Blackie	Chester Morris
Inspector Farraday	Richard Lane
Dorothy Anderson	Janis Carter
Paul Martens	William Wright
Matt Healy	Robert Williams

The Runt	George E. Stone
Eileen Daley	Dorothy Maloney (Malone)
George Daley	Robert E. Scott
Matthews	Lyle Latell
Sergeant McNulty	George McKay
Margaret Dean	Early Cantrell
Jumbo Madigan	Joseph Crehan
Austin	John Tyrrell
Newstand Clerk	Ann Loos
2nd Man	Henry Jordan
Traffic Officer	Ben Taggart

BOSTON BLACKIE BOOKED ON SUSPICION (Col., 1945) 66 M.

Producer, Mikhail Kraike; director, Arthur Dreifuss; author, Malcolm Stuart Boylan; screenplay, Paul Yawitz; art director, Perry Smith; camera, George B. Meehan, Jr.; editor, Richard Fautl.

Boston Blackie	Chester Morris
Gloria Mannard	Lynn Merrick
Inspector Farraday	Richard Lane
Sgt. Matthews	Frank Sully
Jack Higgins	Steve Cochran
The Runt	George E. Stone
Arthur Manleder	Lloyd Corrigan
Wilfred Kittredge	George Carleton
Porter Hadley	George Meader
Alexander Harmon	Douglas Wood
Diz	George Lloyd
Officer Lee	Robert Williams
Policeman	Joseph Palma
Paisley	Dan Stowell
Housekeeper	Jessie Arnold

BOSTON BLACKIE'S RENDEZVOUS (Col., 1945) 64 M.

Producer, Alexis Thurn-Taxis; director, Arthur Dreifuss; author, Fred Schiller; screenplay, Edward Dein; art director, Perry Smith; music director, Mischa Bakaleinikoff; camera, George B. Meehan, Jr.; editor, Aaron Stell.

Boston Blackie	Chester Morris
Sally Brown	Nina Foch
James Cook	Steve Cochran
Inspector Farraday	Richard Lane
The Runt	George E. Stone
Mathews	Frank Sully
Martha	Iris Adrian
Arthur Manleder	Harry Hayden
Patricia Powers	Adelle Roberts
Steve Caveroni	Joe Devlin
Hotel Clerk	Dan Stowell
Dr. Fagle	Phil Van Zandt
Chambermaid	Marilyn Johnson
First Cop	Robert Williams
Second Cop	John Tyrrell
Third Cop	Joseph Palma
Second Bruiser	Dick Alexander

A CLOSE CALL FOR BOSTON BLACKIE (Col., 1946) 60 M.

Producer, John Stone; director, Lew Landers; author, Paul Yawitz; screenplay, Ben Markson, Paul Yawitz; art director, Carl Anderson, Jerome Pycha, Jr.; music director, Mischa Bakaleinikoff; camera, Burnett Guffey; editor, Jerome Thoms.

Boston Blackie	Chester Morris
Gerry Peyton	Lynn Merrick
Inspector Farraday	Richard Lane
Sgt. Matthews	Frank Sully
The Runt	George E. Stone
Mamie Kirwin	Claire Carleton
Smiley Slade	Erik Rolf
Hack Hagen	Charles Lane
John Peyton	Robert Scott
Coroner	Emmett Vogan
Harcourt	Russell Hicks
Josie	Doris Houck
Milk Woman	Ruth Warren
Cab Driver	Jack Gordon

THE PHANTOM THIEF (Col., 1946) 65 M.

Producer, John Stone; director, D. Ross Lederman; author, G. A. Snow; screenplay, Richard Wormser, Richard Weil; art director, Robert Peterson; music director, Mischa Bakaleinikoff; camera, George B. Meehan, Jr.; editor, Al Clark.

Boston Blackie	Chester Morris
Anne Duncan	Jeff Donnell
Inspector Farraday	Richard Lane
Sandra	Dusty Anderson
Runt	George E. Stone
Matthews	Frank Sully
Dr. Nejino	Marvin Mueller
Rex Duncan	Wilton Graff
Eddie Alexander	Murray Alper
Dr. Purcell Nash	Forbes Murray
Jumbo	Joseph Crehan
Police Sgt.	Edward F. Dunn
Patrolman	George Magrill
Police Sgt. #2	Eddie Featherstone
Policeman #1	Edmund Cobb

BOSTON BLACKIE AND THE LAW (Col., 1946) 69 M.

Producer, Ted Richmond; director, D. Ross Lederman; screenplay, Harry J. Essex; art director, Charles Clague; music director, Mischa Bakaleinikoff; camera, George B. Meehan, Jr.; editor, James Sweeny.

Boston Blackie	Chester Morris
Irene	Trudy Marshall
Dianah Moran	Constance Dowling
Inspector Farraday	Richard Lane
The Runt	George E. Stone
Sergeant Matthews	Frank Sully

Lampau (Jani) .... Warren Ashe
Warden Lund .... Selmer Jackson
Clerk .... Fred Graff
Harry Burton (bookie) .... Ted Hecht
Peterson .... Edward Dunn
Reporter .... Ed Fetherstone
Cab Driver .... Frank O'Connor
Cop .... Brian O'Hara

TRAPPED BY BOSTON BLACKIE (Col., 1948) 67 M.

Producer, Rudolph C. Flothow; director, Seymour Friedman; author, Charles Marion, Edward Bock; screenplay, Maurice Tombragel; art director, George Brooks; music director, Mischa Bakaleinikoff; camera, Philip Tannura; editor, Dwight Caldwell.

Boston Blackie .... Chester Morris
Doris Bradley .... June Vincent
Inspector Farraday .... Richard Lane
Joan Howell .... Patricia White
Igor Borio .... Edward Norris
Runt .... George E. Stone
Sergeant Matthews .... Frank Sully
Sandra Doray .... Fay Baker
Mr. Carter .... William Forrest
Mrs. Carter .... Sarah Selby
Mrs. Kenyon .... Mary Currier

Dunn .... Pierre Watkin
Louis .... Ben Welden
Receptionist .... Abigail Adams
Clerk .... Ray Harper

BOSTON BLACKIE'S CHINESE VENTURE (Col., 1949) 59 M.

Producer, Rudolph C. Flothow; director, Seymour Friedman; author-screenplay, Maurice Tombraegel; art director, Paul Palmentola; music director, Mischa Bakaleinikoff; camera, Vincent Farrar; editor, Richard Fantl.

Boston Blackie .... Chester Morris
Mei Ling .... Maylia
Inspector Farraday .... Richard Lane
Bus Guide .... Don McGuire
Red .... Joan Woodbury
Runt .... Sid Tomack
Sergeant Matthews .... Frank Sully
Pop Gerard .... Charles Arnt
Bill Craddock .... Luis Van Rooten
Wong .... Philip Ahn
Rolfe .... Peter Brocco
Ah Hing .... Benson Fong
Reiber .... Edgar Dearing
Chemist .... Fred Sears
Jim .... Pat O'Malley
Bartender .... George Lloyd

BOWERY BOYS

The Bowery Boys have had enormous popularity both in theatrical release and in constant television syndication. Although starting in motion pictures in 1937 in *Dead End,* the acting group did not evolve its final "mongrel" format and cast of characters until 1946. That year they commenced a series of 48 features produced over the next decade for Monogram (Allied Artists) Pictures. Their sixty-minute, black and white, ultra-low-budget second features, have always had an undefinable appeal, stemming from the lower comic sense of slapstick and corny punning dialogue which fills their pictures.

The Bowery Boys consisted of group leader Terence Alyosius ("Slip") Mahoney (Leo Gorcey), Horace Debussey ("Sach") Jones (Huntz Hall), Louie Dumbrowsky (Bernard Gorcey), Whitey (Billy Benedict), Chuck (David Gorcey), Bobby (Bobby Jordan), Gabe (Gabriel Dell), and Butch (Bennie Bartlett, later played by Buddy Gorman). In the mid-1950s, there was Duke (Stanley Clements).

Most of the Boys' operations centered at Louie's ice cream shop in the semi-slums of the Lower East Side. As the series progressed, less was shown of the boys' tenement home life, and more or all of the action focused on their endless activities at Louie's emporium. With Slip as the acknowledged director of the gang's daily lives (in the late 1930s it had been Billy Halop as Tommy who was the group leader), and dumb-witted Sach as the #1 foil, the fellows' personalities soon took on rigid characteristics. Slip would constantly be murdering the English language with his malapropisms, while valiantly trying to live up to his image as den father, lord protector, Casanova at large, and would-be aristocrat of the sleezy soda shop domain; Sach, with his rolling eyes, his fey gestures, his puppy-like loyalty, would often be at odds with Slip in vying for a position of complete loafishness, and having the admiring Boys do all his biddings, no matter how ridiculous or impossible. That Slip would generally become exasperated with Sach and slug him with his hat or fists was to be expected, since the none-too-bright Mahoney had a very low threshold of tolerance for his fellow man, and Sach could always be counted on to take any task assigned or punishment meted out to him with fantastic good graces (as long as he had plenty of chocolate malteds and could be part of the boys' activities, he was content; if one of the heroines by some foolish choice preferred him to Slip, he was in seventh heaven—at least for a moment). Louie was a blessing in disguise for the Bowery Boys. He gave them free reign of his soda shop to carry on their scatterbrained, do-good activities; he fed them for free, and he would be willing to come to their rescue at a moment's notice. That his efforts would generally not be appreciated by his callous comrades mattered not—he had old-country charm, and the dapper over-fifty Jewish-accented proprietor was almost a modern-day Don Quixote. Strangely, the other Bowery Boys had very little to say or do throughout the series, beyond playing extras to the repartee between Slip-Sach-Louie; they could carry out orders, come along for the ride; but never had more than three words at a time to say throughout any one film.

A somewhat perverse enjoyment of *Bowery Boys* films is to judge which entry has the sleeziest sets, the less classy dames or the crummiest villains. That the actors portraying the "Boys" were playing roles of twenty-year-olds when they had passed forty, seemed inconsequential. However, as the years rolled by, and economy-minded Allied Artists further cut back on the slim budgets for the quickie films, the number of supporting players decreased both in quantity and quality. Gone were villains like Douglass Dumbrille, Sheldon Leonard, Nestor Paiva, Hillary Brooke, Martin Kosleck; heroines such as Jane Randolph, Teala Loring, Rosemary La Planche, Adele Jerkins, or such reassuring character performers as Mary Gordon (as Slip's mother), Minerva Urecal, Frankie Darro (as Feathers, Bananas *et al*), Stanley Andrews, and Ida Moore. That the "Bowery Boys" took themselves seriously was all part of the fun, although occasionally an "in" reference to the fact that they were in the films would crop in, such as in *Angels' Alley* where the disgruntled Sach tells Slip at the finale "This is the last time I make a movie with you."

The actors who later became the Bowery Boys first were joined professionally in the Broadway run of Sidney Kingsley's *Dead End* in 1936. Huntz Hall, born in Manhattan in the late teens, attended the Professional Chidrens' School and as a youth was a member of a local singing group. In the early 1930s he was featured on several radio serials, including *Bobby Benson* with Billy Halop. After the finale of the *Bowery Boys* films, he would be seen occasionally in character roles in films and on television, his latest film to date is *The Phynx* (1970). Leo Gorcey, born June 3, 1915, in New York, was the son of Bernard Gorcey, a stage actor who was the original Isaac Cohen in *Abie's Irish Rose*. Gorcey was not originally in the Broadway production of *Dead End* but later joined the cast in the role of "Spit," replacing Charles Duncan. When Swiss-born Bernard Gorcey died in an automobile accident September 11, 1955, the younger Gorcey withdrew from the *Bowery Boys* series and retired to his ranch. Married five times, he had a son and two daughters. He wrote his autobiography, *Original Dead End Yells, Wedding Bells, Cockle Shells and Crazy Spells* in 1967; his last two film roles were cameos in *It's A Mad, Mad, Mad World* (1963) and *The Phynx* (1970). He died June 2, 1969 in Oakland, California.

When Samuel Goldwyn bought the film rights to *Dead End* he hired the youths to repeat their roughneck stage roles. Then the group appeared in such Warner Bros. features as *Crime School* (1938), *Angels With Dirty Faces* (1938), *They Made Me a Criminal* (1939), and *The Return of Dr. X* (1939). Meanwhile, Huntz Hall and others of the crew, minus Leo Gorcey, made *Little Tough Guy* (1938) at Universal, leading to a new splinter group of films produced by that studio. In early 1940, Sam Katzman began producing his inexpensive "East Side Kids" comedies at Monogram Pictures, with Leo Gorcey as the group leader, while Huntz Hall was still at Universal. Hall eventually played in some of the Monogram entries, including *Spooks Run Wild* (1941), *Mr. Wise Guy* (1942), *Come Out Fighting* (1945) as well as appearing in additional Universal features and serials such as *Sea Raiders* (1941) and *Tough as They Come* (1942). Hall received high critical acclaim for his serious role in *A Walk in the Sun* (1946), a World War II drama directed by Lewis Milestone.

In 1946, the perennial youngish "Dead End Kids" reorganized themselves for a new series at Monogram, co-produced by Jan Grippo (the actors' agent) and by Hall and Leo Gorcey. Gorcey turned the segments into a family affair, with brother David and father Bernard added to the repertory group.

When Gorcey retired from the series in 1955, Stanley Clements was elevated to co-starring roles opposite Hall for the remaining seven entries.

In the earlier post-1946 *Bowery Boys* films, the roughnecks were continually engaged in do-good events in their low-class neighborhood. *In Fast Company* concerns taxi warfare; *News Hounds* has Slip as a reporter for the *Post World*, Sach an amateur photographer, and their involvement with a crooked prize fighting fix; *Trouble Makers* has the Boys scouting a local murder gang and bringing them to justice. *Angels' Alley* shows them trying to reform Slip's cousin, employed by car thieves, *Blonde Dynamite* concerns their running an escort bureau and trapping a ring of bank robbers, and *Hold that Baby* deals with a lost child found in a bundle of washing and a rich inheritance involved.

Another familiar format of the *Bowery Boys* was amazing super-ordinary powers suddenly thrust upon Sach: in *Master Minds* Sach develops prophetic powers and is kidnapped by a mad scientist for bizarre experimentation; *Blues Busters* shows Sach having a throat operation and acquiring a good singing voice; *Private Eyes* finds Sach possessing mind reading abilities after he is punched in the nose, and the Boys capitalize on his new talent by taking over a detective agency; in *Jungle Gents* Sach has the unique ability to smell out hidden diamonds and is hired to locate a cache of stolen gems secreted in a jungle cave; *Crashing Las Vegas* reveals Sach with a strange clairvoyant ability to foretell winning number combinations, which allows the group to win a Las Vegas trip; *No Holds Barred* concerns Sach's sudden possession of strange physical powers and becoming a noted wrestler; and *Hold that Hypnotist* has Sach in a state of hypnotic regressions, acquiring a treasure map from Blackbeard the Pirate in 1683.

The locale of the *Bowery Boys* films did switch on some occasions from the sparse, unimaginative sweet shop, but budget-minded Monogram-Allied Artists never allowed for any elaborate sets (the crude slapped-together furnishings of the series had their own peculiar charm): the Boys are in ritzy company at the Jones Mansion in *High Society;* in *Hot Shots* they are television executives —for a brief spell; *Hold that Line* sees the Boys sent to college in the hopes of transforming them into gentlemen; *Loose in London* shows the roughnecks in England when it is thought Sach is a relative of a dying earl; the crew goes out west in *Bowery Buckaroos,* clearing Louie of a murder charge, and *Dig that Uranium* details their frontier adventures exploring desert land they have purchased; *Jungle Gents* focuses on their African safari to hunt diamonds; *Crashing Las Vegas* is set in the gambling capital; *Paris Playboys* follows their French jaunt, where Sach proves to be the double of a French scientist; the gang are in the hoosegoose in *Triple Trouble* and *Jail Busters,* taking bum raps to find the real crooks; and *In the Money* details Sach's transatlantic voyage on a visit to England.

As with other long-running cinema series, the *Bowery Boys* fell back on the service comedy format to enliven their stable of well-used jokes and routines; *Clipped Wings* (the Air Force), *Here Come the Marines; Let's Go Navy;* and *Bowery Batallion* (the Army).

Very often the occult, ghosts, and magic played a large role in *Bowery Boys* episodes. *Ghost Chasers* has Edgar the friendly ghost helping the boys capture a band of crooks; *Bowery to Bagdad* details the Boys' sudden acquisition of Aladdin's lamp and their becoming masters of a most amiable genie; *Bowery Boys Meet the Monsters* brings the do-gooders face to face with a mad doctor and his menagerie of monsters; *Spook Busters* shows them graduating from exterminating school, and practicing their new art at an old "haunted" mansion; *Spook Chasers* centers on the group obtaining an old farm house where crooks have hidden jewels, and their valiant attempts to scare the robbers into leaving the premises; *Up in Smoke* has the offbeat plot of Sach selling his soul to the Devil to obtain gambling information.

Another favorite *Bowery Boys* plot gambit involved the trouble shooters with the sporting world; in *Crazy over Horses* they enter the big horse race when they are forced to accept a race horse in payment for a debt; *Hold that Line* finds them at college with Sach a football player; in *Mr. Hex* Sach is an amateur boxer turned pro; *No Holds Barred* has Sach a proficient wrestler; *Fighing Fools* concerns the boxing game with Slip as an overeager fight manager; and *Jalopy* follows the group's adventures when they invent a new type fuel which they hope will win them a stock car meet.

The *Bowery Boys* must be accorded the distinction of doing much with very little; of protracting a satisfactory formula for two decades of movie making; and for creating a seemingly timeless mileau which obviously bears constant revisiting; for the projection of such characters as good natured Louie, the incredibly dumb but nice "Sach-ali" (as Louie affectionately called him) and the kind hearted tough mug Slip.

Leo Gorcey.

Huntz Hall as Satch Star.

David Gorcey, Huntz Hall, Bennie Bartlett, Leo
Gorcey, Billy Benedict. (Trouble Makers)

Gorcey, Jean Kean. (Angels in Disguise)

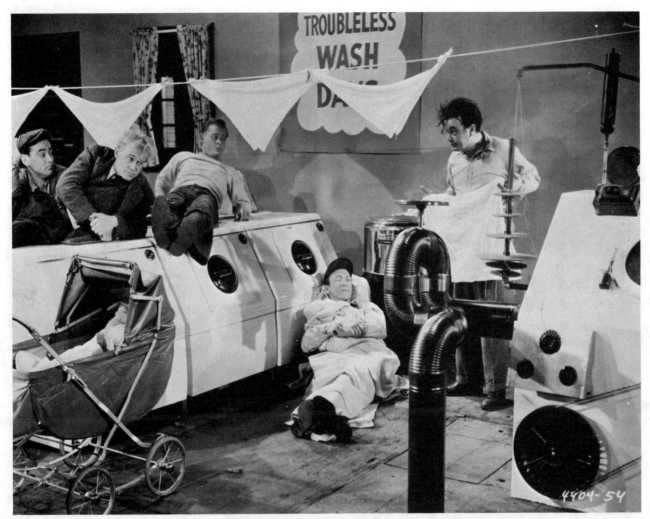

Gorcey, David Gorcey, Billy Benedict, Bartlett, Hall.
(Hold that Baby!)

Bernard Gorcey, Jody Gilbert, Hall. (Blonde Dynamite)

Gorcey, Hall. (Lucky Losers)

Gorcey, Hall. (No Holds Barred)

Hanley Stafford, Lisa Wilson, Hall. (Here Come the Marines)

Hall. (Loose in London)

Gorcey, Ellen Corby. (The Bowery Boys Meet the Monsters)

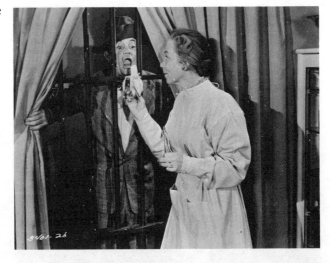

Patrick O'Moore, Bernard Gorcey, David Gorcey, Bartlett, Hall. (Jungle Gents)

Veola Vonn, Leo Gorcey. (Spy Chasers)

Hall, Leo Gorcey. (Jail Busters)

Gorcey, Bartlett, Hall, Leo and David Gorcey. (Dig That Uranium)

*Jimmy Murphy, David Gorcey (kneeling), Hall and
Leo Gorcey, Bob Hopkins. (Crashing Las Vegas)*

Hall, Stanley Clements, Jane Nigh. (Hold that Hypnotist)

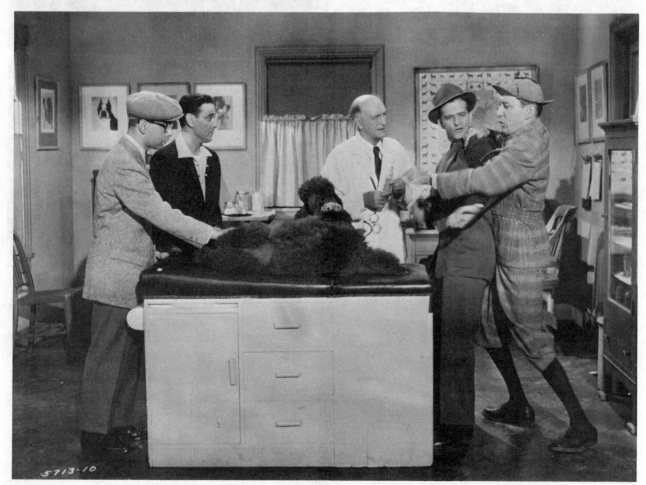

Bennie Bartlett, David Gorcey, Owen McGiveney,
Stanley Clements, Hall. (In the Money)

IN FAST COMPANY (Mon., 1946) 61 M.

Producer, Lindsley Parsons, Jan Grippo; director, Del Lord; author, Martin Mooney; screenplay, Edmond Seward, Tim Ryan, Victor Hammond; music director, Edward Kay; camera, William Sickner; editor, William Austin.

Slip	Leo Gorcey
Sach	Huntz Hall
Bobby	Bobby Jordan
Whitey	Billy Benedict
Mabel Dumbrowski	Judy Clark
Marian McCormick	Jane Randolph
Chuck	David Gorcey
Father Donovan	Charles D. Brown
Steve Trent	Douglas Fowley
Patrick McCormick	Paul Harvey
Sally Turner	Marjorie Woodworth
Mr. Cassidy	Frank Marlowe
Pete	Dick Wessel
Gus	William Ruhl
Tony	Luis Alberni

BOWERY BOMBSHELL (Mon., 1946) 65 M.

Producer, Lindsley Parsons, Jan Grippo; director, Phil Karlson; author-screenplay, Edmond Seward; music director, Edward Kay; camera, William Sickner; editor, William Austin.

Slip	Leo Gorcey
Sach	Huntz Hall
Bobby	Bobby Jordan
Whitey	Billy Benedict
Chuck	David Gorcey
Cathy Smith	Teala Loring
O'Malley	James Burke
Ace Deuce	Sheldon Leonard
Street Cleaner	Vince Barnett
Dugan	William Newell
Prof. Schnackenberger	Milton Parsons
Louie	Bernard Gorcey
Moose	Wm. "Wee Willie" Davis
Featherfingers	Lester Dorr
Mug #1	William Ruhl
O'Hara	Eddie Dunn

LIVE WIRES (Mon., 1946) 64 M.

Producer, Lindsley Parsons, Jan Grippo; director, Phil Karlson; author, Jeb Schary; screenplay, Tim Ryan, Josef Mischel; music director, Dave Milton; camera, William Sickner; editor, Fred Maguire.

Slip	Leo Gorcey
Sach	Huntz Hall
Bobby	Bobby Jordan
Whitey	Billy Benedict
Eddie	William Frambes
Jeanette	Claudia Drake
Mary	Pamela Blake

Mabel	Patti Brill
Patsy Clark	Mike Mazurki
Herbert Sayers	John Eldredge
Stevens	Pat Gleason
Construction Foreman	William Ruhl
George	Rodney Bell
Boyfriend	Bill Christy
Girlfriend	Nancy Brinkman
Barton	Robert E. Keane

SPOOK BUSTERS (Mon., 1946) 68 M.

Producer, Jan Grippo; director, William Beaudine; author, Edmond Seward, Tim Ryan; music director, Edward J. Kay; camera, Harry Neumann; editor, Richard Currier, William Austin.

Slip	Leo Gorcey
Sach	Huntz Hall
Dr. Coslow	Douglass Dumbrille
Bobby	Bobby Jordan
Gabe	Gabriel Dell
Whitey	Billy Benedict
Chuck	David Gorcey
Mignon	Tanis Chandler
Dr. Bender	Maurice Cass
Mrs. Grimm	Vera Lewis
Stiles	Charles Middleton
Brown	Chester Clute
Ivan	Richard Alexander
Louie	Bernard Gorcey
Dean Pettyboff	Charles Millsfield
Herman	Arthur Miles
Police Captain	Tom Coleman

MR. HEX (Mon., 1946) 63 M.

Producer, Jan Grippo; associate producer, Cyril Endfield; director, William Beaudine; author, Jan Grippo; screenplay, Cyril Endfield; music director, Edward J. Kay; art director, David Milton; camera, James Brown; editor, Richard Currier, Seth Larson.

Slip	Leo Gorcey
Sach	Huntz Hall
Bobby	Bobby Jordan
Gabe	Gabriel Dell
Whitey	Billy Benedict
Chuck	David Gorcey
Gloria	Gale Robbins
Bull Lagina	Ben Weldon
Raymond	Ian Keith
Evil Eyes Fagin	Sammy Keith
Louie	Bernard Gorcey
Mob Leader	William Ruhl
Danny The Dip	Danny Beck
Margie	Rita Lynn
Belly Butterworth	Joe Gray
Blackie	Eddie Gribbon

BOWERY BUCKAROOS (Mon., 1947) 66 M.

Producer, Jan Grippo; director, William Beaudine; au-

thor-screenplay, Tim Ryan, Edmond Seward; music director, Edward Kay; art director, Dave Milton; camera, Marcel Le Picard.

Slip	Leo Gorcey
Sach	Huntz Hall
Bobby	Bobby Jordan
Gabe	Gabriel Dell
Whitey	Billy Benedict
Chuck	David Gorcey
Carolyn Briggs	Julie Gibson
Louie	Bernard Gorcey
Blackjack	Jack Norman
Kate Barlow	Minerva Urecal
Luke Barlow	Russell Simpson
Chief Hi-Octane	Chief Yowlachi
Indian Joe	Iron Eyes Cody
Ramona	Rosa Turich
Rufe	Sherman Sanders
Moose	Billy Wilkerson
Jose	Jack O'Shea
Spike	Bud Osborne

HARD BOILED MAHONEY (Mon., 1947) 63 M.

Producer, Jan Grippo; director, William Beaudine; author-screenplay, Cyril Endfield; art director, Dave Milton; camera, Jim Brown.

Slip	Leo Gorcey
Sach	Huntz Hall
Bobby	Bobby Jordan
Whitey	Billy Benedict
Chuck	David Gorcey
Gabe	Gabriel Dell
Eleanor	Teala Loring
Armand	Dan Seymour
Louie	Bernard Gorcey
Alice	Patti Brill
Selena Webster	Betty Compson
Lennie the Meatball	Danny Beck
Dr. Carter	Pierre Watkin
Hasson	Noble Johnson
Professor Quizard	Byron Foulger
Thug	Teddy Pavelec
Police Lieutenant	Pat O'Malley
Police Sergeant	Jack Cheatham

NEWS HOUNDS (Mon., 1947) 68 M.

Producer, Jan Grippo; director, William Beaudine; author, Tim Ryan, Edmond Seward, George Cappy; screenplay, Edward Seward, Tim Ryan; art director, Dave Milton; music director, Edward Kay; camera, Marcel Le Picard; editor, William Austin.

Slip	Leo Gorcey
Sach	Huntz Hall
Bobby	Bobby Jordan
Whitey	Billy Benedict
Chuck	David Gorcey
Gabe	Gabriel Dell
Louie	Bernard Gorcey

John Burke	Tim Ryan
Mark Morgan	Bill Kennedy
Mack Snide	Robert Emmett Keane
Jane Ann Connelly	Christine McIntyre
"Clothes" Greco	Anthony Caruso
Dutch Miller	Ralph Dunn
Judge	John Elliott
Red Kane	Leo Kaye

ANGELS' ALLEY (Mon., 1947) 67 M.

Producer, Jan Grippo; director, William Beaudine; author-screenplay, Edmond Seward, Tim Ryan, Gerald Schnitzer; art director, Dave Milton; music director, Edward J. Kay; camera, Marcel Le Picard; editor, William Austin.

Slip	Leo Gorcey
Sach	Huntz Hall
Ricky	Gabriel Dell
Whitey	Billy Benedict
Chuck	David Gorcey
Jimmy	Frankie Darro
Tony (Piggy) Lucarno	Nestor Paiva
Daisy Harris	Rosemary La Planche
Josie O'Neill	Geneva Gray
"Jag" Harmon	Bennie Bartlett
Willis	John Eldredge
Father O'Hanlon	Nelson Leigh
Boomer	Tommie Menzies
Mrs. Mahoney	Mary Gordon
Jockey Burns	Dick Paxton
Andy Miller	Buddy Gorman
Attorney Felix Crowe	Robert Emmett Keane

JINX MONEY (Mon., 1948) 68 M.

Producer, Jan Grippo; director, William Beaudine; author-screenplay, Edmond Seward, Tim Ryan, Gerald Schnitzer; suggested by story by Jerome T. Gollard; art director, Dave Milton; music director, Edward J. Kay; camera, Marcel Le Picard; editor, William Austin.

Slip	Leo Gorcey
Sach	Huntz Hall
Gabe	Gabriel Dell
Lippy Harris	Sheldon Leonard
Lt. Broderick	Donald MacBride
Candy	Betty Caldwell
Whitey	Billy Benedict
Chuck	David Gorcey
Lullaby Shmo	John Eldredge
Benny "The Meatball"	Ben Welden
Tipper	Lucien Littlefield
Louie	Bernard Gorcey
Butch	Benny Bartlett
Augie	Benny Baker
Jake "Cold Deck" Shapiro	Ralph Dunn
Virginia	Wanda McKay
Officer Rooney	Tom Kennedy
Sgt. Ryan	William Ruhl

SMUGGLERS COVE (Mon., 1948) 66 M.

Producer, Jan Grippo; director, William Beaudine; au-

thor, Talbert Josselyn; screenplay, Edmond Seward, Tim Ryan; music director, Edward J. Kay; camera, Marcel Le Picard; editor, William Austin.

Slip	Leo Gorcey
Sach	Huntz Hall
Gabe	Gabriel Dell
Whitey	Billy Benedict
Chuck	David Gorcey
Butch	Benny Bartlett
Count Petrov Bons	Martin Kosleck
Terrence Mahoney, Esq.	Paul Harvey
Teresa Mahoney	Amelita Ward
Sandra	Jacqueline Dalya
Digger	Eddie Gribbon
Captain Drum	Gene Stutenroth
Dr. Latka	Leonid Snegoff
Franz Leiber	John Bleifer
Karl	Andre Pola
Ryan	William Ruhl
Attorney Williams	Emmett Vogan
Messenger	Buddy Gorman
Building Manager	George Meader

TROUBLE MAKERS (Mon., 1948) 69 M.

Producer, Jan Grippo; director, Reginald Le Borg; author, Gerald Schnitzer; screenplay, Edmond Seward, Tim Ryan, Gerald Schnitzer; music director, Edward J. Kay; camera, Marcel Le Picard; editor, William Austin.

Slip	Leo Gorcey
Sach	Huntz Hall
Gabe	Gabriel Dell
Whitey	Billy Benedict
Chuck	David Gorcey
Feathers	Frankie Darro
Hennessey	Fritz Feld
Ann Prescott	Helen Parrish
"Silky" Thomas	John Ridgely
"Hatchet" Moran	Lionel Stander
Butch	Benny Bartlett
Louie	Bernard Gorcey
Capt. Madison	Cliff Clark
Jones	William Ruhl
Stunt Double (Huntz Hall)	Carey Loftin
Stunt Double (Leo Gorcey)	Frankie Darro

ANGELS IN DISGUISE (Mon., 1949) 63 M.

Producer, Jan Grippo; director, Jean Yarbrough; author-screenplay, Charles B. Marion, Gerald Schnitzer, Bert Lawrence; art director, Dave Milton; music director, Edward Kay; camera, Marcel Le Picard; editor, William Austin.

Slip	Leo Gorcey
Sach	Huntz Hall
Whitey	Billy Benedict
Chuck	David Gorcey
Butch	Benny Bartlett
Gabe Moreno	Gabriel Dell
Louie Dumbrowsky	Bernard Gorcey

Angles	Mickey Knox
Carver	Edward Ryan
Miami	Richard Benedict
Johnny Mutton	Joseph Turkel
Jim Cobb	Ray Walker
Roger T. Harrison	William Forrest
Bertie Spangler	Pepe Hern
Millie	Marie Blake
Johnson (Foreman)	Roy Gordon
Nurse	Jane Adams
Hodges	Don Harvey
Bookkeeper	Tristram Coffin

BLONDE DYNAMITE (Mon., 1950) 66 M.

Producer, Jan Grippo; director, William Beaudine; screenplay, Charles B. Marion; art director, Dave Milton; music director, Edward Kay; camera, Marcel Le Picard; editor, William Austin.

Slip	Leo Gorcey
Sach	Huntz Hall
Joan Marshall	Adele Jergens
Gabe Moreno	Gabriel Dell
Champ	Harry Lewis
Dynamite	Murray Alper
Louie	Bernard Gorcey
Sarah	Jody Gilbert
Whitey	Billy Benedict
Chuck	David Gorcey
Professor	John Harmon
Samson	Michael Ross
Verna	Lynn Davies
Bunny	Beverlee Crane
Tracy	Karen Randle
Mr. Jennings	Stanley Andrews
First Dowager	Constance Purdy
Second Dowager	Florence Auer

FIGHTING FOOLS (Mon., 1949) 69 M.

Producer, Jan Grippo; director, Reginald Le Borg; author-screenplay, Edmond Seward, Gerald Schnitzer, Bert Lawrence; art director, Dave Milton; music director, Edward Kay; camera, William Sickner; editor, William Austin.

Slip Mahoney	Leo Gorcey
Sach	Huntz Hall
Gabe Moreno	Gabriel Dell
Whitey	Billy Benedict
Chuck	David Gorcey
Butch	Benny Bartlett
Johnny Higgins	Frankie Darro
Blinky Harris	Lyle Talbot
Louie	Bernard Gorcey
Boomer	Teddy Infuhr
Guard	Tom Kennedy
Mrs. Higgins	Dorothy Vaughan
Bunny Talbot	Evelyn Eaton
Goon	Frank Moran

HOLD THAT BABY (Mon., 1949) 64 M.

Producer, Jan Grippo; director, Reginald Le Borg; au-

thor-screenplay, Charles B. Marion, Gerald Schnitzer; music director, Edward Kay; camera, William Sickner; editor, William Austin.

Slip Mahoney	Leo Gorcey
Sach Debussey Jones	Huntz Hall
Whitey	Billy Benedict
Chuck	David Gorcey
Butch	Benny Bartlett
Gabe Moreno	Gabriel Dell
Louie Dumbrowsky	Bernard Gorcey
Bananas	Frankie Darro
Cherry Nose Gray	John Kellogg
Gypsy Moran	Max Marx
Laura Andrews	Anabel Shaw
Burton (cop)	Edward Gargan
Joe The Crooner	Meyer Grace
Jonathan Andrews III	Judy and Jody Dunn
Hope Andrews	Florence Auer
Faith Andrews	Ida Moore
First Policeman	William Ruhl

MASTER MINDS (Mon., 1949) 64 M.

Producer, Jan Grippo; director, Jean Yarbrough; screenplay, Charles R. Marion; art director, Dave Milton; music director, Edward Kay; camera, Marcel Le Picard; editor, William Austin.

Slip Mahoney	Leo Gorcey
Sach Debussy Jones	Huntz Hall
Whitey	Billy Benedict
Butch	Bennie Bartlett
Chuck	David Gorcey
Gabe Moreno	Gabriel Dell
Louie Dumbrowsky	Bernard Gorcey
Atlas	Glenn Strange
Dr. Druzik	Alan Napier
Otto	William Yetter
Benny	Kit Guard
Hugo	Skelton Knaggs
Nancy Marlowe	Jane Adams
Juggler	Whitey Roberts
Hoskins (Constable)	Harry Tyler
Woman	Anna Chandler
Mike Barton	Chester Clute
Mrs. Hoskins	Minerva Urecal
Henchman	Stanley Blystone

BLUES BUSTERS (Mon., 1950) 67 M.

Producer, Jan Grippo; director, William Beaudine; screenplay, Charles R. Marion; art director, Dave Milton; music director, Edward Kay; camera, Marcel Le Picard; editor, William Austin.

Slip Mahoney	Leo Gorcey
Sach Debussy Jones	Huntz Hall
Lola Stanton	Adele Jergens
Gabe Moreno	Gabriel Dell
Rick Martin	Craig Stevens
Sally Dolan	Phyllis Coates

Teddy Davis	William Vincent
Louie Dumbrowsky	Bernard Gorcey
Whitey	Billy Benedict
Butch	Buddy Gorman
Chuck	David Gorcey
Bimbo	Paul Bryar
Joe Ricco	Matty King

LUCKY LOSERS (Mon., 1950) 69 M.

Producer, Jan Grippo; director, William Beaudine; screenplay, Charles R. Marion, Bert Lawrence; art director, David Milton; music director, Edward J. Kay; camera, Marcel Le Picard; editor, William Austin.

Slip Mahoney	Leo Gorcey
Sach	Huntz Hall
Countess	Hillary Brooke
Gabe Moreno	Gabriel Dell
Bruce McDermott	Lyle Talbot
Louie Dumbrowsky	Bernard Gorcey
Whitey	William Benedict
Johnny Angelo	Joseph Turkel
Buffer McGee	Harry Tyler
Butch	Buddy Gorman
Chuck	David Gorcey
Chic	Harry Cheshire
Bartender	Frank Jenks
Tom Whitney	Douglas Evans
Carol Thurston	Wendy Waldron
Andrew Stone III	Glen Vernon
2nd Conventioner	Chester Clute
David Thurston	Selmer Jackson

TRIPLE TROUBLE (Mon., 1950) 66 M.

Producer, Jan Grippo; director, Jean Yarbrough; screenplay, Charles R. Marion; art director, Dave Milton; music director, Edward Kay; camera, Marcel Le Picard; editor, William Austin.

Slip Mahoney	Leo Gorcey
Sach	Huntz Hall
Gabe Moreno	Gabriel Dell
Skeets O'Neil	Richard Benedict
Bat Armstrong	Pat Collins
Shirley O'Brien	Lyn Thomas
Louie Dumbrowsky	Bernard Gorcey
Pretty Boy Gleason	Paul Dubov
Benny The Blood	Joseph Turkel
Whitey	William Benedict
Butch	Buddy Gorman
Chuck	David Gorcey
Squirrely Davis	George Chandler
Hobo Barton	Eddie Gribbon
Judge	Jonathan Hale
Warden	Joseph Crehan
Ma Armstrong	Effie Lairch
Murphy	Edward Gargan

BOWERY BATTALION (Mon., 1951) 69 M.

Producer, Jan Grippo; director, William Beaudine;

screenplay, Charles R. Marion; art director, Dave Milton; music director, Edward Kay; camera, Marcel Le Picard; editor, William Austin.

Slip	Leo Gorcey
Sach	Huntz Hall
Frisbie	Donald MacBride
Marsha	Virginia Hewitt
Hatfield	Russell Hicks
Whitey	William Benedict
Louie Dumbrowsky	Bernard Gorcey
Butch	Buddy Gorman
Chuck	David Gorcey
Decker	John Bleifer
Conroy	Al Eben
Recruiting Officer	Frank Jenks
Masters	Selmer Jackson

CRAZY OVER HORSES (Mon., 1951) 65 M.

Producer, Jan Grippo; director, William Beaudine; screenplay, Tim Ryan; camera, Marcel Le Picard; editor, William Austin.

Slip	Leo Gorcey
Sach	Huntz Hall
Whitey	William Benedict
Louie	Bernard Gorcey
Chuck	David Gorcey
Butch	Bennie Bartlett
Duke	Ted de Corsia
Weepin' Willie	Allen Jenkins
Swifty	Mike Ross
Flynn	Tim Ryan
Terry	Gloria Saunders
Mazie	Peggy Wynne
Uniformed Guard	Bob Peoples
Charlie	Pere Launders
Groom	Leo "Ukie" Sherin

GHOST CHASERS (Mon., 1951) 69 M.

Producer, Jan Grippo; director, William Beaudine; screenplay, Charles R. Marion, Bert Lawrence; art director, Dave Milton; camera, Marcel Le Picard; editor, William Austin.

Slip Mahoney	Leo Gorcey
Sach	Huntz Hall
Whitey	William Benedict
Chuck	David Gorcey
Butch	Buddy Gorman
Louie Dumbrowsky	Bernard Gorcey
Cynthia	Jan Kayne
Dr. Granville	Philip Van Zandt
Jack Eagen	Robert Coogan
Gus	Michael Ross
Edgar	Lloyd Corrigan
Leonard	Donald Lawton
1st Reporter	Paul Bryar
2nd Reporter	Pat Gleason
Photographer	Bob Peoples

Mrs. Parelli	Argentina Brunetti
Mrs. Mahoney	Doris Kemper
Madame Zola	Belle Mitchell

LET'S GO NAVY (Mon., 1951) 68 M.

Producer, Jan Grippo; director, William Beaudine; screenplay, Max Adams; art director, Dave Milton; music director, Edward Kay; camera, Marcel Le Picard; editor, William Austin.

Slip Mahoney	Leo Gorcey
Sach	Huntz Hall
Whitey	William Benedict
Chuck	David Gorcey
Louie Dumbrowsky	Bernard Gorcey
Butch	Buddy Gorman
Longnecker	Allen Jenkins
Joe	Tom Neal
Red	Richard Benedict
1st Sailor	Jimmy Cross
2nd Sailor	Bill Chandler
3rd Sailor	Don Gordon
4th Sailor	Neyle Morrow
5th Sailor	Joey Ray
Sailor	Murray Alper
Dalton	Harry Lauter

FEUDIN' FOOLS (Mon., 1952) 63 M.

Producer, Jerry Thomas; director, William Beaudine; screenplay, Bert Lawrence, Tim Ryan; art director, Dave Milton; music director, Edward Kay; camera, Marcel Le Picard; editor, William Austin.

Slip	Leo Gorcey
Sach	Huntz Hall
Butch	Bennie Bartlett
Chuck	David Gorcey
Louie	Bernard Gorcey
Luke Smith	Paul Wexler
Clem Smith	Oliver Blake
Caleb Smith	Bob Easton
Yancy Smith	O. Z. Whitehead
Ellie Mae	Anne Kimbell
Tiny Smith	Dorothy Ford
Pinky	Leo "Ukie" Sherin
Corky	Benny Baker
Big Jim	Lyle Talbot
Traps	Fuzzy Knight

HERE COME THE MARINES (Mon., 1952) 66 M.

Producer, Jerry Thomas; director, William Beaudine; screenplay, Tim Ryan, Charles R. Marion, Jack Crutcher; art director, Martin Obzina; music director, Edward Kay; camera, Marcel Le Picard; editor, William Austin.

Slip	Leo Gorcey
Sach	Huntz Hall
Chuck	David Gorcey
Butch	Bennie Bartlett

Junior	Gil Stratton
Louie	Bernard Gorcey
Corporal Stacy	Murray Alper
Colonel Brown	Hanley Stafford
Capt. Miller	Arthur Space
Lulu Mae	Myrna Dell
Jolly Joe Johnson	Paul Maxey
Sheriff Benson	Tim Ryan
Desmond	William Newell
Croupier	Sammy Finn
Dealer	Buck Russell

HOLD THAT LINE (Mon., 1952) 64 M.

Producer, Jerry Thomas; director, William Beaudine; screenplay, Tim Ryan, Charles R. Marion; art director, Martin Obzina; musical director, Edward Kay; camera, Marcel Le Picard; editor, William Austin.

Slip	Leo Gorcey
Sach	Huntz Hall
Junior	Gil Stratton, Jr.
Chuck	David Gorcey
Butch	Bennie Bartlett
Louie	Bernard Gorcey
Dean Forrester	Taylor Holmes
Billingsley	Francis Pierlot
Stanhope	Pierre Watkin
Biff	John Bromfield
Harold	Bob Nichols
Katie Wayne	Mona Knox
Penny	Gloria Winters
Coach Rowland	Paul Bryar
Asst. Coach	Bob Peoples
Candy Calin	Veda Ann Borg
Professor Grog	Byron Foulger

NO HOLDS BARRED (Mon., 1952) 65 M.

Producer, Jerry Thomas; director, William Beaudine; screenplay, Tim Ryan, Jack Crutcher, Bert Lawrence; art director, Dave Milton; music director, Edward Kay; camera, Ernest Miller; editor, William Austin.

Slip	Leo Gorcey
Sach	Huntz Hall
Pete Taylor	Leonard Penn
Rhonda Nelson	Marjorie Reynolds
Louie	Bernard Gorcey
Chuck	David Gorcey
Butch	Bennie Bartlett
Terrible Tova (wrestler)	Hombre Montana
Gertie	Barbara Gray
The Mauler	Henry Kulky
Stickup Man	Nick Stewart
Challenger (wrestler)	Pat Fraley
Crusher Martin (wrestler)	'Brother' Frank Jares
Barney	Murray Alper

CLIPPED WINGS (AA, 1953) 65 M.

Producer, Ben Schwalb; director, Edward Bernds; au-
thor, Charles R. Marion; screenplay, Charles R. Marion, Elwood Ullman; art director, David Milton; camera, Harry Neumann; editor, Bruce B. Pierce.

Slip	Leo Gorcey
Sach	Huntz Hall
Louie	Bernard Gorcey
Chuck	David Condon
Butch	Bennie Bartlett
W.A.F. Sergeant Anderson	Renie Riano
Lieutenant Moreno	Todd Karns
Dorene	June Vincent
Mildred	Mary Treen
Eckler	Philip Van Zanct
Dupre	Frank Richards
Anders	Michael Ross
Sergeant White	Elaine Riley
Hilda	Jeanne Dean
Allison	Anne Kimbell

JALOPY (AA, 1953) 62 M.

Producer, Ben Schwalb; director, William Beaudine; author, Tim Ryan, Jack Crutcher; screenplay, Tim Ryan, Jack Crutcher, Edward Seward, Jr., Bert Lawrence; art director, David Milton; camera, Harry Neumann; editor, William Austin.

Slip	Leo Gorcey
Sach	Huntz Hall
Chuck	David Gorcey
Butch	Bennie Bartlett
Louie	Bernard Gorcey
Skid Wilson	Bob Lowry
Red Baker	Murray Alper
Bobbie Lane	Jane Easton
Tony Lango	Richard Benedict
Professor Bosgood Elrod	Leon Belasco
Girl	Mona Knox
Announcer	Tom Hanlon

LOOSE IN LONDON (AA, 1953) 62½ M.

Producer, Ben Schwalb; director, Edward Bernds; author-screenplay, Elwood Ullman, Edward Bernds; art director, David Milton, camera, Harry Neumann.

Slip	Leo Gorcey
Sach	Huntz Hall
Chuck	David Gorcey
Louie	Bernard Gorcey
Sir Edgar Whipsnade	John Dodsworth
Aunt Agatha	Norma Varden
Reggie	William Cottrell
Lady Marcia	Angela Greene
Herbert	Rex Evans
Earl of Walsingham	Walter Kingsford
Hoskins	James Logan
Higby	Alex Fraser
Tall Girl	Joan Shawlee
Steward	James Fairfax
Sir Talbot	Wilbur Mack

PRIVATE EYES (AA, 1953) 64 M.

Producer, Ben Schwalb; director, Edward Bernds; screenplay, Elwood Ullman, Edward Bernds; art director, David Milton; camera, Carl Guthrie; editor, Lester A. Sansom.

Slip .... Leo Gorcey
Sach .... Huntz Hall
Chuck .... David Condon
Butch .... Bennie Bartlett
Louie .... Bernard Gorcey
Herbie .... Rudy Lee
Myra Hagen .... Joyce Holden
Damon .... Robert Osterloh
Graham .... William Forrest
Soapy .... William Phillips
Al .... Gil Perkins
Chico .... Peter Mamakos
Karl .... Lee Van Cleef
Oskar .... Lou Lubin
Patient .... Emil Sitka

BOWERY BOYS MEET THE MONSTERS (AA, 1954) 65½ M.

Producer, Ben Schwalb; director, Edward Bernds; screenplay, Elwood Ullman, Edward Bernds; art director, David Milton; camera, Harry Neumann; editor, William Austin.

Slip .... Leo Gorcey
Sach .... Huntz Hall
Louie .... Bernard Gorcey
Chuck .... David Gorcey
Butch .... Bennie Bartlett
Derek .... John Dehner
Anton .... Lloyd Corrigan
Grissom .... Paul Wexler
Amelia .... Ellen Corby
Francine .... Laura Mason
Gorgo .... Norman Bishop
Cosmos .... Steve Calvert
Herbie .... Rudy Lee
Officer Martin .... Paul Bryar
O'Meara .... Pat Flaherty
Skippy Biano .... Jack Dimond

JUNGLE GENTS (AA, 1954) 64 M.

Producer, Ben Schwalb; director, Edward Bernds; screenplay, Elwood Ullman, Edward Bernds; art director, David Milton; camera, Harry Neumann.

Slip .... Leo Gorcey
Sach .... Huntz Hall
Chuck .... David Gorcey
Butch .... Bennie Bartlett
Louie .... Bernard Gorcey
Grimshaw .... Patrick O'Moore
Dr. Goebel .... Rudolph Anders
Dan Shanks .... Harry Cording
Malaka .... Woody Strode

Tarzana .... Laurette Luez
Rangori .... Joel Fluellen
Trader Holmes .... Eric Snowden
Lomax .... Murray Alper
Tarzan .... Jett Norman (Clint Walker)

PARIS PLAYBOYS (AA, 1954) 62 M.

Producer, Ben Schwalb; director, William Beaudine; screenplay, Elwood Ullman, Edward Bernds; art director, David Milton; camera, Harry Neumann; editor, Lester A. Sansom.

Slip .... Leo Gorcey
Sach ⎫
Le Beau ⎬ .... Huntz Hall
Louie .... Bernard Gorcey
Mimi .... Veola Vonn
Gaspard .... Steven Geray
Vidal .... John Wengraf
Celeste .... Marianne Lynn
Chuck .... David Condon
Butch .... Bennie Bartlett
Pierre .... Alphonse Martell
Cambon .... Gordon Clark

BOWERY TO BAGDAD (AA, 1955) 64 M.

Producer, Ben Schwalb; director, Edward Bernds; screenplay, Elwood Ullman, Edward Bernds; art director, David Milton; music director, Marlin Skiles; camera, Harry Neumann; editor, John C. Fuller.

Slip .... Leo Gorcey
Sach .... Huntz Hall
Chuck .... David Gorcey
Butch .... Bennie Bartlett
Louie .... Bernard Gorcey
Velma .... Joan Shawlee
Dolan .... Robert Bice
Gus .... Richard Wessel
Canarsie .... Rayford Barnes
Tiny .... Michael Ross
Genii .... Eric Blore
Selim .... Rick Vallin
Abdul .... Paul Marion
Claire .... Jean Willes
Caliph .... Charlie Lung
Man .... Leon Burbank

HIGH SOCIETY (AA, 1955) 61 M.

Producer, Ben Schwalb; director, William Beaudine; author, Elwood Ullman, Edward Bernds; screenplay, Bert Lawrence, Jerome S. Gottler; music director, Marlin Skiles; camera, Harry Neumann; editor, John C. Fuller.

Slip .... Leo Gorcey
Sach .... Huntz Hall
Clarissa .... Amanda Blake
Louie .... Bernard Gorcey
Chuck .... David Condon

Butch	Bennie Bartlett
Stuyvesant	Dayton Lummis
Terwilliger	Ronald Keith
Frisbie	Gavin Gordon
Cosgrove	Addison Richards
Marten	Kem Dibbs
Palumbo	David Barry
Baldwin	Paul Harvey

Jeannette	Mary Beth Hughes
Mac (Slim McKenzie)	Raymond Hatton
Joe Hody	Myron Healey
Frank Loomis	Richard Powers
Ron Haskell	Harry Lauter
Indian	Paul Fierro
Chief	Francis McDonald
Olaf	Frank Kenks
Tex	Don Harvey
Shifty Robertson	Carl Switzer

JAIL BUSTERS (AA, 1955) 61 M.

Producer, Ben Schwalb; director, William Beaudine; screenplay, Edward Bernds, Elwood Ullman; art director, David Milton; music director, Marlin Skiles; camera, Carl Guthrie; editor, William Austin.

Slip	Leo Gorcey
Sach	Huntz Hall
Louis	Bernard Gorcey
Jenkins	Barton MacLane
Ed Lannigan	Anthony Caruso
Warden Oswald	Percy Helton
Chuck	David Gorcey
Butch	Bennie Bartlett
Gus	Murray Alper
Big Greenie	Michael Ross
Dr. Fordyce	Fritz Feld
Bowman	Lyle Talbot
Marty	Henry Kulky

CRASHING LAS VEGAS (AA, 1956) 62 M.

Producer, Ben Schwalb; director, Jean Yarbrough; screenplay, Jack Townley; art director, David Milton; camera, Harry Neumann; editor, George White.

Slip	Leo Gorcey
Sach	Huntz Hall
Butch	Jimmy Murphy
Chuck	David Gorcey
Carol	Mary Castle
Sam	Nicky Blair
Oggy	Mort Mills
Tony	Don Haggerty
1st Policeman	Dick Foote
2nd Policeman	Don Marlowe
Mrs. Kelly	Doris Kemper
Wiley	Jack Rice
Bellboy	Jack Grinnage
Police Sergeant	Terry Frost

SPY CHASERS (AA, 1955) 61 M.

Producer, Ben Schwalb; director, Edward Bernds; screenplay, Bert Lawrence, Jerome S. Gottler; art director, David Milton; music director, Marlin Skiles; camera, Harry Neumann; editor, John C. Fuller.

Slip	Leo Gorcey
Sach	Huntz Hall
Louie	Bernard Gorcey
Chuck	David Gorcey (Condon)
Butch	Bennie Bartlett
Colonel Baxis	Leon Askin
King Rako	Sig Ruman
Lady Zelda	Veola Vonn
Princess Ann	Lisa Davis
Little Girl	Linda Bennett
George	Frank Richards
Michael	Paul Burke
Boris	Richard Benedict

FIGHTING TROUBLE (AA, 1956) 61 M.

Producer, Ben Schwalb; director, George Blair; screenplay, Elwood Ullman; art director, David Milton; music director, Buddy Bregman; camera, Harry Neumann; editor, William Austin.

Sach	Huntz Hall
Duke	Stanley Clements
Mae	Adele Jergens
Handsome Hal	Joseph Downing
Mrs. Kelly	Queenie Smith
Bates	John Bleifer
Arbo	Tomas B. Henry
Chuck	David Gorcey
Dolly	Laurie Mitchell
Butch	Danny Welton
Smith	Charles Williams
McBride	Clegg Hoty
Conroy	William Boyett
Vance	Tim Ryan
Evans	Michael Ross
Max Kling	Benny Burt
Hawaiian Girl	Ann Griffith
Vic	Rick Vallin

DIG THAT URANIUM (AA, 1956) 61 M.

Producer, Ben Schwalb; director, Edward Bernds; screenplay, Elwood Ullman, Bert Lawrence; camera, Ellsworth Fredericks.

Slip	Leo Gorcey
Sach	Huntz Hall
Louie	Bernard Gorcey
Chuck	David Gorcey
Butch	Bennie Bartlett

HOT SHOTS (AA, 1956) 61 M.

Producer, Ben Schwalb; director, Jean Yarbrough; author, Jack Townley; screenplay, Jack Townley, Elwood

Ullman; art director, David Milton; music director, Marlin Skiles; camera, Harry Neumann; editor, Neil Brunnenkant.

Sach (Horace DeBussy Jones)	Huntz Hall
Duke (Stanislaus Coveleske)	Stanley Clements
Connie Forbes	Joi Lansing
Myron	Jimmy Murphy
Chuck	David Gorcey
Mrs. Kelly	Queenie Smith
Joey Munroe	Philip Phillips
P. M. Morley	Robert Shayne
George Slater	Mark Dana
Karl	Henry Rowland
Tony	Dennis Moore
Mrs. Taylor	Isabel Randolph
Henry (Bartender)	Frank Marlowe

SPOOK CHASERS (AA, 1957) 62 M.

Producer, Ben Schwalb; director, George Blair; screenplay, Elwood Ullman; art director, David Milton; camera, Harry Neumann; editor, Neil Brunnenkant.

Sach	Huntz Hall
Duke	Stanley Clements
Chuck	David Gorcey
Myron	Jimmy Murphy
Mike Clancy	Percy Helton
Dolly Owens	Darlene Fields
Blinky	Eddie LeRoy
Harry Shelby	Bill Henry
Snap	Peter Mamakos
Ziggie	Ben Welden
Lt. Harris	Robert Shayne
Ernie	Robert Christopher

HOLD THAT HYPNOTIST (AA, 1957) 61 M.

Producer, Ben Schwalb; director, Austen Jewell; screenplay, Dan Pepper; art director, David Milton; camera, Harry Neumann; editor, George White.

Sach	Huntz Hall
Duke	Stanley Clements
Cleo	Jane Nigh
Dr. Noble	Robert Foulk
Morgan	James Flavin
Mrs. Kelly	Queenie Smith
Chuck	David Condon
Myron	Jimmy Murphy
Gale	Murray Alper
Clerk	Dick Elliott
Blackbeard	Mel Welles

LOOKING FOR DANGER (AA, 1957) 62 M.

Producer, Ben Schwalb; director, Austen Jewell; screenplay, Elwood Ullman; art director, David Milton; camera, Harry Neumann.

Sach	Huntz Hall
Duke	Stanley Clements
Blinky	Eddie LeRoy

Chuck	David Condon
Myron	Jimmy Murphy
Ahmed	Richard Avonde
Wolff	Otto Reichow
Sidi-Omar	Michael Granger
Hassan	Peter Mamakos
Shareen	Lili Kardell
Zarida	Joan Bradshaw
Mustapha	George Khoury
Wetzel	Henry Rowland
Mike Clancy	Percy Helton
Watson	Harry Strang
Harper	Paul Bryar
Sari	Jane Burgess
Bradfield	John Harmon
Waiter	Michael Vallon

UP IN SMOKE (AA, 1958) 61 M.

Producer, Richard Heermance; director, William Beaudine; author, Elwood Ullman, Bert Lawrence; screenplay, Jack Townley; art director, David Milton; music director, Marlin Skiles; camera, Harry Neumann.

Sach	Huntz Hall
Duke	Stanley Clements
Mabel	Judy Bamber
Blinky	Eddie LeRoy
Chuck	David Gorcey
Tony	Ric Roman
Satan	Byron Foulger
Mike	Dick Elliott
Sam	Ralph Sanford
Al	Joe Devlin
Policeman	James Flavin
Friendly Frank	Earle Hodgins
Desk Sergeant	John Mitchum
Police Clerk	Jack Mulhall
Dr. Bluzak	Fritz Feld
Drugist	Wilbur Mack
Bernie	Benny Rubin

IN THE MONEY (AA, 1958) 61 M.

Producer, Richard Heermance; director, William Beaudine; author, Al Martin; screenplay, Al Martin, Elwood Ullman; art director, David Milton; music director, Marlin Skiles; camera, Harry Neumann; editor, Neil Brunnenkant.

Sach	Huntz Hall
Duke	Stanley Clements
Chuck	David Gorcey
Blinky	Eddie LeRoy
Clarke	Leonard Penn
Babs	Patricia Donahue
Cummings	John Dodsworth
Inspector Saunders	Paul Cavanagh
Inspector White	Leslie Denison
Bellboy	Ashley Cowan
Dowager	Norman Varden
Mike	Dick Elliott
Dr. Smedley	Owen McGiveney
Randall	Ralph Gamble
Reggie	Patrick O'Moore
Girl	Pamela Light

CHARLIE CHAN

A welcome change of pace from the assembly-line group of American and British detective series was Earl Derr Biggers' (1884–1933) famous Chinese sleuth, Charlie Chan, first introduced to the reading public in a serialized version of the novel *The House Without a Key* (1925). Five more Chan books appeared; only the last, *Keeper of the Keys* (1932), was not filmed. In 1926, Pathé filmed a serial version of *The House Without a Key* with Japanese actor George Kuwa as Chan. In 1928, Universal turned *The Chinese Parrot* into a motion picture with Kamiyama Sojin, another Japanese performer, as the detective from Honolulu. The first sound film with Charlie Chan was *Behind that Curtain* (1929) in which Fox Films reconstructed the novel as a starring vehicle for Warner Baxter and Lois Moran. English actor E. L. Park had the insignificant role of Charlie Chan. Then Fox produced *Charlie Chan Carries On* (1931) starring Swedish actor Warner Oland, and continued on for sixteen additional entries, before the player's death in 1938. Scotch-descended character actor Sidney Toler successfully carried on as Chan beginning with . . . *In Honolulu* (1938) and made ten more *Charlie Chan* entries at Fox. Then the series lay dormant for two years, until Monogram Pictures picked up the property, with Toler continuing on for eleven low-budget segments at that studio. When he died in 1947, film and television character actor Roland Winters assumed the part, and portrayed Chan for six dismal productions before the series disappeared in 1949. (On radio, Walter Connolly, Ed Begley, Santos Ortego played Charlie Chan, with Leon Janney as number one son. On television, J. Carrol Naish appeared as Chan in *The New Adventures of Charlie Chan*, 39 half-hour episodes filmed in England during the 1957–58 season.)

Universal Pictures, which acquired rights to the *Chan* property, is currently preparing a two-hour telefeature on *Charlie* as a series pilot with Marvin Miller as Chan.

Perhaps the most essential ingredient which has insured the continued popularity of the *Charlie Chan* films has been the oft-quoted abundance of aphorisms which abound in all the Chan films, particularly from the mid 1930s onward. Spoken in pidgin English by the lethargic-seeming Chan, the not so bon mots of the assorted scriptwriters created such verbal gems as "Must not too soon come to conclusion," "Too many mixed drinks make big headaches," "Silence is golden, except in police station," "Tombstones often engraved with words of wisdom," "Confucius has said 'a wise man questions himself, a fool, others,'" "Ancient adage say—music soothe savage beast," and "Hasty deduction like ancient egg—look good from outside."

One of the more offhanded and contradictory factors of the Chan series was the excessive utilization of members of Charlie's family to help wrap up the case at hand. *The Black Camel* showed Chan with his family of ten childen and wife at the breakfast table; the chaos of the situation sending the overwhelmed detective back to the less hectic sanctity of his criminal investigations. In *Charlie Chan's Chance*, son #11 is born. . . . *In Paris* saw Keye Luke's first appearance as helpful but inexperienced number one son Lee. . . . *At the Circus* had the quaint sleuth taking his family to the big top; . . . *At the Olympics* number two son, Charlie, Jr. (Layne Tom, Jr.) showed up; in . . . *In Honolulu* Victor Sen Yung was seen as number two son, Jimmy, with Layne Tom, Jr. now as Tommy. . . .'s *Murder Cruise* found Layne Tom, Jr. as Willie Chan. . . . *In Secret Service* saw Benson Fong as number three son Tommy and Marianne Quon as Iris Chan; Frances Chan was in *Black Magic* as daughter Frances; Edwin Luke as number four son Eddie in *Jade Mask*, and Victor Sen Yung reappeared as Tommy in *Shanghai Chest*, with Keye Luke back as Lee Chan in *Feathered Serpent* and the final entry, *Sky Dragon*.

. . . *Secret Service* introduced Negro actor Manton Moreland as chauffeur Birmingham, who served as an obvious comic foil to an increasing extent in the final "Charlie Chan" episodes.

To vary the background locale from the metropolitan area, beginning with . . . *In London* Charlie went on a world tour, stopping off at Paris, Cairo, Shanghai, Monte Carlo, Honolulu, Panama, Mexico, with forays to Reno and to Manhattan. Being a 20th Century-Fox programmer entry, rear projection served as the basis for most of the Oriental sleuth's traveling, save when an atmospheric backlot standing set offered necessary exotic appeal.

As a contrast to the seemingly imperturbable, portly Charlie Chan, there would be such gumshoe detectives and policemen as Sergeant Kelly (William Demarest) in . . . *At the Opera*, or the country bumpkin sheriff Tombstone Fletcher in . . . *In Reno* or the stuffy Britisher Detective Sergeant Thacker (E. E. Clive) in . . . *In London*. Most conspicuous in his several appearances was the French police inspector (Harold Huber) whose over-exaggerated gestures and mannerisms detracted from such "Chan" chapters as . . . *At Monte Carlo* and . . . *In City in Darkness*. Ironically when Huber portrayed New York Inspector Nelson in . . . *On Broadway* he turned in a fairly subtle performance.

The pre-1935 Fox "Charlie Chan" films were not burdened with the later standardized formats and routines that lessened the excitement of the films. Since Chan's sons did not appear as father's best helper until . . . *In Shanghai* (1935), Charlie had more script freedom to pursue his suspects all on his own. In these earlier productions, Chan was more energetic in actively tracking the culprits, and there would be many scene changes as he hunted the villains. As the series crystallized, such gimmicks as the lights going out at the crucial

moment, with a piercing scream and another victim found dead when the lights went on again, became obligatory. As the years went on, Chan would increasingly putter around, politely talking with the various people involved in the case. He would remain extremely cool in spite of sudden emotional outbursts by the suspects, and would hardly bat an eye when barely escaping near death or coming upon the latest homicide victim. By the early 1940s, Chan no longer personally risked his life to trap the guilty party. Rather, he would resort to gathering the suspects together, reconstructing the crime, and hoping the wrongdoer would reveal himself.

In retrospect, the best of the *Charlie Chan* canon are considered: . . . *In Egypt* which has such virtues as a nicely honed sinister quality, an intelligent murderer, and such supporting players as Rita Casino (Hayworth). The weird case gets underway when a high priest's tomb is opened, and Charlie Chan as the special agent of a French museum is asked to solve the rash of crimes and deaths surrounding the expedition. . . . *At the Opera* was a felicitous blend of the mystery and musical genre with unintentional high camp bridging the two styles most successfully. Oscar Levant composed a special "opera" "Carnival" for utilization in the lavish film (by series standards). And there was Boris Karloff as Gravelle; a baritone suffering from aphasia, who escapes from a mental asylum to visit his old haunts, still filled with grandiose artistic vanity. Seen in the bizarre musical setting are Gravelle's diva wife, Mme. Lilli Rochelle (Margaret Irving), his daughter Mlle. Kitty (Charlotte Henry). Representing the law were staid Inspector Regan (Guy Usher) and his snappy, down to earth assistant Sergeant Kelly (William Demarest).

One of the best Chan films is . . . *At Treasure Island*, which has a well contrived plot, several believable red herrings, a good supporting cast, and most of all a realistic characterization for the killer. The case starts when a man is found dead in a plane just landing in San Francisco; the clues deriving from Dr. Zodiac (Gerald Mohr) lead Charlie and Jimmy (Victor Sen Yung) to the great fair at Treasure Island. Among those present are Rhadina (Cesar Romero), famous magician; his wife Myra (June Gale), and the assistant Eve Cairo (Pauline Moore), who possesses genuine psychic powers.

. . . *On Broadway* featured a zesty cast, including Murdock (J. Edward Bromberg), a newspaper editor; Speed Patton (Donald Woods), an ace reporter; Buzz Moran (Leon Ames), the crime ring chief; and Johnny Burke (Douglas Fowley), the head henchman and operator of a nightclub. The film is blessed with a brisk plot involving a hidden diary, with Lee Chan (Keye Luke) suspected of murder, and the spotlight of suspicion darting around the assembled suspects.

Sidney Toler's last Chan entry at Fox, *Castle in the Desert,* also has several engaging scenes. The story is set in a medieval castle situated 35 miles into the Mojave Desert, where eccentric millionaire Manderley (Douglass Dumbrille) resides with his wife Lucretia (Lenita Lane). The weekend guests gathered there provide a wide variety of interesting suspects for the murders that soon occur, and such locales as the gloomy subterranean torture dungeon heighten the mood of the production.

The best of the series performers was Warner Oland, born October 3, 1880, in Ulmea, Sweden. Educated in Boston, the 5'11" actor received his dramatic training at Dr. Curry's Acting School. After excelling on the stage, he turned to the cinema; one of his earliest roles was in *Sin* (Fox, 1915) opposite Theda Bara. He portrayed a number of Oriental villains in the silent cinema, often in Pearl White Pathé serials. One of his offbeat acting assignments was as the cantor father in the trend-setting *The Jazz Singer* (1927) with Al Jolson. In talking films, he appeared in such productions as *Chinatown Nights* (1929), *The Mysterious Dr. Fu Manchu* (1929), *The Vagabond King* (1930). Three of his best non-Charlie Chan stints in the 1930s were: *Dishonored* (1931), *Shanghai Express* (1932), and *The Painted Veil* (1935). While preparing scenes for . . . *At The Arena* he became ill and was found wandering the streets. He died soon thereafter on August 6, 1938. He had been married to Edith Shearn since 1908.

Sidney Toler was born April 28, 1874, in Warrensburg, Missouri. After graduating from the University of Kansas, he took up acting, and appeared in such plays as *Canary Dutch, Lulu Belle, Tommy* and others, as well as writing the drama, *Belle of Richmond.* His film debut was in *Madame X* (1929), followed by supporting character parts in a string of films including *Blonde Venus* (1932), *The Narrow Corner* (1933), *Massacre* (1934), *Call of the Wild* (1935), *The Gorgeous Hussey* (1936), and *King of Chinatown* (1939). After assuming the Charlie Chan role, his outside assignments were limited to a few token appearances in motion pictures like *A Night to Remember* (1943) and *White Savage* (1943). He died February 12, 1947; he had been married to Viva Tattersal.

The last cinema Charlie Chan to date was Roland Winters, born November 22, 1904, in Boston, Massachusetts. He began in the theatre in 1928 and by 1933 was a seasoned supporting player. At that time, he went into radio work, performing in assorted audio series like *Henry Aldrich, The Kate Smith Show* and *The Kay Kyser Program.* His cinema debut was in *13 Rue Madaleine* (1946) with James Cagney. Among his non-Charlie Chan film roles were *The West Point Story* (1950), *She's Working Her Way Through College* (1952), *Jet Pilot* (1957), *Blue Hawaii* (1961), and *Follow That Dream* (1962). In television, he was best noted for his role as the boss on *Meet Millie* in the early 1950s; during the 1969 Broadway season he returned to the Broadway stage in the musical *Minnie's Boys.*

Warner Oland, Dorothy Revier, Bela Lugosi. (The Black Camel)

Oland. (. . . In Shanghai)

Oland, Arthur Stone, Stepin Fetchit. (. . . In Egypt)

Russell Hicks, Oland. (. . . . In Shanghai)

Oland and Keye Luke. (. . . At Monte Carlo)

Luke, Oland, Shirley Deane, John McGuire. (. . . At the Circus)

Toler, Phyllis Brooks, John King. (. . . In Honolulu)

Sidney Toler.

Kay Linaker, Ricardo Cortez, Toler, Sen Yung. (. . . In Reno)

*Douglass Dumbrille, Sen Yung, Harold Goodwin,
Toler. (. . . At Treasure Island)*

Douglass Dumbrille, Victor Sen Yung, Toler, Steven Geray. (Castle in the Desert)

Robert Lowery, Marjorie Weaver, Toler, Lionel Atwill. (. . .'s Murder Cruise)

C. Henry Gordon, Toler, Archie Twitchell, Michael
Visaroff, Ted Osborn, Joan Valerie, Harold Goodwin.
Marguerite Chapman at table. (At the Wax Museum)

Sen Yung, Marjorie Weaver, Toler. (Murder Over
New York)

Victor Sen Yung, Toler. (Castle in the Desert)

Tim Ryan, Winters, George Eldridge. (The Shanghai Chest)

Roland Winters.

Sen Yung, Winters. (The Golden Eye)

Winters, Tim Ryan, Luke, Gaylord Pendleton, Milburn Stone, Noel Neill. (Sky Dragon)

CHARLIE CHAN

BEHIND THAT CURTAIN (Fox, 1929) 72 M.

Director, Irving Cummings; author, Earl Derr Biggers; screenplay, Clarke Silvernail; camera, Conrad Wells, Dave Ragin, Vincent Farrar; editor, Alde Gaetano.

John Beetham	Warner Baxter
Eve Mannering	Lois Moran
Sir Frederic Bruce	Gilbert Emery
Sir George Mannering	Claude King
Eric Durand	Philip Strange
Sondanese Servant	Boris Karloff
Habib Hanna	Jamiel Hassen
Scotland Yard Inspector	Peter Gawthorne
Alf Pornick	John Rogers
Hilary Gatt	Montague Shaw
Gatt's Clerk	Finch Smiles
Neinah	Mercedes De Valasco
Charlie Chan	E. L. Parks

CHARLIE CHAN CARRIES ON (Fox, 1931) 76 M.

Director, Hamilton MacFadden; author, Earl Derr Biggers; screenplay, Philip Klein, Barry Connors; camera, George Schneiderman; editor, Al Degaetano.

Charlie Chan	Warner Oland
Mark Kenaway	John Garrick
Palema Potter	Marguerite Churchill
Max Minchin	Warren Hymer
Sadie	Marjorie White
John Ross	C. Henry Gordon
Patrick Tait	William Holden
Captain Ronald Keane	George Brent
Inspector Duff	Peter Gawthorne
Dr. Lofton	John T. Murray
Elmer Benbow	John Swon
Mrs. Benbow	Goode Montgomery
Walter Honeywood	Jason Robards
Inspector Hanley	Lumsden Hare
Mrs. Luce	Zeffie Tiltbury
Sybil Conway	Betty Francisco
Kent	Harry Beresford
Martin	John Rogers
Eben	J. C. Davis

BLACK CAMEL (Fox, 1931) 71 M.

Director, Hamilton MacFadden; author, Earl Derr Biggers; screenplay, Hugh Stange, Barry Conners, Philip Klein; editor, Al De Saetano.

Charlie Chan	Warner Oland
Julie O'Neil	Sally Eilers
Tarneverro	Bela Lugosi
Shelah Fane	Dorothy Revier
Robert Fyfe	Victor Varconi
Jimmy Bradshaw	Robert Young
Rita Ballou	Marjorie White
Wilkie Ballou	Richard Tucker
Thomas MacMaster	J. M. Kerrigan
Mrs. MacMaster	Mary Gordon
Van Horn	C. Henry Gordon
Anna	Violet Dunn
Alan Jaynes	William Post, Jr.
Jessop	Dwight Frye
Smith	Murray Kinnell
Kashimo	Otto Yamaoka
Luana	Rita Roselle
Chief of Police	Robert Homans
Housekeeper	Louise Mackintosh

CHARLIE CHAN'S CHANCE (Fox, 1932) 73 M.

Producer, Joseph August; director, John Blystone; author, Earl Derr Biggers; screenplay, Barry Connors, Philip Klein; sound, Albert Protzman; editor, Alex Troffey.

Charlie Chan	Warner Oland
Barry Kirk	Ralph Morgan
Inspector Fife	H. B. Warner
Shirley Marlowe	Marion Nixon
Gloria Garland	Linda Watkins
John Douglas	Alexander Kirland
Inspector Flannery	James Kirkwood
Kenneth Dunwood	James Todd
Paradise	Charles McNaughton
Li Gung	Edward Peil, Jr.
Garrick Enderly	Herbert Bunsten

CHARLIE CHAN'S GREATEST CASE (Fox, 1933) 71 M.

Director, Hamilton MacFadden; author, Earl Derr Biggers; adaptor, Lester Cole, Marion Orth; camera, Ernest Palmer; music director, Samuel Kaylin; editor, Alex Troffey.

Charlie Chan	Warner Oland
Carlotta Eagan	Heather Angel
The Beachcomber	Roger Imhof
John Quincy Winterslip	John Warburton
Harry Jennison	Walter Byron
Brade	Ivan Simpson
Barbara Winterslip	Virginia Cherrill
Captain Hallett	Francis Ford
Dan Winterslip	Robert Warwick
Amos Winterslip	Frank McGlynn
Minerva Winterslip	Clara Blandick
Captain Arthur Cope	Claude King
James Eagen	William Stack
Arlene Compton	Gloria Roy
Steve Letherbee	Cornelius Keefe

CHARLIE CHAN'S COURAGE (Fox, 1934) 72 M.

Director, George Hadden, Eugene Forde; screenplay, Seton I. Miller; camera, Hal Mohr; music director, Samuel Kaylin.

Charlie Chan	Warner Oland
Paula Graham	Drue Leyton
Bob Crawford	Donald Woods
Martin Thorne	Murray Kinnell

J. P. Madden ⎫	Paul Harvey
Jerry Delaney ⎭	
Maydorf	Jerry Jerome
Professor Gamble	Harvey Clark
Will Holley	Si Jenks
Victor Jordan	Jack Carter
Wong	James Wang
Mr. Crawford	Reginald Mason
Mrs. Jordan	Virginia Hammond
Constable Brackett	De Witt C. Jennings
Hewitt	Francis Ford

CHARLIE CHAN IN LONDON (Fox, 1934) 79 M.

Producer, John Stone; director, Eugene Forde; screenplay, Phillip MacDonald; camera, L. W. O'Connell; music director, Samuel Kaylin.

Charlie Chan	Warner Oland
Pamela Gray	Drue Leyton
Hugh Gray	Douglas Walton
Geoffrey Richmond	Alan Mowbray
Lady Mary Bristol	Mona Barrie
Neil Howard	Raymond Milland
Major Jardine	George Barraud
Bunny Fothergill	Paul England
Becky Fothergill	Madge Bellamy
Jerry Garton	Walter Johnson
Phillips	Murray Kinnell
Detective Sergeant Thacker	E. E. Clive
Alice Rooney	Elsa Buchanan
Sir Lionel Bashford	David Torrence
RAF Commandant	Claude King
Flight Commander King	Reginald Sheffield
Kemp	Perry Ivins
Lake	John Rogers
Secretary (Miss Jones)	Helena Grant
Doctor	Montague Shaw
Nurse	Phillis Coghlan
Housemaid	Margaret Mann

CHARLIE CHAN IN PARIS (Fox, 1935) 70 M.

Producer, Sol M. Wurtzel; director, Lewis Seiler; author, Philip MacDonald; screenplay, Edward T. Lowe, Stuart Anthony; camera, Ernest Palmer; music director, Samuel Kaylin.

Charlie Chan	Warner Oland
Yvette Lamartine	Mary Brian
Max Corday	Erik Rhodes
Dufresno	John Miljan
Victor	Thomas Beck
Renee	Ruth Peterson
Henri Latouche	Murray Kinnell
Renaud	Minor Watson
M. Lamartine	Henry Kolker
Lee Chan	Keye Luke
Bedell	Perry Ivins
Concierge	John M. Qualen
Nardi	Dorothy Appleby
Gendarme	Harry Cording

CHARLIE CHAN IN EGYPT (Fox, 1935) 65 M.

Producer, Edward T. Lowe; director, Louis King; screenplay, Robert Ellis, Helen Logan; camera, Daniel B. Clark; music director, Samuel Kaylin; editor, Alde Gaetano.

Charlie Chan	Warner Oland
Carol Arnold	Pat Paterson
Tom Evans	Thomas Beck
Nayda	Rita Cansino (Hayworth)
Dr. Anton Racine	Jameson Thomas
Prof. John Thurston	Frank Conroy
Edfu Ahmad	Nigel De Brulier
Soueida	Paul Porcasi
Dragonman	Arthur Stone
Snowshoes	Stepin Fetchit
Barry Arnold	James Eagles
Dr. Jaipur	Frank Reicher
Prof. Arnold	George Irving
Snowshoes' Friend	Anita Brown

CHARLIE CHAN IN SHANGHAI (Fox, 1935) 70 M.

Producer, John Stone; director, James Tinling; author-screenplay, Robert Ellis, Helen Logan, Joseph Hoffman; camera, Rudolph Mate.

Charlie Chan	Warner Oland
Diana Woodland	Irene Hervey
Philip Nash	Charles Locher (Jon Hall)
Lee Chan	Keye Luke
James Andrews	Russell Hicks
Chief of Police	Halliwell Hobbes
Dakin	Neil Fitzgerald
Burke	Fredrik Vogeding
Chauffeur	Harry Strang
Taxi-Driver	Max Wagner
Belden	Pat O'Malley

CHARLIE CHAN'S SECRET (20th, 1936) 71 M.

Producer, John Stone; director, Gordon Wiles; screenplay, Robert Ellis, Helen Logan, Joseph Hoffman; camera, Rudolph Mate; editor, Nick De Maggio.

Charlie Chan	Warner Oland
Alice Lowell	Rosina Lawrence
Dick Williams	Charles Quigley
Fred Gaige	Edward Trevor
Janice Gaige	Astrid Allwyn
Henrietta Lowell	Henrietta Crosman
Allen Coleby	Jerry Miley
Baxter	Herbert Mundin
Carlotta	Gloria Roy
Professor Bowan	Arthur E. Carew
Warren T. Phelps	Jonathan Hale
Ulrich	Egon Brecher
Morton	Ivan (Dusty) Miller
Harris	William N. Bailey
Fingerprint Man	James T. Mack
Coroner	Landers Stevens
Boat Captain	Francis Ford

CHARLIE CHAN AT THE CIRCUS (20th, 1936) 72 M.

Producer, John Stone; director, Harry Lachman; screenplay, Robert Ellis, Helen Logan; music director, Samuel Kaylin; camera, Daniel B. Clark; editor, Alex Troffey.

Charlie Chan	Warner Oland
Lee Chan	Keye Luke
Tim	George Brasno
Tiny	Olive Brasno
Gaines	Francis Ford
Louise Norman	Shirley Deane
Hal Blake	John McGuire
Marie Norman	Maxine Reiner
Tom Holt	J. Carrol Naish
Joe Kinney	Paul Stanton
Dan Farrell	Boothe Howard
Nellie Farrell	Drue Leyton
Lieutenant Macy	Wade Boteler
Su Toy	Shia Jung
Ticket Taker (Mike)	Francis Farnum

CHARLIE CHAN AT THE RACE TRACK (20th, 1936) 70 M.

Associate producer, John Stone; director, H. Bruce Humberstone; screenplay, Robert Ellis, Helen Logan, Edward T. Lowe; author, Lou Breslow, Saul Elkins; camera, Harry Jackson; music director, Samuel Kaylin; editor, Nick De Maggio.

Charlie Chan	Warner Oland
Lee Chan	Keye Luke
Alice Fenton	Helen Wood
Bruce Rogers	Thomas Beck
George Chester	Alan Dinehart
Bagley	Gavin Muir
Catherine Chester	Gloria Roy
Warren Fenton	Jonathan Hale
Denny Barton	G. P. Huntley, Jr.
Major Kent	George Irving
Eddie Brill	Junior Coghlan
"Tip" Collins	Frankie Darro
Mooney	John Rogers
"Streamline" Jones	John H. Allen
Al Meers	Harry Jans
Chief of Police	Robert Warwick
Second Purser	Jack Mulhall
Gangster	Paul Fix

CHARLIE CHAN AT THE OPERA (20th, 1936) 66 M.

Associate producer, John Stone; director, H. Bruce Humberstone; author, Bess Meredith; screenplay, Scott Darling, Charles S. Belden; camera, Lucien Androit; music director, Samuel Kaylin; editor, Alex Troffey.

Charlie Chan	Warner Oland
Gravelle	Boris Karloff
Lee Chan	Keye Luke
Mlle. Kitty	Charlotte Henry

Phil Childers	Thomas Beck
Mme. Lilli Rochelle	Margaret Irving
Enrico Barelli	George Gaye
Mme. Lucretia Barelli	Nedda Harrigan
Mr. Whitely	Frank Conroy
Inspector Regan	Guy Usher
Sergeant Kelly	William Demarest
Mr. Arnold	Maurice Cass
Morris	Tom McGuire

CHARLIE CHAN AT THE OLYMPICS (20th, 1937) 71 M.

Associate producer, John Stone; director, H. Bruce Humberstone; author, Paul Burger; screenplay, Robert Ellis, Helen Logan; music director, Samuel Kaylin; camera, Daniel B. Clark; editor, Fred Allen.

Charlie Chan	Warner Oland
Yvonne Roland	Katherine De Mille
Betty Adams	Pauline Moore
Richard Masters	Allan Lane
Lee Chan	Keye Luke
Arthur Hughes	C. Henry Gordon
Cartwright	John Eldredge
Zaraka	Morgan Wallace
Hopkins	Jonathan Hale
Charlie Chan, Jr.	Layne Tom, Jr.
Inspector Strasser	Fredrik Vogeding
Chief Scott	Andrew Tombes
Dr. Burton	Howard Hickman
Colonel	Edward Keane
Navy Commander	Selmer Jackson
Radio Announcer	Don Brodie

CHARLIE CHAN ON BROADWAY (20th, 1937) 68 M.

Producer, John Stone; director, Eugene Ford; screenplay, Charles S. Belden, Jerry Cady; author, Art Arthur, Robert Ellis, Helen Logan; camera, Harry Jackson; editor, Al De Gaetano.

Charlie Chan	Warner Oland
Murdock	J. Edward Bromberg
Joan Wendall	Joan Marsh
Billie Bronson	Louise Henry
Marie Collins	Joan Woodbury
Speed Patton	Donald Woods
Johnny Burke	Douglas Fowley
Inspector Nelson	Harold Huber
Lee Chan	Keye Luke
Buzz Moran	Leon Ames
Thomas Mitchell	Marc Lawrence
Ling Tse	Toshie Mori
Reporter	Creighton Hale
Policeman	Jack Dougherty
Desk Man	Lon Chaney, Jr.

CHARLIE CHAN AT MONTE CARLO (20th, 1938) 71 M.

Producer, John Stone; director, Eugene Ford; screen-

play, Charles Pelden, Jerry Cady; author, Robert Ellis, Helen Logan; camera, Daniel B. Clark; music director, Samuel Kaylin; editor, Nick De Maggio.

Charlie Chan	Warner Oland
Lee Chan	Keye Luke
Evelyn Gray	Virginia Field
Karnoff	Sidney Blackmer
French Police Inspector	Harold Huber
Joan Karnoff	Kay Linaker
Gordon Chase	Robert Kent
Paul Savarin	Edward Raquelo
Al Rogers	George Lynn
Cab Driver	Louis Mercier
Pepito	George Davis
Ludwig	John Bleifer
Renault	Georges Renavent
Gendarme	George Sorrel

CHARLIE CHAN IN HONOLULU (20th, 1938) 65 M.

Associate producer, John Stone; director, H. Bruce Humberstone; author, Charles Belden; screenplay, Charles Belden; art director, Richard Day, Haldane Douglas; music director, Samuel Kaylin; camera, Charles Clarke; editor, Nick De Maggio.

Charlie Chan	Sidney Toler
Judy Hayes	Phyllis Brooks
Lee Chan	Sen Yung
Al Hogan	Eddie Collins
Randolph	John King
Mrs. Carol Wayne	Claire Dodd
Dr. Cardigan	George Zucco
Capt. Johnson	Robert Barrat
Johnnie McCoy	Marc Lawrence
Detective Arnold	Richard Lane
Tommy	Layne Tom, Jr.
Wing Foo	Philip Ahn
Inspector	Paul Harvey
Sailor	Dick Alexander

CHARLIE CHAN IN RENO (20th, 1939) 70 M.

Producer, John Stone; director, Norman Foster; author, Philip Wylie; screenplay, Frances Hyland, Albert Ray, Robert E. Kent; camera, Virgil Miller; editor, Fred Allen.

Charlie Chan	Sidney Toler
Dr. Ainsley	Ricardo Cortez
Vivian Wells	Phyllis Brooks
Sheriff Tombstone Fletcher	Slim Summerville
Curtis Whitman	Kane Richmond
James Chan	Sen Yung
Mary Whitman	Pauline Moore
Cab Driver	Eddie Collins
Mrs. Russell	Kay Linaker
Jeanne Bently	Louise Henry
Wally Burke	Robert Lowery
Chief of Police	Charles D. Brown
Choy-Wong	Iris Wong

George Bently	Morgan Conway
Night Clerk	Hamilton MacFadden

CHARLIE CHAN AT TREASURE ISLAND (20th, 1939) 59 M.

Producer, Edward Kaufman; director, Norman Foster; author, John Larkin; screenplay, John Larkin; camera, Virgil Miller; editor, Norman Colbert.

Charlie Chan	Sidney Toler
Fred Rhadini	Cesar Romero
Eve Cairo	Pauline Moore
James Chan	Sen Yung
Pete Lewis	Douglas Fowley
Myra Rhadini	June Gale
Thomas Gregory (Stuart Salsbury	Douglass Dumbrille
Stella Essex	Sally Blane
Bessie Sibley	Billie Seward
Elmer Keiner	Wally Vernon
Chief Kilvaine	Donald MacBride
Redley	Charles Halton
The Turk (Abdul)	Trevor Bardette
Paul Essex	Louis Jean Heydt
Dr. Zodiac	Gerald Mohr
Doctor	John Elliott

CHARLIE CHAN IN THE CITY OF DARKNESS (20th, 1939) 75 M.

Associate producer, John Stone; director, Herbert I. Leeds; screenplay, Robert Ellis, Helen Logan; author, Gina Kaus, Ladislaus Fodor; camera, Virgil Miller; editor, Harry Reynolds.

Charlie Chan	Sidney Toler
Marie Dubon	Lynn Bari
Tony Madero	Richard Clarke
Marcel	Harold Huber
Antoine	Pedro de Cordoba
Charlotte Rondell	Dorothy Tree
Romaine	C. Henry Gordon
Petroff	Douglass Dumbrille
Belescu	Noel Madison
Louis Sentinelli	Leo Carroll
Pierre—assistant to Sentinelli	Lon Chaney, Jr.
Max	Louis Mercier
Alex	George Davis
Lola	Barbara Leonard
Landlady	Adrienne d'Ambricourt
Captain	Fredrik Vogeding
Gendarmes	Alphonse Martell
	Eugene Borden

CHARLIE CHAN IN PANAMA (20th, 1940) 67 M.

Producer, Sol M. Wurtzel; director, Norman Foster; screenplay, John Larkin, Lester Ziffren; camera, Virgil Miller; editor, Fred Allen.

Charlie Chan	Sidney Toler
Kathi Lenesch	Jean Rogers

Cliveden Compton	Lionel Atwill
Jennie Finch	Mary Nash
Jimmy Chan	Sen Yung
Richard Cabot	Kane Richmond
Lt. Montero	Chris-Pin Martin
Dr. Grosser	Lionel Royce
Stewardess	Helen Ericson
Manolo	Jack La Rue
Governor Webster	Edwin Stanley
Captain Lewis	Don Douglas
Achmed Halide	Frank Puglia
Godley	Addison Richards
Dr. Fredericks	Edward Keane
Officer	Lane Chandler
Suspicious Sailor	Eddie Acuff
Plant Worker	Ed Gargan
Drunken Sailor	Jimmy Aubrey

CHARLIE CHAN'S MURDER CRUISE (20th, 1940) 75 M.

Associate producer, John Stone; director, Eugene Ford; author, Earl Derr Biggers; screenplay, Robertson White, Lester Ziffren; camera, Virgil Miller; editor, Harry Reynolds.

Charlie Chan	Sidney Toler
Paula Drake	Marjorie Weaver
Doctor Suderman	Lionel Atwill
Jimmy Chan	Sen Yung
Dick Kenyon	Robert Lowery
James Ross	Don Beddoe
Professor Gordon	Leo Carroll
Susie Watson	Cora Witherspoon
Mrs. Pendleton	Kay Linaker
Coroner	Harlan Briggs
Mr. Walters	Charles Middleton
Mrs. Walters	Claire DuBrey
Walter Pendleton	Leonard Mudie
Wilkie	James Burke
Buttons	Richard Keene
Willie Chan	Layne Tom, Jr.
Inspector Duff	Montague Shaw
Guard	Harry Strang
Officer	Walter Miller

CHARLIE CHAN AT THE WAX MUSEUM (20th, 1940) 63 M.

Associate producer, Walter Morosco, Ralph Dietrich; director, Lynn Shores; screenplay, John Larkin; art di,-rector, Richard Day, Lewis Creber; camera, Virgil Miller; editor, Emil Newman.

Charlie Chan	Sidney Toler
Jimmy Chan	Sen Yung
Dr. Cream	C. Henry Gordon
Steve McBirney	Marc Lawrence
Lily Latimer	Joan Valerie
Mary Bolton	Marguerite Chapman
Tom Agnew	Ted Osborn
Dr. Otto Von Brom	Michael Visaroff
Mrs. Rocke	Hilda Vaughn

Willie Fern	Charles Wagenheim
Carter Lane	Archie Twitchell
Grenock	Edward Marr
Insp. O'Matthews	Joe King
Edwards	Harold Goodwin

MURDER OVER NEW YORK (20th, 1940) 65 M.

Producer, Sol M. Wurtzel; director, Harry Lachman; screenplay, Lester Ziffren; camera, Virgil Miller; editor, Louis Loeffler.

Charlie Chan	Sidney Toler
Patricia Shaw	Marjorie Weaver
David Elliott	Robert Lowery
George Kirby	Ricardo Cortez
Inspector Vance	Donald MacBride
Herbert Fenton	Melville Cooper
June Preston	Joan Valerie
Ralph Percy	Kane Richmond
Jimmy Chan	Sen Yung
Richard Jeffery	John Sutton
Boggs	Leyland Hodgson
Butler	Clarence Muse
Hugh Drake	Frederick Worlock
Ramullah	Lal Chand Mehra
Gilroy	Frank Coghlan, Jr.

DEAD MEN TELL (20th, 1941) 60 M.

Associate producer, Walter Morosco, Ralph Dietrich; director, Harry Lachman; screenplay, John Larkin; camera, Charles Clarke; editor, Harry Reynolds.

Charlie Chan	Sidney Toler
Kate Ransome	Sheila Ryan
Steve Daniels	Robert Weldon
Jimmy Chan	Sen Yung
Jed Thomasson	Don Douglas
Laura Thursday	Kay Aldridge
Charles Thursday	Paul McGrath
Bill Lydig	George Reeves
Captain Kane	Truman Bradley
Patience Nodbury	Ethel Griffies
Dr. Anne Bonney	Lenita Lane
Gene La Farge	Milton Parsons

CHARLIE CHAN IN RIO (20th, 1941) 60 M.

Producer, Sol M. Wurtzel; director, Harry Lachman; screenplay, Samuel G. Engel, Lester Ziffren; music and lyrics, Mack Gordon, Harry Warren; music director, Emil Newman; art director, Richard Day; camera, Joseph P. MacDonald; editor, Alexander Troffey.

Charlie Chan	Sidney Toler
Joan Reynolds	Mary Beth Hughes
Grace Ellis	Cobina Wright, Jr.
Clark Denton	Ted North
Alfredo Marana	Victor Jory
Chief Souto	Harold Huber
Jimmy Chan	Victor Sen Yung

Ken Reynolds	Richard Derr
Lola Dean	Jacqueline Dalya
Helen Ashby	Kay Linaker
Paul Wagner	Truman Bradley
Bill Kellogg	Hamilton MacFadden
Rice	Leslie Denison
Lili	Iris Wong
Armando	Eugene Borden
Margo	Ann Codee

CASTLE IN THE DESERT (20th, 1942) 62 M.

Producer, Ralph Dietrich; director, Harry Lachman; screenplay, John Larkin; camera, Virgil Miller; editor, John Brady.

Charlie Chan	Sidney Toler
Brenda Hartford	Arleen Whelan
Carl Detheridge	Richard Derr
Manderley	Douglass Dumbrille
Watson King	Henry Daniell
Walter Hartford	Edmund MacDonald
Jimmy Chan	Sen Yung
Lucretia Manderley	Lenita Lane
Madame Saturnie	Ethel Griffies
Fletcher	Milton Parsons
Dr. Retling	Steve Geray
Prof. Gleason	Lucien Littlefield
Body Guard	Paul Kruger
Bus Driver	George Chandler
Wigley (Hotel Manager)	Oliver Prickett (Blake)

CHARLIE CHAN IN SECRET SERVICE (Mon., 1944) 63 M.

Producer, Philip N. Krasne, James S. Burkett; director, Phil Rosen; author-screenplay, George Callahan; music director, Karl Hajos; editor, Martin G. Cohn.

Charlie Chan	Sidney Toler
Inez	Gwen Kenyon
Birmingham	Manton Moreland
Jones	Arthur Loft
Iris Chan	Marianne Quon
Mrs. Winters	Lela Tyler
Tommie Chan	Benson Fong

THE CHINESE CAT (Mon., 1944) 65 M.

Producer, Philip N. Krasne, James S. Burkett; director, Phil Rosen; author-screenplay, George Callahan; art director, Dave Milton; camera, Ira Morgan; editor, Fred Allen.

Charlie Chan	Sidney Toler
Tommie Chan	Benson Fong
Birmingham	Manton Moreland
Harvey Dennis	Weldon Heyburn
Leah Manning	Joan Woodbury
Recknick	Ian Keith
Tom Manning	Sam Flint
Deacon	Cy Kendall

Catlen	Anthony Warde
Salos	Dewey Robinson
Carl / Kurt	John Davidson
Mrs. Manning	Betty Blythe

CHARLIE CHAN IN BLACK MAGIC (Mon., 1944) 67 M.

Producer, Philip N. Krasne, James S. Burkett; director, Phil Rosen; author-screenplay, George Callahan; camera, Arthur Martinelli; editor, John Link.

Charlie Chan	Sidney Toler
Birmingham	Mantan Moreland
Frances Chan	Frances Chan
Matthews	Joe Crehan
Justine Bonner	Jacqueline DeWit
Rafferty	Ralph Peters
Norma Duncan	Helen Beverley
Paul Hamlin	Frank Jaquet
Bonner	Dick Gordon
Tom Starkey	Charles Jordan
Vera Starkey	Claudia Dell
Harriet Green	Geraldine Wall
Charles Edwards	Harry Depp
Dawson	Edward Earle

THE JADE MASK (Mon., 1945) 66 M.

Producer, James S. Burkett; director, Phil Rosen; screenplay, George Callahan; art director, Dave Milton; camera, Harry Neumann; editor, Dick Currier.

Charlie Chan	Sidney Toler
Birmingham	Manton Moreland
Tommy	Edwin Luke
Jean	Janet Warren
Louise	Edith Evanson
Meeker	Hardie Albright
Harper	Frank Reicher
Roth	Cyril Delevanti
Mack	Alan Bridge
Stella	Dorothy Granger
Peabody	Joe Whitehead

THE SCARLET CLUE (Mon., 1945) 65 M.

Producer, James B. Burkett; director, Phil Rosen; author-screenplay, George Callahan; camera, William A. Sickner; editor, Richard Currier.

Charlie Chan	Sidney Toler
Tommy Chan	Benson Fong
Birmingham Brown	Mantan Moreland
Diane Hall	Helen Devereaux
Captain Flynn	Robert Homans
Mrs. Marsh	Virginia Brissac
Ralph Brett	Stanford Jolley
Wilbur Chester	Reid Kilpatrick
Willie Rand	Jack Norton
Sgt. McGraw	Charles Sherlock
Gloria Bayne	Janet Shaw

Herbert Sinclair	Milt Kibbee
Ben	Ben Carter
Hulda Swenson	Victoria Faust
Nelson	Charles Jordan
Horace Carlos	Leonard Mudie
Detective	Kernan Cripps

THE SHANGHAI COBRA (Mon., 1945) 64 M.

Producer, James B. Burkett; director, Phil Karlson; author, George Callahan; screenplay, George Callahan, George Wallace Sayre; camera, Vince Farrar; editor, Ace Herman.

Charlie Chan	Sidney Toler
Tommy Chan	Benson Fong
Birmingham	Mantan Moreland
Insp. Harry Davis	Walter Fenner
Ned Stewart	James Cardwell
Paula Webb	Joan Barclay
Jarvis	James Flavin
John Adams (Jan Van Horn)	Addison Richards
Bradford Harris (Hume)	Arthur Loft
Morgan	Gene Stutenroth
Taylor	Joe Devlin
Walter Fletcher	Roy Gordon
Lorraine	Janet Warren

THE RED DRAGON (Mon., 1945) 64 M.

Producer, James B. Burkett; director, Phil Rosen; author-screenplay, George Callahan; camera, Vincent Farrar; editor, Ace Herman.

Charlie Chan	Sidney Toler
Inspector Luis Carvero	Fortunio Bonanova
Tommy Chan	Benson Fong
Alfred Wyans	Robert E. Keane
Chattanooga Brown	Willie Best
Marguerite Fontan	Carol Hughes
Countess Irena	Marjorie Hoshelle
Joseph Bradish	Barton Yarborough
Edmond Slade	George Meeker
Charles Masack	Don Costello
Prentiss	Charles Trowbridge
Josephine	Mildred Boyd
Iris	Jean Wong
Dorn	Donald D. Taylor

DARK ALIBI (Mon., 1946) 61 M.

Producer, James S. Burkett; director, Phil Karlson; screenplay, George Callahan; art director, Dave Milton; camera, William A. Sickner.

Charlie Chan	Sidney Toler
Tommy Chan	Benson Fong
Birmingham	Mantan Moreland
June Harley	Teala Loring
Hugh Kenzie	George Holmes
Thomas Harley	Edward Earle
Carter	Ben Carter

Emily Evans	Joyce Compton
Miss Petrie	Janet Shaw
Mrs. Foss	Edna Holland
Morgan	John Eldredge
Thompson	William Ruhl
Johnson	Milton Parsons
Danvers	Ray Walker
Warden Cameron	Russell Hicks
Slade	Anthony Warde
Foggy	Tim Ryan
Barker	Frank Marlowe
Brand	George Eldredge

SHADOWS OVER CHINATOWN (Mon., 1946) 64 M.

Producer, James S. Burkett; director, Terry Morse; original screenplay, Raymond Schrock; camera, William Sickner; editor, Ralph Dixon.

Charlie Chan	Sidney Toler
Birmingham	Mantan Moreland
Jimmy	Victor Sen Yung
Mary Conover	T. Chandler
Jeff Hay	John Galaudet
Mike Rogan	Paul Bryar
Jack Tilford	Bruce Kellogg
Capt. Allen	Alan Bridge
Mrs. Conover	Mary Gordon
Joan Mercer	Dorothy Granger
Cosgrove	Jack Norton
Jenkins	Charlie Jordan

DANGEROUS MONEY (Mon., 1946) 66 M.

Producer, James S. Burkett; director, Terry Morse; screenplay, Miriam Kissinger; camera, William Sickner; editor, William Austin.

Charlie Chan	Sidney Toler
Jimmy Chan	Victor Sen Young
Chattanooga	Willie Best
Captain Black	Joseph Crehan
P. T. Burke	Dick Elliott
Cynthia Martin	Elaine Lange
Laura Erickson	Amira Moustafa
Rona Simmonds	Gloria Warren
George Brace	Joe Allen, Jr.
Tao Erickson	Rick Vallin
Harold Mayfair	Bruce Edwards
Professor Martin	Emmett Vogan
Freddie Kirk	John Harmon
Mrs. Whipple	Alan Douglas
Reverend Whipple	Leslie Denison
Big Ben	Dudley Dickerson
Scott Pearson	Tristram Coffin
Pete	Rito Punay
Ship's Doctor	Selmer Jackson

THE TRAP (Mon., 1947) 62 M.

Producer, James S. Burkett; director, Howard Brether-

ton; screenplay, Miriam Kissinger; musical director, Edward J. Kay; camera, James Brown; editor, Ace Herman.

Charlie Chan	Sidney Toler
Birmingham	Mantan Moreland
Jimmy Chan	Victor Sen Young
Adelaide	Tanis Chandler
Rick Daniels	Larry Blake
Sgt. Reynolds	Kirk Alyn
Clementine	Rita Quigley
Marcia	Anne Nagel
Ruby	Helen Gerald
Cole King	Howard Negley
Mrs. Thorn	Lois Austin
San Toy	Barbara Jean Wong
Mrs. Weebles	Minerva Urecal
Madge Mudge	Margaret Brayton
Winifred	Bettie Best
Lois	Jan Bryant
Doc Brandt	Walden Boyle

THE CHINESE RING (Mon., 1947) 68 M.

Producer, James S. Burkett; director, William Beaudine; screenplay, Scott Darling; camera, William Sickner; editor, Ace Herman.

Charlie Chan	Roland Winters
Birmingham	Mantan Moreland
Sergeant Davidson	Warren Douglas
Tommy	Victor Sen Young
Peggy Cartwright	Louise Currie
Capt. Kong	Philip Ahn
Armstrong	Byron Foulger
Capt. Kelso	Thayer Roberts
Princess Mei Ling	Jean Wong
Lilly Mae	Chabing
Sergeant	Paul Bryar
Dr. Hickey	George L. Spaulding
Stenographer	Charmienne Harker
Hotel Clerk	Thornton Edwards

DOCKS OF NEW ORLEANS (Mon., 1948) 64 M.

Producer, James S. Burkett; director, Derwin Abrahams; screenplay, W. Scott Darling; camera, William Sickner.

Charlie Chan	Roland Winters
Rene	Virginia Dale
Birmingham	Mantan Moreland
Captain McNally	John Gallaudet
Tommy	Victor Sen Young
Nita Aguirre	Carol Forman
Grock	Douglas Fowley
Swendstrom	Harry Hayden
Pereaux	Howard Negley
Von Scherbe	Stanley Andrews
Henri Castanaro	Emmett Vogan
La Fontaine	Boyd Irwin
Thompson	Rory Mallinson
Dansiger	George J. Lewis

THE SHANGHAI CHEST (Mon., 1948) 56 M.

Producer, James S. Burkett; director, William Beaudine; screenplay, W. Scott Darling, Sam Newman; story, Sam Newman; camera, William Sickner.

Charlie Chan	Roland Winters
Birmingham	Mantan Moreland
Lt. Ruark	Tim Ryan
Tommy Chan	Victor Sen Young
Phyllis	Deannie Best
Ed Seward	Thristram Coffin
Vic Armstrong	John Alvin
District Attorney Bronson	Russell Hicks
Judge Armstrong	Pierre Watkin
Tony Pindello	Philip Van Zandt
Mr. Grail	Milton Parsons
Bates	Olaf Hytten
Walter Somerville	Erville Alderson
Finley	George Eldredge
Custodian	Louis Mason

THE MYSTERY OF THE GOLDEN EYE (Mon., 1948) 68 M.

Producer, James S. Burkett; director, William Beaudine; screenplay, W. Scott Darling; camera, William Sickner.

Charlie Chan	Roland Winters
Evelyn	Wanda McKay
Birmingham	Mantan Moreland
Tommy Chan	Victor Sen Young
Bartlett	Bruce Kellogg
Lt. Ruark	Tim Ryan
Teresa (Nursing sister)	Evelyn Brent
Driscoll	Ralph Dunn
Mrs. Driscoll	Lois Austin
Manning	Forrest Taylor
Pete	Lee "Lasses" White
1st Miner	Edmund Cobb

THE FEATHERED SERPENT (Mon., 1948) 68 M.

Producer, James S. Burkett; director, William Beaudine; author-screenplay, Oliver Drake; camera, William Sickner.

Charlie Chan	Roland Winters
Lee Chan	Keye Luke
Tommy Chan	Victor Sen Yung
Birmingham	Mantan Moreland
John Stanley	Robert Livingston
Pedro	Martin Garralaga
Professor Paul Evans	Nils Asther
Sonia Cabot	Carol Forman
Joan Farnsworth	Beverly Jons
Capt. Juan	George J. Lewis
Professor Farnsworth	Leslie Dennison
Diego	Jay Silverheels

SKY DRAGON (Mon., 1949) 64 M.

Producer, James S. Burkett; director, Lesley Selander;

author, Clint Johnston; screenplay, Oliver Drake, Clint Johnston; camera, William Sickner.

Charlie Chan	Roland Winters
Lee Chan	Keye Luke
Birmingham	Mantan Moreland
Jane Marshall	Noel Neill
Lt. Ruark	Tim Ryan
Wanda LaFern	Iris Adrian
Marie Burke	Elena Verdugo
Tim Norton	Milburn Stone
Andy Barrett	Lyle Talbot
John Anderson	Paul Maxey
Don Blake	Joel Marston
William French	John Eldredge
Mr. Tibbets	Eddie Parks
Lena	Louise Franklin
Ed Davidson	Lyle Latell
Stacey	George Eldredge
Watkins	Bob Curtis

CRIME DOCTOR

One of the more popular pre-World War II radio shows was Max Martin's *Crime Doctor* whose unlikely but engaging promise revolved around Dr. Ordway the ex-gangster turned psychiatrist who was a specialist in the diseases of the human mind, especially the criminal mind. Ray Collins was heard in the title role on radio (later replaced by House Jameson, Everett Sloane, and John McIntire) with Edgar Stehli as District Attorney Miller and Walter Greaza as Inspector Ross. Near the close of each half hour program, the announcer would solemnly state: "Dr. Ordway will be back in exactly 47 seconds with the solution to tonight's case."

It was natural that Columbia Pictures, with more than its share of low-budget films on its production slate, would look for other projects to bolster its lineup of profitable quickie series such as *Boston Blackie, Lone Wolf, The Whistler,* and *Blondie.*

To headline this new detective series, veteran film star Warner Baxter was contracted to play the semi-sophisticated title role. Baxter was born March 29, 1892, in Columbus, Ohio. He made his film debut in 1922 in Paramount's *Her Own Money.* For his zesty performance as the Cisco Kid in *In Old Arizona* (1929), he won an Academy Award, and subsequently played the cowboy hero-bandit in several other westerns. Baxter returned to more sophisticated roles in the mid-1930s, costarring with Myrna Loy in *To Mary—With Love* (1936), with Loretta Young in *Wife, Doctor, and Nurse* (1938) and with Ingrid Bergman in *Adam Had Four Sons* (1940). Having recovered from a nervous breakdown in the early 1940s, Baxter assumed the less-than-breezy *Crime Doctor* series, allowing him at the age of 51 to retain a respectable footing in Hollywood's cinema hierarchy at the easy price of a non-physically-taxing two films a year. Each quickie was photographed in less than four weeks of backlot work.

The initial entry, *Crime Doctor,* was released in the fall of 1943, a trim 66-minute black and white programmer, which established the background for the remaining nine film entries. Master criminal Phil Moran (Warner Baxter) is conked on the head by his henchmen when he tries to dupe them of their share in a recent $200,000 robbery. Left for dead, Moran wakes up in a hospital unaware of his past identity. Dr. Carey (Ray Collins) encourages him to make a new start in life. Under the name of Robert Ordway he studies medicine, specializing in psychiatry and enjoying considerable success in rehabilitating criminals. Years later, due to his work on the state parole board, a former gang member recognizes him and tries to force the doctor to reveal the hiding place of the loot from the robbery of a decade ago. When Ordway is then hit on the head and his past comes vividly alive, he is forced to deal with the threat to his career. The facts of his past lead to a trial in which the jury must determine if the new doctor must pay for his old crimes.

The remaining *Crime Doctor* pictures paid decreasing attention to the fact that Ordway had once been a crook. Instead, the entries concentrated on capers of a prestigious physician-criminologist who had an astute sense of the criminal mind. In at least three of the films, Dr. Ordway is on vacation: in . . .'s *Courage* he is among the California swimming pool set; in *The Millerson Case* the scripters have Dr. Ordway taking his first vacation in five years (!) with a fishing trip to a rural community in the Blue Ridge Mountains of West Virginia, and in . . .'s *Warning* he is enjoying a change of climate in Paris. For the other films, Columbia utilized its functional backlot big city street locales, as well as the pedestrian interior sets the Gower Street Studio so inexpensively tossed together to serve for its unique interior decoration style.

Usually in each *Crime Doctor* episode, it is the prime suspect or chief victim who comes to Dr. Ordway seeking his expert assistance, thus setting into motion the criminal hunt.

In . . .'s *Strangest Case* Ordway is asked to aid Jimmy Trotter (Lloyd Bridges) accused of having murdered his former employers; in *Shadows in the Night* Lois Garland (Nina Foch) resides in an eerie household filled with supposed ghosts and eccentric humans; in . . .'s *Courage* Ordway investigates the death of Kathleen Carson's (Hillary Brooke) husband and the unexplained fate of his previous wives; in . . .'s *Warning* an artist's model is murdered with art dealer Frederick Malone (Miles Mander) as the leading suspect; in *Just Before Dawn* demented Karl Ganss (Martin Kosleck) leads Ordway on a merry chase with several creative murders tossed in along the way; in . . .'s *Man Hunt* the doctor must solve the mystery involving Irene Cotter (Ellen Drew), her murdered fiance, and the sudden appearance of her "twin" sister; in *The Millerson Case* a rash of typhoid fever masks the murder of rural physician Sam Millerson (Griff Barnett); in . . .'s *Gamble* Ordway is among the European art circles with the heroine's father Maurice Duval (Eduardo Ciannelli) and attorney Jules Daudet (Steven Geray) the most likely homicide suspects; and in . . .'s *Diary* parolee Steve Carter (Stephen Dunne) claims he was framed by co-executives at his store for arson and later murder.

Unlike the radio version of *Crime Doctor* there were no recurrent police inspector roles in the motion picture series. Rather a variety of law enforcement officials were used as contrast to the brilliant deductions and sleuthing of Ordway. At best, the contract players assigned these thankless parts gave some dimension to their nondescript roles, bolstering the flow of the sometimes stodgy plotlines. Many were capable police detectives like Captain Wheeler (Leon Ames) in *Crime Doctor* or Inspector Dawes (John Litel) in . . .'s *Warning*. Others were professionally unimaginative like Inspector Manning (William Frawley) in . . .'s *Man Hunt* or Inspector Burns (Charles D. Brown) in *Just Before Dawn* or Captain Birch (Emory Parnell) in . . .'s *Warning* or the sheriff (Charles Wilson in *Shadows of the Night*. Most sophisticated was Marcel Journet (Jacques Morrell) chief inspector of the Paris police in . . . *Gamble*.

Because of Baxter's obvious middle age, producers of the *Crime Doctor* series wisely left the romantic interest to others in the films, with the leading lady usually just the victim in the case whom Dr. Ordway helps in a purely professional manner.

Many of the series were not even reviewed by the trade or general newspapers, considered just bottom of the double bill product from Columbia Pictures. The supporting cast and guest co-stars in *Crime Doctor* films were occasionally Columbia contract players with a future such as Nina Foch or Lloyd Bridges or respected character actors such as Eduardo Ciannelli or John Litel; but generally they were just ordinary players fulfilling their studio contract in the programmers.

In between his chores as Dr. Ordway, Baxter turned out such other minor Columbia films as *A Gentleman from Nowhere* (1947), *Prison Warden* (1949), *The Devil's Henchman* (1949) and *State Penitentiary* (1950), his final film. Baxter died May 7, 1951, of cranial surgery following a long bout with advanced arthritis.

In line with the onrush of competing television, it is unlikely that the *Crime Doctor* series would have lasted much longer than it did, serving merely as a quantity entry for undemanding audiences at double feature theaters.

Warner Baxter, Dewey Robinson. (Crime Doctor)

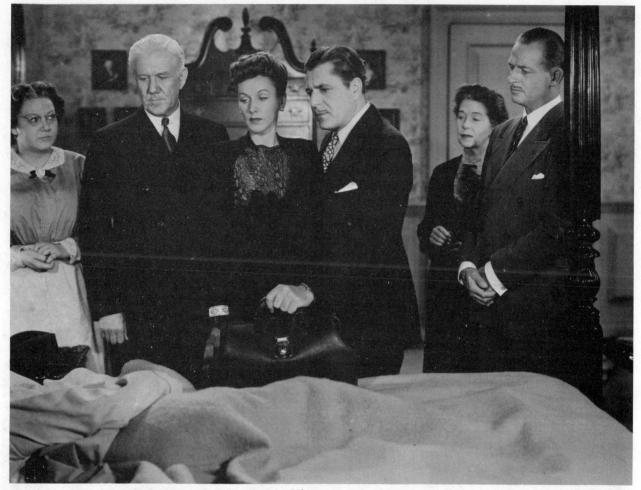

Gloria Dickson, Sam Flint, Rose Hobart, Baxter, Virginia Brissac, Reginald Denny. (. . .'s Strangest Case)

Nina Foch, Baxter. (Shadows in the Night)

Baxter, Lupita Tovar, Anthony Caruso. (. . .'s Courage)

Baxter, Miles Mander. (. . .'s Warning)

Baxter, Byron Foulger. (Just Before Dawn)

Baxter and Steven Geray. (. . .'s Gamble)

Eduardo Ciannelli, Baxter. (. . .'s Warning)

Baxter and Geray. (. . .'s Gamble)

Cliff Clark, Baxter, Stephen Dunne, Adele Jergens,
Robert Armstrong. On floor: Lois Maxwell (?). (. . .'s
Diary)

Lois Maxwell, Baxter, Don Beddoe, Whit Bissell.
(. . .'s Diary)

CRIME DOCTOR

CRIME DOCTOR (Col., 1943) 66 M.

Producer, Ralph Cohn; director, Michael Gordon; screenplay, Graham Baker, Louise Lantz; camera, James S. Brown, Jr.; musical score, Lee Zahler; editor, Dwight Caldwell.

Dr. Robert Ordway	Warner Baxter
Grace Fielding	Margaret Lindsay
Three Fingers	John Litel
Dr. Carey	Ray Collins
Joe	Harold Huber
Nick	Don Costello
Capt. Wheeler	Leon Ames
Betty	Constance Worth
Pearl	Dorothy Tree
Myrtle	Vi Athens

CRIME DOCTOR'S STRANGEST CASE (Col., 1943) 68 M.

Producer, Rudolph C. Flothow; director, Eugene J. Forde; screenplay, Eric Taylor; camera, James S. Brown; art director, George Van Marten; editor, Dwight Caldwell.

Dr. Robert Ordway	Warner Baxter
Mrs. Trotter	Lynn Merrick
Jimmy Trotter	Lloyd Bridges
Mrs. Burns	Rose Hobart
Rief	Barton MacLane
Patricia Cornwell	Virginia Brissac
Mrs. Keppler	Gloria Dickson
Paul Ashley	Reginald Denny
Addison Burns	Sam Flint
Malory	Jerome Cowan
Betty Watson	Constance Worth
Yarnell	Thomas Jackson
Walter Burns	George Lynn

SHADOWS IN THE NIGHT (Col., 1944) 67 M.

Producer, Rudolph C. Flothow; director, Eugene J. Forde; story-screenplay, Eric Taylor; art director, John Dala; set director, Sidney Clifford; assistant director, Richard Monroe; editor, Dwight Caldwell.

Dr. Robert Ordway	Warner Baxter
Lois Garland	Nina Foch
Frank Swift	George Zucco
Frederick Gordon	Minor Watson
Stanley Carter	Lester Matthews
Nick Kallus	Ben Weldon
Jess Hilton	Edward Norris
Sheriff	Charles Wilson
Doc Stacey	Charles Halton
Adele Carter	Jeanne Bates

CRIME DOCTOR'S COURAGE (Col., 1945) 70 M.

Producer, Rudolph C. Flothow; director, George Sher-

man; screenplay, Eric Taylor; camera, L. W. O'Connell; art director, John Dala; editor, Dwight Caldwell.*

Dr. Robert Ordway	Warner Baxter
Kathleen Carson	Hillary Brooke
Jeffers Jerome	Jerome Cowan
Bob Rencoret	Robert Scott
John Massey	Lloyd Corrigan
Capt. Birch	Emory Parnell
Gordon Carson	Stephen Crane
Butler	Charles Arnt
Miguel Bragga	Anthony Caruso
Dolores Bragga	Lupila Tovar
David Lee	Dennis Moore
Luga	King Kong Kashay
Detec. Fanning	Jack Carrington

CRIME DOCTOR'S WARNING (Col., 1945) 69 M.

Producer, Rudolph C. Flothow; director, William Castle; story-screenplay, Eric Taylor; camera, L. W. O'Connell; assistant director, Leonard Shapiro; music director, Paul Sawtell; editor, Dwight Caldwell.

Dr. Robert Ordway	Warner Baxter
Inspector Dawes	John Litel
Connie Mace	Dusty Anderson
Clive Lake	Coulter Irwin
Frederick Malone	Miles Mander
Jimmy Gordon	John Abbott
Nick Petroni	Eduardo Ciannelli
Mrs. Wellington	Alma Kruger
Robert MacPherson	J. M. Kerrigan
Joseph Duval	Franco Corsaro

CRIME DOCTOR'S MAN HUNT (Col., 1946) 61 M.

Producer, Rudolph C. Flothow; director, William Castle; story, Eric Taylor; screenplay, Leigh Brackett; camera, Philip Tannura; art director, Hans Radon; set director, George Montgomery; assistant director, Carl Hiecke; music director, Mischa Bakaleinikoff; editor, Dwight Caldwell.

Dr. Robert Ordway	Warner Baxter
Irene Cotter	Ellen Drew
Inspector Manning	William Frawley
Bigger	Frank Sully
Ruby Farrell	Claire Carleton
Waldo	Bernard Nedell
Sgt. Bradley	Jack Lee
Gerald Cotter	Francis Pierlot
Philip Armstrong	Myron Healy
Marcus Leblanc	Olin Howlin
Alfredi	Ivan Triesault
Tom	Paul E. Burns
Martha	Mary Newton
Herrera	Leon Lenoir

JUST BEFORE DAWN (Col., 1946) 65 M.

Producer, Rudolph C. Flothow; director, William Castle;

screenplay, Eric Taylor, Aubrey Wisbert; camera, Philip Tannura; editor, Dwight Caldwell.

Dr. Robert Ordway	Warner Baxter
Claire Foster	Adelle Roberts
Karl Ganss	Martin Kosleck
Harriet Travers	Mona Barrie
Casper	Marian Miller
Inspector Burns	Charles D. Brown
Jack Swain	Craig Reynolds
Clyde Travers	Robert Barrat
Alexander Gerard	Milton Graff
Dr. Steiner	Charles Lane
Allan S. Tobin	Charles Arnt
Armand Morcel	Ted Hecht
Connie Day	Peggy Converse
Florence White	Irene Tedrow
Walter Cummings	Thomas Jackson

THE MILLERSON CASE (Col., 1947) 72 M.

Producer, Rudolph C. Flothow; director, George Archainbaud; authors, Gordon Rigby, Carlton Sand; screenplay, Raymond L. Schrock; art director, Harold MacArthur; camera, Philip Tannura; music director, Mischa Bakaleinikoff; editor, Dwight Caldwell.

Dr. Robert Ordway	Warner Baxter
Belle Englehart	Nancy Saunders
Sheriff Akers	Clem Bevans
Doc Sam Millerson	Griff Barnett
Jud Rookstool	Paul Guilfoyle
Ezra Minnich	James Bell
Dr. Wickersham	Addison Richards
Bye Minnich	Mark Dennis
Dr. Prescott	Robert Stevens
Lt. Callahan	Eddie Parker
Hank Nixon	Vic Potel
Jeremiah Dobbs	Eddy Waller
Squire Tuttle	Russell Simpson
Emma Millerson	Sarah Padden
Eadie Rookstool	Barbara Pepper
Ella Minnich	Frances Morris

CRIME DOCTOR'S GAMBLE (Col., 1947) 66 M.

Producer, Rudolph C. Flothow; director, William Castle; screenplay, Edward Boch; story, Raymond L. Schrock; camera, Philip Tannura; art director, George Brooks; set director, Louis Diage; assistant director, Carter De Haven; music director, Mischa Bakaleinikoff; editor, Dwight Caldwell.

Dr. Robert Ordway	Warner Baxter
Mignon	Micheline Cheirel
Henri Jardin	Roger Dann
Jules Daudet	Steven Geray
Jacques Morrell	Marcel Journet
Maurice Duval	Eduardo Ciannelli
Anton Geroux	Maurice Marsac
Louis Chabonet	Henri Letondal
Theodore	Jean Delval
Auctioneer	Leon Lenoir
Brown	Wheaton Chambers
Otheilly	Emory Parnell
Paul Romaine	George Davis

CRIME DOCTOR'S DIARY (Col., 1949) 61 M.

Producer, Rudolph C. Flothow; director, Seymour Friedman; story, David Dressler; screenplay, Edward Anhalt; camera, Vincent Farrar; art director, Harold MacArthur; set director, George Montgomery; assistant director, Earl Bellamy; editor, Jerome Thoms.

Dr. Robert Ordway	Warner Baxter
Steve Carter	Stephen Dunne
Jane Darrin	Lois Maxwell
Inez Grey	Adele Jergens
"Goldie" Harrigan	Robert Armstrong
Philip Bellem	Don Beddoe
Pete Bellem	Whit Bissell
Insp. Manning	Cliff Clark
Roma	Lois Fields
Anson	George Meeker
Mac	Crane Whitley
Louise	Claire Carleton
Warden	Selmer Jackson
Blane	Sid Tomack

DR. CHRISTIAN

One of the most universally accepted film series to be produced by the American cinema was *Dr. Christian* as portrayed by the distinguished Danish actor Jean Hersholt in a group of six modestly budgeted black and white feature films made by RKO Pictures between 1939 and 1941. Shot inexpensively at the home studio in Culver City, the unpretentious sentimental series centered around beloved Dr. Paul Christian, the past middle-age physician practicing in River's End, Minnesota, a storybook small midwestern town filled with all the homey virtues and stereotypes of the then accepted Americana of pre-World War II. Devoted to humanitarian causes, the wise Dr. Christian was not only a superb country doctor (with almost miraculous medical-surgical prowess) but a never ending optimist as to the goodness of mankind and the aspirations of his townfolk. Whether there was a civic crisis involving the town council or a near tragedy among the local populace, Dr. Christian was sure to become involved, offering ultrasound advice and capable of bringing the best out of people and situations.

The multi-media success history of the *Dr. Christian* property is closely tied to the career of Jean Hersholt; himself a great humanitarian, founder of the Motion Picture Relief Fund, president of the Academy of Motion Picture Arts & Sciences and winner of three Academy Awards for humanitarian causes. Born July 12, 1896, in Copenhagen, Hersholt came to the United States in 1913, an already seasoned cinema performer. Before and while under contract to Universal Pictures in California, he appeared in a variety of one-reelers.

In 1919, he joined the American Lifegraph Co., Portland, Oregon, as a film director and actor. During the 1920s, he rose to film prominence with finely etched performances in *Four Horsemen of the Apocalypse* (1920) with Rudolph Valentino, *Tess of the Storm Country* (1922) with Mary Pickford, Eric von Stroheim's *Greed* (1923) and *Abie's Irish Rose* (1927) with Nancy Carroll. In 1931, he signed a long-term contract with MGM and became one of its outstanding character players along with Lewis Stone. He appeared in such films as *Sins of Madelon Claudet* (1931) with Helen Hayes, *Grand Hotel* (1932) with Greta Garbo, and *Men In White* (1934) with Clark Gable.

In 1935, a Canadian named Dionne gained world fame when he became the father of quintuplets. Twentieth Century-Fox Films decided to make a film on the subject, and Hersholt was hired to portray Canadian doctor Allan Dafoe, on the basis of his performance as Dr. Hochberg in *Men In White*. (Will Rogers had been signed for the Dafoe role, but was killed in a plane crash that year.) A trio of motion pictures involving Dr. Dafoe and the quintuplets appeared: *The Country Doctor* (1936), *Reunion* (1936) and *Five of a Kind* (1938). The boxoffice success of these films convinced Hersholt and entertainment executives that an intriguing further series could be based on the career of the country doctor.

However, necessary rights to Dr. Dafoe's life story were not available, and a new leading figure was created, "Dr. Christian." The title was chosen partly because it was Scandinavian and justified

Hersholt's accent, and also because Hans Christian Andersen was the actor's favorite author. The radio series which introduced Dr. Christian to the public debuted on CBS network in the 1937 season, and the half-hour show was heard every Wednesday night at 10 P.M. for 15 years. It was estimated that the show attracted a weekly listening audience of 20 million people. The theme song was *Rainbow on the River*.

In 1938, RKO Pictures bought film rights to the heart-warming series and began production with *Meet . . .* released in October 1939. The 68-minute programmer introduced cinema audiences to the familiar cast of characters from the radio show: Mrs. Hastings (Maude Eburne), Dr. Christian's well meaning, practical housekeeper; Judy Price (Dorothy Lovett) the young, pert nurse; Roy Davis (Robert Baldwin) the pleasant town pharmacist in love with Judy; and George Browning (Edgar Kennedy) the well to do irascible grocer. The homey atmosphere of River's End came vividly alive in all its wholesome unreality. Dr. Christian's unpretentious, sprawling house, with its sliding doors, rooms cluttered with medical paraphernalia; complimented the country flavor of the small town with its modest homes and simple stores.

Unlike his big city cinema counterpart, Dr. Kildare, Dr. Christian's medical practice reflected its rural roots. Certainly expert in his medical knowledge (in *Meet . . .* he performs a most delicate operation brilliantly, despite the lack of proper equipment; in *The Courageous . . .* he combats a rash of spinal meningitis among the squatters), Dr. Christian maintained a simple professional office at home, unhampered by neo-pharmaceutical equipment or smart medical terminology. Probably his most essential basic tool was his constant pipe, allowing him to puff away and meditate on the ramifications of his patient's medical and emotional problems.

The plots of the six B-quality films were slight, unencumbered affairs, much stronger on soap opera than on cinematic storytelling. *Meet . . .* dealt with the good doctor's philanthropic attempts to get the town a new hospital; *The Courageous . . .* centered on his campaign to rid River's End of its slums; *. . . Meets the Women* revolved around his efforts to combat a quack doctor with a dangerous weight reducing pill formula; *Remedy for Riches* had him investigating a phony oil land discovery in town; *Melody for Three* showed

him in the kindly role of matchmaker trying to reunite a divorced couple who have a musically talented son; and *They Meet Again* detailed his valiant efforts to prove a man's innocence of a crime and to find the real culprit.

All of the films relied on unsophisticated wholesome basics for comedy relief. In *The Courageous . . .* the good samaritan must diplomatically avoid the pursuing advances of rich Mrs. Stewart (Vera Lewis); and in *Remedy for Riches* Dr. Christian accidentally spoils the cake his housekeeper had prepared for the bazaar contest and bakes the prize-winning entry himself. In each film, there is mention of how overworked the past-middle-aged Dr. Christian is, and the need for him to take a vacation. But always some new crisis prevents it; often a situation arises forboding potential professional humiliation for his standing in the community; in *Meet . . .* the unthinking town's mayor tries to have him removed as the town's health officer; in *. . . Meets the Women* the diet-conscious ladies revolt against Dr. Christian's warnings of quackery and accuse him of being old-fashioned and unsuitable to be their family physician.

The romantic interest in the series was quietly supplied by Roy Davis's constant courting of Judy Price, and the rivalry of new visitors to town to spark Judy's interest, such as con artist Tom Stewart (Warren Hull) in *Remedy for Riches*. Music played an important role in the series's last two entries: in *Melody for Three* the doctor's part-time nurse Mary Stanley (Fay Wray) is divorced from orchestra conductor Antoine Pirelle (Walter Woolf King) and they have a son Billy (Schuyler Standish), a violin prodigy, allowing for some attractive arrangements of Brahms Hungarian Dances; and in *They Meet Again* nine-year-old Janie Webster (Anne Bennett) is competing for a state musical scholarship, leaving the story open for her to nicely sing arias from *Il Traviata*, etc.

With the July 1941 release of *They Meet Again* the *Dr. Christian* film series came to a close. As with most movie series, the entries were not well received by film critics, who complained here of the pedestrian stories, unexciting direction, and the "phlegmatic" acting of star Jean Hersholt. Hersholt had become frustrated with playing the same character in each film, and was not unhappy to conclude the series, to devote himself to war work. Because the radio series required only a half hour of rehearsal and a half hour of air time per week, he continued with the show through 1953.

He collaborated with radio script writer Ruth Adam Knight and the novel *Dr. Christian's Office* appeared in August 1943.

A natural entry for weekly television, Ziv Television prepared a 39-episode half-hour series of *Dr. Christian* in 1956 with MacDonald Carey as young Dr. Mark Christian, the big-city-doctor nephew of Dr. Christian. Although dying of cancer and weighing only 95 pounds at the time, Hersholt made a guest appearance in the opening episode of the video series, introducing his nephew as the focal point of the show. Hersholt died June 2, 1956. The video series never gained momentum, largely due to its updated, pseudo sophisticated flavor that retained none of the nostalgic qualities of the radio and motion picture series.

Jean Hersholt, as Dr. Christian.

Vera Lewis, George Meader, Hersholt. (The Courageous . . .)

Edgar Kennedy, Lelah Taylor, Hersholt, Heinie Conklin, Frank Albertson. (. . . Meets the Women)

Hersholt, Walter Catlett. (Remedy for Riches)

Walter Woolf King, Fay Wray, Hersholt. (Melody
for Three)

Hersholt, Anne Bennett, Barton Yarborough, Dorothy
Lovett. (They Meet Again)

Schuyler Standish, Maude Eburne, Hersholt. (Melody
for Three)

DR. CHRISTIAN

MEET DR. CHRISTIAN (RKO, 1939) 68 M.

Producer, William Stephens; associate producer, Monroe Shaff; director, Bernard Vorhaus; original story, Harvey Gates; screenplay, Ian McLellan Hunter, Ring Lardner, Jr., Harvey Gates; camera, Robert Pittack; assistant director, Gordon S. Griffith; costumes, Bridgehouse; editor, Edward Mann.

Dr. Christian	Jean Hersholt
Judy Price	Dorothy Lovett
Roy Davis	Robert Baldwin
Anne Hewitt	Enid Bennett
John Hewitt	Paul Harvey
Marilee	Marcia Mae Jones
Don Hewitt	Jackie Moran
Mrs. Hastings	Maude Eburne
Bud	Frank Coghan, Jr.
Patsy Hewitt	Patsy Lee Parsons
Mrs. Minnows	Sarah Edwards
Cars	John Kelly
Benson	Eddie Acuff

THE COURAGEOUS DR. CHRISTIAN (RKO, 1940) 67 M.

Producer, William Stephens; director, Bernard Vorhaus; associate producer, Monroe Shaff; screenplay, Ring Lardner, Jr., Ian McLellan Hunter; art director, Bernard Herstrum; assistant director, Gordon S. Griffith; costumes, Bridgehouse; editor, Edward Mann.

Dr. Paul Christian	Jean Hersholt
Judy Price	Dorothy Lovett
Roy Davis	Robert Baldwin
Dave Williams	Tom Neal
Mrs. Hastings	Maude Eburne
Mrs. Stewart	Vera Lewis
Harry Johnson	George Meader
Jack Williams	Bobby Larson
Ruth Williams	Babette Bentley
Sam	Reginald Barlow
Martha	Jacqueline de River
Tommy Wood	Edmund Glove
Jane Wood	Mary Davenport
Grandpa	Earle Ross

DR. CHRISTIAN MEETS THE WOMEN (RKO, 1940) 68 M.

Producer, William Stephens; associate producer, Monroe Shaff; director, William McGann; screenplay, Marian Orth; camera, John Alton; sets, Earl Wooden; music director, C. Bakaleinikoff; assistant director, Gordon S. Griffith; costumes, Monroe Friedman.

Dr. Paul Christian	Jean Hersholt
Judy Price	Dorothy Lovett
George Browning	Edgar Kennedy
Prof. Kenneth Parker	Rod LaRocque
Bill Ferris	Frank Albertson
Kitty Browning	Marilyn Merrick
Mrs. Hastings	Maude Eburne
Carol Compton	Veda Ann Borg

Martha Browning	Lelah Tyler
Dr. Webster	William Gould
Ed the plumber	Heine Conklin
Annie	Phyllis Kennedy
The Mason twins	Bertha Priestley
	Diedra Vale

REMEDY FOR RICHES (RKO, 1940) 60 M.

Producer, William Stephens; director, Erle C. Kenton; screenplay, Lee Loeb; camera, John Alton; art director, Bernard Harzbrun; assistant director, Glenn Cork; music director, C. Bakaleinikoff; editor, Paul Wetherwax.

Dr. Paul Christian	Jean Hersholt
Judy Price	Dorothy Lovett
George Browning	Edgar Kennedy
D. B. (Emerson) Vanderveer	Jed Prouty
Clem	Walter Catlett
Roy Davis	Robert Baldwin
Tom Stewart	Warren Hull
Mrs. Hastings	Maude Eburne
Gertrude Purdy	Margaret McWade
Abby Purdy	Halline Hill
Mrs. Gattle	Renie Riano
Harvey Manning	Barry Macollum
Eddie	Lester Scharff
Prudence Penny	Herself

MELODY FOR THREE (RKO, 1941) 67 M.

Producer, William Stephens; director, Erle C. Kenton; original screenplay, Walter Ferris, Leo Loeb; camera, John Alton; music director, C. Bakaleinikoff; assistant director, Glenn Cork; editor, Edward Mann.

Dr. Paul Christian	Jean Hersholt
Mary Stanley	Fay Wray
Antoine Pirelle	Walter Woolf King
Billy Stanley	Schuyler Standish
Nancy Higby	Patsy Lee Parsons
Mrs. Hastings	Maude Eburne
Gladys McClelland	Astrid Allwyn
Mrs. Higby	Irene Ryan
Red Bates	Donnie Allen
Clarence	Leon Tyler
Mickey	Andrew Tombes
Mrs. Mitchell	Irene Shirley
Mr. Simpson	Alexander Leftwich

THEY MEET AGAIN (RKO, 1941) 69 M.

Producer, William Stephens; director, Erle C. Kenton; original story, Peter Milne; screenplay, Peter Milne, Maurice Leo; music director, C. Bakaleinikoff; editor, Alexander Troffey.

Dr. Paul Christian	Jean Hersholt
Judy Price	Dorothy Lovett
Roy Davis	Robert Baldwin
Mrs. Hastings	Maude Eburne
Robert Webster	Neil Hamilton
Janie Webster	Anne Bennett
Messenger	Leon Tyler

and: Frank Melton, Barton Yarborough

DR. KILDARE

At the opposite end of the cinema stereotype from small town doctors such as Dr. Christian was the screen's depiction of the urban physician. And the epitome of the modern, medically sophisticated yet socially naive M.D. was Dr. Kildare. Based on a Max Brand work, Dr. James Kildare first appeared in a 1938 Paramount gangster melodrama, *Internes Can't Take Money,* starring Joel McCrea and Barbara Stanwyck. Later that year, Metro-Goldwyn-Mayer Studios acquired the property, restructured the format to insert all the needed ingredients for a successful series entry, and began production of what evolved as a fifteen-film black and white series over the next nine years. In marked contrast to McCrea's rugged, straightforward portrayal, MGM molded the series so that a more pliable, good natured physician could play the key role. MGM utilized contract male lead Lew Ayres for nine films, then Philip Dorn, followed by Van Johnson in a carbon-copy part, and finally James Craig. Although quickly churned out, the *Dr. Kildare* films—through the Van Johnson entries—were all well-mounted motion pictures, filled with solid production values and stocked with such MGM starlets as Lana Turner, Ava Gardner and Marilyn Maxwell. A most professional stock company of contract players was always in full view to depict the innumerable problems found at Blair General Hospital—providing the balance between tears and laughters. And of course, there was the dominating presence of Lionel Barrymore (1878–1954) as gruff but lovable Dr. Leonard Gillespie. (On television, Richard Chamberlain was Kildare and Raymond Massey appeared as Dr. Gillespie, in 132 hour-length episodes and 58 half-hour chapters, between 1961–1966).

As *Dr. Kildare* developed, it proved that the most essential element insuring audience acceptance of the series was the presence of Lionel Barrymore, portraying the senior physician at Blair, and mentor of the young Dr. Kildare. The veteran stage, radio, and film actor (soon after the series started he was permanently confined to a wheelchair due to arthritis) added the contrasting note of warmth, paternalism and experience, needed to gain audience appeal. Gillespie's keen eye, surface cynicism, and his eccentric behavior gave each chapter of the series the necessary focal point and bridge. In fact, after Lew Ayres was replaced in the series, the Dr. Gillespie role became even more crucial to the property's well being. Surrounding the two doctors at the Hospital was a gallery of soon familiar (stereo)types. There were Nurse Mary Lamont (Laraine Day), Kildare's girlfriend; Superintendent of Nurses Molly Bird (Alma Kruger) who brooked no backtalk from Dr. Gillespie or funny business from anyone; Dr. Walter Carew (Walter Kingsford) head of the hospital; floor Nurse Parker (Nell Craig); Sally (Marie Blake) the switchboard operator; Joe Wayman (Nat Pendleton) the ambulance driver—later Hobart Genet (Rags Ragland)—and the orderly Vernon Briggs (Red Skelton). Emma Dunn and Samuel S. Hinds appeared as Kildare's parents.

Young . . . has Kildare coping with his parents' fond hope that he will follow in the father's country medical practice, but he wants to find himself in the big city. At Blair General Hospital, he comes into conflict with his superiors in treating a patient. He wins the point, and is taken on as assistant by brilliant Dr. Gillespie. In *Calling . . .*, Dr. Gillespie transfers Kildare to the downtown out-patient department, so that he will gain some needed practical experience. Here he trips into a jam helping a gangster who has been shot, becomes involved with Rosalie (Lana Turner), a gun moll, and endures complications with the oversuspicious police.

The Secret of . . . finds lovable, irritable Dr. Gillespie pushing himself beyond his strength, seeking to uncover the final cure for pneumonia. He asks Kildare to assist him, so that although the two doctors differ in years and techniques, they share an unabiding enthusiasm for the project. When Dr. Gillespie collapses from exhaustion (his illness is diagnosed as incurable cancer) Kildare assumes the responsibilities for the testing, and also supervises the treatment of a traumatic shock victim, Nancy Messenger (Helen Gilbert).

. . .'s Strange Case depicts Kildare's budding romance with nurse Mary Lamont (Laraine Day). Brilliant surgeon Gregory Lane (Shepperd Strudwick) had been courting her, which makes the situation touchy, when Kildare must prove the senior surgeon's competence in the treatment of a case that went bad. Once again, it is crusty old Dr. Gillespie who proves to be master of the situation. In *. . . Goes Home*, Dr. Kildare has just been appointed as resident assistant to Dr. Gillespie at the Byng State Hospital, when he learns that his physician father is on the point of collapse from overwork. Kildare returns home to help out with the patient overload. The townfolk at first do not appreciate his new medical procedures. However, when Kildare makes an astute diagnosis regarding one of the town's leading citizens, he gains public support, and is able to help fund a new medical clinic for the area.

. . .'s Crisis finds Mary Lamont's brother Douglas (Robert Young) coming to Manhattan to get financial support for a system of training centers for youths he wants to establish. Dr. Kildare diagnosis that Douglas may have a form of epilepsy; he does not tell Mary for fear she will call off their pending marriage. It is peppery Dr. Gillespie who discovers that Douglas's illness is due to a repercussion from an old injury, and is not a hereditary problem.

The People vs. . . . took the medical series into the courtroom. Dr. Kildare had performed an emergency operation on Frances Marlowe (Bonita Granville), whose leg was injured in an automobile accident. Later, the skating star developed paralysis and sued Dr. Kildare and Blair General for $100,000, claiming gross negligence. It is rambunctious Dr. Gillespie who determines that she has a tumor on the spine, and an operation saves the day.

. . .'s Wedding Day revolves around the much-awaited Kildare-Lamont marriage which ends in tragedy when Mary is struck by a truck and dies. Testy Dr. Gillespie sparks the disillusioned Kildare into a new lease on life. (The starkness of the tragedy is somewhat lightened by many recurring humorous episodes throughout the film, such as the orchestra leader Constanzo Labardi (Nils Asther) who learns that the buzzing in his ears is caused by eating too much spaghetti.)

. . .'s Victory shows the young doctor's spiritual recovery, although he still pines for his lost Mary. A flashy debutante, Cookie Charles (Ann Ayars), is brought into Blair General with a broken piece of glass wedged in her heart. Kildare falls in love with the brash, fast talking society girl, and there are hints of a pending marriage. In the course of the film, Kildare gallantly saves a colleague and a hospital nurse from a sudden explosion.

In *Calling Dr. Gillespie*, the respected, older physician has a new assistant, a young Dutch surgeon, Dr. John Hunter Gerniede (Philip Dorn), who has a bent for psychiatry. The film focuses on a homicidal maniac Roy Todwell (Phil Brown) suffering from *dementia praecox*. One memorable suspenseful sequence finds the killer late one night stalking the shadowy corridors of Blair General, with Dr. Gillespie as his intended victim.

In *Dr. Gillespie's New Assistant*, Dr. Gillespie is on the verge of a physical breakdown, and agrees to appoint a new helper. The three new house surgeons are Dr. Randall (Red) Adams (Van Johnson), Dr. Lee Wong How (Keye Luke) and Dr. Dennis Lindsay (Richard Quine). They are on trial, each having a very touchy medical case to diagnose. Although they fail to crack their cases, Dr. Gillespie agrees to give them another chance. Meanwhile, Dr. Lee Wong How joins the Nationalist Chinese Army (the *Dr. Kildare* series was now taking on a topical approach, since Willis Goldbech was directing the films, and a new cast of characters had entered the scene).

Dr. Gillespie's Criminal Case finds the venerable senior physician relying on the vigorous assistance of both Drs. Red Adams (Van Johnson) and Lee Wong How (Keye Luke) (the latter back at the hospital after working with the Chinese Nationalist Army) in soothing Marcia Bradburn's (Donna Reed) romance with Sergeant Orisin (Michael Duane) with the hospital in chaos over psychopathic convict patient Roy Todwell (John Craven).

Three Men in White sees Dr. Gillespie trying to choose between Adams (Johnson) and Lee Wong How (Luke) for the coveted assistantship—referred to at Blair as the Gillespie sweepstakes. Among the medical cases at hand, are Mary Jones (Patricia Barker) suffering from a severe sugar insulin allergy and Joan Brown (Ava Gardner) whose mother has advanced arthritis. Lee Wong How leaves again to work in China.

Between Two Women has Dr. Red Adams still being chased by Ruth Edley (Marilyn Maxwell), the social worker. Adams has his first real test as a surgeon, displaying a good sense of physical diagnosis and bedside manner. He helps patient Edna (Gloria DeHaven) overcome her fixation about not eating. For a change, Gillespie does not partake of his lengthy tirades of wisdom; instead he gives his diagnosis with neatness and dispatch. Sidelights of the film have Edna, a chorus girl, singing *I'm in the Mood for Love,* and Sally (Marie Blake) the switchboard operator, undergoing complicated surgery, from which she fully recovers.

Dark Delusion, which climaxed the series, has Dr. Tommy Coalt (James Craig, born James Meador February 12, 1912, in Nashville, Tennessee) as Gillespie's blunt protege, being guided in the tricky diagnosis and treatment of Cynthia Grace (Lucille Bremer), a wealthy socialite who is suffering from a blood clot. Gillespie advises Coalt in his off-duty romancing of the girl, and tries to help the fledgling doctor decide whether to marry her and move to a small town to practice, or to stay in the metropolitan surrounding.

Lew Ayres (Lewis Ayer) was born December 28, 1907, in Minneapolis, the son of a court reporter. When his mother remarried, he moved to California with her. As an accomplished banjo player he tried to break into show business when he graduated from high school. He obtained his first screen work as an extra in a Vitaphone short. A term contract with Pathé Studios eventually led to a role opposite Greta Garbo in *The Kiss* (1929). His most famous part was in the antiwar film *All Quiet on the Western Front* (1930), followed by such roles as *State Fair* (1933), *Last Train from Madrid* (1937) and *Holiday* (1939). After doing nine *Dr. Kildare* films, he was dropped from the series because MGM felt that his much publicized belief as a conscientious objector who refused to bear arms in World War II would hurt the box-office value of the property. (Ayres eventually served in a distinguished capacity with the medical corps overseas during the war.) After being discharged from his war work, Ayres appeared in such independent parts as *The Dark Mirror* (1946), *Johnny Belinda* (1948) and *Donovan's Brain* (1953). His book *Altars of the East* was published in 1956, and a documentary film with the same title was made of his religious tours throughout the world. Recently, Ayres has been seen in *Advise and Consent* (1962) and *The Carpetbaggers* (1964), and guest-starring on various television series. He has been married to Lola Lane, Ginger Rogers, and Diana Hall.

Of the others who played Dr. Gillespie's chief assistant, the most noted was Van Johnson (born Charles Van Johnson in Newport, Rhode Island on August 25, 1916), the son of a plumber. After a stage career including such musicals as *New Faces of 1937, Too Many Girls,* and *Pal Joey,* Johnson went to Hollywood and began his career with a role in *Murder in the Big House* (1941). After obtaining his MGM contract, he was seen in such studio productions as *A Guy Named Joe* (1943), *Easy to Wed* (1946), *Battleground* (1949), *Plymouth Adventure* (1952), and *Brigadoon* (1954). As a freelance player he later played in *Subway in the Sky* (1959), *Divorce American Style* (1967), *Where Angels Go . . . Trouble Follows* (1968), *The Price of Power* (1969), and others. He is a frequent television performer, and he often tours in summer stock. He was married to Eve Abbott and they have a child Schuyler.

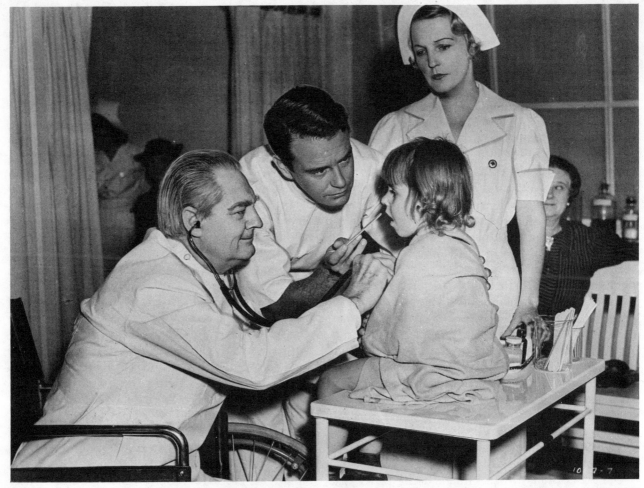

Lionel Barrymore, Lew Ayres, Janice Chambers, Brenda Fowler. (Young Dr. Kildare)

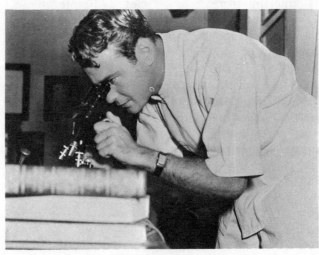

Ayres. (Young . . .)

Jo Ann Sayers, Lynne Carver, Ayres. (Young . . .)

Lionel Atwill, Helen Gilbert, Ayres. (The Secret of . . .)

Nat Pendleton, Ayres. (Calling . . .)

Pendleton and Ayres. (The Secret of . . .)

Barrymore, Laraine Day, Ayres. (. . .'s Strange Case)

Arthur Ayles with Ayres. (. . . Goes Home)

Robert Young, Laraine Day, Barrymore, Ayres. (. . .'s Crisis)

Diana Lewis, Tom Conway, Ayres, Laraine Day. (The
People vs. . . .)

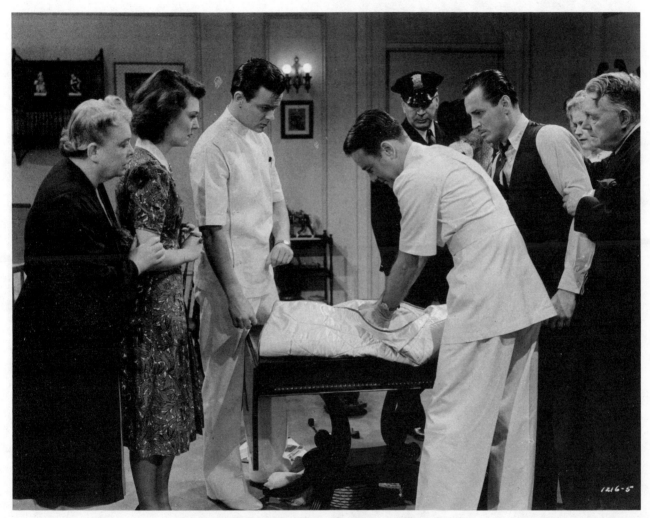

Grace Stafford, Charlotte Wynters, Robert Sterling, Ayres, Paul Kruger, William Bakewell, Tom Stevenson. (. . .'s Victory)

Alma Kruger, Susan Peters, Van Johnson, Barrymore, Horace (Stephen) McNally. (Dr. Gillespie's New Assistant)

John Craven, Henry O'Neill, Edward Earle, Van Johnson, Grant Withers, Edward Keane, Barrymore, Matt Moore, George Lynn. (Dr. Gillespie's Criminal Case)

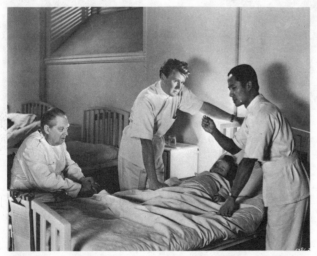

Barrymore, Van Johnson, Luke. (Dr. Gillespie's Criminal Case)

Van Johnson, Marilyn Maxwell, Alma Kruger, Gloria De Haven, Barrymore, Marie Blake, Luke. (Between Two Women)

Barrymore and James Craig. (Dark Delusion)

DR. KILDARE

INTERNES CAN'T TAKE MONEY (Par., 1937) 79 M.

Producer, Benjamin Glazer; director, Alfred Santell; author, Max Brand; screenplay, Rian James, Theodore Reeves; art director, Hans Dreier, Roland Anderson; music director, Boris Morros; music, Gregory Stone; camera, Theodore Sparkuhl; editor, Doane Harrison.

Janet Haley .... Barbara Stanwyck
Jimmie Kildare .... Joel McCrea
Hanlon .... Lloyd Nolan
Innes .... Stanley Ridges
Interne Weeks .... Lee Bowman
Stooly Martin .... Barry Macollum
Jeff .... Irving Bacon
Interne Jones .... Gaylord Pendleton
Dr. Fearson .... Pierre Watkin
Grote .... Charles (Levison) Lane
Haines .... James Bush
Interne .... Nick Lukats
Dr. Riley .... Anthony Nace
Sister Superior .... Fay Holden
Eddie .... Frank Bruno
Bit .... Ellen Drew
First Mug .... Jack Mulhall
Nurse .... Priscilla Lawson

YOUNG DR. KILDARE (MGM, 1938) 81 M.

Director, Harold Bucquet; author, Max Brand; screenplay, Willis Goldbeck, Harry Ruskin; camera, John Seitz; editor, Elmo Vernon.

Dr. James Kildare .... Lew Ayres
Dr. Leonard Gillespie .... Lionel Barrymore
Alice Raymond .... Lynne Carver
Wayman .... Nat Pendleton
Barbara Chanler .... Jo Ann Sayers
Dr. Steve Kildare .... Samuel S. Hinds
Mrs. Martha Kildare .... Emma Dunn
Dr. Walter Carew .... Walter Kingsford
Mrs. Chanler .... Nella Walker
Mr. Chanler .... Pierre Watkin
John Hamilton .... Truman Bradley
Dr. Lane Porteus .... Monty Wooley
Bates .... Don Castle
Vickery .... Phillip Terry
Joiner .... Roger Converse
Collins .... Donald Barry
First Lodger .... James Mason
Waiter .... Murray Alper

CALLING DR. KILDARE (MGM, 1939) 86 M.

Director, Harold S. Bucquet; author, Max Brand; screenplay, Harry Ruskin, Willis Goldbeck; art director, Cedric Gibbons; music director, David Snell; camera, Alfred Gilks, Lester White; editor, Robert J. Kern.

Dr. James Kildare .... Lew Ayres

Dr. Leonard Gillespie .... Lionel Barrymore
Mary Lamont .... Laraine Day
Rosalie .... Lana Turner
Dr. Stephen Kildare .... Samuel S. Hinds
Alice Raymond .... Lynne Carver
Joe Wayman .... Nat Pendleton
Mrs. Martha Kildare .... Emma Dunn
Dr. Walter Carew .... Walter Kingsford
John Galt .... Harlan Briggs
Harry Galt .... Henry Hunter
Sally .... Marie Blake
Collins .... Donald Barry
Crandall .... Reed Hadley
Mrs. Thatcher .... Aileen Pringle
Jenny .... Ann Todd

THE SECRET OF DR. KILDARE (MGM, 1939) 84 M.

Director, Harold S. Bucquet; author, Max Brand; screenplay, Willis Goldbeck, Harry Ruskin; art director, Cedric Gibbons; music director, David Snell; camera, Alfred Gilks; editor, Frank Hull.

Dr. James Kildare .... Lew Ayres
Dr. Leonard Gillespie .... Lionel Barrymore
Paul Messenger .... Lionel Atwill
Mary Lamont .... Laraine Day
Nancy Messenger .... Helen Gilbert
Joe Wayman .... Nat Pendleton
Nora .... Sara Haden
Dr. Stephen Kildare .... Samuel S. Hinds
Mrs. Martha Kildare .... Emma Dunn
John Archley .... Grant Mitchell
Dr. Walter Carew .... Walter Kingsford
Molly Byrd .... Alma Kruger
Charles Herron .... Robert Kent
Nurse Parker (Nosey) .... Nell Craig
Conover .... George Reed
Sally .... Marie Blake
Mrs. Roberts .... Martha O'Driscoll
Collins .... Donald Barry
Mike Ryan .... Frank Orth
Attendant .... Byron Foulger

DR. KILDARE'S STRANGE CASE (MGM, 1940) 76 M.

Director, Harold S. Bucquet; author, Max Brand, Willis Goldbeck; screenplay, Harry Ruskin, Willis Goldbeck; art director, Cedric Gibbons; music director, David Snell; camera, John Seitz; editor, Gene Ruggiero.

Dr. James Kildare .... Lew Ayres
Dr. Leonard Gillespie .... Lionel Barrymore
Mary Lamont .... Laraine Day
Dr. Gregory Lane .... Shepperd Strudwick
Dr. Stephen Kildare .... Samuel S. Hinds
Martha Kildare .... Emma Dunn
Dr. Walter Carew .... Walter Kingsford
Molly Byrd .... Alma Kruger
Henry Adams .... John Eldredge

Nosey	Nell Craig
Conover	George H. Reed
Antonio	Paul Porcasi
Fog Horn	Horace MacMahon
Sally	Marie Blake
Florence	Marcia Mae Jones
Dr. Squires	Charles Waldron
Mike Ryan	Frank Orth
Mrs. Adams	Fay Helm

DR. KILDARE GOES HOME (MGM, 1940) 78 M.

Director, Harold S. Bucquet; author, Max Brand, Willis Goldbeck; screenplay, Harry Ruskin, Willis Goldbeck; music director, David Snell; camera, Harold Rosson; editor, Howard O'Neill.

Dr. James Kildare	Lew Ayres
Dr. Leonard Gillespie	Lionel Barrymore
Mary Lamont	Laraine Day
Dr. Davidson	John Skelton
George Winslow	Gene Lockhart
Dr. Stephen Kildare	Samuel S. Hinds
Mrs. Martha Kildare	Emma Dunn
Joe Wayman	Nat Pendleton
Dr. Walter Carew	Walter Kingsford
Molly Byrd	Alma Kruger
Nurse Parker	Nell Craig
Conover	George H. Reed
Sally	Marie Blake
Collins	Henry Wadsworth
Joiner	Tom Collins
Mr. Brownlee	Donald Briggs
Interne	Arthur O'Connell

DR. KILDARE'S CRISIS (MGM, 1940) 75 M.

Director, Harold S. Bucquet; author, Max Brand, Willis Goldbeck; screenplay, Harry Ruskin, Willis Goldbeck; music director, David Snell; art director, Cedric Gibbons; camera, John Seitz; editor, Gene Ruggiero.

Dr. James Kildare	Lew Ayres
Douglas Lamont	Robert Young
Dr. Leonard Gillespie	Lionel Barrymore
Mary Lamont	Laraine Day
Mrs. Martha Kildare	Emma Dunn
Joe Wayman	Nat Pendleton
Tommy	Bobs Watson
Dr. Walter Carew	Walter Kingsford
Molly Byrd	Alma Kruger
Nurse Parker	Nell Craig
Mike Ryan	Frank Orth
Sally	Marie Blake
Conover	George Reed
Foghorn Murphy	Horace MacMahon
Betty	Ann Morriss
John Root	Frank Sully
Orderly	Byron Foulger
Clifford Genet	Eddie Acuff

THE PEOPLE VS. DR. KILDARE (MGM, 1941) 78 M.

Director, Harold S. Bucquet; author, Lawrence P. Bachmanor, Max Brand; screenplay, Willis Goldbeck, Harry Ruskin; camera, Clyde DeVinna; editor, Ralph Winters.

Dr. James Kildare	Lew Ayres
Dr. Leonard Gillespie	Lionel Barrymore
Mary Lamont	Laraine Day
Frances Marlowe	Bonita Granville
Vernon Briggs	"Red" Skelton
Mr. Channing	Tom Conway
Dr. Walter Carew	Walter Kingsford
Molly Byrd	Alma Kruger
Dan Morton	Chick Chandler
Fay Lennox	Diana Lewis
Clifford Genet	Eddie Acuff
Sally	Marie Blake
Nurse Parker	Nell Craig
Mr. Reynolds	Paul Stanton
Mike Ryan	Frank Orth
Policeman	Grant Withers
Juror Bit	Anna Q. Nilsson
Jury Foreman	Dwight Frye

DR. KILDARE'S WEDDING DAY (MGM, 1941) 82 M.

Director, Harold S. Bucquet; original story, Ormond Ruthven, Laurence P. Bachmann; screenplay, Willis Goldbeck, Harry Ruskin; music, Bronislau Kaper; camera, George Folsey; editor, Conrad A. Nervig.

Dr. James Kildare	Lew Ayres
Dr. Leonard Gillespie	Lionel Barrymore
Mary Lamont	Laraine Day
Vernon Briggs	"Red" Skelton
Mrs. Bartlett	Fay Holden
Dr. Walter Carew	Walter Kingsford
Molly Byrd	Alma Kruger
Dr. Stephen Kildare	Samuel S. Hinds
Mrs. Martha Kildare	Emma Dunn
Constanzo Labardi	Nils Asther
Dr. Lockberg	Miles Mander
Nurse Parker	Nell Craig
Mike Ryan	Frank Orth
Clifford Genet	Eddie Acuff
Nurse	Ann Doran
Jennie	Connie Gilchrist
Policeman	Ralph Byrd

DR. KILDARE'S VICTORY (MGM, 1942) 92 M.

Director, W. S. Van Dyke, II; author, Joseph Harrington; screenplay, Harry Ruskin, Willis Goldbeck; camera, William Daniels; editor, Frank E. Hull.

Dr. James Kildare	Lew Ayres
Dr. Leonard Gillespie	Lionel Barrymore
Dr. Roger Winthrop	Robert Sterling
Edith "Cookie" Charles	Ann Ayars
Annabelle Kirke	Jean Rogers

Molly Byrd	Alma Kruger
Dr. Walter Carew	Walter Kingsford
Nurse Parker	Nell Craig
Willie Brooks	Edward Gargan
Sally	Marie Blake
Mike Ryan	Frank Orth
Conover	George H. Reed
Clifford Genet	Eddie Acuff
Sam Z. Cutler	Barry Nelson
Boy	Kirby Grant

CALLING DR. GILLESPIE (MGM, 1942) 82 M.

Director, Harold S. Bucquet; author, Kubec Glasmon; screenplay, Willis Goldbeck, Harry Ruskin; art director, Cedric Gibbons; music director, Daniele Amfitheatrof; camera, Ray June; editor, Elmo Vernon.

Dr. Leonard Gillespie	Lionel Barrymore
John Hunter Gerniede	Philip Dorn
Marcia Bradburn	Donna Reed
Roy Todwell	Phil Brown
Molly Byrd	Alma Kruger
Emma Hope	Mary Nash
Dr. Walter Carew	Walter Kingsford
Joe Wayman	Nat Pendleton
Dr. Ward O'Kenwood	Charles Dingle
Nurse Parker	Nell Craig
"Bubbles"	Robin Raymond
Sally	Marie Blake
Frank Marshall Todwell	Jonathan Hale
Mrs. Marshall Todwell	Nana Bryant
Lieut. Clifton	Emmett Vogan
Sergt. Hartwell	Pat McVey
Mrs. Brown	Hillary Brooke
Clifford Genet	Eddie Acuff
Susan Prentiss	Ruth Tobey
Girl Bit	Ava Gardner

DR. GILLESPIE'S NEW ASSISTANT (MGM, 1942) 87 M.

Director, Willis Goldbeck; story, Daniele Amfitheatrof; screenplay, Harry Ruskin, Willis Goldbeck, Lawrence P. Bachmann; art director, Cedric Gibbons; camera, George Folsey; editor, Ralph Winters.

Dr. Leonard Gillespie	Lionel Barrymore
Dr. Randall Stuart	Van Johnson
Dr. Dennis Lindsay	Richard Quine
Mrs. Howard Young	Susan Peters
Molly Byrd	Alma Kruger
Howard Young	Stephen H. McNally
Joe Wayman	Nat Pendleton
Dr. Edwin Carew	Walter Kingsford
Dr. Lee Wong How	Keye Luke
Nurse Parker	Nell Craig
Sally	Marie Blake
Mike Ryan	Frank Orth
Mrs. Black	Rose Hobart
Iris Headley	Ann Richards
Jimmy James	Pamela Blake
Husband	Paul Fix

DR. GILLESPIE'S CRIMINAL CASE (MGM, 1943) 89 M.

Director, Willis Goldbeck; screenplay, Martin Berkeley, Harry Ruskin, Lawrence P. Bachmann; music director, Daniele Amfitheatrof; art director, Cedric Gibbons; camera, Nobert Brodine; editor, Laurie Vejar.

Dr. Leonard Gillespie	Lionel Barrymore
Dr. Randall Adams	Van Johnson
Marcia Bradburn	Donna Reed
Dr. Lee Wong How	Keye Luke
Roy Todwell	John Craven
Alvin F. Peterson	William Lundigan
Dr. Walter Carew	Walter Kingsford
Ruth Edly	Marilyn Maxwell
Sergt. Pat J. Orisin	Michael Duane
Joe Wayman	Nat Pendleton
Molly Byrd	Alma Kruger
Sally	Marie Blake
Warden Kenneson	Henry O'Neill
Nurse Parker	Nell Craig
Dr. Post	Arthur Loft
Briggs	Milton Kibbee
Chaperon	Aileen Pringle
Margaret	Margaret O'Brien
Waddy	Grant Withers

THREE MEN IN WHITE (MGM, 1944) 85 M.

Director, Willis Goldbeck; screenplay, Martin Berkeley, Harry Ruskin; music director, Nathaniel Shilkret; art director, Cedric Gibbons, Harry McAfee; camera, Ray June; editor, George Hively.

Dr. Leonard Gillespie	Lionel Barrymore
Dr. Randall Adams	Van Johnson
Ruth Edley	Marilyn Maxwell
Dr. Lee Wong How	Keye Luke
Jean Brown	Ava Gardner
Molly Byrd	Alma Kruger
Hobart Genet	Rags Ragland
Nurse Parker	Nell Craig
Dr. Walter Carew	Walter Kingsford
Conover	George H. Reed
Mary Jones	Patricia Barker

BETWEEN TWO WOMEN (MGM, 1945) 83 M.

Director, Willis Goldbeck; screenplay, Harry Ruskin; music, David Snell; art director, Cedric Gibbons, Edward Carfagno; camera, Harold Rosson; editor, Adrienne Fazan.

Dr. Leonard Gillespie	Lionel Barrymore
Dr. Red Adams	Van Johnson
Ruth Edley	Marilyn Maxwell
Edna	Gloria DeHaven
Tobey	Keenan Wynn
Dr. Lee Wong How	Keye Luke
Molly Byrd	Alma Kruger
Eddie Harmon	Tom Trout
Dr. Edwin Carew	Walter Kingford
Sally	Marie Blake

Nurse Parker	Nell Craig	Cynthia Grace	Lucille Bremer
Nurse Thorsen	Shirley Patterson	Mrs. Selkirk	Jayne Meadows
Nurse Morgan	Edna Holland	Teddy Selkirk	Warner Anderson
Dr. Norman	Ralph Brooke	Dr. Evans Biddle	Henry Stephenson
Marion	Lorraine Miller	Molly Byrd	Alma Kruger
Orderly	Eddie Acuff	Dr. Lee Wong How	Keye Luke
		Dr. Sanford Burson	Art Baker
		Wyndham Grace	Lester Matthews
		Sally	Marie Blake
		Napoleon	Ben Lessy
		Miss Rowland	Geraldine Wall
		Nurse Parker	Nell Craig
		Conover	George Reed
		Nurse Workman	Mary Currier
		Interne	Clarke Hardwicke
		Mild Little Man	Eddie Parks
		Minister	John Burton

DARK DELUSION (MGM, 1947) 90 M.

Producer, Carey Wilson; director, Willis Goldbeck; author-screenplay, Jack Andrews, Harry Ruskin; art director, Cedric Gibbons, Stan Rogers; music director, David Snell; camera, Charles Rosher; editor, Gene Ruggiero.

Dr. Leonard Gillespie	Lionel Barrymore
Dr. Tommy Coalt	James Craig

ELLERY QUEEN

For a phenomenally successful detective series in the printed media, *Ellery Queen* has had a most checkered cinema career. In 1928, Frederic Dannay and Manfred B. Lee (cousins) collaborated on a detective novel, *The Roman Hat Mystery*. They used the pseudonym Ellery Queen both for the author of their joint book and for its main character, the mystery novelist son of a Manhattan police inspector. Whenever the competent Inspector Queen was unable to solve a baffling crime by the standard procedures, Ellery would step in with his brilliant deductive methods, and soon unravel the case via top-notch analytical reasoning. In 1935–36 Republic Pictures—more noted for its serials and western action features—released two modest films about Ellery Queen, then dropped the programmer subject from its production schedule. Not until 1940 did Columbia Pictures pick up the property and begin its seven-entry black and white series. The aimed-at sophistication of the Ellery Queen novels was missing from the Columbia series, and with decreasing audience appeal, the studio dropped the project in mid 1942. (On radio *Ellery Queen's Armchair Detective Theatre* featured Hugh Marlowe, Larry Dobkin, Carleton Young and Sidney Smith among others as Ellery Queen, with Santos Ortego and later Bill Smith as Inspector Queen; Marion Shorkly and then Barbara Terrell were heard as Nikki; and Howard Smith, Ted De Corsica and Ed Latimer as Sergeant Velie. One gimmick of the radio show was to have a celebrity guest attend the radio broadcast and try to solve the crime before Ellery Queen revealed the denouement—a variation of the device used in the *Queen* books. Among those who played Ellery Queen on live and filmed television in the early 1950s were George Nader, Lee Bowman, Lee Phillips, and the best of the lot, Hugh Marlowe. Universal Studios is currently preparing a two-hour telefeature of *Ellery Queen*, which may wind up as a new video series.)

Some of the nine *Ellery Queen* films were based on the novels, although greatly disguised and distorted in presentation. The "challenge to the reader" gambit of the books (the reader, having been given all the needed facts, was told he should now be able to solve the case) was eliminated from the films. As in the books, Ellery remains a well-bred fiction writer, who does not always agree with the more mundane police methods of his law enforcement executive father. Columbia Pictures utilized both Inspector Queen (Charley Grapewin) and dumb Sergeant Velie (James Burke) in all their entries. Both were well cast in their roles as the tolerant senior policeman who patiently waded through the myriad of clues and his well-meaning but addled gumshoe assistant. Columbia's one inspired touch in their *Ellery Queen* features (scripted by Eric Taylor) was the addition of Nikki Porter (Margaret Lindsay) as a freelance mystery writer who goes to work for Ellery as his secretary. She added a bubbling note of pretty distraction, since more often than not the plots called for her to do some amateur sleuthing to help out boss Ellery. (The casting highlights of the Republic *Ellery Queen* films had been the presence of Guy Usher as Inspector Queen in its first effort, and Wade Boteler in the same role in their second film).

Of the four who played Ellery Queen, Ralph

Bellamy was most nearly the image of the smart detective. Born June 17, 1905, in Chicago, he began an acting career in stock and eventually on Broadway. His theatrical credits over the next five decades have included: *Town Boy, Roadside, Tomorrow the World, State of the Union, Detective Story,* and his greatest stage performance in *Sunrise at Campobello.* His film debut was in: *The Secret Six* (1931) for MGM, followed by roles in such films as *Rebecca of Sunnybrook Farm* (1932), *The Awful Truth* (1937), *His Girl Friday* (1940), *Guest in the House* (1944), *The Court-Martial of Billy Mitchell* (1955), *Sunrise at Campobello* (1960), *The Professionals* (1966) and *Rosemary's Baby* (1968). On television, he has appeared in such series as the early 1950s *Man Against Crime,* the recent *The Survivors* and *The Most Deadly Game.* Previously wed to Alice Delbridge, Catherine Willard, Ethel Smith, he is now married to Alice Murphy. Stage actor Donald Cook (1901–1961) who played Ellery in the initial Republic film of the series was competent in the role, but lacked the vitality so necessary for the part. The next Republic *Ellery Queen* featured snappy Eddie Quillan (born, March 31, 1907, in Philadelphia), an ex-vaudevillan who had made his film debut in *Up and at 'Em* (1922). It was an unfortunate case of contra-casting.

After four *Ellery Queen* episodes at Columbia, the studio replaced Bellamy with William Gargan (born July 17, 1905, in Brooklyn), who was too phlegmatic to give the dying series any renewed signs of life. (The stage performer has appeared in *Aloma of the South Seas, The Animal Kingdom* and most recently *The Best Man.* His film debut was in *Misleading Lady* (1932), followed by roles in such productions as *British Agent* (1934), *They Knew what they Wanted* (1940), *The Bells of St. Mary's* (1945), and *The Rawhide Years* (1956). On television, his most noted appearance was in *Martin Kane, Private Eye,* a mid 1950s video series. After combatting a siege of throat cancer, Gargan went on the lecture circuit, and wrote his autobiography "Why Me?" (1969).

The Spanish Cape Mystery has Ellery on vacation with his cohort Judge Macklin (Berton Churchill) at Spanish Cape. While there, he becomes involved in four murders, as well as finding romance with Stella Godfrey (Helen Twelvetrees). A strange plot twisting has loud mouth, philosophizing local sheriff Moley (Harry Stubbs) as the focal point of the story and the one who solves the murders, when Ellery bows out of the scene. The supporting cast, filled with such veteran performers as Betty Blythe, George Cleveland and Jack LaRue, gave the story some flavor. Republic's other well-photographed followup, *The Mandarin Mystery,* was sadly played for laughs with crime detector Queen tracking down the thief who had taken a $50,000 Chinese Mandarin postage stamp, which leads to two murders. Jo Temple (Charlotte Henry) who was originally entrusted with the prized stamp, becomes Ellery's love interest.

. . ., *Master Detective,* the first Columbia "Queen," has the novel setting of a health resort, where John Braun (Fred Niblo), a wealthy physical culturist is recuperating from what turns out to be a fatal illness. When he threatens to disinherit his relatives and associates, the murder mystery is set into motion. There is a three-pronged search for Braun's murderer as Inspector Queen, Ellery, and Nikki Porter (another mystery writer who is looking for story material) become entangled in the case. In the course of events, there is a vanishing body, missing X-rays, a lost will, and a disappearing ambulance, plus a mad man who busily digs up graves. At the finale, ever-helpful Nikki promises to become Ellery's secretary.

. . .'s *Penthouse Mystery* concerns Gordon Cobb (Noel Madison), a famed Oriental ventriloquist who is entrusted with a fortune in jewels by a wealthy group in China. Cobb is obliged to smuggle the gems into the United States, to sell them so the funds can be used to aid China's war effort. Shortly after his arrival in Manhattan, he is found dead in his penthouse hotel room. Once again, super-smart, super-chic Ellery intercedes in the case assigned to his father, and unsorts the clues and suspects, which include: Lois Ling (Anna May Wong), influential contact for the Chinese cause; Count Brett (Eduardo Ciannelli), a crook teamed up with Walsh (Russell Hicks), a one-time partner of Cobb; and Jim Ritter (Theodore Von Eltz), a card-sharp magician. Also involved in the caper is Sanders (Frank Albertson), a newspaperman posing as a bellboy.

. . . *The Perfect Crime* is set into motion when John Matthews (Douglass Dumbrille) sells shady stocks, which bankrupts Ray Jardin (H. B. Warner), father of Matthews's son's fiancee Marian (Linda Hayes). When the son Walter (John Beal) disappears, senior Matthews asks Ellery for aid. With an overabundance of diluted red herrings and no real clues for the viewers, the film is only noteworthy for its able supporting cast.

. . . The Murder Ring finds Mrs. Stack (Blanche Yurka), owner of Stack Memorial Hospital, requesting Inspector Queen and Ellery to investigate strange goings on at her private hospital. When Mrs. Stack is injured in a car accident and after an emergency operation, she is found strangled to death, the line up of suspects include John Stack (Leon Ames) who covets his mother's money; Dr. Janney (George Zucco), the medical director at the hospital; Nurse Fox (Charlotte Wynters); and Miss Tracy (Mona Barrie), the head nurse who is in love with John Stack.

A Close Call . . . , which initiated the sober detecting of William Gargan as Ellery Queen, picks up steam when Ellery is asked to check on two unwanted visitors at Fawn Lake estate who are blackmailing the owner Alan Rogers (Ralph Morgan). Ellery thinks he has outwitted Nikki into staying out of the case, but she becomes part of the melee when Marie Rogers (Kay Linaker), one of Rogers's long-lost daughters, arrives at Ellery's office and Nikki eagerly volunteers her help. Soon blackmailers Bates (Andrew Tombes) and Corday (Charles Judele) are entangled in the adventure, with two murders occurring.

Desperate Chance . . . sees Mrs. Norman Hadley (Charlotte Wynters) asking Ellery to trace her missing banker husband, whom she thought dead —now it seems he may be alive in San Francisco. Meantime, George Belden (Noel Madison) and his burlesque queen wife Adele (Lillian Bond) leave New York for San Francisco with stolen $100 bills. Ellery finds Hadley (John Litel) who confesses he once served a prison term, and the caper sideshoots to the Silver Star Club run by Ray Stafford (Morgan Conway) where Adele is now an entertainer. Along the helter-skelter path, assorted homicides occur.

The final Ellery Queen entry, *Enemy Agents Meet . . .* , had diamonds being smuggled from Holland to Egypt to the United States with Gestapo agents and the U.S. Marines in deadly combat to obtain the precious gems being shipped in a mummy's case. When Paul Gillette (Gilbert Roland) is killed after bringing the valuables into this country, Ellery and his father enter the case, with the scene shifting from a swank jewelry shop to an art gallery to an athletic club and a cemetery. A slambang fistfight climaxes the story, giving excessive action to a very lowbrow entry.

Helen Twelvetrees, Director Lewis D. Collins, and Donald Cook. (The Spanish Cape Mystery)

Franklin Pangborn, Anthony Meritt, Wade Boteler, Eddie Quillan, Charlotte Henry.

Margaret Lindsay, Ralph Bellamy.

Joe Yule, Bellamy, Margaret Lindsay. (. . . and the
Perfect Crime)

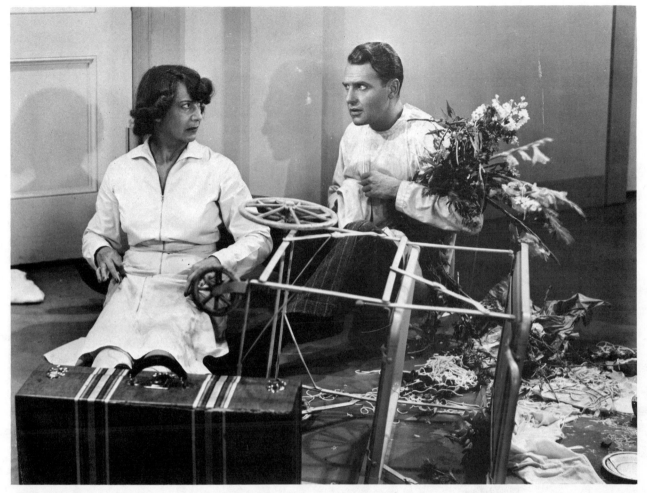

Claire DuBrey, Bellamy. (. . . and the Murder Ring)

Charlie Grapewin, Bellamy, Margaret Lindsay, Anna May Wong. (. . .'s Penthouse Mystery)

John Beal, H. B. Warner, Margaret Lindsay, Ralph Bellamy, Spring Byington, Sidney Blackmer, Walter Kingsford.

Margaret Lindsay, Gargan. (Enemy Agents Meet . . .)

William Gargan, Margaret Lindsay, Claire DuBrey, Charley Grapewin.

Jack LaRue, Lilian Bond, Gargan, Margaret Lindsay, Charlie Grapewin.

ELLERY QUEEN

THE SPANISH CAPE MYSTERY (Rep., 1935) 65 M.

Producer, M. H. Hoffman; director, Lewis D. Collins; author, Ellery Queen; screenplay, Albert DeMond; camera, Gilbert Warrenton; editor, Jack Ogilvie.

Stella Godfrey	Helen Twelvetrees
Ellery Queen	Donald Cook
Judge Macklin	Berton Churchill
Godfrey	Frank Sheridan
Moley	Harry Stubbs
Inspector Queen	Guy Usher
Kummer	Huntley Gordon
Mrs. Godfrey	Betty Blythe
DuPre	Olaf Hytten
Mrs. Constable	Ruth Gillette
Gardner	Jack LaRue
Tiller	Frank Leigh
Mrs. Munn	Barbara Bedford
Hendricks	Donald Kerr
Jorum	George Cleveland

THE MANDARIN MYSTERY (Rep., 1936) 63 M.

Producer, Nat Levine; director, Ralph Staub; author, Ellery Queen; screenplay, John F. Larkin, Rex Taylor, Gertrude Orr, Cortland Fitzsimmons; camera, Jack Marta; music, Harry Gray.

Ellery Queen	Eddie Quillan
Josephine Temple	Charlotte Henry
Martha Kirk	Rita Le Roy
Inspector	Wade Boteler
Mellish	Franklin Pangborn
Dr. Alexander Kirk	George Irving
Irene Kirk	Kay Hughes
Guffy	William Newell
Donald Trent	George Walcott
Bronson	Edwin Stanley
Reporter	Edgar Allen
Craig	Anthony Merrill
Reporter	Richard Beach
First Detective	Monte Vandergrift

ELLERY QUEEN, MASTER DETECTIVE (Col., 1940) 69 M.

Producer, Larry Darmour; director, Kurt Neumann; author, Ellery Queen; screenplay, Eric Taylor; camera, James S. Brown, Jr.; editor, Dwight Caldwell.

Ellery Queen	Ralph Bellamy
Nikki Porter	Margaret Lindsay
Inspector Queen	Charley Grapewin
Sergeant Velie	James Burke
Doctor James Rogers	Michael Whalen
Barbara Braun	Marsha Hunt
John Braun	Fred Niblo
Doctor Prouty	Charles Lane
Lydia Braun	Ann Shoemaker

Cornelia	Marian Martin
Rocky Taylor	Douglas Fowley
Zachary	Morgan Wallace
Amos	Byron Foulger
Valerie Norris	Katharine DeMille
Flynn	Lee Phelps

ELLERY QUEEN'S PENTHOUSE MYSTERY (Col., 1941) 69 M.

Producer, Larry Darmour; director, James Hogan; author, Ellery Queen; screenplay, Eric Taylor; camera, James S. Brown, Jr.; editor, Dwight Caldwell.

Ellery Queen	Ralph Bellamy
Nikki Porter	Margaret Lindsay
Inspector Queen	Charley Grapewin
Lois Ling	Anna May Wong
Sergeant Velie	James Burke
Count Brett	Eduardo Ciannelli
Sanders	Frank Albertson
Sheila Cobb	Ann Doran
Gordon Cobb	Noel Madison
Doc Prouty	Charles Lane
Walsh	Russell Hicks
McGrath	Tom Dugan
Roy	Mantan Moreland
Jim Ritter	Theodore Von Eltz

ELLERY QUEEN AND THE PERFECT CRIME (Col., 1941) 68 M.

Producer, Larry Darmour; director, James Hogan; author, Ellery Queen; screenplay, Eric Taylor; music, Lee Zahler; camera, James S. Brown, Jr.; editor, Dwight Caldwell.

Ellery Queen	Ralph Bellamy
Nikki Porter	Margaret Lindsay
Inspector Queen	Charley Grapewin
Carlotta Emerson	Spring Byington
Ray Jardin	H. B. Warner
Sergeant Velie	James Burke
John Mathews	Douglass Dumbrille
Walter Mathews	John Beal
Marian Jardin	Linda Hayes
Anthony Rhodes	Sidney Blackmer
Henry	Walter Kingsford
Lee	Honorable Wu
Doctor Prouty	Charles Lane

ELLERY QUEEN AND THE MURDER RING (Col., 1941) 70 M.

Producer, Larry Darmour; director, James Hogan; author, Ellery Queen; screenplay, Eric Taylor, Gertrude Purcell; music, Lee Zahler; camera, James S. Brown, Jr.; editor, Dwight Caldwell.

Ellery Queen	Ralph Bellamy
Nikki Porter	Margaret Lindsay
Inspector Queen	Charley Grapewin

Miss Tracy	Mona Barrie
Page	Paul Hurst
Sergeant Velie	James Burke
Dr. Janney	George Zucco
Mrs. Stack	Blanche Yurka
Thomas	Tom Dugan
John Stack	Leon Ames
Alice Stack	Jean Fenwick
Dr. Williams	Olin Howland
Dr. Dunn	Dennis Moore
Miss Fox	Charlotte Wynters

CLOSE CALL FOR ELLERY QUEEN (Col., 1942) 65 M.

Producer, Larry Darmour; director, James Hogan; author, Ellery Queen; screenplay, Eric Taylor; camera, James S. Brown, Jr.; editor, Dwight Caldwell.

Ellery Queen	William Gargan
Nikki Porter	Margaret Lindsay
Inspector Queen	Charley Grapewin
Alan Rogers	Ralph Morgan
Margo Rogers	Kay Linaker
Stewart Cole	Edward Norris
Sergeant Velie	James Burke
Lester Younger	Addison Richards
Corday	Charles Judel
Bates	Andrew Tombes
Housekeeper	Claire DuBrey
Marie Dubois	Michael Cheirel
Fisherman	Ben Weldon
Butler	Milton Parson

DESPERATE CHANCE FOR ELLERY QUEEN (Col., 1942) 70 M.

Producer, Larry Darmour; director, James Hogan; author, Ellery Queen; screenplay, Eric Taylor; camera, James S. Brown, Jr.; assistant director, Carl Hiecke; editor, Dwight Caldwell.

Ellery Queen	William Gargan
Nikki Porter	Margaret Lindsay
Inspector Queen	Charley Grapewin
Norman Hadley	John Litel
Adele Belden	Lillian Bond
Sergeant Velie	James Burke
Tommy Gould	Jack LaRue
Ray Stafford	Morgan Conway
George Belden	Noel Madison
Captain Daley	Frank Thomas
Mrs. Norman Hadley	Charlotte Wynters

ENEMY AGENTS MEET ELLERY QUEEN (Col., 1942) 64 M.

Producer, Larry Darmour; director, James Hogan; author, Ellery Queen; screenplay, Eric Taylor; camera, James S. Brown, Jr.; editor, Dwight Caldwell.

Ellery Queen	William Gargan
Nikki Porter	Margaret Lindsay
Inspector Richard Queen	Charley Grapewin
Mrs. Von Dorn	Gale Sondergaard
Paul Gillette	Gilbert Roland
Heinrich	Sig Rumann
Sergeant Velie	James Burke
Morse	Ernest Dorian
Helm	Felix Basch
Commodore Bang	Minor Watson
Commissioner Bracken	John Hamilton
Sergeant Stevens	James Seay
Reece	Louis Donath
Sailor	Dick Wessel

THE FALCON

In the early 1940s, RKO found it advantageous, as did the other major Hollywood film studios, to promulgate motion picture series which would advantageously utilize its contract players, serve as a showcase for new performers, and most importantly help meet their exhibitor booking needs at the least possible expense for the studio. Thus RKO acquired the rights to a Michael Arlen detective story, dealing with the debonair Falcon. In six years, the studio churned out thirteen black and white entries, the first four starring George Sanders, and the balance featuring Sanders's real life brother Tom Conway. After a lapse of two years, independent Film Craft bought "The Falcon" and turned out three quickie entries in 1948–49 with John Calvert in the leading role. (On television, Charles McGraw portrayed Mike Waring, the Falcon, in 39 half-hour episodes syndicated during the 1954–55 video season. On radio, the Falcon was played by James Meighan, Les Damon, Berry Kroeger, Les Tremayne, George Petrie, with Joan Banks as Nancy, and Ethel Everett as Renee.)

Stylistically, *The Falcon* tried to retain a well-bred approach to the tried and true formula, with Sanders and Conway, arch prototypes of the aristocratic amateur detective. The Falcon (Sanders played Gay Falcon, Conway was Tom Falcon, and Calvert was Mike Waring) would much rather spend his time hobnobbing with society and exchanging witty repartee with sophisticated female members of the 400 set. Each episode saw the well posed Britisher swearing off further investigating work, and pledging to take a much wanted vacation to some fashionable spot, only to have his plans drastically altered by a damsel in distress. Usually near the film's finale, the next production's leading lady would make a token appearance requesting the Falcon's eloquent assistance. And being a perfect gentleman, how could he refuse? To supply the prerequisite comedy interest, there were the Falcon's cronies Goldy (Allen Jenkins—later Don Barclay, Vince Barnett, and the best one, Edward Brophy) and Bates (Edward Gargan). As the on-the-spot plodding police inspector, there was Mike O'Hara (James Gleason) and later Inspector Timothy Donovan (Cliff Clark).

After Sanders left *The Falcon* series to concentrate on higher-class projects, his semi-lookalike brother Tom Conway replaced him to good advantage in these second feature productions. Thomas Charles Sanders was born September 15, 1904, in St. Petersburg, Russia. Shortly before the Bolshevik revolution, the British-origin family returned to England. After attending a succession of boarding schools, he worked as a rancher in South Africa for six years. When his brother George achieved success on the stage in the early 1930s, he persuaded Tom to try the acting profession. To avoid cashing in on his brother's fame, he adopted the stage name of Conway. After repertory work in Manchester and a period of radio acting, Conway followed Sanders to Hollywood and began making featured appearance in such films as *Sky Murder* (1941), *Lady Be Good* (1941), and *Rio Rita* (1942). Then came *The Falcon* series which elevated him to second-string male stardom, and it was the peak of his professional career. Following his RKO stint, he returned to featured roles (often as the other man or as the villain) in films like *One*

Touch of Venus (1950), *Prince Valiant* (1954), and *Voodoo Woman* (1959). On radio, Conway was heard as Sherlock Holmes and The Saint; on an early television series he portrayed Inspector Mark Sabre. Then Conway dropped into obscurity until early 1965 when he was discovered ill and destitute, living in a cheap Venice, California, boarding house. He admitted he had squandered his one-million-dollar film salary and that drinking and eye trouble had been great problems. He died April 22, 1967, at the age of 63, from a liver ailment. His second wife was former actress Queenie Leonard.

John Calvert, born in New Treilan, Indiana, was originally a theology student, but instead preferred the stage and performing his magico act. After small roles in assorted RKO Films like *Bombardier* (1943) and in other independent studio productions, he gained some prominence in *The Falcon* series. Later he toured with his magician act, and produced-starred in a television series, *The Sea Fox*.

The Gay . . . shows Gay (George Sanders) asked to guard a famous diamond worn by a guest at a society function. The diamond owner is murdered, and Goldy (Allen Jenkins), the Falcon's chauffeur, is suspected—especially after a second homicide occurs. After two more murders the Falcon unravels the fake jewel insurance scheme and wraps up the case. Midst the chaos, the suave Falcon has been refereeing the jealous rivalry of Helen Reed (Wendy Barrie) and Elinor (Anne Hunter) for his attention.

In *A Date With* . . . , the Falcon is on the verge of marrying Helen Reed (Wendy Barrie) when he becomes implicated in the mysterious disappearance of Waldo Sampson (Alec Craig) who has perfected a synthetic diamond. After being kidnapped, escaping and kidnapped again by the rowdy gang involved, and being wrongly arrested for murder, the Falcon ties up the loose ends of the case. At the finale, he and Helen are on their way again.

. . . *Takes Over* deals with Moose Malloy (Ward Bond) imprisoned on a false charge, and escaping from jail after five years. Goldy is on the spot at the wrong time, and finds himself having to drive Moose away from the murder scene. Meanwhile, the Falcon has agreed to protect Lindsey Marriot (Hans Conried) while the latter is ransoming a necklace stolen from his girl friend Diana Kenyon (Helen Gilbert). The seemingly extraneous seg-

ments of this caper all fit together, when it is discovered that one of the supposed victims is really someone else in disguise. This story came from Raymond Chandler's novel *Farewell My Lovely*, which was remade as a Dick Powell vehicle, *Murder My Sweet* (1944) (with the detective role being restored to the Philip Marlowe character).

. . . *'s Brother* concerns Gay's efforts to help his brother Tom (Tom Conway) just back from the Bahamas, break up an Axis conspiracy bent on upsetting United States-South American relations. When Gay is fatally wounded, Tom promises his dying brother that he will take up the cause where Gay left off. This entry, which marked the turning point of the series, is a baffling conglomeration of crimes and clues, without the usual compensating humor or characterization.

. . . *Strikes Back* sees the Falcon tricked by pretty Mia Bruger (Rita Corday), knocked unconscious and when he recovers, finding himself accused by the police of murdering a bank messenger and stealing war bonds. He escapes to a country hotel to follow clues, and discovers that Mia has been killed. By prying further, he unearths a war bond racket. This entry particularly emphasizes Conway's abilty to give the Falcon role the necessary ease and polish needed to carry off the light hearted dialogue, and showing the amusing philandering of *The Falcon*.

. . . *and the Co-Eds* has the sleuth called upon to investigate the mysterious death of Professor Jamieson at Bluecliff Seminary. Miss Keyes (Barbara Brown), head of the school, is most anxious to avoid scandal, but when other sinister deaths occur, she cannot pass them off as accidents. The more logical than usual plot involves Mary Phoebus (Isabel Jewell), the music teacher; Vicky Gaines (Jean Brooks) of the drama department; Dr. Graelich (George Givot), a psychology lecturer; and Marguerita Serena (Rita Corday), one of the moody, hysterical pupils there. This entry is noteworthy for its exceptionally good photography, especially shots of the seaside.

. . . *In Danger* concerns a small passenger plane which crash lands at an airport, but there are neither passengers nor pilot aboard. The Falcon is asked to hunt the passenger(s) who took some valuable securities from Stanley Palmer (Clarence Kolb), the millionaire whose plane it was. Before the caper is completed, several murders occur, linked together in the subversion of a large government contract. Distracting from the too obvious plot, is the Falcon's romance with Bonnie Caldwell (Amelita Ward).

. . . *In Hollywood* finds the Falcon vacationing in the cinema capital where he happens on a corpse, the former actor-husband of studio fashion designer Roxanna (Jean Brooks). She is about to marry prominent film director, Hoffman (Konstantin Shayne). The suspenseless script is greatly aided by Gordon Douglas's tongue-in-cheek direction, and a peppery cast including Billie (Veda Ann Borg), a garrulous taxi driver; Peggy (Barbara Hale), a dancing star; Louie (Sheldon Leonard), an ex-convict on the loose; Lili (Rita Corday), a foreign film actress; with McBride (Emory Parnell) and Higgins (Frank Jenks) as dumb cops.

The Falcon goes south of the border in . . . *In Mexico.* He must uncover the alleged New York City murder of an art gallery proprietor over Humphrey Wade's (Bryant Washburn) portrait of Mexican Dolores Ybarra (Cecilia Callejo). The Falcon is accompanied by Wade's daughter Barbara (Martha Vickers), hoping to find out if Wade is really dead. The aristocratic sleuth has three murders to solve, which necessitates a trip to an inn a few hundred miles from Mexico City. There Raquel (Mona Maris) is the specialty dancer who knows too much about the case. The film boasts the scenic background of a large lakeside, and there are two Mexican songs performed for diversion.

In . . . *Out West,* the Falcon is dining at the crowded Flamingo Club when Tex Irwin (Lyle Talbot), a millionaire rancher collapses and dies on the dance floor. Also present are Vanessa Drake (Carole Gallagher), his fiancee, and Irwin's ex-wife (Joan Barclay). The Falcon follows Vanessa to Irwin's ranch, and he in turn is trailed by reliable Inspector Donovan (Cliff Clark) and Hayde (Don Douglas), Irwin's attorney. Before cleverly untangling the clues, two attempts are made on the Falcon's life and he is kidnapped when he discovers that Irwin died of rattlesnake poisoning and that much money was stolen from his wallet. Conway again demonstrates a suave nonchalance, making discernment and shrewdness his trademark as the Falcon.

. . . *In San Francisco* is a mild adventure concerning silk smugglers in the Golden Gate City and the Falcon's determination to bring the gang responsible to justice. . . .'s *Alibi* centers on Joan Meredith (Rita Corday), social secretary to Mrs. Peabody (Esther Howard), a flighty rich widow whose famous jewel collection is always being stolen. Joan fears she will be blamed and asks the Falcon's help. Before the fadeout, three murders transpire, and the sleuth finds himself jailed on a homicide charge. Compared to other segments, this is a slow moving, easy who-done-it.

. . .'s *Adventure* has the Falcon rescuing Brazilian Luisa Braganza (Madge Meredith) from a kidnap attempt, and he falls into a plot to get her father's formula for preparing synthetic industrial diamonds. The Falcon is blamed for her father's death, and before the conclusion, another victim has died of a "heart attack" and the Falcon has had to hop a train to Florida with the police hot on his trail.

The Devil's Cargo is a lightweight entry, focusing on Ramon Delgado (Paul Marion) who allegedly killed a racetrack operator in a dispute over Margo (Rochelle Hudson), the former's wife. Before surrendering to the police, Delgado asks Michael Waring's help. Later he dies of poisoning in jail. At opposite ends of the pole, are the standard police forces headed by Lt. Hardy (Roscoe Karns) and the sinister criminal lawyer Tom Mallon (Theodore Van Eltz). A sidelight of the film has the Falcon performing magic tricks (a professional skill of actor Calvert). *Appointment with Murder* has an international background around stolen paintings. Herein, the Falcon is an insurance investigator searching in Hollywood and Italy for paintings stolen and for which his insurance firm has already paid substantial claims. *Search for Danger* is a double murder mystery, solved through conversation rather than much needed action. The Falcon tracks down the absconding partner of a gambling pair (Albert Dekker and Ben Weldon as Kirk and Gregory), which leads to murder and a stolen $100,000.

Wendy Barrie, George Sanders. (The Gay Falcon

*Amelita Ward, Richard Davies, Elaine Shepard, Clar-
ence Kolb, Conway.* (. . . in Danger)

Sanders, Ed Brophy. (. . . Takes Over)

Tom Conway, Jane Randolph. (. . . Strikes Back)

Cliff Clark, Conway, Jean Brooks, Richard Davies.
(. . . in Danger)

Richard Martin, Conway. (. . . in Danger)

*Richard Corday, Robert Clarke, Veda Ann Borg,
Conway, Barbara Hale, John Abbott, Emory Parnell,
Jean Brooks. On ground: Konstantin Shayne. (. . .
in Hollywood)*

Steve Winston, Lee Trent, Wheaton Chambers, Ed Gargan, Clark, Conway. (. . . Out West)

Conway, Sharyn Moffett, Edward S. Brophy. (. . . in San Francisco)

John Mylong, Conway, Brophy. (. . . in San Francisco)

Myrna Dell, Calvert. (Search for Danger)

Roscoe Karns, Paul Regan, John Calvert. (Devil's Cargo)

THE FALCON

THE GAY FALCON (RKO, 1941) 67 M.

Producer, Howard Benedict; director, Irving Reis; author, Michael Arlen; screenplay, Lynn Root, Frank Fenton; camera, Nicholas Musuraca; music, Paul Sawtell; art director, Van Nest Polglase; editor, George Crone.

Falcon	George Sanders
Helen Reed	Wendy Barrie
Goldy	Allen Jenkins
Elinor	Anne Hunter
Maxine	Gladys Cooper
Bates	Edward S. Brophy
Waldeck	Arthur Shields
Weber	Damian O'Flynn
Retana	Turhan Bey
Grimes	Eddie Dunn
Mrs. Gardiner	Lucile Gleason
Jerry	Willie Fung
Herman	Hans Conreid
Bit	Virginia Vale

A DATE WITH THE FALCON (RKO, 1941) 63 M.

Producer, Howard Benedict; director, Irving Reis; author, Michael Arlen; screenplay, Lynn Root, Frank Fenton; camera, Robert DeGrasse; editor, Harry Marker.

Falcon	George Sanders
Helen Reed	Wendy Barrie
O'Hara	James Gleason
Goldy	Allen Jenkins
Rita Mara	Mona Maris
Max	Victor Kilian
Dutch	Frank Moran
Needles	Russ Clark
Bates	Ed Gargan
Waldo Sampson ⎫ H. Sampson ⎬	Alec Craig
Louie	Frank Martinelli
Hotel Clerk	Hans Conried
Girl on Plane	Elizabeth Russell

THE FALCON TAKES OVER (RKO, 1942) 63 M.

Producer, Howard Benedict; director, Irving Reis; author, Raymond Chandler; screenplay, Lynn Root, Frank Fenton; art director, Albert S. D'Agostino, F. M. Gray; music director, C. Bakaleinikoff; camera, George Robinson; editor, Harry Marker.

Falcon	George Sanders
Ann Riordan	Lynn Bari
Mike O'Hara	James Gleason
Jonathan G. (Goldy) Locke	Allen Jenkins
Diana Kenyon	Helen Gilbert
Moose Malloy	Ward Bond
Bates	Edward Gargan
Jessie Florian	Ann Revere
Jerry	George Cleveland
Grimes	Harry Shannon

Lindsey Marriot	Hans Conried
Bartender	Mickey Simpson
Laird Burnett	Selmer Jackson
Jules Amthor	Turhan Bey

THE FALCON'S BROTHER (RKO, 1942) 63 M.

Producer, Maurice Geraghty; director, Stanley Logan; screenplay, Stuart Palmer, Craig Rice; camera, Russell Metty; music, Roy Webb; art director, Albert S. D'Agostino, Walter E. Keller; editor, Mark Robson.

Falcon	George Sanders
Tom	Tom Conway
Marcia	Jane Randolph
Goldy	Don Barclay
Carmelita	Amanda Varela
Valdez	George Lewis
Diane	Gwili Andre
Nolan	Cliff Clark
Bates	Edward Gargan
Paul	James Newill
Arlette	Charlotte Wynters
Savitski	Andre Charlot
Grimes	Eddie Dunn
Miss Ross	Mary Halsey
Steamship Official	Richard Martin
Victory Gown Model ⎫ Spanish Girl ⎬	Kay Aldridge

THE FALCON STRIKES BACK (RKO, 1943) 66 M.

Producer, Maurice Geraghty; director, Edward Dmytryk; author, Stuart Palmer; screenplay, Edward Dein, Gerald Geraghty; camera, Jack McKenzie; music director, C. Bakaleinikoff; art director, Albert S. D'Agostino, Walter E. Keller; editor, George Crone.

Falcon	Tom Conway
Gwynne Gregory	Harriet Hilliard
Marcia Brooks	Jane Randolph
Smiley Dugan	Edgar Kennedy
Goldy	Cliff Edwards
Mia Bruger	Rita Corday
Rickey Davis	Erford Gage
Mrs. Lipton	Wynne Gibson
Jerry	Richard Leo
Bruno Steffen	Andre Charlot
Inspector Donovan	Cliff Clark
Bates	Ed Gargan
Hotel Clerk (Argyle)	Byron Foulger
Bit	Joan Barclay
Hobo (Cecil)	Frank Faylen
Hobo	Jack Norton

THE FALCON AND THE CO-EDS (RKO, 1943) 68 M.

Producer, Maurice Geraghty; director, William Clemens; author, Ardel Wray; screenplay, Ardel Wray, Gerald Geraghty; camera, Roy Hunt; art director, Albert S. D'Agostino; music director, C. Bakaleinikoff; editor, Theron Warth.

Falcon	Tom Conway
Vicky Gaines	Jean Brooks
Marguerita Serena	Rita Corday
Jane Harris	Amelita Ward
Mary Phoebus	Isabel Jewell
Dr. Anatole Graelich	George Givot
Inspector Timothy Donovan	Cliff Clark
Bates	Ed Gargan
Miss Keyes	Barbara Brown
2nd Ugh	Juanita Alvarez
1st Ugh	Ruth Alvarez
3rd Ugh	Nancy McCullum
Beanie Smith	Patti Brill
Co-Ed	Dorothy Malone (y)

THE FALCON IN DANGER (RKO, 1943) 69 M.

Producer, Maurice Geraghty; director, William Clemens; screenplay, Fred Niblo, Jr., Craig Rice; camera, Frank Redman; music director, C. Bakaleinikoff; art director, Albert S. D'Agostino, Walter E. Keller; editor, George Crone.

Falcon	Tom Conway
Iris Fairchild	Jean Brooks
Nancy Palmer	Elaine Shepard
Bonnie Caldwell	Amelita Ward
Insp. Timothy Donovan	Cliff Clark
Bates	Ed Gargan
Stanley Harris Palmer	Clarence Kolb
Morley	Felix Basch
Ken Gibson	Richard Davies
Georgie Morley	Richard Martin
Evan Morley	Erford Gage
Grimes	Eddie Dunn
Bit	Russell Wade
Mechanic	Bruce Edwards
Hysterical Girl	Joan Barclay
Manager of Casino	Jack Mulhall

THE FALCON IN HOLLYWOOD (RKO, 1944) 67 M.

Producer, Maurice Geraghty; director, Gordon Douglas; screenplay, Gerald Geraghty; camera, Nicholas Musuraca; music director, C. Bakaleinikoff; art director, Albert D'Agostino, L. O. Croxton; editor, Gene Milford.

Falcon	Tom Conway
Peggy	Barbara Hale
Billie	Veda Ann Borg
Dwyer	John Abbott
Louie	Sheldon Leonard
Hoffman	Konstantin Shayne
McBride	Emory Parnell
Higgins	Frank Jenks
Roxana	Jean Brooks
Lili	Rita Corday
Ed Johnson	Walter Soderling
Nagari	Usaf Ali
Perc Saunders	Robert Clarke

THE FALCON IN MEXICO (RKO, 1944) 70 M.

Producer, Maurice Geraghty; director, William Berke; screenplay, George Worthing Yates, Gerald Geraghty; camera, Frank Redman; art director, Albert S. D'Agostino; music director, C. Bakaleinikoff; editor, Joseph Noriega.

Falcon	Tom Conway
Raquel	Mona Maris
Barbara Wade	Martha MacVicar (Vickers)
Manuel Romero	Nestor Paiva
Paula Dudley	Mary Currier
Dolores Ybarra	Cecilia Callejo
James Winthrop Hughes (Lucky Diamond)	Emory Parnell
Anton	Joseph Vitale
Don Carlos Ybarra	Pedro de Cordoba
Pancho Romero	Fernando Alvarado
Humphrey Wade	Bryant Washburn
Mexican Detective	George Lewis
Mexican Doctor	Julian Rivero
Singers	Juanita and Ruth Alvarez

THE FALCON OUT WEST (RKO, 1944) 64 M.

Producer, Maurice Geraghty; director, William Clemmons; screenplay, Billy Jones, Morton Grant; camera, Barry Wild; art director, Albert S. D'Agostino, Alfred Herman; music director, C. Bakaleinikoff; editor, Gene Milford.

Falcon	Tom Conway
Vanessa Drake	Carole Gallagher
Marion	Barbara Hale
Mrs. Irwin	Joan Barclay
Inspector Donovan	Cliff Clark
Bates	Ed Gargan
Caldwell	Minor Watson
Hayden	Don Douglas
Tex Irwin	Lyle Talbot
Dusty	Lee Trent
Orchestra Leader	Lawrence Tierney

THE FALCON IN SAN FRANCISCO (RKO, 1945) 65 M.

Producer, Maurice Geraghty; director, Joseph H. Lewis; author, Robert Kent; screenplay, Robert Kent, Ben Markson; camera, Virgil Miller, William Sickner; music director, C. Bakaleinikoff; editor, Ernie Leadlay.

Falcon	Tom Conway
Joan Marshall	Rita Corday
Goldie	Edward S. Brophy
Annie Marshall	Sharyn Moffett
Doreen Temple	Faye Helm
De Forrest	Robert Armstrong
Rickey	Carl Kent
Dalman	George Holmes
Peter Vantine	John Mylong
Cop	Edmund Cobb
Beautiful Girl	Myrna Dell
Mrs. Peabody	Esther Howard

THE FALCON'S ALIBI (RKO, 1946) 62 M.

Producer, William Berke; director, Ray McCarey; story, Dane Lussior, Manny Seff; screenplay, Paul Yawitz; camera, Frank Redman; music director, C. Bakaleinikoff; art director, Albert S. D'Agostino, Lucius Croxton; editor, Philip Martin, Jr.

Falcon	Tom Conway
Joan Meredith	Rita Corday
Goldie Locke	Vince Barnett
Lola Carpenter	Jane Greer
Nick	Elisha Cook, Jr.
Metcalf	Emory Parnell
Inspector Blake	Al Bridge
Gloria Peabody	Esther Howard
Baroness Lena	Jean Brooks
Det. Williams	Edmund Cobb
Girl With Falcon	Myrna Dell

THE FALCON'S ADVENTURE (RKO, 1946) 61 M.

Producer, Herman Schlom; director, William Berke; screenplay, Aubrey Wisberg; additional dialogue, Robert E. Kent; camera, Harry Wild, Frank Redman; editor, Marvin Coil.

Falcon	Tom Conway
Luisa Braganza	Madge Meredith
Goldie Locke	Edward S. Brophy
Kenneth Sutton	Robert Warwick
Doris Blanding	Myrna Dell
Benny	Steve Brodie
Denison	Ian Wolfe
Helen	Carol Forman
Inspector Cavanaugh	Joseph Crehan
Mike Geary	Phil Warren
Paolo	Tony Barrett
Duncan	Harry Harvey
Lieutenant Evans	Jason Robards
Crew Member	Dave Sharpe

THE DEVIL'S CARGO (FC, 1948) 61 M.

Producer, Philip N. Krasne; director, John F. Link; screenplay, Don Martin; original story, Robert Tallman, Jason James; camera, Walter Strange; music, Karl Hajos; editor, Asa Boyd Clark.

Falcon	John Calvert
Margo	Rochelle Hudson
Lt. Hardy	Roscoe Karns

Morello	Lyle Talbot
Naga	Tom Kennedy
Bernie	Paul Regan
Tom Mallon	Theodore Van Eltz
Ramon Delgado	Paul Marion

APPOINTMENT WITH MURDER (FC, 1948) 67 M.

Producer-director, Jack Bernhard; story, Joel Malone, Harold Swanton; camera, Walter Strange; music, Karl Hajos; editor, Asa Boyd Clark.

Falcon	John Calvert
Lorraine	Catherine Craig
Norton	Jack Reitzen
Fred Muller	Lyle Talbot
Count Dalo	Robert Conte
Donatti	Fred Brocco
Minecci	Ben Welden
Farella	Carlos Schipa
Italian woman	Ann Demitri
Customs officer	Pat Lane
Butler	Eric Wilton
Baggage Clerk #1	Robert Nadell
Baggage Clerk #2	Michael Mark
Miss Connors	Carole Donne
Thug #1	Gene Carrick
Thug #2	Frank Richards
Guard	Carl Sklover
Detective	Jay Griffith
Hotel Clerk	Jack Chife

SEARCH FOR DANGER (FC, 1949) 62 M.

Producer-director, Don Martin; original story, Jerome Epstein; screenplay, Don Martin; camera, Paul Ivans; music, Karl Hajos; editor, Asa Boyd Clark.

Falcon	John Calvert
Kirk	Albert Dekker
Wilma	Myrna Dell
Gregory	Ben Weldon
Inspector	Douglas Fowley
Perry	Michael Mark
Elaine	Anna Cornell
Cooper	James Griffith
Larry Andrews	Mauritz Hugo
Morris Jason	Peter Brocco
Jaifer	Peter Michael
Drunk	Jack Daly
Thug	Billy Nelson

FRANCIS, THE TALKING MULE

Only Hollywood could dramatically prove that a talking mule was worth more revenue at the box-office than a super spectacular. Thus it was when Universal-International in 1950 began its famous and highly profitable series (it saved the Hollywood studio from bankruptcy) on *Francis, the Talking Mule*. Seven of these one-joke black and white programmers were tossed out by Universal, all save the last modest entry, in 1956, co-starred singer-dancer Donald O'Connor, and were directed by Arthur Lubin; and each showcased a rising studio starlet. Cinema trend predictors were amazed that the *Francis* films captured the imagination of sophisticated audiences, who found the verbose army animal a most engaging screen star.

Based on David Stern's (pseudonym for Peter Stirling) 1946 novel, the major premise and charm of *Francis* was that an Army mule could not only talk articulately, but that it could have a tremendous amount of common sense and native intelligence, making its human compatriot, Peter Stirling, look like a dunce by comparison. Moreover, the mule even had a patronizing attitude toward his cohort!

To play the brash, boyish Peter Stirling, Universal tapped one of its long-time contract players, Donald O'Connor, who had made his film debut in *Melody for Two* (1937), a Warner Bros. musical with Patricia Ellis. O'Connor was born of show business parents in Chicago on August 28, 1925. The family vaudeville act of singing-dancing-acrobatics played the Keith Circuit and other

houses in the diminishing live show market of the mid-1930s. Eventually a Paramount screen test and contract was forthcoming, and O'Connor was cast in a rash of above average films there, usually as the star's younger brother or as the leading player as a child. He appeared in such vehicles as *Men with Wings* (1938) and *Beau Geste* (1939). When he outgrew children's parts, Paramount dropped his option, and O'Connor returned to vaudeville with his family, touring Australia. In 1941, he was signed by Universal Pictures, becoming the house teenager. He shone in a number of unmemorable musicals, co-starred with such personalities as Gloria Jean in *Get Hep to Love* (1942), with the Andrews Sisters in *Give Out Sisters* (1942), with Deanna Durbin in *Something in the Wind* (1947) and with Olga San Juan in *Are You With It?* (1948).

By the late 1940s, O'Connor's career had reached another snag and the *Francis* series proved a boost to his fortune and fame, if not to his sense of artistic integrity. He balked after doing six of the *Francis* vehicles, and refused to continue in the series, which saw Francis getting more fan mail than he. This was especially irksome when, on outside loan, he was performing in such outstanding films as *Singin' In The Rain* (1952) with Gene Kelly. O'Connor's most recent film to date (his 47th) is *That Funny Feeling* (1965). He has since continued with his nightclub and television appearances.

Mickey Rooney, whose famous career somewhat

parallels O'Connor's, was contracted for the seventh and final Francis entry. Unfortunately, his dynamic personality clashed with the ambiance of the series, and critics not only lambasted the declining quality of the *Francis* magic, but harped on the poor choice of the replacement leading man.

To provide the off-screen voice for the mule, Universal quietly hired Chill Wills, who lent the appropriate homespun accent to the wise-cracking words of wisdom uttered by Francis . . . and the studio left it a mystery for the public to guess who was doing the mule's talking. In . . . *Joins the Wacs,* Wills had an on-screen acting role as well, as crusty General Kaye. For . . . *in the Haunted House* Paul Frees supplied the mule's voice.

The storylines for the *Francis* films did not tax the viewer's intelligence. In fact, the premises utilized for most of the series were downright implausible, but no one seemed to care. In *Francis,* the army mule becomes friendly with a rather simplistic second lieutenant in the U.S. Army (Peter Stirling, played by Donald O'Connor), on duty with the armed forces in World War II Burma. Francis is responsible for the destruction of Japanese outposts, and Peter unwittingly becomes a hero. In . . . *Goes to the Races* Peter, after saving an atomic plant from destruction with the fortuitous help of Francis, is rewarded with a scholarship to West Point. Peter has academic and romantic problems at the Point until Francis shows up as a mascot of the football team. Once again, the mule ingeniously helps his pal win the gal. In . . . *Covers the Big Town,* Peter is a novice reporter at a big-city newspaper, who through the aid of his friend Francis becomes an outstanding newspaper reporter. The mule had wisely made friends with the police horses. One scene in this film had Francis testifying in court under oath, to prove the innocence of Peter on a homicide charge. In . . . *Joins the Wacs* Peter, army lieutenant, is ordered to a WAC base headed by Major Simpson (Lynn Bari), a group out to prove their prowess as camouflage experts. The mule helps his friend lead the WACs to victory. In . . . *In the Navy* the talking animal is afraid he will be auctioned off as surplus merchandise and sends for his army pal. O'Connor in a dual role, plays Peter

and a two-fisted, girl-chasing war hero sailor Slicker Donovan.

In the final entry, . . . *In the Haunted House,* David Prescott (Mickey Rooney) is informed by Francis that a murder occurred near MacLeod Castle. When David reports the crime, he is arrested as a suspect and has a hard time proving that his informant is a mule. He and Francis eventually solve the caper.

Contrary to the critical disapproval heaped on many film series, movie reviewers were generally enthused about the amusing possibilities inherent in *Francis,* noting the fine interplay between the very undumb animal and its wide eyed, naive companion. As the series continued, it became obvious that the potential of the premise was limited and that the increasingly repetitious clichés of service comedy were harming the pace of each production. The growing presence of inferior dialogue also hindered matters.

Geared strictly as economic ventures to quickly produce revenue, the *Francis* films were all made on Universal's backlot; none of the entries were in color; all ranged between 80 and 91 minutes in length.

The supporting casts for the *Francis* films were never of heavyweight caliber. *Francis* and . . . *Joins the Wacs* boasted Zasu Pitts and Lynn Bari in recurring roles. Contract player Tony Curtis was in the original *Francis,* Paul Burke, David Janssen and Clint Eastwood had supporting roles in . . . *In the Navy.* Mamie Van Doren was the most flamboyant of the Universal starlets (Patricia Medina, Piper Laurie, Lori Nelson, Nancy Guild, Julia Adams, Martha Hyer, Virginia Welles) to appear in a *Francis* film, . . . *Joins the Wacs.*

At one point in his blossoming career, Francis was almost replaced. After the initial film, a year elapsed before the second entry was ready to shoot. And meanwhile, Francis had been standing around, growing fatter. Jimmy Phillips, trainer for the mule star, was ordered to make the animal lose the excess poundage—he did. Francis's career continued and he went on to win the first Patsy Award in 1951.

After Francis expired in 1956, Arthur Lubin, who directed six of the entries, went on to create television's *Mr. Ed, the Talking Horse.*

Donald O'Connor. (Francis)

O'Connor. (Francis)

O'Connor and Patricia Medina. (Francis)

Zasu Pitts, O'Connor. (Francis)

(Francis Goes to the Races) *O'Connor.*

O'Connor. (. . . **Covers the Big Town**)

Lori Nelson, O'Connor. (. . . **Goes to West Point**)

O'Connor and Chill Wills. (. . . Joins the WACS)

Richard Erdman, O'Connor, Clint Eastwood, Martin Milner, Phil Garris. (. . . in the Navy)

Mickey Rooney. (. . . in the Haunted House)

FRANCIS

FRANCIS (Univ., 1949) 90 M.

Producer, Robert Arthur; director, Arthur Lubin; author-screenplay, David Stern; art director, Bernard Herzbrun, Richard H. Fields; music, Frank Skinner; camera, Irving Glassberg; editor, Milton Carruth.

Peter Stirling	Donald O'Connor
Maureen Gelder	Patricia Medina
Valerie Humpert	Zazu Pitts
Colonel Hooker	Ray Collins
General Stevens	John McIntire
Colonel Plepper	Eduard Franz
Major Nadel	Howland Chamberlin
Colonel Saunders	James Todd
Colonel Carmichael	Robert Warwick
Sgt. Chillingbacker	Frank Faylen
Captain Jones	Tony Curtis
Major Garber	Mikel Conrad
Major Richards	Loren Tindall
Francis, The Talking Mule	(voice) Chill Wills

FRANCIS GOES TO THE RACES (Univ., 1951) 88 M.

Producer, Leonard Goldstein; director, Arthur Lubin; author, David Stern; screenplay, Oscar Brodny, David Stern; art director, Bernard Herzbrun, Emrich Nicholson; music, Frank Skinner; camera, Irving Glassberg; editor, Milton Carruth.

Peter Stirling	Donald O'Connor
Frances Travers	Piper Laurie
Col. Travers	Cecil Kellaway
Frank Daner	Jesse White
Mallory	Barry Kelley
Rogers	Hayden Rorke
Harrington	Vaughn Taylor
Head Steward	Larry Keating
Dr. Marberry	Peter Brocco
Dr. Quimby	Don Beddoe
First Mug	Ed Max
Second Mug	Jack Wilson
Sam	Bill Walker
Jockey	George Webster
Francis, The Talking Mule	(voice) Chill Wills

FRANCIS GOES TO WEST POINT (Univ., 1952) 81 M.

Producer, Leonard Goldstein; director, Arthur Lubin; author-screenplay, Oscar Brodney; art director, Bernard Herzbrun, Eric Orbom; music director, Joseph Gershenson; camera, Carl Guthrie; editor, Milton Carruth.

Peter Stirling	Donald O'Connor
Barbara	Lori Nelson
Cynthia	Alice Kelley
Wilbur Van Allen	William Reynolds
William Norton	Palmer Lee (Gregg Palmer)

Corporal Ransom	James Best
Coach Chadwick	Otto Hulett
Colonel Daniels	Les Tremayne
Corporal Thomas	David Janssen
Francis, The Talking Mule	(voice) Chill Wills

FRANCIS COVERS THE BIG TOWN (Univ., 1953) 86 M.

Producer, Leonard Goldstein; director, Arthur Lubin; screenplay, Oscar Brodney; art director, Bernard Herzbrun, Richard H. Riedel; camera, Carl Guthrie; editor, Milton Carruth.

Peter Stirling	Donald O'Connor
Alberta Ames	Nancy Guild
Maria Scola	Yvette Dugay
Tom Henderson	Gene Lockhart
Chief Hansen	William Harrigan
Salvatore Scola	Silvio Minciotti
Jefferson Garnet	Lowell Gilmore
Dan Austin	Larry Gates
Dr. Goodrich	Hanley Stafford
District Attorney Evans	Gale Gordon
Judge Stanley	Forrest Lewis
Parker	Michael Ross
Mason	Louis Mason
Jones	Charles J. Flynn
Francis, The Talking Mule	(voice) Chill Wills

FRANCIS JOINS THE WACS (Univ., 1954) 95 M.

Producer, Ted Richmond; director, Arthur Lubin; author, Herbert Baker; screenplay, Devery Freeman; art director, Alexander Golitzen, Robert Clatworthy; camera, Carl Guthrie; editor, Ted J. Kent, Russell Schoengarth.

Peter Stirling	Donald O'Connor
Captain Parker	Julia Adams
General Benjamin "Mustard Ben" Kaye	Chill Wills
Corporal Bunky Hilstrom	Mamie Van Doren
Major Louise Simpson	Lynn Bari
Lt. Valerie Humpert	Zasu Pitts
Kate	Mara Corday
Marge	Karen Kadler
Lt. Dickson	Allison Hayes
Sergeant Kipp	Joan Shawlee
Bessie	Elsie Holmes
Lt. Burke	Patti McKaye
General's Aide	Anthony Radecki
Jeep Driver	Richard Deems
Blue Soldier	Sam Woody
Francis, The Talking Mule	(voice) Chill Wills

FRANCIS IN THE NAVY (Univ., 1955) 80 M.

Producer, Stanley Rubin; director, Arthur Lubin; author-screenplay, Devery Freeman; art director, Alexander Golitzen, Bill Newberry; music director, Joseph Gershenson; camera, Carl Guthrie; editor, Milton Carruth, Ray Snyder.

Lt. Peter Stirling ⎱ .... Donald O'Connor
Slicker Donovan ⎰
Betsy Donevan .... Martha Hyer
Murphy .... Richard Erdman
Commander Hutch .... Jim Backus
Lieutenant Anders .... David Janssen
Jonesy .... Clint Eastwood
Rick .... Martin Milner
Tate .... Paul Burke
Stover .... Phil Garris
Francis, The Talking Mule ...... (voice) Chill Wills

FRANCIS IN THE HAUNTED HOUSE (Univ., 1956) 80 M.

Producer, Robert Arthur; director, Charles Lamont; author-screenplay, Herbert Margolis, William Raynor; art director, Alexander Golitzen, Richard H. Riedel; music director, Joseph Gershenson; camera, George Robinson; editor, Milton Carruth.

David Prescott .... Mickey Rooney
Lorna MacLeod .... Virginia Welles
Chief Martin .... James Flavin
Neil Frazer .... Paul Cavanagh
Lorna Ann .... Mary Ellen Kaye
Lt. Hopkins .... David Janssen
Mayor Hargrove .... Ralph Dumke
District Attorney Reynolds .... Richard Gaines
Jason .... Richard Deacon
Sgt. Arnold .... Dick Winslow
Hugo .... Timothy Carey
Mrs. MacPherson .... Helen Wallace
Malcolm .... Charles Horvath
Howard Grisby .... Edward Earle
Edward Ryan .... John Maxwell
Francis, The Talking Mule .... (voice) Paul Frees

HOPALONG CASSIDY

Of all the western film series turned out by Hollywood in the 1930s, none was initially so successful and enduring as *Hopalong Cassidy*, starring William Boyd. The reasons are many: Boyd, a clean cut handsome actor (6'1", 170 pounds, blonde-silver hair, blue eyes) portrayed a gentlemanly, chivalrous cowboy who did everything in a well-mannered method, rarely spent (wasted) time courting the fickle heroines, was a good rider and all-around athlete. Boyd had the good fortune of working for two major film studios (Paramount, United Artists) which had excellent theatrical distribution and publicity facilities. Thus the *Hopalong Cassidy* entries were always available in prime market booking situations for patrons of all ages, who declared Boyd to be the epitome of their cowboy heroes, enjoyed the fairly intelligent scripting of the chapters, the beautifully photographed stories, and appreciated the above-average supporting cast. All 66 of these black and white western features were of much higher caliber than their western series competition, and with their longer-than-average running times for western series, made a mark with the audience as prestigious, carefully prepared episodes. (On radio, Boyd was heard as Hopalong Cassidy, with Andy Clyde as his sidekick California. On television, the duo appeared in 52 half-hour, black and white segments between 1951–1952.)

William Lawrence Boyd was born June 5, 1898, near Cambridge, Ohio, one of five children of a laborer. His family moved to the Oklahoma territory when he was seven. He was a teenager when his parents died, he quit school in Tulsa, and went to work as a surveyor and tool dresser in the booming oil fields nearby. He tried to enlist in the army for World War I, but an athlete's heart disqualified him. He went to Arizona and took a job as a hotel manager. While there, he met and married heiress Ruth Miller. They had a son, but were soon divorced. He headed to California where for a spell he ran the Post Exchange at March Field in Riverside. Then he moved on to Hollywood, where he landed a bit part in a Cecil B. DeMille film, *Why Change Your Wife?* (1919). This led to other roles, and a growing professional friendship with DeMille. Boyd became a romantic lead in the cinema, starring in such productions as *Road to Yesterday* (1925), *The Volga Boatman* (1926), *The Last Frontier* (1926) (his first western), and *Two Arabian Knights* (1927). His talking film debut was in *Lady of the Pavement* (1928). In the early 1930s, Boyd was the victim of a Hollywood scandal connected with another actor with the same name (who soon thereafter was forced to use the acting name of William "Stage" Boyd). The public and producers confused the two persons, and Boyd's career suffered a great reversal. Then along came the *Hopalong Cassidy* films and a new career for Boyd, who after 1935 made only a few non-Cassidy entries, such as *Racing Luck* (1935), *Go Get 'Em Haines* (1936) and a guest appearance in DeMille's *The Greatest Show on Earth* (1952). During World War II, Boyd was a frequent U.S.O. tour performer. After switching from theatrical to television filming with the *Cassidy* series in the early 1950s, and engineering the merchandising involved with the tremendous Hopalong vogue of the time, Boyd retired in 1955 from show business. He now lives in California with his fourth wife, Grace Brady, whom he married in 1937. (He had married actress Elinor Faire in 1926, divorced 1929; married film player Dorothy Sebastian in 1930, divorced 1936.)

Boyd has summed up his Hoppy role as "It's like a vacation. I ride my horse 'Topper,' chase rustlers and outlaws, shoot my six shooters and do the things that every kid—and man too—in America would want to do."

Clarence Edward Mulford (1883–1956) had begun his *Hopalong Cassidy* book series in 1912 with *Hopalong Cassidy* and wrote 25 others. In 1935, producer Harry "Pop" Sherman bought the rights to these stories from Mulford and prepared to film a feature. He offered Boyd the role of the wholesome Bar 20 ranch foreman (the part ironically was finally played by arch heavy Charles Middleton). Instead, Boyd elected to portray Hopalong (who received his nickname because of a gun wound in the leg—by the second *Cassidy* film the wound had healed and Boyd limped no more). Thus Paramount released *Hop-a-long Cassidy* in 1935 (it was reissued the following year as *Hopalong Cassidy Enters*) and found it had a good formula on its hands, giving birth to a new feature series which would continue at breakneck speed for the next thirteen years. Boyd received $30,000 for the initial six *Hopalong* productions; by 1938 he was receiving a $100,000 annual salary.

In 1942, after 41 Paramount *Hopalong* films, Sherman and his prize oater series moved to United Artists for production and distribution. Then in 1944 came a two-year hiatus, during which time, Boyd by mortgaging all his assets, managed to acquire all the production and television rights to the *Cassidy* property, retaining Sherman in a purely financial capacity. Sherman no longer was involved in overseeing production. By the time Boyd switched his series to television, he was in complete production control, reaping the profits from the sale of the features to television syndication in the late 1940s. The last dozen *Hopalong* features were also reedited into short films, and strung out to fill up the new video series package Boyd created in 1951–1952. (An amusing Hollywood satire of the Boyd-Cassidy vogue was made as a MGM comedy *Callaway Went Thataway* [1951] with Fred MacMurray, Dorothy McGuire, and Howard Keel.)

The evolution of the *Hopalong Cassidy* film

canon, points up the lack of finesse in the early entries. Nevertheless, even the first efforts had well conceived scripts which offered a realistic picture of ranch life, with its boring, repetitious chores and rambunctious horseplay. In keeping with the Mulford books, the first batch of *Cassidy* entries were rather slow moving, with little gunplay or hard horse riding. There were vigorous climaxes, surrounded by good buildups, and the appearance of rousing music for the finale. That many establishing scene shots were constantly reused seemed to bother no one. Typical of this phase was *The Eagle's Brood* in which the grandson of Il Toro, a famous Mexican bandit, is the object of a hunt by Big Henry's gang, with Cassidy and the men of the Bar 20 Ranch intervening to protect the youth.

As the series developed, the productions increased in length—many chapters being over 70 minutes—with much more time devoted to the performance of fancy stunt work (usually performed by Boyd, who had become a seasoned rider by then and no longer required stuntman Cliff Lyons to do his tough scenes on and off horseback). As in *Bar 20 Rides Again* Hopalong was slow to speak, but quick to act. Another example of this period was *Heart of Arizona* in which there is a well executed sequence showing the preparation for the long chase. *Hills of Old Wyoming* shows Cassidy's imperturbability and resourcefulness when he confronts and eventually pacifies the hostile Indians, who are getting stirred up at a tribal war dance. *Hopalong Rides Again* shows to full advantage the fine outdoor scenery utilized by the series. This episode has ranch foreman Cassidy and his men trekking to the Black Buttes Canyons in their attempt to deliver a herd of cattle on time.

By the mid 1940s, when Boyd had full reign on *Hopalong*, the series showed noticeable deterioration in quality, with the financial shortcuts all too evident. The number of extras in the scenes had been greatly reduced, the care in setting up imaginative camera angles had disappeared, and the scripting was quite inferior. Typical of this phase was *Sinister Journey,* in which a most lackadaisical Hoppy befriends a railroad clerk falsely accused of murder—the paucity of action here was most pronounced.

There were several innovations in the *Cassidy* films. For a startling change, the hero was no longer dressed all in white, riding a black horse, but quite the reverse, with a dark-clad Hoppy astride the all white Topper. Since Boyd was in his mid-

30s when he began the series, it was decided to focus the romantic facets of the films as well as some of the more rugged scenes on a younger side-kick, and to bring in some comedy relief for the series, a third crusty partner was added, thus originating the trio western formula which became so popular in the late 1930s and 1940s.

George "Gabby" Hayes (1885–1969), who had played screen villains and sidekicks interchangably, first appeared in the *Hoppy* films as a character actor-villain (Uncle Ben in *Hop-Along Cassidy,* Spike in *The Eagle's Brood,* and Shanghai in *Call of the Prairie*). Then in *Bar 20 Rides Again* he assumed the role of Windy Holliday, a part he played for nineteen entries, until he left the series in 1939. Then came Britt Wood as Speedy Mac-Ginnis in *Range War,* followed by veteran funny-man Andy Clyde (1892–1967) as California Jack Carlson; he stayed with the series till its conclusion, and then joined Boyd in the television chapters. Usually, Hayes-Wood-Clyde would play the cantankerous older member of the trio, who was the cook and general all-around helper; filled with salty experience they brooked no nonsense from the villains, and always were around to assist their pals.

Boyd's first young screen partner was James Ellison (born 1910) who played in eight series entries as Johnny Nelson, followed by Russell Hayden (born 1912) as Lucky Jenkins, a part he portrayed for five years. Then came Brad King in *Outlaws of the Desert* as the new Johnny Nelson, followed after five chapters by Jay Kirby as Breezy Travers. *False Colors* introduced Jimmy Rogers as himself for four films, with Rand Brooks as the next to play Lucky Jenkins, through the final theatrical feature, *False Paradise,* in 1948. It was the scripters' ploy to have the young gunslinger helper of Hoppy usually be accused of some murder or crime, and Hoppy and the boys having to prove his innocence. Then too, the romantic lead was more suitable to courting the variety of young heroines who popped up in the films, although a rule of the *Hoppy* films was never to let the romancing go on for long or get too serious. In fact, Lucky's (Johnny, Breezy) infatuations were the source for much of the comic bantering in the series, with the finale of several entries devoted to Hoppy and Windy (or California) poking mild fun at their lovelorn comrade in arms.

Not to bore viewers with the sameness of locale, Cassidy would travel to new terrain in the series,

as in *In Old Mexico* which had him south of the border capturing the murderer of his friend's son. As a gimmick in the plot of *The Frontiersman* Hoppy is aided by a schoolhouse full of rambunctious children (played by the St. Brendan's Boys Choir, who sing several numbers). *Outlaws of the Desert* is set in Arabia, where Hoppy has been commissioned to buy Arabian steeds. Some of the entries had unusual local color: *Riders of the Timberlane* and *Lumberjack* are set in lumber camps (the latter in the High Sierras); *Law of the Pampas* is situated in South America where Hoppy is selling his boss's herd of cattle. A most unusual locale for gunplay was found in *The Marauders,* set in an old church, where Hoppy and his pals have taken refuge during a storm, becoming involved with local crooks.

A few *Hoppy* entries have unusual plotlines, getting away from the standard cattle rustlers and fair damsel in distress routine: *Unexpected Guest* concerns the legatees of a will, who are being murdered one by one; *Silent Conflict* involves a quack medicine man and his niece who hypnotize Lucky and steal the funds from the cooperative cattle drive Hoppy is heading; Hoppy has a dual role in *Texas Masquerade* in which he poses as a Boston lawyer recently come west on business; in *Sunset Trail* the crux of the film is a tense poker game Hoppy must win.

Occasionally the script allowed Hoppy to be something other than the foreman of the Bar 20 Ranch. In *Santa Fe Marshal* he is the legal authority of that town; and he is a sheriff in *Hoppy Serves a Writ, Forty Thieves,* and *Wide Open Town.* In *Riders of the Deadline, Three Men From Texas* and *Border Patrol* Hoppy and his sidekicks are Texas Rangers. *Texas Trails* finds Hoppy drilling volunteers when the United States declares war on Spain, and Gabby is seen as the troop bugler.

The earlier *Hopalong Cassidy* films were noted for some fine character actors who popped up in good parts: Clara Kimball Young in *Three on the Trail, Hills of Old Wyoming* and *The Frontiersman;* Evelyn Brent in *Hopalong Cassidy Returns* and *Wide Open Town;* Natalie Moorhead in *Heart of Arizona;* Evelyn Venable in *The Frontiersman;* Sidney Toler in *Law of the Pampas;* Marjorie Rambeau in *Santa Fe Marshal;* Anna Q. Nilsson in *Riders of the Timberline;* Antonio Moreno in *Undercover Man,* and Betty Blythe in *Bar 20.*

For comedy relief and musical interludes, the *Cassidy* films relied on first Chill Wills and his Avalon Boys, then the Kingsmen, and later the Jim Wakely trio.

The series served as a testing ground for such later stars as James Craig (in *Pride of the West*), George Reeves (who, beginning with *Colt Comrades*, played minor hero-villain roles in the series), Robert Mitchum (in *Hoppy Serves a Writ* and several others), and Lee J. Cobb (*North of the Rio Grande* and *Rustler's Valley*). And to round out the villain parts, usually Roy Barcroft, Morris Ankrum or Victor Jory would be on hand.

Most of the heroines—whose roles were most passive in the *Hopalong Cassidy* films—were performers who quickly disappeared from the Hollywood scenes. Occasionally there would be players like Joan Woodbury (*The Eagle's Brood*), Judith Allen (*Texas Trail*), Jan Clayton (*In Old Mexico, Sunset Trail, The Showdown*), or Barbara Britton (*Secrets of the Wasteland*), who would go on to better acting careers.

Chill Wills (rear), William Boyd, James Mason. (Bar 20 Rides Again)

Boyd, Hayes, Steve Clemente, Russell Hayden. (Hills of Old Wyoming)

John St. Polis (tied up), Boyd. (Rustler's Valley)

Russell Hayden, Jan Clayton, Charlotte Wynters (third left), Boyd, Jerry Jerome (rear), Maurice Cass, George Reeves. (Sunset Trail)

Hayden, Boyd, George Hayes. (Pride of the West)

Francis McDonald, Boyd, Eddie Dean. (Range War)

Hayden, Boyd, Steffi Duna. (Law of the Pampas)

Boyd, Charlotte Wynters. (Renegade Trail)

Andy Clyde, Victor Jory, Hayden, Boyd, Hank Bell.
(Border Vigilantes)

Evelyn Brent (l.), Boyd, Morris Ankrum, Bernice Kay
(later Cara Williams), Ed Cassidy, Russell Hayden.
(Wide Open Town)

George J. Lewis, Andy Clyde, Luli Deste, King, Boyd,
Forrest Stanley, Jean Phillips. (Outlaws of the Desert)

Andy Clyde, Boyd, Barbara Britton, Hal Price (in
hole), Keith Richards, Brad King, Gordon Hart. (Secrets of the Wasteland)

Boyd, Andy Clyde, Keith Richards. (Secrets of the Wasteland)

Boyd, George Reeves, Jay Kirby. (Colt Comrades)

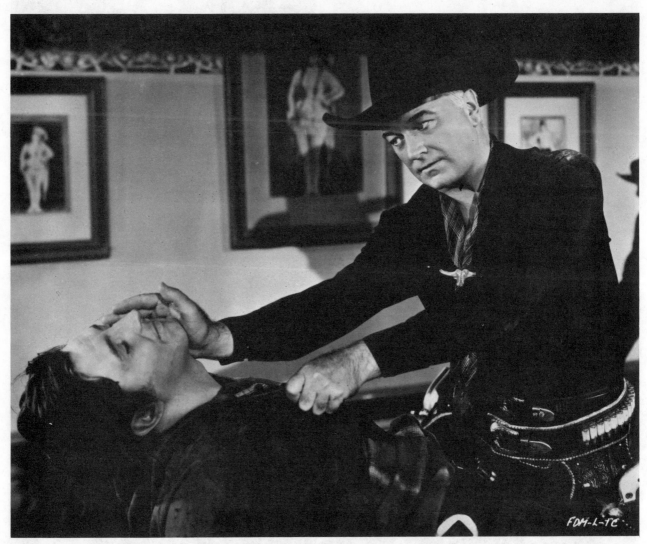

Robert Mitchum, Boyd. (Hoppy Serves a Writ [?])

Andy Clyde, Jimmy Rogers, Boyd, Herman Hack,
Jack Rockwell, Robert Mitchum, Anthony Warde.
(Riders of the Deadline)

Boyd, Jane Randolph. **(Fool's Gold)**

Boyd, Rand Brooks, Andy Clyde. **(The Marauders)**

HOP-ALONG CASSIDY (HOP-ALONG CASSIDY ENTERS) (Par., 1935) 62 M.

Producer, Harry Sherman; director, Howard Bretherton; story, Clarence E. Mulford; screenplay-adaptation, Doris Schroeder; camera, Archie Stout; editor, Edward Schroeder.

Bill Cassidy	William Boyd
Johnny Nelson	Jimmy Ellison
Mary Meeker	Paula Stone
Jim Meeker	Robert Warwick
Buck Peters	Charles Middleton
Red Connors	Frank McGlynn, Jr.
Pecos Jack Anthony	Kenneth Thomson
Uncle Ben	George Hayes
Tom Shaw	James Mason
Frisco	Frank Campeau
Hall	Ted Adams
Salem, the cook	Willie Fung
Doc Riley	Franklin Farnum
Party Guest	John Merton

THE EAGLE'S BROOD (Par., 1935) 59 M.

Producer, Harry Sherman; director, Howard Bretherton; story, Clarence E. Mulford; screenplay, Doris Schroeder, Harrison Jacobs; camera, Archie Stout; editor, Edward Schroeder.

Hop-Along Cassidy	William Boyd
Johnny Nelson	Jimmy Ellison
El Toro	William Farnum
Big Henry	Addison Richards
Spike	George Hayes
Dolores	Joan Woodbury
Mike	Frank Shannon
Dolly	Dorothy Revier
Steve	Paul Fix
Pop	Al Lydell
Ed	John Merton
Pablo	George Mari
Estaban	Juan Torena
Sheriff	Henry Sylvester

BAR 20 RIDES AGAIN (Par., 1935) 62 M.

Producer, Harry Sherman; director, Howard Bretherton; story, Clarence Mulford; screenplay, Doris Schroeder, Gerald Geraghty; camera, Archie Stout; editor, Edward Schroeder.

Hop-Along Cassidy	William Boyd
Johnny Nelson	Jimmy Ellison
Margaret Arnold	Jean Rouverol
Windy	George Hayes
Nevada (George Perdue)	Harry Worth
Red Connors	Frank McGlynn, Jr.
Jim Arnold	Howard Lang
Clarrisa Peters	Ethel Wales
Gil	Paul Fix

Buck Peters	J. P. McGowan
Herb Layton	Joe Rickson
Cinco	Al St. John
Carp	John Merton
Elbows	Frank Layton
Chill Wills and his Avalon Boys	Themselves

CALL OF THE PRAIRIE (Par., 1936) 65 M.

Producer, Harry Sherman; director, Howard Bretherton; story, Clarence E. Mulford; screenplay, Doris Schroeder, Vernon Smith; camera, Archie Stout; editor, Edward Schroeder.

Hopalong Cassidy	William Boyd
Johnny Nelson	Jimmy Ellison
Linda McHenry	Muriel Evans
Shanghai	George Hayes
Sandy McQueen	Chester Conklin
Sam Porter	Al Bridge
Tom	Hank Mann
Wong	Willie Fung
Buck Peters	Howard Lang
Slade	Al Hill
Arizona	John Merton
Hoskins	Jim Mason
Chill Wills and his Avalon Boys	Themselves

THREE ON THE TRAIL (Par., 1936) 67 M.

Producer, Harry Sherman; associate producer, George Green; director, Howard Bretherton; story, Clarence Mulford; screenplay, Doris Schroeder, Vernon Smith; camera, Archie Stout; editor, Edward Schroeder.

Hop-Along Cassidy	William Boyd
Johnny Nelson	Jimmy Ellison
Pecos Kane	Onslow Stevens
Mary Stevens	Muriel Evans
Windy	George Hayes
J. P. Ridley	Claude King
Buck Peters	William Duncan
Rose Peters	Clara Kimball Young
Idaho	Ernie Adams
Jim Trask	Ted Adams
Sam Corwin	John St. Polis
Kit Thorpe	Al Hill
Lewis	John Rutherford
Conchita	Lita Cortez

HEART OF THE WEST (Par., 1936) 60 M.

Producer, Harry Sherman; associate producer, George Green; director, Howard Bretherton; story, Doris Schroeder; music-lyrics, Sam Coslow, Victor Young; camera, Archie Stout; editor, Edward Schroeder.

Hop-Along Cassidy	William Boyd
Johnny Nelson	Jimmy Ellison
Windy	George Hayes
Sally Jordan	Lynn Gabriel
Big John Trumbull	Sydney Blackmer

Jim Jordan .... Charles Martin
Tom Paterson .... John Rutherford
Johnson .... Warner Richmond
Whitey .... Walter Miller
Saxon .... Ted Adams
Barton .... Fred Kohler
Tim Grady .... Robert McKenzie

HOPALONG CASSIDY RETURNS (Par., 1936) 71 M.

Producer, Harry Sherman; associate producer, Eugene Strong; director, Nat Watt; story, Clarence E. Mulford; screenplay, Harrison Jacobs; camera, Archie Stout; editor, Robert Warwick.

Hopalong Cassidy .... William Boyd
Windy Halliday .... George Hayes
Mary Saunders .... Gail Sheridan
Lilli Marsh .... Evelyn Brent
Blackie .... Stephen Morris
Buddy Cassidy .... William Janney
Peg Leg Holden .... Irving Bacon
Bob Claiborne .... Grant Richards
Robert Saunders .... John Beck
Benson .... Ernie Adams
Luke .... Al St. John
Buck .... Joe Rickson
Davis .... Ray Whitley
Dugan .... Claude Smith

TRAIL DUST (Par., 1936) 77 M.

Producer, Harry Sherman; associate producer, Eugene Strong; director, Nate Watt; story, Clarence E. Mulford; screenplay, Al Martin; musical arrangements, Charles Bradshaw; camera, Archie Stout; editor, Robert Warwick.

Hopalong Cassidy .... William Boyd
Johnny Nelson .... James Ellison
Windy .... George Hayes
Tex .... Stephen Morris
Beth .... Gwynne Shipman
Lanky .... Britt Wood
Red .... Earl Askam
Hank .... John Beach
Wilson .... Ted Adams
Al .... Al. St. John
Officer .... Kenneth Harlan

BORDERLAND (Par., 1937) 82 M.

Producer, Harry Sherman; associate producer, Eugene Strong; director, Nate Watt; story, Clarence E. Mulford; screenplay, Harrison Jacobs; camera, Archie Stout; editor, Robert Warwick.

Hopalong Cassidy .... William Boyd
Johnny Nelson .... James Ellison
Windy .... George Hayes
Loco .... Stephen Morris
Molly Rand .... Charlene Wyatt
Grace Rand .... Nora Lane
Col. Gonzales .... Trevor Bardette
Dandy Morgan .... Al Bridge
Tom Parker .... George Chesboro

HILLS OF OLD WYOMING (Par., 1937) 79 M.

Producer Harry Sherman; supervisor, Harry Knight; director, Nate Watt; story, Clarence E. Mulford; screenplay, Maurice Geraghty; camera, Archie Stout; editor, Robert Warwick.

Hopalong Cassidy .... William Boyd
Windy .... George Hayes
Lucky Jenkins .... Russell Hayden
Alice Hutchins .... Gail Sheridan
Andrews .... Morris Ankrum
Ma Hutchins .... Clara Kimball Young
Thompson .... Earle Hodgins
Lone Eagle .... Steve Clemente
Chief Big John Tree .... Chief Big Tree
Saunders .... John Beach
Peterson .... George Chesebro
Daniels .... Paul Gustine
Steve .... Leo MacMahon
Smiley, the cook .... John Powers
Deputy-henchman .... James Mason

NORTH OF THE RIO GRANDE (Par., 1937) 65 M.

Producer, Harry Sherman; director, Nate Watt; story, Clarence E. Mulford; screenplay, Jack O'Donnell; camera, Russell Harlan; editor, Robert Warwick.

Hopalong Cassidy .... William Boyd
Windy .... George Hayes
Lucky Jenkins .... Russell Hayden
Henry Stoneham ⎫
Lone Wolf   ⎬ .... Stephen Morris
Faro Annie .... Bernadene Hayes
Crowder .... John Rutherford
Mary Cassidy .... Lorraine Randall
Bull .... Walter Long
Goodwin .... Lee Cobb
Clark .... John Beach
Plunkett .... Al Ferguson
Joe .... Lafe McKee

RUSTLER'S VALLEY (Par., 1937) 60 M.

Producer, Harry Sherman; director, Nate Watt; screenplay, Harry O. Hoyt; camera, Russell Harlan; editor, Robert Warwick.

Hopalong Cassidy .... William Boyd
Windy Halliday .... George Hayes
Lucky Jenkins .... Russell Hayden
Clem Crawford .... John St. Polis
Cal Howard .... Lee Cobb
Glen Randall .... Stephen Morris
Agnes Randall .... Muriel Evans

Taggart .... Ted Adams
Joe .... Al Ferguson
Boulton .... John Beach

HOPALONG RIDES AGAIN (Par., 1937) 65 M.

Producer, Harry Sherman; director, Lesley Selander; story, Clarence E. Mulford; screenplay, Norman Houston; camera, Russell Harlan; editor, Robert Warwick.

Hopalong Cassidy .... William Boyd
Windy Halliday .... George Hayes
Lucky Jenkins .... Russell Hayden
Buck Peters .... William Duncan
Laura Peters .... Lois Wilde
Artie Peters .... Billy King
Nora Blake .... Nora Lane
Professor Hepburn .... Harry Worth
Blackie .... John Rutherford
Keno .... Ernie Adams
Rider .... Frank Ellis

TEXAS TRAIL (Par., 1937) 58 M.

Producer, Harry Sherman; director, David Selman; story, Clarence E. Mulford; screenplay, Jack O'Donnell, Jack Mersereau; camera, Russell Harlan; editor, Robert Warwick.

Hopalong Cassidy .... William Boyd
Windy Halliday .... George Hayes
Lucky Jenkins .... Russell Hayden
Barbara Allen .... Judith Allen
Black Jack Carson .... Alexander Cross
Hawks .... Robert Kortman
Boots .... Billy King
Brad .... Rafael Bennett
Major McCready .... Karl Hackett
Shorty .... Jack Rockwell
Jordan .... Philo McCullough
Smokey .... John Beach

HEART OF ARIZONA (Par., 1938) 68 M.

Producer, Harry Sherman; director, Lesley Selander; associate producer, J. D. Trop; story, Clarence E. Mulford; screenplay, Norman Houston, Harrison Jacobs; camera, Russell Harlan; editor, Sherman Rose.

Hopalong Cassidy .... William Boyd
Windy .... George Hayes
Lucky .... Russell Hayden
Buck Peters .... John Elliott
Artie .... Billy King
Belle Starr .... Natalie Moorhead
Jacqueline Starr .... Dorothy Short
Dan Ringo .... Stephen Alden Chase
Sheriff Hawley .... John Beach
Trimmer Windler .... Lane Chandler
Twister .... Leo MacMahon

BAR 20 JUSTICE (Par., 1938) 70 M.

Producer, Harry Sherman; associate producer, J. D. Trop; director, Lesley Selander; story, Clarence E. Mulford; screenplay, Arnold Belgard, Harrison Jacobs; art director, Lewis J. Rachmil; camera, Russell Harlan; editor, Robert Warwick.

Hopalong Cassidy .... William Boyd
Windy Halliday .... George Hayes
Lucky Jenkins .... Russell Hayden
Slade .... Paul Sutton
Ann Dennis .... Gwen Gaze
Frazier .... Pat O'Brien
Perkins .... Joseph DeStefani
Buck Peters .... William Duncan
Pierce .... Walter Long
Ross .... H. Bruce Mitchell
Dennis .... John Beach

PRIDE OF THE WEST (Par., 1938) 56 M.

Producer, Harry Sherman; director, Lesley Selander; story, Clarence E. Mulford; screenplay, Nate Wyatt; camera, Russell Harlan; editor, Robert Warwick.

Hopalong Cassidy .... William Boyd
Windy Halliday .... George Hayes
Lucky Jenkins .... Russell Hayden
Mary Martin .... Charlotte Field
Sheriff Tom Martin .... Earle Hodgins
Dick Martin .... Billy King
Caldwell .... Kenneth Harlan
Saunders .... Glenn Strange
Nixon .... James Craig
Detective .... Bruce Mitchell
Sing Loo .... Willie Fung
Townsman .... George Morrell

IN OLD MEXICO (Par., 1938) 62 M.

Producer, Harry Sherman; director, Edward D. Venturini; story, Clarence E. Mulford; screenplay, Harrison Jacobs; art director, Lewis J. Rachmil; camera, Russell Harlan; editor, Robert Warwick.

Hopalong Cassidy .... William Boyd
Windy Halliday .... George Hayes
Lucky .... Russell Hayden
The Fox .... Paul Sutton
Don Carlos Gonzales .... Allan Garcia
Anita Gonzales .... Jan Clayton
Colonel Gonzales .... Trevor Bardette
Janet Leeds .... Betty Amann
Elena .... Anna Demetrio
Burk .... Glenn Strange
Pancho .... Tony Roux

SUNSET TRAIL (Par., 1938) 60 M.

Producer, Harry Sherman; director, Lesley Selander; story Clarence E. Mulford; screenplay, Norman Houston; art director, Lewis J. Rachmil; camera, Russell Harlan; editor, Robert Warwick.

Hopalong Cassidy	William Boyd
Windy	George Hayes
Lucky	Russell Hayden
Ann Marsh	Charlotte Wynters
Dorrie Marsh	Jan Clayton
Monte Keller	Robert Fiske
Abigail Snodgrass	Kathryn Sheldon
E. Prescott Furbush	Maurice Cass
Steve Dorman	Anthony Nace
John Marsh	Kenneth Harlan
Superintendent	Alphonse Ethier
Bouncer	Glenn Strange
Stage Driver	Jack Rockwell
Patrol Captain	Tom London
Bonnie	Claudia Smith

THE FRONTIERSMAN (Par., 1938) 74 M.

Producer, Harry Sherman; director, Lesley Selander; story, Clarence E. Mulford; screenplay, Norman Houston, Harrison Jacobs; art director, Lewis J. Rachmil; camera, Russell Harlan; editor, Sherman Rose.

Hopalong Cassidy	William Boyd
Windy	George Hayes
Lucky	Russell Hayden
June Lake	Evelyn Venable
Buck Peters	William Duncan
Amanda Peters	Clara Kimball Young
Mayor Judson Thorpe	Charles A. (Tony) Hughes
Artie Peters	Dickie Jones
Sutton	Roy Barcroft
Miss Snook	Emily Fitzroy
Quirt	John Beach
School Kids	St. Brendan Boys Choir
	(led by Robert B. Mitchell)

PARTNERS OF THE PLAINS (Par., 1938) 70 M.

Producer, Harry Sherman; director, Lesley Selander; story, Clarence E. Mulford; screenplay, Harrison Jacobs; art director, Lewis Rachmil; camera, Russell Harlan; editor, Robert Warwick.

Hopalong Cassidy	William Boyd
Baldy	Harvey Clark
Lucky Jenkins	Russell Hayden
Lorna Drake	Gwen Gaze
Aunt Martha	Hilda Plowright
Ronald Harwood	John Warburton
Scar Lewis	Al Bridge
Doc Galer	Al Hill
Sheriff	Earle Hodgins
Mr. Benson	John Beach

CASSIDY OF BAR 20 (Par., 1938) 56 M.

Producer, Harry Sherman; director, Lesley Selander; story, Clarence E. Mulford; screenplay, Norman Houston;

art director, Lewis Rachmil; camera, Russell Harlan; editor, Sherman Rose.

Hopalong Cassidy	William Boyd
Lucky Jenkins	Russell Hayden
Pappy	Frank Darien
Nora Blake	Nora Lane
Clay Allison	Robert Fiske
Tom Dillon	John Elliott
Mary Dillon	Margaret Marquis
Ma Caffrey	Gertrude W. Hoffman
Jeff Caffrey	Carleton Young
Judge Belcher	Gordon Hart
Sheriff Hawley	Edward Cassidy

RANGE WAR (Par., 1939) 64 M.

Producer, Harry Sherman; director, Lesley Selander; author, Josef Montaigue; screenplay, Sam Robins; camera, Russell Harlan; editor, Sherman A. Rose.

Hopalong Cassidy	William Boyd
Lucky Jenkins	Russell Hayden
Buck Collins	Willard Robertson
Jim Marlow	Matt Moore
Jose	Pedro de Cordoba
Ellen Marlow	Betty Moran
Speedy MacGinnis	Britt Wood

LAW OF THE PAMPAS (Par., 1939) 72 M.

Producer, Harry Sherman; associate producer, Joseph W. Engel; director, Nate Watt; screenplay, Harrison Jacobs; art director, Lewis J. Rachmil; camera, Russell Harlan; music, Victor Young; editor, Carroll Lewis.

Hopalong Cassidy	William Boyd
Lucky Jenkins	Russell Hayden
Chiquita	Steffi Duna
Don Fernando Rameriez	Sidney Toler
Ralph Merritt	Sidney Blackmer
Jose Valdez	Pedro de Cordoba
Buck Peters	William Duncan
Dolores Rameriez	Anna Demetrio
Curly	Eddie Dean
Slim	Glenn Strange
Ernesto (Tito) Valdez	Jo Jo La Savio
A Gaucho	Tony Roux
Bolo Carrier	Martin Garralaga

SILVER ON THE SAGE (Par., 1939) 66 M.

Producer, Harry Sherman; associate producer, J. D. Trop; director, Lesley Selander; story, Clarence E. Mulford; screenplay, Maurice Geraghty; art director, Lewis J. Rachmil; music director, Boris Morros; camera, Russell Harlan; editor, Robert Warwick.

Hopalong Cassidy	William Boyd
Windy Halliday	George Hayes
Lucky Jenkins	Russell Hayden
Brennan—Talbot	Stanley Ridges

Hamilton	Frederick Burton
Ethel	Ruth Rogers
Marshal	Jack Rockwell
Ewing	Roy Bancroft
Pierce	Ed Cassidy
Martin	Jim Corey
Baker	Sherry Tanzey
Bartender	Bruce Mitchell

RENEGADE TRAIL (Par., 1939) 61 M.

Producer, Harry Sherman; director, Lesley Selander; screenplay, John Rathmell; camera, Russell Harlan.

Hopalong Cassidy	William Boyd
Windy Halliday	George Hayes
Lucky Jenkins	Russell Hayden
Mary Joyce	Charlotte Wynters
Smoky Joslin	Russell Hopton
Joey Joyce	Sonny Bupp
Slim	Jack Rockwell
Stiff Hat Bailey	Roy Barcroft
Traynor	John Merton
Haskins	Bob Kortman
Riders	The King's Men

SANTA FE MARSHAL (Par., 1940) 65 M.

Producer, Harry Sherman; director, Lesley Selander; screenplay, Harrison Jacobs; art director, Lewis Rachmil; music, John Leopold; camera, Russell Harlan; editor, Sherman A. Rose.

Hopalong Cassidy	William Cassidy
Lucky Jenkins	Russell Hayden
Ma Burton	Marjorie Rambeau
Paula Bates	Bernadene Hayes
Doc Bates	Earle Hodgins
Axel	Britt Wood
Blake	Kenneth Harlan

THE SHOWDOWN (Par., 1940) 65 M.

Producer, Harry Sherman; director, Howard Bretherton; author, Jack Jungmeyer; screenplay, Harold Daniel Kusel; art director, Lewis J. Rachmil; music, John Leopold; camera, Russell Harlan; editor, Carrol Lewis.

Hopalong Cassidy	William Cassidy
Lucky Jenkins	Russell Hayden
Speedy	Britt Wood
Baron Rendor	Morris Ankrum
Sue Willard	Jan Clayton
Colonel White	Wright Kramer
Harry Cole	Donald Kirk
Bowman	Roy Barcroft
Johnson	Kermit Maynard
Snell	Walter Shumway
Riders	The King's Men

HIDDEN GOLD (Par., 1940) 61 M.

Producer, Harry Sherman; director, Lesley Selander;

screenplay, Jack Mersereau, Gerald Geraghty; art director, Lewis J. Rachmil; music director, Irving Talbot; camera, Russell Harlan; editor, Carrol Lewis.

Hopalong Cassidy	William Boyd
Lucky	Russell Hayden
Speedy	Britt Wood
Jane Colby	Ruth Rogers
Hendricks	Roy Barcroft
Ed Colby	Minor Watson
Matilda Purdy	Ethel Wales
Sheriff Cameron	Lee Phelps
Ward Ackerman	George Anderson
Stage Driver	Jack Rockwell
Logan	Eddie Dean
Fleming	Raphael Bennett

STAGECOACH WAR (Par., 1940) 63 M.

Producer, Harry Sherman; director, Lesley Selander; author, Norman Houston, Harry F. Olmstead; screenplay, Norman Houston, Harry F. Olmstead; camera, Russell Harlan; editor, Sherman A. Rose.

Hopalong Cassidy	William Boyd
Lucky Jenkins	Russell Hayden
Shirley Chapman	Julie Carter
Neal Holt	Harvey Stephens
Jeff Chapman	J. Farrell MacDonald
Speedy	Britt Wood
Smiley	Rad Robinson
Quince Cobalt	Eddy Waller
Twister Maxwell	Frank Lackteen
Mart Gunther	Jack Rockwell
Tom	Eddie Dean
Bandits	The King's Men

THREE MEN FROM TEXAS (Par., 1940) 70 M.

Producer, Harry Sherman; associate producer, Joseph W. Engel; director, Lesley Selander; screenplay, Norton S. Parker; art director, Lewis J. Rachmil; music, Victor Young; camera, Russell Harlan; editor, Sherman A. Rose.

Hopalong Cassidy	William Boyd
Lucky Jenkins	Russell Hayden
California	Andy Clyde
Morgan	Morris Ankrum
Andrews	Morgan Wallace
Pico	Thornton Edwards
Paquita	Esther Estrella
Thompson	Davison Clark
Gardner	Dick Curtis

DOOMED CARAVAN (Par., 1941) 62 M.

Producer, Harry Sherman; director, Lesley Selander; author, Johnson McCulley, J. Benton Cheney; screenplay, Johnston McCulley, J. Benton Cheney; art director, Lewis J. Rachmil; camera, Russell Harlan; editor, Carrol Lewis.

Hopalong Cassidy	William Boyd

Lucky Jenkins	Russell Hayden
California Jack	Andy Clyde
Jane Travers	Minna Gombell
Stephen Westcott	Morris Ankrum
Diana Westcott	Georgia Hawkins

Jud Carter	Dennis Moore
Sheriff Blake	Henry Hall
Ben Pendleton	Britt Wood

IN OLD COLORADO (Par., 1941) 66 M.

Producer, Harry Sherman; director, Howard Bretherton; screenplay, Norton S. Parker, Russell Hayden, J. Benton Cheney; art director, Lewis J. Rachmil; camera, Russell Harlan.

Hopalong Cassidy	William Boyd
Lucky Jenkins	Russell Hayden
California	Andy Clyde
Myra Woods	Margaret Hayes
Joe Weller	Morris Ankrum
Ma Woods	Sarah Padden
Nosey Haskins	Cliff Nazarro
George Davidson	Stanley Andrews
Hank Merritt	James Seay
Jack Collins	Morgan Wallace
Burton	Weldon Heyburn
Blackie Reed	Glenn Strange
Jim Stark	Eddy Waller
Vender	Philip Van Zandt

BORDER VIGILANTES (Par., 1941) 62 M.

Producer, Harry Sherman; director, Derwin Abrams; author-screenplay, J. Benton Cheney; camera, Russell Harlan; editor, Carrol Lewis.

Hopalong Cassidy	William Boyd
Lucky Jenkins	Russell Hayden
California Carlson	Andy Clyde
Henry Logan	Victor Jory
Dan Forbes	Morris Ankrum
Helen Forbes	Frances Gifford
Aunt Jenifer Forbes	Ethel Wales
Jim Yager	Tom Tyler
Ed Stone	Hal Taliaferro
Henry Weaver	Jack Rockwell
Lafe Willis	Britt Wood
Wagon Driver	Hank Worden
Banker Stevens	Edward Earle
Liveryman	Hank Bell

PIRATES ON HORSEBACK (Par., 1941) 69 M.

Producer, Harry Sherman; associate producer, Joseph W. Engel; director, Lesley Selander; screenplay, J. Benton Cheney, Ethel La Blanche; art director, Lewis J. Rachmil; editor, Fred Feitshans, Jr.

Hopalong Cassidy	William Boyd
Lucky Jenkins	Russell Hayden
California	Andy Clyde
Trudy Pendleton	Eleanor Stewart
Ace Gibson	Morris Ankrum
Bill Watson	William Haade

WIDE OPEN TOWN (Par., 1941) 78 M.

Producer, Harry Sherman; associate producer, Lewis J. Rachmil; director, Lesley Selander; art director, Ralph Berger; music director, Irving Talbot, John Leopold; camera, Sherman A. Rose.

Hopalong Cassidy	William Boyd
Lucky Jenkins	Russell Hayden
California	Andy Clyde
Belle Langtry	Evelyn Brent
Steve Fraser	Victor Jory
Jim Stuart	Morris Ankrum
Joan Stuart	Bernice Kay

OUTLAWS OF THE DESERT (Par., 1941) 66 M.

Producer, Harry Sherman; associate producer, Lewis J. Rachmil; director, Howard Bretherton; screenplay, J. Benton Cheney, Bernard McConville; art director, Ralph Berger; camera, Russell Harlan; editor, Carrol Lewis.

Hopalong Cassidy	William Boyd
California	Andy Clyde
Johnny	Brad King
Sheik Suleiman	Duncan Renaldo
Charles Grant	Forest Stanley
Marie Karitza	Luli Deste
Nickie Karitza	Albert Morin
Susan Grant	Jean Phillips
Mrs. Jane Grant	Nina Guilbut
Major	George Woolsley
Yussuf	George Lewis
Faran El Kalar	Joan Del Val
Ali	Jamuel Hassor

RIDERS OF THE TIMBERLINE (Par., 1941) 59 M.

Producer, Harry Sherman; associate producer, Lewis J. Rachmil; director, Lesley Selander; screenplay, J. Benton Cheney; art director, Ralph Berger; music director, Irvin Talbot; music, John Leopold; camera, Russell Harlan; editor, Fred Feitschans, Jr.

Hopalong Cassidy	William Boyd
Johnny Nelson	Brad King
California	Andy Clyde
Kerrigan	J. Farrel McDonald
Elaine	Eleanor Stewart
Donna	Anna Q. Nilsson
Yatos	Edward Keene
Petrie	Hal Talliaferro
Slade	Tom Tyler
Baptiste	Victor Jory
Larry	Mickey Eissa

SECRETS OF THE WASTELAND (Par., 1941) 66 M.

Producer, Harry Sherman; associate producer, Lewis J. Rachmil; director, Derwin Abrahams; screenplay, Gerald Geraghty; camera, Russell Harlan; editor, Fred Feitschans, Jr.

Hopalong Cassidy	William Boyd
Johnny Nelson	Brad King
California	Andy Clyde
Jennifer Kendall	Barbara Britton
Salters	Douglas Fawley
Clay Elliott	Keith Richards
May Soong	Soo Young
Professor Birdsall	Gordon Hart
Professor Stubbs	Hal Price
Doy Kee	Lee Tung Foo
Clanton	Earl Gunn
Hollister	Ian MacDonald
Williams	John Rawlings
Quan	Richard Loo
Yeng	Roland Got
Sheriff	Jack Rockwell

STICK TO YOUR GUNS (Par., 1941) 63 M.

Producer, Harry Sherman; associate producer, Lewis J. Rachmil; director, Lesley Selander; screenplay, J. Benton Cheney; camera, Russell Harlan; editor, Earl Moser.

Hopalong Cassidy	William Boyd
Johnny Nelson	Brad King
California	Andy Clyde
June Winters	Jacqueline Holt
Winters	Henry Hall
Buck	Joe Whitehead
Frenchy	Bob Card
Pete	Jimmy Wakely
Skinny	Johnny Bond
Bow Wow	Dick Rinehart
Tex	Jack Smith
Red	Jack Trent
Lanky	Homer Holcomb
Waffles	Tom London
Ed	Mickey Eissa
Riders	Jim Wakely Trio

TWILIGHT ON THE TRAIL (Par., 1941) 58 M.

Producer, Harry Sherman; associate producer, Lewis J. Rachmil; director, Howard Bretherton; screenplay, J. Benton Cheney, Ellen Corby, Cecile Kramer; camera, Russell Harlan; editor, Fred Feitschans, Jr.

Hopalong Cassidy	William Boyd
Johnny Nelson	Brad King
California	Andy Clyde
Brent	Jack Rockwell
Lucy	Wanda McKay
Kerry	Norma Willis
Drake	Robert Kent
Gregg	Tom London

Steve	Frank Austin
Stage Driver	Clem Fuller
Drummer	Johnny Powers
Riders	The Jim Wakely Trio

UNDERCOVER MAN (UA, 1942) 68 M.

Producer, Harry Sherman; director, Lesley Selander; screenplay, J. Benton Cheney; music director, Irvin Talbot; art director, Ralph Berger; camera, Russell Harlan; editor, Carroll Lewis.

Hopalong Cassidy	William Boyd
California	Andy Clyde
Breezy Travers	Jay Kirby
Tomas Gonzales	Antonio Moreno
Miguel	Chris-Pin Martin
Louise Saunders	Nora Lane
Dolores Gonzales	Esther Estrella
Bob Saunders	Alan Baldwin
Rosita Lopez	Eva Puig
Captain John Hawkins	Jack Rockwell
Ed Carson	John Vosper
Chavez	Tony Roux
Bert	Pierce Lyden
Jim, a rancher	Ted Wells
Cortez	Martin Garralaga
Caballero	Joe Dominguez
Sheriff Blackton	Earle Hodgins

COLT COMRADES (UA, 1943) 67 M.

Producer, Harry Sherman; associate producer, Lewis J. Rachmil; director, Lesley Selander; screenplay, Michael Wilson; art director, Ralph Berger; camera, Russell Harlan; editor, Sherman A. Rose.

Hopalong Cassidy	William Boyd
California	Andy Clyde
Johnny Nelson	Jay Kirby
Lin Whitlock	George Reeves
Lucy Whitlock	Gayle Lord
Wildcat Willy	Earle Hodgins
Jebb Hardin	Victor Jory
Joe Brass	Douglas Fowley
Varney	Herb Rawlinson

BAR 20 (UA, 1943) 54 M.

Producer, Harry Sherman; associate producer, Lewis J. Rachmil; director, Lesley Selander; screenplay, Morton Grant, Norman Houston, Michael Wilson; art director, Ralph Berger; camera, Russell Harlan; editor, Carroll Lewis.

Hopalong Cassidy	William Boyd
California	Andy Clyde
Lin Bradley	George Reeves
Marie Stevens	Dustin Farnum
Mark Jackson	Victor Jory
Slash	Douglas Fowley
Mrs. Stevens	Betty Blythe

Richard Adams .... Bob Mitchum
One Eye .... Francis McDonald
Tom .... Earle Hodgins

LOST CANYON (UA, 1943) 61 M.

Producer, Harry Sherman; director, Lesley Selander; author, Clarence E. Mulford; screenplay, Harry O. Hoyt; art director, Ralph Berger; camera, Russell Harlan; editor, Sherman A. Rose.

Hopalong Cassidy .... William Boyd
Breezy Travers .... Jay Kirby
California .... Andy Clyde
Laura .... Lola Lane
Jeff Burton .... Douglas Fowley
Clark .... Herbert Rawlinson
Rogers .... Guy Usher
Haskell .... Carl Hackett

HOPPY SERVES A WRIT (UA, 1943) 67 M.

Producer, Harry Sherman; associate producer, Lewis J. Rachmil; director, George Archainbaud; screenplay, Gerald Geraghty; music director, Irwin Talbot; camera, Russell Harlan; editor, Sherman A. Rose.

Hopalong Cassidy .... William Boyd
California .... Andy Clyde
Johnny Travers .... Jay Kirby
Tom Jordan .... Victor Jory
Steve Jordan .... George Reeves
Jean Hollister .... Jan Christy
Greg Jordan .... Hal Taliaferro
Ben Hollister .... Forbes Murray
Rigney .... Bob Mitchum
Storekeeper Danvers .... Byron Foulger
Jim Belnap (clerk) .... Earle Hodgins
Tod Colby .... Roy Barcroft
Card Player .... Ben Corbett

BORDER PATROL (UA, 1943) 64 M.

Producer, Harry Sherman; associate producer, Lewis Rachmil; director, Lesley Selander; screenplay, Michael Wilson; music director, Irvin Talbot; camera, Russell Harlan; editor, Sherman A. Rose.

Hopalong Cassidy .... William Boyd
California Carlson .... Andy Clyde
Johnny Travers .... Jay Kirby
Orestes Krebs .... Russell Simpson
Inez .... Claudia Drake
Don Enrique .... Cliff Parkinson

THE LEATHER BURNERS (UA, 1943) 66 M.

Producer, Harry Sherman; director, Joseph Henabery; story, Bliss Lomax; screenplay, Jo Pagano; music director, Irvin Talbot; art director, Ralph Berger; camera, Russell Harlan; editor, Carroll Lewis.

Hopalong Cassidy .... William Boyd
California Carlson .... Andy Clyde
Johnny .... Jay Kirby
Dan Slack .... Victor Jory
Sam Bucktoe .... George Givot
Sharon Longstreet .... Shelley Spencer
Bobby Longstreet .... Bobby Larson
Harrison Brooke .... George Reeves
Lafe .... Hal Taliaferro
Bart .... Forbes Murray

FALSE COLORS (UA, 1943) 65 M.

Producer, Harry Sherman; associate producer, Lewis J. Rachmil; director, George Archainbaud; screenplay, Bennett Cohen; art director, Ralph Berger; camera, Russell Harlan; editor, Fred Berger.

Hopalong Cassidy .... William Boyd
California Carlson .... Andy Clyde
Jimmy Rogers .... Jimmy Rogers
Bud Lawton and Kit Mayer .... Tom Seidel
Faith Lawton .... Claudia Drake
Mark Foster .... Douglass Dumbrille
Rip Austin .... Bob Mitchum
Sonora .... Glenn Strange
Lefty .... Pierce Lyden
Sheriff Clem Martin .... Roy Barcroft
Judge Stevens .... Sam Flint
Lawyer Jay Griffin .... Earle Hodgins
Jed Stevers .... Elmer Jerome
Townsman .... Tom London
Bar Spectator .... Dan White
Denton Towsman .... George Morrell

RIDERS OF THE DEADLINE (UA, 1943) 68 M.

Producer, Harry Sherman; associate producer, Lewis J. Rachmil; director, Lesley Selander; screenplay, Bennett Cohen; art director, Ralph Berger; camera, Russell Harlan; editor, Fred Berger.

Hopalong Cassidy .... William Boyd
California Carlson .... Andy Clyde
Jimmy .... Jimmy Rogers
Tim Mason .... Richard Crane
Sue .... Frances Woodward
Crandall .... William Halligan
Madigan .... Tony Warde
Drago .... Bob Mitchum
Tex .... Jim Bannon
Martin .... Hugh Prosser
Captain Jennings .... Herbert Rawlinson
Calhoun .... Montie Montana
Sourdough .... Earle Hodgins
Kilroy .... Bill Beckford
Sanders .... Pierce Lyden

MYSTERY MAN (UA, 1944) 58 M.

Producer, Harry A. Sherman; director, George Archainbaud; screenplay, J. Benton Cheney; music director, Irvin Talbot; camera, Russell Harlan.

Hopalong Cassidy	William Boyd
California Carlson	Andy Clyde
Jimmy Rogers	Jimmy Rogers
Bud Trilling	Don Costello
Bert Rogan	Francis McDonald
Sheriff Sam Newhall	Forrest Taylor
Diane Newhall	Eleanor Stewart
Marshall Ted Blane	Jack Rockwell
Red	Pierce Lyden
Bill	John Merton
Joe	Bill Hunter
Tom Hanlon	Bob Burns
Tex	Ozie Waters
Bank Robber	Art Mix
Townsman	George Morrell
Bar 20 Boy	Bob Baker
Deputy Ed	Hank Bell

FORTY THIEVES (UA, 1944) 60 M.

Producer, Harry A. Sherman; director, Lesley Selander; screenplay, Michael Wilson, Bernie Kamins; camera, Russell Harlan.

Hopalong Cassidy	William Boyd
California Carlson	Andy Clyde
Jimmy Rogers	Jimmy Rogers
Tad Hammond	Douglass Dumbrille
Katherine Reynolds	Louise Currie
Jerry Doyle	Kirk Alyn
Buck Peters	Herbert Rawlinson
Judge Reynolds	Robert Frazer
Ike Simmons	Glenn Strange
Sam Garms	Jack Rockwell
Joe Garms	Bob Kortman

TEXAS MASQUERADE (UA, 1944) 59 M.

Producer, Harry A. Sherman; associate producer, Lewis J. Rachmil; director, George Archainbaud; screenplay, Norman Houston, Jack Lait, Jr.; art director, Ralph Berger; camera, Russell Harlan; editor, Walter Hannemann.

Hopalong Cassidy	William Boyd
California Carlson	Andy Clyde
Jimmy Rogers	Jimmy Rogers
Virginia Curtis	Mady Correll
Ace Maxson	Don Costello
J. K. Trimble	Russell Simpson
James Corwin	Nelson Leigh
Sam Nolan	Francis McDonald
John Martindale	J. Farrell MacDonald
Mrs. Martindale	June Pickerell
Jeff	John Merton
Al	Pierce Lyden
Rowbottom	Robert McKenzie
Sykes	Bill Hunter
Oldtimer	George Morrell

LUMBERJACK (UA, 1944) 65 M.

Producer, Harry A. Sherman; associate producer, Lewis

J. Rachmil; director, Lesley Selander; screenplay, Norman Houston; camera, Russell Harlan.

Hopalong Cassidy	William Boyd
California Carlson	Andy Clyde
Jimmy Rogers	Jimmy Rogers
Buck	Herbert Rawlinson
Julie	Ellen Hall
Abbey	Ethel Wales
Keeper	Douglass Dumbrille
Fenwick	Francis McDonald
Jordan	John Whitney
Taggart	Hal Taliaferro
Slade	Henry Wills
Big Joe	Charles Morton
Mrs. Williams	Frances Morris
Sheriff	Jack Rockwell
Justice	Bob Burns

THE DEVIL'S PLAYGROUND (UA, 1946) 62 M.

Producer, Lewis J. Rachmil; director, George Archainbaud; musical director, David Chudnow; art director, Harvey D. Gillett; camera, Mack Stengler; editor, Fred W. Berger.

Hopalong Cassidy	William Boyd
California Carlson	Andy Clyde
Lucky Jenkins	Rand Brooks
Mrs. Evans	Elaine Riley
Judge Morton	Robert Elliott
Sheriff	Joseph J. Greene
Roberts	Francis McDonald
Curly	Ned Young
Daniel	Earle Hodgins
U.S. Marshal	George Eldredge
Wolfe	Everett Shields
Dwarf	John George

FOOL'S GOLD (1947) 65 M.

Producer, Lewis J. Rachmil; director, George Archainbaud; screenplay, Doris Schroeder; music, David Chudnow; art director, Harvey T. Gillett; camera, Mack Stengler; editor, Fred W. Berger.

Hopalong Cassidy	William Boyd
California	Andy Clyde
Lucky	Rand Brooks
Jessie Dixon	Jane Randolph
Professor Dixon	Robert E. Keane
Bruce Landy	Stephen Barclay
Duke	Harry Cording
Sandler	Earle Hodgins
Colonel Jed Landy	Forbes Murray
Blackie	William Davis
Sergeant	Benny Corbett
Speed	Fred S. Toones
Barton	Bob Bentley
Lieutenant Anderson	Glen B. Gallagher

HOPPY'S HOLIDAY (UA, 1947) 60 M.

Producer, Lewis J. Rachmil; director, George Archainbaud; author, Ellen Corby, Cecile Kremer; screenplay, J. Benton Cheney, Bennett Cohen, Ande Lamb; music, David Chudnow; art director, Harvey T. Gillett; camera, Mack Stengler; editor, Fred W. Berger.

Hopalong Cassidy .... William Boyd
California Carlson .... Andy Clyde
Lucky Jenkins .... Rand Brooks
Mayor .... Andrew Tombes
Hotel clerk .... Jeff Corey
    and: Mary Ware, Leonard Penn, Donald Kirke, Hollis
        Bane, Gil Patric, Frank Henry

MARAUDERS (UA, 1947) 63 M.

Producer, Lewis J. Rachmil; director, George Archainbaud; author, Charles Belden; screenplay, Charles Belden; music, David Chudnow; camera, Mack Stengler; editor, McLure Capps.

Hopalong Cassidy .... William Boyd
California Carlson .... Andy Clyde
Lucky Jenkins .... Rand Brooks
Black .... Ian Wolfe
Susan .... Dorinda Clifton
Mrs. Crowell .... Mary Newton
Black .... Harry Cording
Clerk .... Earle Hodgins
Oil Driller .... Dick Bailey

UNEXPECTED GUEST (UA, 1947) 59 M.

Producer, Lewis J. Rachmil; director, George Archainbaud; screenplay, Ande Lamb; art director, Harvey T. Gillett; music, David Chudnow; camera, Mack Stengler; editor, Fred W. Berger.

Hopalong Cassidy .... William Boyd
California .... Andy Clyde
Lucky .... Rand Brooks
Miss Hackett .... Una O'Connor
Potter .... John Parrish
Joshua .... Earle Hodgins
Ogden .... Robert B. Williams

DANGEROUS VENTURE (UA, 1947) 59 M.

Producer, Lewis J. Rachmil; director, George Archainbaud; screenplay, Doris Schroeder; music, David Chudnow; art director, Harvey T. Gillett; camera, Mack Stengler; editor, Fred W. Berger.

Hopalong Cassidy .... William Boyd
California Carlson .... Andy Clyde
Lucky Jenkins .... Rand Brooks
Xeoli .... Fritz Leiber
Doctor Atwood .... Douglas Evans
Morgan .... Harry Cording
Sue Harmon .... Betty Alexander
Kane .... Francis McDonald

Jose .... Neyle Morrow
Talu .... Patricia Tate
Stark .... Bob Faust

SINISTER JOURNEY (UA, 1948) 60 M.

Exec. producer, William Boyd; producer, Lewis J. Rachmil; director, George Archainbaud; author-screenplay, Doris Schroeder; art director, Jerome Pycha, Jr.; music director, Darrel Calker; camera, Mack Stengler; editor, Fred W. Berger.

Hopalong Cassidy .... William Boyd
California Carlson .... Andy Clyde
Lucky Jenkins .... Rand Brooks
Mrs. Garvin .... Elaine Riley
Lee Garvin .... John Kellogg

SILENT CONFLICT (UA, 1948) 61 M.

Producer, Lewis J. Rachmil; director, George Archainbaud; author-screenplay, Charles Belden; music, Ralph Stanley; art director, Jerome Pycha, Jr.; camera, Mack Stengler; editor, Fred W. Berger.

Hopalong Cassidy .... William Boyd
California Carlson .... Andy Clyde
Lucky Jenkins .... Rand Brooks
Rene Richards .... Virginia Belmont
Doc Richards .... Earle Hodgins
Speed Blaney .... James Harrison
Randall .... Forbes Murray
Clerk .... John Butler
Yardman .... Herbert Rawlinson
First Rancher .... Richard Alexander
Second Rancher .... Don Haggerty

STRANGE GAMBLE (UA, 1948) 61 M.

Exec. Producer, William Boyd; producer, Lewis J. Rachmil; director, George Archainbaud; author-screenplay, Doris Schroeder; art director, Jerome Pycha, Jr.; camera, Mack Stengler; editor, Fred W. Berger.

Hopalong Cassidy .... William Boyd
California Carlson .... Andy Clyde
Lucky Jenkins .... Rand Brooks
Nora .... Elaine Riley
    and: William Leicester, Joan Barton, James Craven,
        Joel Friedkin, Herbert Rawlinson

BORROWED TROUBLE (UA, 1948) 60 M.

Producer, Lewis J. Rachmil; director, George Archainbaud; screenplay, Charles Belden; music director, Darrill Calker; camera, Mack Stengler; editor, Fred W. Berger.

Hopalong Cassidy .... William Boyd
California Carlson .... Andy Clyde
Lucky Jenkins .... Rand Brooks
Mrs. Garvin .... Elaine Riley
Lee Garvin .... John Kellogg

Teacher .... Helen Chapman

THE DEAD DON'T DREAM (UA, 1948) 62 M.

Exec. Producer, William Boyd; producer, Lewis J. Rachmil; director, George Archainbaud; author-screenplay, Francis Rosenwald; art director, Jerome Pycha, Jr.; music, Ralph Stanley; camera, Mack Stengler; editor, Fred W. Berger.

Hopalong Cassidy .... William Boyd
California Carlson .... Andy Clyde
Lucky Jenkins .... Rand Brooks
Jeff Potter .... John Parrish
Earl Wesson .... Leonard Penn
Mary Benton .... Mary Tucker
Bert Lansing .... Francis McDonald
Duke .... Richard Alexander

Larry Potter .... Bob Gabriel
Jesse Williams .... Stanley Andrews
Sheriff Thompson .... Forbes Murray
Deputy .... Doug Haggerty

FALSE PARADISE (UA, 1948) 60 M.

Exec. Producer, William Boyd; producer, Lewis J. Rachmil; director, George Archainbaud; author-screenplay, Harrison Jacobs; art director, Jerome Pycha, Jr.; music, Ralph Stanley; camera, Mack Stengler; editor, Fred W. Berger.

Hopalong Cassidy .... William Boyd
California Carlson .... Andy Clyde
Lucky Jenkins .... Rand Brooks
    and: Joel Friedkin, Elaine Riley, Kenneth MacDonald,
        Don Haggerty, Cliff Clark

JAMES BOND

In 1963, a well-endowed British-made satirical super spy thriller, *Dr. No*, went into theatrical release, with relatively little fanfare. However, the public took the film and its star, Sean Connery, to heart, and a new cinema vogue of cold war espionage adventure films blossomed forth, flowering the land with imitation super heroes of all varieties. Yet, it was the Ian Fleming–*James Bond* films and not the slew of imitations that proved ultimately most successful. Between 1963–70, seven lavishly produced color-widescreen 007 adventures appeared, with additional *James Bond* epics slated for future production. It even caused the revival of theatrical series thrillers, a genre thought killed by television's competition.

Britisher Ian Fleming (who died August 12, 1964) had been writing his series of brisk sex and violence James Bond secret agent novels since 1950 when *Casino Royale* appeared. A loyal but relatively small coterie of devotees for the series developed, but it was not until the late 1950s when John F. Kennedy and other notables let it be known that they were partial to the Bond books, that the Bond craze developed. Thereafter, international film producers Harry Saltzman and Albert Broccoli purchased film rights to all the Bond novels save *Casino Royale* (which had gone almost unnoticed when dramatized in the mid-1950s on *Climax* on American television, with Barry Nelson as James Bond) which producer Charles K. Feldman owned, and *Thunderball*, which writer-producer Kevin McClory claimed via a law suit.

After bringing the first three Bond films to the screen, Saltzman and Broccoli reached a compro-mise coproducing agreement with McClory and turned out *Thunderball* in time for a mammoth Christmas, 1965 release. However, no accord could be attained with Feldman, who spent huge sums on his Columbia Pictures release (all the other Bond films were mass distributed by United Artists) trying to find a new formula for his Fleming property to counteract the absence of Sean Connery. What resulted in *Casino Royale* was an unwieldy multi directional lampoon, weakly mocking the *James Bond* series. David Niven archly portrayed Sir James Bond brought out of retirement, with Joanna Pettet as his daughter Mata Bond (via Mata Hari) and Woody Allen as his wayward nephew Jimmy Bond. The disjointed effort was only distinguished by a lively Burt Bacharach score.

Having completed his leading role in *You Only Live Twice* (1967), Connery refused additional 007 films. He wanted more challenging parts. Connery was born August 25, 1930, in Edinburgh, Scotland, the son of a lorry driver. He quit school at age 13 to become a milkman. Upon reaching military age, he served for three years as an able seaman, then as a member of an anti-aircraft carrier squadron. Once a civilian again, he was employed at such odd jobs as bricklayer, boxer, and lifeguard. When he began taking courses in commercial art, he earned part of his tuition by modeling. His theatrical debut was as a chorus replacement in a British touring company of *South Pacific*. After a stint in repertory and with a Shakespearian group, he appeared on BBC television in such productions as *Requiem for a Heavyweight* and *Anna*

Karenina. His cinema debut was in *No Road Back* (1956). He had a leading (singing) part in "Darby O'Gill and the Little People" (1959) a Walt Disney film, and was a villain in *Tarzan's Greatest Adventure* (1959). Once stereotyped by the "James Bond" films, he found it difficult to obtain non super spy roles. He did, however, appear in such dramatic productions as *The Hill* (1965), *A Fine Madness* (1967) and *The Molly Maguires* (1970), romantic stories like *Woman of Straw* and *Marne* (both 1964), or westerns like *Shalako* (1968). None of them were commercial successes. Connery is married to actress Diane Cilento. They reside in a West London suburb with their two children, Giovanna Volpe (Miss Cilento's daughter by a previous marriage) and Jason.

On Her Majesty's Secret Service was released in 1970 with George Lazenby as the famed secret agent. (Born September 5, 1939, in Goulburn, Australia, the son of a railway worker, Lazenby's first job was as an apprentice motor mechanic. After working as a car salesman in various Australian cities, he went to England in mid 1964 and soon became a male model. *Secret Service* was his film debut.)

For *Diamonds Are Forever,* filmed in Las Vegas and Hollywood in the spring of 1971, Sean Connery was lured back to the James Bond role by $1 million plus salary (which he donated to Scottish educational charities).

Dr. No cost $1.5 million to make, and grossed over $5.5 million. Each subsequent production was more lavish in its overall production values, with huge sums expended on fantastic Ken Adam's sets, precise gimmicks and gadgets, and a host of breathtaking special effects. It is estimated that the seven Bond films to date have earned over $125 million in rentals, with *Thunderball* the highest grossing, at $27 million.

Richard Maibaum has concocted most of the Saltzman-Broccoli *James Bond* screenplays, embroidering wild intricacies on the Fleming originals, setting the pace for mad plotlines, briskly filled with violence, sex, and grandiose adventure —all played tongue in cheek.

In *Dr. No,* Bond is sent by M (Bernard Lee) to Kingston, Jamaica, to investigate the disappearance of another British agent, leading 007 eventually to Crab Key, an island retreat where demonic Dr. No (Joseph Wiseman) is engaged in counter-United States missile activity, while working for SPECTRE (Special Executive for Counter-Terrorism, Revenge and Extortion).

From Russia With Love again has Bond fighting SPECTRE, which now is busily nurturing British-Russian hostility, so they can steal a special Lektor decoding machine from the Soviet cryptographic headquarters in Istanbul.

Goldfinger concerns Bond's valiant efforts to offset Auric Goldfinger's (Gert Frobe) diabolic master plot to explode a nuclear device within Fort Knox and thus contaminate the United States gold resources.

Thunderball finds SPECTRE again challenging the free world by hijacking a huge NATO nuclear bomber, and threatening to detonate the bombs in Miami and Cape Kennedy unless a £100 million ransom in diamonds is quickly paid.

Casino Royale sees the American, British, French, and Russian secret services joining forces to stave off SMERSH (Smyert Spionam, the Soviet organ of vengeance, meaning "death to spies") and forcing Sir James Bond out of retirement to handle the job of utilizing Evelyn Trimble's (Peter Sellers) foolproof, baccarat gambling system to outbid SMERSH's attempt to restock their financial coffers at the expense of the world.

You Only Live Twice has Bond tracking down SPECTRE's arch villain Ernst Stavro Blofeld (Donald Pleasance) in his Japanese coastal hideout where he has been fostering American-Russian friction by intercepting space capsules from each of the countries.

In *On Her Majesty's Secret Service* Bond is again pitted against SPECTRE's Blofield (here, Telly Savalas) who from his Institute of Physiological Research headquarters in Switzerland hopes to take over the world through biological warfare.

All the Saltzman-Broccoli *James Bond* films benefitted from an increasingly flavorful put-on atmosphere, best handled by director Terence Young. Besides Monty Norman's vibrating Bond theme music, the pulsating film scores by John Barry, there was the hard beat theme song, such as *Goldfinger* by Leslie Bricusse and Anthony Newley Beginning with *From Russia With Love* there was an elaborate, tightly paced pre-credit sequence, far removed from the film's plot, in which Bond undergoes, in five minutes, a lifetime of harrowing violence and sex. More and more gimmicks appeared in the entries, such as the Aston Martin car, the specially fitted attaché case, a collapsible helicopter, etc. As the Bond series went on, 007 would be heard mouthing all sorts of Bondisms, patriotic platitudes and chic bedroom talk with a bevy of sensuous gals, albeit villainesses or heroines. Super cool Bond was absolutely at ease lashing out at a foe with a karate chop, tangling with wrongdoers on a ski slope, or romancing such lovelies as Tatiana Romanova (Daniela Bianchi) in a speedboat finale in *From Russia With Love*. Each film ended with a credit card announcing the next Bond entry.

The stock company of players for the James Bond series included M, the British secret service chief (Bernard Lee; in *Casino Royale* it was John Huston), Miss Moneypenny, M's bachelor secretary who was in love with Bond (Lois Maxwell; in *Casino Royale* it was Barbara Bouchet).

The colorful gallery of Bondian villains include the inscrutable "Dr. No" (Joseph Wiseman) with his gloved, radioactive-burned hand; the stony faced blonde killer Red Grant (Robert Shaw) and the frumpy but deadly matron Rosa Klebb (Lotta Lenya), former head of SMERSH, both dazzling in *From Russia With Love; Goldfinger* had the triple threat of stocky, sinister Auric Goldfinger (Gert Frobe), his indestructible Korean iron henchman

Odd-Job (Harold Sakata), and their flashy female cohort Pussy Galore (Honor Blackman); *Thunderball* revealed oily-smooth SPECTRE agent and international blackmailer Largo (Adolfo Celi) and his chief helper, glamorous playgirl Domino (Claudine Auger); *Casino Royale* had the vapid shenanigans of arch enemies Vesper Lynd (Ursula Andress), the richest spy in the world, and the eccentric ninkenpoop Dr. Noah, alias Jimmy Bond (Woody Allen); in *You Only Live Twice* there were the fey sinister ambiguities of SPECTRE head Blofeld (Donald Pleasance) and such deadly helpers as Helga Brandt (Karin Dor); *On Her Majesty's Secret Service* returned Blofeld in a less subtle and cruder version (Telly Savalas) and his no nonsense Institute overseer, Irma Bunt (Ilse Steppart).

Perhaps the most fetching and showy of all the Bond heroines was Tracy (Diana Rigg) in *On Her Majesty's Secret Service*. She could equal Bond on the ski slopes, in bed; match his wisecracks, and out-cool his hippest behavior.

Sean Connery.

John Kitzmiller, Ursula Andress, Connery. (Dr. No)

Joseph Wiseman, Connery. (Dr. No)

Lotte Lenya, Robert Shaw. (From Russia With Love

Connery, Daniela Bianchi. (From Russia With Love)

Connery, Honor Blackman. (Goldfinger)

Connery, Daniela Bianchi, Robert Shaw. (From Russia With Love)

Connery and Aston-Martin. (Goldfinger)

Gert Frobe, Connery. (Goldfinger)

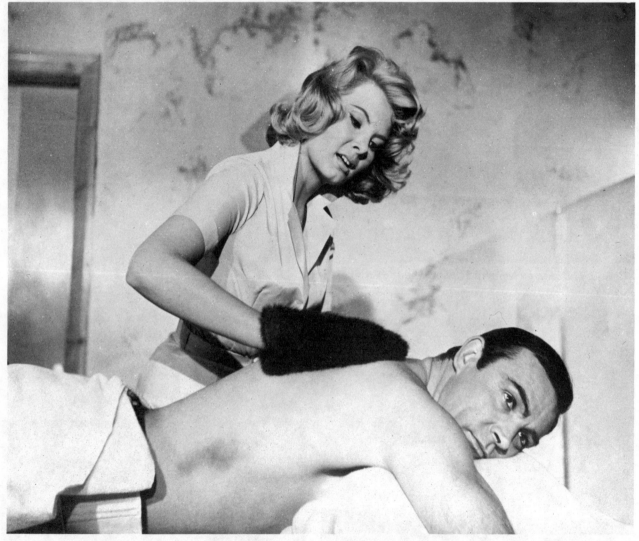

Molly Peters, Connery. (Thunderball)

Adolfo Celi, Connery. (**Thunderball**)

Connery. (You Only Live Twice)

Rik Van Nutter, Connery. (Thunderball)

Connery. (You Only Live Twice)

Connery, Donald Pleasence. (You Only Live Twice)

David Niven. (Casino Royale)

Telly Savalas, George Lazenby. (On Her Majesty's Secret Service)

Diana Rigg, Lazenby. (On Her Majesty's Secret Service)

JAMES BOND

DR. NO (UA, 1963) 111 M.

Producer, Harry Saltzman, Albert R. Broccoli; director, Terence Young; author, Ian Fleming; screenplay, Richard Maibaum, Joanna Harwood, Berkley Mather; musical director, John Barry; camera, Ted Moore; editor, Peter Hunt.

James Bond	Sean Connery
Felix Leiter	Jack Lord
Dr. No	Joseph Wiseman
Honey	Ursula Andress
Miss Taro	Zena Marshall
Sylvia	Eunice Gayson
Secretary	Lois Maxwell
Photographer	Margaret LeWars
Quarrel	John Kitzmiller
"M"	Bernard Lee
Professor Dent	Anthony Dawson

FROM RUSSIA WITH LOVE (UA, 1964) 118 M.

Producer, Harry Saltzman, Albert R. Broccoli; director, Terence Young; author, Ian Fleming; screenplay, Richard Maibaum; adaptation, Johanna Harwood; camera, Ted Moore; art director, Syd Cain; music, John Barry; assistant director, David Anderson; editor, Peter Hunt.

James Bond	Sean Connery
Tatiana Romanova	Daniela Bianchi
Kerim Bey	Pedro Armendariz
Rosa Klebb	Lotte Lenya
Red Grant	Robert Shaw
"M"	Bernard Lee
Sylvia	Eunice Gayson
Morzeny	Walter Gotell
Vavra	Francis de Wolff
Train Conductor	George Pastell
Kerim's Girl	Nadja Regin
Miss Moneypenny	Lois Maxwell
Vida	Aliza Gur
Zora	Martine Beswick
Kronsteen	Vladek Sheybal
Benz	Peter Bayliss
Belly Dancer	Leila

GOLDFINGER (UA, 1965) 108 M.

Producer, Harry Saltzman, Albert R. Broccoli; director, Guy Hamilton; author, Ian Fleming; screenplay, Richard Maibaum, Paul Dehn; camera, Ted Moore; special effects, John Stears, Frank George; music director, John Barry; production designer, Ken Adam; art director, Peter Murton; editor, Peter Hunt.

James Bond	Sean Connery
Goldfinger	Gert Frobe
Pussy Galore	Honor Blackman
Jill Masterson	Shirley Eaton
Tilly Masterson	Tania Mallett
Odd-Job	Harold Sakata

"M"	Bernard Lee
Solo	Martin Benson
Felix Leiter	Cec Linder
Simmons	Austin Willis
Miss Moneypenny	Lois Maxwell
Midnight	Bill Nagy
Capungo	Alf Joint
Old Lady	Varley Thomas
Bonita	Nadja Regin
Sierra	Raymond Young
Smithers	Richard Vernon
Brunskill	Denis Cowles
Mr. Ling	Burt Kwouk

THUNDERBALL (UA, 1965) 125 M.

Producer, Kevin McClory; director, Terence Young; author, Ian Fleming; story, Kevin McClory, Jack Whittingham, Ian Fleming; screenplay, Richard Maibaum, John Hopkins, camera, Ted Moore; art director, Ken Adam; music director, John Barry; editor, Peter Hunt.

James Bond	Sean Connery
Domino	Claudine Auger
Emilio Largo	Adolfo Celi
Fiona	Luciana Paluzzi
Felix Leiter	Rik Van Nutter
"M"	Bernard Lee
Paula	Martine Beswick
Count Lippe	Guy Doleman
Patricia	Molly Peters
"Q"	Desmond Llewelyn
Moneypenny	Lois Maxwell
Foreign Secretary	Roland Culver
Pinder	Earl Cameron
Major Derval	Paul Stassino

YOU ONLY LIVE TWICE (UA, 1967) 117 M.

Producer, Albert R. Broccoli, Harry Saltzman; director, Lewis Gilbert; author, Ian Fleming; screenplay, Roald Dahl; camera, Freddie Young; assistant director, William Cartlidge; production designer, Ken Adam; art director, Harry Pottle; music director, John Barry; special effects, John Stears; editor, Peter Hunt.

James Bond	Sean Connery
Aki	Akiko Wakabayashi
Tiger Tanaka	Tetsuro Tamba
Kissy Suzuki	Mie Hama
Osato	Teru Shimada
Helga Brandt	Karin Dor
Miss Moneypenny	Lois Maxwell
"Q"	Desmond Llewelyn
Henderson	Charles Gray
Chinese Girl	Tsai Chin
"M"	Bernard Lee
Blofeld	Donald Pleasence
American President	Alexander Knox
President's Aide	Robert Hutton
SPECTRE 3	Burt Kwouk
SPECTRE 4	Michael Chow

CASINO ROYALE (Col., 1967) 131 M.

Producer, Charles K. Feldman, Jerry Bresler; directors, John Huston, Ken Hughes, Val Guest, Robert Parrish, Joe McGrath; additional sequences, Val Guest; author, Ian Fleming; screenplay, Wolf Mankowitz, John Law; Michael Sayers; special effects, Cliff Richardson, Roy Whybrow; music director, Burt Bacharach; set decorator, Terence Morgan, camera, Jack Hildyard; editor, Bill Lenny.

Evelyn Tremble .... Peter Sellers
Vesper Lynd .... Ursula Andress
Sir James Bond .... David Niven
Le Chiffre .... Orson Welles
Mata Bond .... Joanna Pettet
The Detainer .... Daliah Lavi
Jimmy Bond (Dr. Noah) .... Woody Allen
Agent Mimi (Lady Fiona McTarry) ..... Deborah Kerr
Ransome .... William Holden
Le Grand .... Charles Boyer
McTarry .... John Huston
Smernov .... Kurt Kasznar
Himself .... George Raft
French Legionnaire .... Jean-Paul Belmondo
Cooper .... Terence Cooper
Moneypenny .... Barbara Bouchet
Buttercup .... Angela Scoular
Eliza .... Gabriella Licudi
Heather .... Tracey Crisp
Frau Hoffner .... Anna Quayle
"Q" .... Geoffrey Bayldon
"Q's" Assistant .... John Wells
British Army Officer .... Richard Wattis
Polo .... Ronnie Corbett

Taxi Driver .... Bernard Cribbins
Casino Director .... Colin Gordon
Fang Leader .... Tracy Reed

ON HER MAJESTY'S SECRET SERVICE (UA, 1970) 140 M.

Producer, Harry Saltzman, Albert Broccoli, director, Peter Hunt; scenario, Richard Maibaum; additional dialogue, Simon Raven; camera, Michael Reed; special effects, John Stears; music, John Barry; assistant director, Frank Ernst; editor, John Glen.

James Bond .... George Lazenby
Tracy .... Diana Rigg
Ernst Stavros Blofeld .... Telly Savalas
Irma Bunt .... Ilse Steppat
Marc Ange Draco .... Gabriele Ferzetti
Grunther .... Yuri Borienko
Campbell .... Bernard Horsfall
Sir Hilary Bray .... George Baker
M .... Bernard Lee
Miss Moneypenny .... Lois Maxwell
Q .... Desmond Llewelyn
Ruby .... Angela Scoular
Janitor .... Norman McGlenn
Manuel .... Brian Worth
Tousaint .... Geoffrey Chesire
Che Che .... Irvin Allen
Felsen .... Les Crawford
Braun .... George Cooper
Nancy .... Catherina von Schell

JUNGLE JIM

In 1948, ace economy producer Sam Katzman created a highly profitable film package. Knowing that ex-Olympic swimming star Johnny Weissmuller was at liberty after his withdrawal from the *Tarzan* film series, he approached the former "King of the Jungle" and offered him a financially attractive contract to star in a *Jungle Jim* series for Columbia Pictures. Based on the popular 1920s Alex Raymond, King Features Syndicate comic strip, the jungle hero had served previously as the basis for a 12-chapter Universal series (1936) starring Grant Withers and Betty Jane Rhodes. Katzman realized that Weissmuller had built-in publicity value from his 16 years as "Tarzan" and that his new role as a jungle man with clothes would fit right into the public image and the lucrative kiddie matinee boxoffice demands. Between 1948 and 1955, a dozen *Jungle Jim* programmers appeared with excellent threatrical returns. Later in 1956, Weissmuller starred in a 26-episode half-hour television series of *Jungle Jim* shows, which included Martin Huston, Norman Frederic and Tamba the chimp in the cast. (On radio in the early 1950s, a 15-minute *Jungle Jim* series was aired, with Matt Crowley as Jungle Jim, Juano Hernandez as Kolu the guide, and Frances Hale as Shanghai Lil.)

The robust star of *Jungle Jim,* Johnny Weissmuller, was born June 2, 1904, in Chicago. As a child he became a sports enthusiast, and was especially fond of swimming. At the University of Chicago he was a swimming star, and until he turned a professional athlete in 1929, he entered and won a host of amateur free style swimming events. He competed in the 1924 and 1928 world Olympics, setting 75 new official world speed records. After appearing in several Grantland Rice sports short subjects films, and having a thankless role as an Adonis figure in *Glorifying the American Girl* (1929), he was tested for the Tarzan role by MGM. Weissmuller was already a shoo-in for the part, because of his amazing physique, leonine head, and the fact that he fitted the popular conception of the Edgar Rice Burroughs hero. He made his debut in *Tarzan, the Ape Man* (1932) and appeared in a dozen additional *Tarzan* films, before bowing out of the series in 1948, after completing *Tarzan and the Mermaids* for RKO.

It was at this low point in Weissmuller's career that Katzman came to the rescue. Weissmuller was no longer suitable for vine-swinging roles, due to age and overweight, and no producer would think of casting him for other parts. His foray outside the jungle domain in *Swamp Fire* (1946), a low-budget Pine-Thomas Production for Paramount had faded quickly at the boxoffice. (Weissmuller made brief cameo appearances in *Stage Door Canteen* [1943] and *The Phynx* [1970].) Thus the *Jungle Jim* role extended his cinema career another decade. When he retired from show business in the late 1950s, he joined a swimming pool franchise company, heading the Chicago-based Johnny Weismuller Swimming Pool Firm. He currently resides in Ft. Lauderdale, Florida, where he is in charge of the Swimming Hall of Fame. (His biography, *Water, World and Weissmuller,* appeared in 1967.) He has been married five times—to Lupe Velez, Camille Louier, Bobbe Arnst, Beryl Scott, and Allene Gates. He and Allene Gates have three children: Wendy, John, and Heide. John Jr. made a brief stab at acting, appearing to minimal advantage in such films as *Andy Hardy Comes Home* (1958).

The plots of the *Jungle Jim* films were generally absurd—at best exotically campy. In the series, Weissmuller was established as an African white hunter, who takes pains to risk his life on the slightest pretext, whether interfering between warring humans or jumping into the midst of a savage animal combat. In these landlubbing adventures, he is surrounded by his pets: Caw-Caw (a crow), Skipper (the dog) and later by Tamba (the chimp—a near relative of Cheetah from his *Tarzan* days). His human companion was Kolu the native. (On the television *Jungle Jim* series, besides his native guide, Jim had an adolescent son tagging along on his treks.) In the last three entries, Weissmuller no longer played Jungle Jim, but appeared as himself. Everything basically remained the same.

To keep the quickie productions within ultralow budgets, Katzman made frequent use of any available stock footage from the Columbia Pictures library, especially from the old Frank Buck travel documentaries. The scripters thought nothing of blending juvenile fiction with the most improbable characterizations and unlikely topical subjects. *Savage Mutiny* had a childish approach to the cold war situation; *Mark of the Gorilla* involved Nazi-buried loot; *Cannibal Attack* has Jungle Jim at odds with members of a foreign government trying to steal cobalt deposits. Any similarity with the African terrain and natives were purely coincidental. In *Devil Goddess* the natives looked more like South Seas islanders, and the heroine was garbed in the Burmese mode. In most entries, the villains were overly evil, but unduly stupid, being easily routed by the simplistic native forces.

Unlike his *Tarzan* days, Weissmuller as Jungle Jim was allowed a modicum of dialogue beyond grunting and yelling. Nevertheless, he was still taciturn, short on romancing the heroines, and more eager to battle the culprits and animals than tackle an intelligent discussion.

In the initial *Jungle Jim,* a young scientist Hilary Parker (Virginia Grey) seeks a valuable drug to combat polio. Bruce Edwards (George Reeves) is the American who joins the group, actually hunting gold and other treasure buried with the secret of the medicine.

In *The Lost Tribe* a seedy hotel owner, Calhoun (Joseph Vitale), and a ship's captain, Rawling (Ralph Dunn), are the villainous team, plotting to abscond with the treasure of the fabulous land of Dzamm. In combatting the crooks, Jungle Jim's gorilla friends come to his aid. And the plotline allowed for a lengthy fight with clawing tigers, slashing sharks, raging lions, and hungry crocodiles. Many of these sequences were to reappear in later episodes.

Captive Girl has Jungle Jim encountering a mysterious white girl, Joan (Anita Lhoest), whose missionary parents have been killed, she having grown up in the jungle. He rescues her from a scheming witch doctor. In *Mark of the Gorilla*, Jim tracks gold thieves disguised as gorillas and he releases a native princess held by the culprits. *Pygmy Island* shows Jim leading an American army detachment in search of a W.A.C. captain (Ann Savage) lost in the jungle while ferreting out materials required for war supplies. Enemy agents attack the search party, but are routed by Jim in alliance with a tribe of white pygmies. A la Tarzan, Jim fights a crocodile and a gorilla, escaping with a herd of elephants.

Fury of the Congo details Jim's efforts to assist a native tribe, whose members have been enslaved by a narcotics gang, and forced by them to hunt the Okongo, a mysterious animal which is the source of a powerful drug. *Jungle Manhunt* centers on football player Bob Miller (Bob Waterfield) missing in the jungle, as well as cut throat white men who are exploiting native labor to process synthetic diamonds. In *The Forbidden Land* Jim has to oppose a greedy ivory hunter and a gang of money-hungry natives who are utilizing a "giant sized man" to overturn the district commissioner's regime.

Voodoo Tiger has Jim and Phyllis Bruce (Jean Byron), an anthropologist working for the British Museum on tribal customs, becoming enmeshed in the jungle manhunt for Nazi war criminals who know the whereabouts of stolen art treasures. Wilder than most *Jungle Jim* entries, this film sees Jim getting the better of Nazis, headhunters, and gangsters.

In *Savage Mutiny* Jim must evacuate tribesmen from a small coastal African island which is to be the site for A-bomb testing. Enemy agents stir up trouble by keeping the natives on the island. *Valley of the Headhunters* focuses on Jim's efforts to help a government representative obtain agreements with African tribal chiefs regarding valuable mineral deposits. *Killer Ape* details Jim's discovery that the Wazuli tribesmen are selling animals to white hunters gathering ingredients to produce bacterial warfare drugs. When a villager is killed, Jim is suspected of the crime, and must prove that the villains were behind both the murder and the illegal experimenting with the animals. The film's opening sequence, in which tribesmen hit crocodiles on the snout, make it most unlikely juvenile fare.

Jim smashes a diamond smuggling ring in *Jungle Man-Eaters*. *Cannibal Attack* centers on Weissmuller's investigation of a gang of mining and cargo thieves. He discovers that Luora (Judy Walsh), whose mother was princess of a tribe of former cannibals, is implicated in a scheme to sell cobalt to foreign powers. She is supported by Rovak (Bruce Cowling), the tribal ruler whose men don crocodile skins when they rob. In the more exotic *Jungle Moon Men,* Weissmuller escorts Ellen Mackey (Jean Byron), an expert on ancient Egyptian gods, into the country of the pygmy moon men, where they are captured. They eventually escape from the natives, ruled over by Oma (Helen Stanton), a blonde priestess, who has the secret of eternal life. *Devil Goddess* finds Weissmuller guiding a father and daughter explorer team into the volcanic homeland of a fire worshipping tribe where the scientists hope to locate a missing colleague. Weissmuller and his companions must escape from the area with the buried treasure before the volcano erupts.

Holmes Herbert, Virginia Grey, Johnny Weissmuller, Rick Vallin. (Jungle Jim)

Weissmuller, Myrna Dell. (The Lost Tribe)

Anita Lhoest, Rick Vallin, Weissmuller. (Captive Girl)

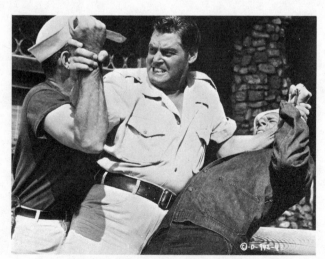

Weissmuller. (The Lost Tribe)

Neyle Morrow, Onslow Stevens, Weissmuller, Trudy Marshall, Suzanne Dalbert. (Mark of the Gorilla)

David Bruce, Weissmuller. (Pygmy Island)

Bruce, Weissmuller. **(Pygmy Island)**

Weissmuller, Bob Waterfield, Sheila Ryan, Rick Vallin. **(Jungle Manhunt)**

Sherry Moreland, Weissmuller. **(Fury of the Congo)**

Steven Rich, Weissmuller, George Eldridge. **(Valley of Headhunters)**

Nick Stuart, Paul Marion, Weissmuller, Nestor Paiva,
Rory Mallinson. (Killer Ape)

Richard Stapley, Weissmuller. (Jungle Man-Eaters)

JUNGLE JIM

JUNGLE JIM (Col., 1948) 73 M.

Producer, Sam Katzman; director, William Berke; author-screenplay, Carroll Young; art director, Paul Palmcutola; music director, Mischa Bakaleinikoff; camera, Lester White; editor, Aaron Stell.

Jungle Jim	Johnny Weissmuller
Hilary Parker	Virginia Grey
Bruce Edwards	George Reeves
Zia	Lita Baron
Kolu	Rick Vallin
Commissioner	Holmes Herbert
Chief Devil Doctor	Tex Mooney

THE LOST TRIBE (Col., 1949) 72 M.

Producer, Sam Katzman; director, William Berke; story-screenplay, Arthur Hoerl, Don Martin; music director, Mischa Bakaleinikoff; camera, Ira H. Morgan; editor, Aaron Stell.

Jungle Jim	Johnny Weissmuller
Norina	Myrna Dell
Li Wanna	Elena Verdugo
Calhoun	Joseph Vitale
Captain Rawling	Ralph Dunn
Chot	Paul Marion
Zoron	Nelson Leigh
Whip Wilson	George J. Lewis
Dojek	Gil Perkins
Cullen	George DeNormand
Eckle	Wally West
Lerch	Rube Schaffer

CAPTIVE GIRL (Col., 1950) 73 M.

Producer, Sam Katzman; director, William Berke; author-screenplay, Carroll Young; art director, Paul Palmentola; music director, Mischa Bakaleinikoff; camera, Ira H. Morgan.

Jungle Jim	Johnny Weissmuller
Barton	Buster Crabbe
Joan	Anita Lhoest
Mahala	Rick Vallin
Hakim	John Dehner
Silva	Rusty Wescoatt
Missionary	Nelson Leigh

MARK OF THE GORILLA (Col., 1950) 68 M.

Producer, Sam Katzman; director, William Berke; author-screenplay, Carroll Young; art director, Paul Palmentola; music director, Mischa Bakaleinikoff; camera, Ira H. Morgan; editor, Henry Batista.

Jungle Jim	Johnny Weissmuller
Barbara Bentley	Trudy Marshall

Nyobi	Suzanne Dalbert
Brandt	Onslow Stevens
Kramer	Robert Purcell
Gibbs	Pierce Lyden
Head Ranger	Neyle Morrow
Warden Bentley	Selmer Jackson

PYGMY ISLAND (Col., 1950) 69 M.

Producer, Sam Katzman; director, William Berke; author-screenplay, Carroll Young; art director, Paul Palmentola; music director, Mischa Bakaleinikoff; camera, Ira H. Morgan; editor, Jerome Thomas.

Jungle Jim	Johnny Weissmuller
Capt. Ann Kingsley	Ann Savage
Major Bolton	David Bruce
Leon Marko	Steven Geray
Kruger	William Tannen
Novak	Tris Coffin
Makuba	Billy Curtis
Captain	Tommy Farrell
Lucas	Pierce Lyden
Anders	Rusty Wescoatt
Tembo	Billy Barty

FURY OF THE CONGO (Col., 1951) 69 M.

Producer, Sam Katzman; director, William Berke; author-screenplay, Carroll Young; art director, Paul Palmentola; music director, Mischa Bakaleinikoff; camera, Ira H. Morgan; editor, Richard Fantl.

Jungle Jim	Johnny Weissmuller
Leta	Sherry Moreland
Ronald Cameron	William Henry
Grant	Lyle Talbot
Professor Dunham	Joel Friedkin
Barnes	George Eldredge
Magruder	Rusty Wescoatt
Raadi	Paul Marion
Mahara	Blanca Vischer
Allen	Pierce Lyden
Guard	John Hart

JUNGLE MANHUNT (Col., 1951) 66 M.

Producer, Sam Katzman; director, Lew Landers; author-screenplay, Samuel Newman; art director, Paul Palmentola; music director, Mischa Bakaleinikoff; camera, William Whitney; editor, Henry Batista.

Jungle Jim	Johnny Weissmuller
Bob Miller	Bob Waterfield
Anne Lawrence	Sheila Ryan
Bono	Rick Vallin
Dr. Mitchell Heller	Lyle Talbot
Maklee Chief	William P. Wilkerson
The Chimp	Tamba

JUNGLE JIM IN THE FORBIDDEN LAND (Col., 1952) 65 M.

Producer, Sam Katzman; director, Lew Landers; author-screenplay, Samuel Newman; art director, Paul Palmentola; music director, Mischa Bakaleinikoff; camera, Fayte Brown; editor, Henry Batista.

Jungle Jim .... Johnny Weissmuller
Linda Roberts .... Angela Greene
Denise .... Jean Willes
Commissioner Kingston .... Lester Matthews
Doctor Edwards .... William Tannen
Fred Lewis .... George Eldredge

VOODOO TIGER (Col., 1952) 67 M.

Producer, Sam Katzman; director, Spencer G. Bennet; author-screenplay, Samuel Newman; art director, Paul Palmentola; music director, Mischa Bakaleinikoff; camera, William Whitley; editor, Gene Havlick.

Jungle Jim .... Johnny Weissmuller
Phyllis Bruce .... Jean Byron
Abel Peterson .... James Seay
Shalimar .... Jeanne Dean
Wombulu .... Charles Howath
Major Bill Green .... Robert Bray
Carl Weiner .... Michael Fox

SAVAGE MUTINY (Col., 1953) 73 M.

Producer, Sam Katzman; director, Spencer G. Bennet; screenplay, Sol Shor; art director, Paul Palmentola; camera, William Whitley; editor, Henry Batista.

Jungle Jim .... Johnny Weissmuller
Joan Harris .... Angela Greene
Major Walsh .... Lester Matthews
Dr. Parker .... Nelson Leigh
Chief Wamai .... Charles Steven
Emil Bruno .... Leonard Penn

VALLEY OF THE HEADHUNTERS (Col., 1953) 67 M.

Producer, Sam Katzman; director, William Berke; author-screenplay, Samuel Newman; art director, Paul Palmentola; music director, Mischa Bakaleinikoff; camera, William Whitley; editor, Gene Havlick.

Jungle Jim .... Johnny Weissmuller
Ellen Shaw .... Christine Larson
Arco .... Robert C. Foulk
Lt. Barry .... Steven Ritch
Mr. Bradley .... Nelson Leigh
Pico Church .... Joseph Allen, Jr.
Commissioner Kingston .... George Eldredge

KILLER APE (Col., 1953) 68 M.

Producer, Sam Katzman; director, Spencer G. Bennet;

author-screenplay, Carroll Young, Arthur Hoerl; music director, Mischa Bakaleinikoff; art director, Paul Palmentola; editor, Gene Havlick; camera, William Whitley.

Jungle Jim .... Johnny Weissmuller
Shari .... Carol Thurston
Norley .... Ray Corrigan
Man Ape .... Max Palmer
Ramada .... Burt Wenland
Andrews .... Nestor Paiva
Mahara .... Paul Marion
Achmed .... Eddie Foster
Perry .... Rory Mallinson
Maron .... Nick Stuart
The Chimp .... Tamba

JUNGLE MAN-EATERS (Col., 1954) 68 M.

Producer, Sam Katzman; director, Lee Sholem; screenplay, Samuel Newman; music director, Mischa Bakaleinikoff; art director, Paul Palmentola; camera, Henry Freulich; editor, Gene Havlick.

Jungle Jim .... Johnny Weissmuller
Bonnie .... Karin Booth
Bernard .... Richard Stapley
Zuwaba .... Bernard Hamilton
Latour .... Gregory Gay
Kingston .... Lester Matthews
Zulu .... Paul Thompson
Chief Boganda .... Vince M. Townsend, Jr.
N'Gala .... Louise Franklin

CANNIBAL ATTACK (Col., 1954) 69 M.

Producer, Sam Katzman; director, Lee Sholem; screenplay, Carroll Young; art director, Paul Palmentola; music director, Mischa Bakaleinikoff; camera, Henry Freulich; editor, Edwin Bryant.

Johnny Weissmuller .... Johnny Weissmuller
Luora .... Judy Walsh
Arnold King .... David Bruce
Rovak .... Bruce Cowling
Commissioner .... Charles Evans
John King .... Stevan Darrell
Jason .... Joseph A. Allen, Jr.

JUNGLE MOON MEN (Col., 1955) 70 M.

Producer, Sam Katzman; director, Charles S. Gould; author, Jo Pagano; screenplay, Dwight V. Babcock; art director, Paul Palmentola; music director, Mischa Bakaleinikoff; camera, Henry Freulich; editor, Henry Batista.

Johnny Weissmuller .... Johnny Weissmuller
Ellen Mackey .... Jean Byron
Oma .... Helen Stanton
Bob Prentice .... Bill Henry
Santo .... Myron Healey
Damu .... Billy Curtis

DEVIL GODDESS (Col., 1955) 70 M.

Producer, Sam Katzman; director, Spencer G. Bennet; author, Dwight Babcock; screenplay, George Plympton; art director, Paul Palmentola; music director, Mischa Bakaleinikoff; camera, Ira H. Morgan; editor, Aaron Stell.

Johnny Weissmuller	Johnny Weissmuller
Nora Blakely	Angela Stevens
Prof. Carl Blakely	Selmer Jackson
Nels Comstock	William Tannen
Joseph Leopold	Ed Hilton
Ralph Dixon	William M. Griffith

THE LONE WOLF

Like the fictional creation *Boston Blackie, The Lone Wolf* has had a long literary life and has popped up continually in the motion picture medium. Ben Lyon was most notable among the performers who played Louis Joseph Vance's crime-solving sleuth in the silent films. Columbia astutely revived the series in 1935 with dapper Melvyn Douglas as the suave ex-jewel thief turned gentleman benefactor, and produced another entry in 1938 with continental Francis Lederer as the Lone Wolf. In each instance, the Lone Wolf, although a retired international crook, saw fit to reembrace his old profession and outdistance the law for one (good) reason or another. Then the series settled down for a nine-entry format (1939–1945) with charming Warren William as the whimsical leading man. The property lay dormant for three years, and was revived again by Columbia as a quickie vehicle for stolid Gerald Mohr who performed in two undistinguished installments, with Ron Randell walking through the part in the final Columbia entry. (On television, Louis Hayward appeared as Michael Lanyard, the Lone Wolf, in a 39-episode half hour series in 1954 entitled "Streets of Danger.")

As with his fellow sleuths The Falcon and Boston Blackie, Michael Lanyard (known as the Lone Wolf for his prowess in engineering and executing daring jewel robberies) has undergone a change of heart. No longer a member of the criminal underworld, he is a respectable, upper-class citizen, with vast experience in the world of crime and its methods. He often is called upon by those in a jam who know of his past reputation. Likewise, the police, recalling his criminal record, instantly assume he is the primary culprit in the case at hand—which conveniently allows the storyline to get underway. Columbia had utilized successfully in their *Boston Blackie* films a formula of heavy comedy emphasis to bolster the potentially weak mystery action line. Thus to complement the suave playboy personality of the Lone Wolf, the studio used a buffoon foil, Jamison the butler, himself an ex pickpocket (Raymond Walburn in the first two 1930s entries was Jenkins the butler; with Eric Blore taking over in . . . *Spy Hunt* for ten entries, and Alan Mowbray tackling the part for the finale entry in 1949). Jamison would not only add his humorous, British serving class approach to events, but often he would become a co-partner in aiding his employer to restore sanity to the situation, or sometimes he was the prime source of focal action himself, as in *Secrets of* . . . .

Columbia wasted little budget on supporting casts in the series, relying on its handy assortment of contract players to fill the stock roles in the stories, with Don Beddoe, Lloyd Bridges, Ann Savage, Victory Jory, and Sheldon Leonard doing yeoman's work again as supporting players. A pleasant, if accidental, exception to this economy rule was . . . *Spy Hunt* which boasted star (lets) Rita Hayworth and Ida Lupino as the women in the case, and young Virginia Weidler as the Lone Wolf's daughter, a rather obnoxious, nosey chip off the old block. Like other studios that varied background locales to pep up the monotonous quality of their series, the *Lone Wolf* chapters had the freelance "detective" turn up in Paris, Alexandria, London, Mexico, Washington, D.C., and Miami—all courtesy of the special effects department with its rear screen projection.

There was a wide divergence among the actors who portrayed the Lone Wolf. The first was Melvyn Douglas, born Helvyn Hesselberg in Macon, Georgia, April 5, 1901. After a spell on the New York stage, he made his film debut in *Tonight or Never* (1931). Among his other roles are: *The Vampire Bat* (1933), *Ninotchka* (1939), *Two Faced Woman* (1941), *Sea of Grass* (1947), *Americanization of Emily* (1964), *Hotel* (1967) and *I Never Sang for My Father* (1970). For his role in *Hud* (1963), he won a best supporting actor Oscar.

Francis Lederer was born in Prague on November 6, 1906. His film debut was in the German-made *Lulu* (1928); his Hollywood film debut occurred with *Pursuit of Happiness* (1934). The European stage actor was later seen in such films as *Confessions of a Nazi Spy* (1939), *A Voice in the Wind* (1944), *The Return of Dracula* (1956), and *Terror Is a Man* (1958).

Gerald Mohr was born in New York May 11, 1914. A CBS radio announcer in his teens, he was a member of Orson Welles's Mercury Theatre. His film debut was in *Lady of Burlesque* (1941), with later roles in *Tall Men* (1951), *Sirocco* (1951), *The Eddie Cantor Story* (1953), and *Angry Red Planet* (1959). On radio he starred in *The Adventures of Philip Marlowe* and on television starred in *Foreign Intrigue*. His last cinema role was in *Funny Girl* (1968); he died November 13, 1968.

Australian-born Ron Randell (October 8, 1920) was a radio performer before his film debut in *Pacific Adventure* (1946). Alternating with stage and television work, he has been seen in such films as *The Loves of Carmen* (1948), *Kiss Me Kate* (1953), *The Longest Day* (1961), and *Savage Pampas* (1966).

Warren William was most associated with the role of the Lone Wolf. Born Warren William Krech in Aiken, Minnesota, on December 2, 1895, he was the son of a newspaper publisher. Although destined for a journalism career, he instead went to the Academy of Dramatic Arts in New York. His stage debut was in *Mrs. Jimmie Thompson* (1920). He appeared opposite Pearl White in a Pathe-produced serial and by the advent of talking pictures returned to filmmaking full time, starring in *Expensive Women* (1931), *Dark Horse* (1932), *Gold Diggers of 1933* (1933), *Cleopatra* (1934),

and *Imitation of Life* (1934) among others. By 1937, he had slipped to leading supporting player roles as in *The Firefly* (1937), *Arsene Lupin Returns* (1938), *Lillian Russell* (1940), *The Wolf Man* (1941), and *The Private Affairs of Bel Ami* (1947), his last role. William died September 24, 1948, of multiple myeloma, which had curtailed his film career for the previous five years. He was married to Helen Nelson.

. . . *Returns* has dapper Michael Lanyard (Melvyn Douglas) reentering the world of crime by stealing a famous emerald pendant belonging to Marcia Stewart (Gail Patrick), but when he falls in love with her on first sight he returns the jewelry and takes a photo of her instead. However, the crooked team of Morphews (Douglass Dumbrille) and Mollison (Henry Mollison) want the Lone Wolf to assist them with a heist, and plant incriminating evidence about the Lone Wolf to blackmail him into helping. Throughout this light-hearted romance mystery, the poise of the suave Lone Wolf is shown in sharp contrast to the new breed of American thieves.

. . . *In Paris* has Lanyard (Francis Lederer) discovering Princess Thania (Frances Drake) hiding in his Paris bedroom. She is desperately trying to get back from the Grand Duke Gregor (Walter Kingsford) and his cohorts, the crown jewels which her mother had sold to raise money for her homeland. The Grand Duke plans to denounce the Queen Mother (Ruth Robinson) at the coronation ceremony of the young King and then seize the throne. Before the Lone Wolf recovers the jewels and sets the political harmony right again, he and the Princess are kidnapped, and he is almost killed in a knife-throwing gambit. The inept dialogue, unconvincing Ruritanian romance, and the fake atmosphere did little to ingratiate critics or audiences.

. . . *Spy Hunt,* which overflows with screwball comedy, concerns an espionage ring at large in the nation's capital, which kidnaps the Lone Wolf (Warren William) in order to force him to help them steal a secret anti-aircraft plan from the War Department's safe. Involved in the yarn are Val Carson (Ida Lupino), the romantic blonde in Lanyard's life, Karen (Rita Hayworth) as the femme fatale moll, and Patricia (Virginia Weidler) as the Lone Wolf's precocious child—not seen or heard from in future episodes.

. . . *Strikes* has the importuned sleuth solving two murders and clearing up the mystery and theft of a pearl necklace sought by two rival gangland crowds. . . . *Meets a Lady* deals with socialite Joan Bradley (Jean Muir) about to marry again, when her worthless (assumed to be ex) husband Bob Pennion (Warren Hull) turns up and tries to abscond with her $100,000 necklace. Clay Beaudine (Victor Jory) is a pal of Pennion, on hand to stir up trouble. Once again, the Lone Wolf proves he is a slicker who outslicks the crooks, and can cross and doublecross the police when he has to.

. . . *Takes a Chance* gets underway when Lanyard and Jamison are accused of homicide after a private detective is murdered on the fire escape outside their hotel room. With a telegram as a clue, the duo work hard to piece together the facts, which concern the shipment of American currency plates being transported in a burglar-proof carrier invented by Johnny Baker (Lloyd Bridges). When Johnny is kidnapped and trapped in the poison-filled special carrier on a streamlined train, the Lone Wolf jumps into action to save the day.

. . . *Keeps a Date* is set in Miami, where the Lone Wolf and Jamison arrive from Havana. At the airport they rescue Pat Lawrence (Frances Robinson) from two hoodlums, who were after the ransom money she is carrying to bail out millionaire Cyrus Colby. This segment is particularly lacking in pacing and decent performances. *Secrets of* . . . concerns the recent arrival of a steamship with the famed Napoleon gems aboard; the Lone Wolf is asked to prevent a possible robbery. Meanwhile, jewel robbers mistake Jamison for his employer and force the affable servant to assist with their planned theft of the valuables. Lanyard is left to help both his employer and employee and set everything right. The two ladies in the case are Helen de Leon (Ruth Ford), the mysterious beauty aboard the ship, and Bubbles Deegan (Marlo Dwyer), a gun moll.

One Dangerous Night deals with a gangster blackmailing three women and preparing to elope with a fourth. He is shot dead in the presence of the female trio. The Lone Wolf finds the body, is suspected of the murder, and is chased by the police and the gunmen associates of the blackmailer. Improbable clues and an overabundance of incidents detract from the twist finale.

Passport to Suez has the Lone Wolf in Alexandria, Egypt, spying on the Germans for the English in the early part of the African campaign. The plot is set into motion when the Germans tell Lanyard that Jamison will die if he does not steal specified documents from the British Embassy. The subplot focuses on Donald (Robert Stanford), Jamison's son who is in the British navy, and his girl friend Valerie King (Ann Savage) who is a spy, posing as a newspaper reporter. Also intertwined in the case are Johnny Booth (Sheldon Leonard) as an all knowing cafe proprietor, and a trio of secret agents, Rembrandt (Lou Merrill), Cezanne (Jay Novello), and Whistler (Sig Arno).

The Notorious . . . had the then timely touch of Lanyard (Gerald Mohr), after serving in the armed forces during World War II, rejoining Jamison, and promptly becoming implicated in a museum jewel theft. It is on the eve of his reunion with girlfriend Carla Winter (Janis Carter) that he must leave her to clear up the mystery. A small highlight of the film has Lanyard and Jamison disguised as high potentates. While a group of foreign emissaries are being held captive, the dapper Lone Wolf uses glib repartee and polished maneuvering to restore the jewels and tidy up the sordid fragments.

. . . *In London* shows Scotland Yard perturbed by the daring robbery of some world-famous diamonds. Lanyard is immediately suspected but denies all knowledge of the heist. Meanwhile, Sir John Kelmscott (Vernon Steele), famous jewel collector, confides in the Lone Wolf that he urgently needs £10,000 and persuades Lanyard to arrange for the sale of some of his collection. When Kelmscott's butler Robards (Tom Stevenson) is killed, a tie-in to the stolen diamonds becomes apparent, and Lanyard speedily wraps up the loose ends. Concerned in the story are Monty Beresford (Alan Napier), a double-crossing theatrical manager on the lam, and Lily (Queenie Leonard), the maid who knows too much.

. . . *In Mexico* centers on the murder of a croupier of a gambling casino in the south-of-the-border capital, with Lanyard suspected of the foul play. Sharon Montgomery (Sheila Ryan), the wife of a wealthy diamond merchant, is implicated in a jewel robbery and the Lone Wolf is accused of the heist.

. . . *And His Lady* verges on comedy melodrama with Lanyard (Ron Randell) accepting a newspaper assignment to cover the public exhibition of a famous diamond. When the gem disappears, he is accused and has a difficult time staying away from the police long enough to capture the real crooks.

Frances Drake, Lederer. (. . . In Paris)

Leona Maricle, Francis Lederer, Frances Drake. (The Lone Wolf in Paris)

Joan Perry, Alan Baxter, Astrid Allwyn, William. (. . . Strikes)

Jean Muir, Roger Pryor. (. . . Meets a Lady)

Ed Gargan, Eddie Laughton, William, Jed Prouty,
Thurston Hall, Henry Herbert, Don Beddoe, Lester
Matthews. (. . . Keeps a Date)

Marlo Dwyer, John Harmon, Victor Jory, Blore.
(Secrets of . . .)

Ann Savage and Warren William. (Passport to Suez)

Robert Stanford, Ann Savage, Sheldon Leonard, Eric Blore. Kneeling: William, Sig Arno, Staley Price. Body: Jay Novello. (Passport to Suez)

John Abbott, Gerald Mohr, Olaf Hytten. (The Notorious . . .)

Winifred Harris, Jacqueline de Wit, Mohr, Blore.
(. . . in Mexico)

Blore, Alan Napier, Evelyn Ankers, Mohr. (. . . in
London)

Ron Randell, Alan Mowbray. (. . . and His Lady)

THE LONE WOLF RETURNS (Col., 1935) 69 M.

Director, R. William Neill; author, Louis Joseph Vance; screenplay, Joseph Krurngold, Bruce Manning, Robert O'Connell; camera, Henry Freulich; editor, Viola Lawrence.

Michael Lanyard (Lone Wolf)	Melvyn Douglas
Marcia Stewart	Gail Patrick
Liane	Tala Birell
Mollison	Henry Mollison
Crane	Thurston Hall
Jenkins	Raymond Walburn
Morphew	Douglass Dumbrille
Aunt Julie	Nana Bryant
McGowan	Robert Middlemass
Benson	Robert E. O'Connor
Bit Man	Arthur Rankin

THE LONE WOLF IN PARIS (Col., 1938) 66 M.

Director, Albert S. Rogell; author, Louis Joseph Vance; screenplay, Arthur T. Horman; camera, Lucien Ballard.

Michael Lanyard	Francis Lederer
Princess Thania	Frances Drake
Jenkins	Olaf Hytten
Grand Duke Gregor	Walter Kingsford
Baroness Cambrell	Leona Maricle
Marquis de Meyervon	Albert Van Dekker
M. Fromont	Maurice Cass
Davna	Bess Flowers
Queen Regent	Ruth Robinson
King	Pio Peretti
Mace	Eddie Fetherston
Guard	Dick Curtis
Otto	Al Herman

THE LONE WOLF SPY HUNT (Col., 1939) 67 M.

Associate producer, Joseph Sistrom; director, Peter Godfrey; author, Louis Joseph Vance; screenplay, Jonathan Latimer; art director, Lionel Banks; music director, Morris Stoloff; camera, Allen G. Siegler; editor, Otto Meyer.

Michael Lanyard	Warren William
Val Carson	Ida Lupino
Karen	Rita Hayworth
Patricia Lanyard	Virginia Weidler
Gregory	Ralph Morgan
Sergeant Devan	Tom Dugan
Inspector Thomas	Don Beddoe
Jameson	Leonard Carey
Jenks	Ben Welden
Senator Carson	Brandon Tynan
Marie Templeton	Helen Lynd
Sergeant	Irving Bacon
Charlie Fenton (Drunk)	Jack Norton
Heavy Leader # 1	Marc Lawrence
Butler	James Craig

THE [obscured]

Produ[...] thor, Dal[...] Segall, Albe[...] Clark.

Michael Lanyard	
Delia Jordan	
Jamison	
Jim Ryder	
Binnie Weldon	
Emil Garlick	
Ralph Bolton	
Conroy	
Dickens	
Stanley Young	
Phillip Jordan	
Alberts	
Dorgan	
Pete (Bartender)	M[...]
Third Cop	E[...]

THE LONE WOLF MEETS A LADY (Col., 19[...] 71 M.

Producer, Ralph Cohn; director, Sidney Salkow; author, Louis Joseph Vance; screenplay, John Larkin; camera, Henry Freulich; editor, Al Clark.

Michael Lanyard	Warren William
Joan Bradley	Jean Muir
Jamison	Eric Blore
Clay Beaudine	Victor Jory
Pete Rennick	Roger Pryor
Bob Pennion	Warren Hull
Inspector Crane	Thurston Hall
Dickens	Fred A. Kelsey
Peter Van Wyck	Robert E. Keane
Mrs. Pennion	Georgia Caine
Arthur Trent	William Forrest
Rose Waverly	Marla Shelton
McManus	Bruce Bennett
Pappakontus	Luis Alberni

THE LONE WOLF TAKES A CHANCE (Col., 1941) 76 M.

Producer, Ralph Cohn; director, Sidney Salkow; author, Sidney Salkow, Earl Felton; screenplay, Sidney Salkow, Earl Felton; camera, John Stumar; editor, Viola Lawrence.

Michael Lanyard	Warren William
Gloria Foster	June Storey
Frank Jordan	Henry Wilcoxon
Jamison	Eric Blore
Inspector Crane	Thurston Hall
Sheriff Haggerty	Don Beddoe
Evelyn Jordan	Evalyn Knapp
Dickens	Fred Kelsey

230

Vic Hilton
Dr. Hooper Tu[...]
Johnny Baker
Conductor
Brakeman
Wallace
Projectionis[...]
Cop # 1

THE [obscured]
65 [...]

Pro[...]
play[...]
mus[...]

	William Forrest
...man	Walter Kingsford
	Lloyd Bridges
	Ben Taggart
	Richard Fiske
	Regis Toomey
	Irving Bacon
	Tom London

...LONE WOLF KEEPS A DATE (Col., 1941) ...M.

...ducer, Ralph Cohn; director, Sidney Salkow; screen-... Sidney Salkow, Earl Fenton; camera, Barney McGill; ...c director, Morris Stoloff; editor, Richard Fastl.

...ichael Lanyard	Warren William
...atricia Lawrence	Frances Robinson
...cotty	Bruce Bennett
Jamison	Eric Blore
Inspector Crane	Thurston Hall
Captain Moon	Jed Prouty
Dickens	Fred Kelsey
Big Joe Brady	Don Beddoe
Mr. Lee	Lester Matthews
Chimp	Edward Garran
Measles	Eddie Laughton
Mrs. Colby	Mary Servess
Santos	Francis McDonald

SECRETS OF THE LONE WOLF (Col., 1941) 67 M.

Producer, Jack Fier; director, Edward Dmytryk; story-screenplay, Stuart Palmer; music director, Morris Stoloff.

Michael Lanyard	Warren William
Helene de Leon	Ruth Ford
Paul Benoit	Roger Clark
Dapper Dan Streever	Victor Jory
Jamison	Eric Blore
Inspector Crane	Thurston Hall
Dickens	Fred Kelsey
Col. Costals	Victor Kilian
Bubbles Deegan	Marlo Dwyer
Deputy Duval	Lester Scharff
Benjamin Evans	Irving Mitchell
Bernard	John Harmon
Bob Garth	Joe McGunn

ONE DANGEROUS NIGHT (Col., 1943) 77 M.

Producer, David Chatkin; director, Michel Gordon; author, Arnold Phillips, Max Nosseck; screenplay, Donald Davis; art director, Lionel Banks; music director, Morris Stoloff; camera, L. W. O'Connell; editor, Viola Lawrence.

Michael Lanyard	Warren William
Eve Andrews	Marguerite Chapman
Jamison	Eric Blore
Jane Merrick	Mona Barrie
Sonia	Tala Birell
Patricia	Margaret Hayes

Vivian	Ann Savage
Inspector Crane	Thurston Hall
Sidney	Warren Ashe
Dickens	Fred Kelsey
Hertzog	Frank Sully
Mac	Eddie Marr
Harry Cooper	Gerald Mohr
Arthur	Louis Jean Heydt
John Sheldon	Roger Clark
Dr. Eric	Gregory Caye
Drunk	Ed Laughton

PASSPORT TO SUEZ (Col., 1943) 71 M.

Producer, Wallace MacDonald; director, Andre DeToth; screenplay, John Stone; story, Alden Nash; camera, L. W. O'Connell; music director, Morris Stoloff; editor, Mel Thorsen.

Michael Lanyard	Warren William
Valerie King	Ann Savage
Jamison	Eric Blore
Donald Jamison	Robert Stanford
Johnny Booth	Sheldon Leonard
Fritz	Lloyd Bridges
Karl	Gavin Muir
Rembrandt	Lou Merrill
Sir Roger Wembley	Frederic Worlock
Cezanne	Jay Novello
Whistler	Sig Arno
Wembley Man # 2	Frank O'Connor

THE NOTORIOUS LONE WOLF (Col., 1946) 64 M.

Director, D. Ross Lederman; original story; William J. Bowers; screenplay, Martin Berkeley, Edward Dein

Michael Lanyard	Gerald Mohr
Carla Winter	Janis Carter
Jamison	Eric Blore
Lal Bara	John Abbott
Inspector Crane	William Davidson
Stanley	Don Beddoe
Rita Hale	Adelle Roberts
Dick Hale	Robert Scott
Harvey Beaumont	Peter Whitney
Prince of Rapur	Olaf Hytten
Adam Wheelright	Ian Wolfe
Olga	Edith Evanson
Assistant Hotel Manager	Maurice Cass
Jones	Eddie Acuff
Lili	Virginia Hunter

THE LONE WOLF IN LONDON (Col., 1947) 68 M.

Producer, Ted Richmond; director, Leslie Goodwins; author, screenplay, Brenda Weisberg, Arthur E. Orloff; art director, Robert Peterson; music director, Mischa Bakaleinikoff; camera, Henry Freulich; editor, Henry Batista.

Michael Lanyard	Gerald Mohr

Ann Kelmscott .... Nancy Saunders
Jamison .... Eric Blore
Iris Chatham .... Evelyn Ankers
David Woolerton .... Richard Fraser
Lily .... Queenie Leonard
Monty Beresford .... Alan Napier
Garvey .... Denis Green
Inspector Broome .... Frederic Worlock
Henry Robards .... Tom Stevenson
Sir John Kelmscott .... Vernon Steele
Bruce Tang .... Paul Fung
Mitchum .... Guy Kingsford

THE LONE WOLF IN MEXICO (Col., 1947) 69 M.

Producer, Sanford Cummings; director, D. Ross Lederman; author, Louis Joseph Vance; screenplay, Maurice Tombragel, Martin Goldsmith; art director, Charles Clague; music director, Mischa Bakaleinikoff; camera, Allen Siegler; editor, William Lyon.

Michael Lanyard .... Gerald Mohr
Sharon Montgomery .... Sheila Ryan
Liliane Dumont .... Jacqueline de Wit
Jamison .... Eric Blore
Carlos Rodriguez .... Nestor Paiva
Henderson .... John Gallaudet
Leon Dumont .... Bernard Nedell
Mrs. Van Weir .... Winifred Harris
Emil .... Peter Brocco

Charles Montgomery .... Alan Edwards
Captain Mendez .... Fred Godoy
Watchman .... Theodore Gottlieb

THE LONE WOLF AND HIS LADY (Col., 1949) 60 M.

Producer, Rudolph C. Flothow; director, John Hoffman; author, Edward Dein; screenplay, Malcolm Stuart Boylan; art director, Sturges Carue; music director, Mischa Bakaleinikoff; camera, Philip Tannura; editor, James Sweeney.

Michael Lanyard .... Ron Randell
Grace Duffy .... June Vincent
Jamison .... Alan Mowbray
Inspector Crane .... William Frawley
Marta Frishbie .... Collette Lyons
John J. Murdock .... Douglass Dumbrille
Tanner .... James Todd
Van Groot .... Steven Geray
Steve Taylor .... Robert H. Barrat
Fisher .... Arthur Space
Joe Brewster .... Philip Van Zandt
Bill Slovak .... Jack Overman
Sergeant Henderson .... Lee Phelps
Lt. Martin .... Robert H. Williams
Tex Talbot .... Fred Sears
Ava Rockling .... William Newell
Paul Braud .... George Tyne
4th Cop .... Lane Chandler

MA AND PA KETTLE

When Betty MacDonald's bestselling novel *The Egg and I* (1945) was transformed into a Universal Pictures production in 1947 starring Claudette Colbert and Fred MacMurray, the film turned out to be an unexpected goldmine. Besides grossing $5.5 million in United States-Canadian film rentals alone, *The Egg and I* was the springboard for one of the studio's most successful hillbilly series, *Ma and Pa Kettle*.

The Egg and I deals with a city girl who marries a chicken farmer and finds life on the farm more than she bargains for, and almost calls the marriage quits. Marjorie Main and Percy Kilbride were seen to good advantage as a middle-aged married couple, filled with all the vulgar good-natured virtues of plain-living, hard-working country folk. In this well-mounted black and white picture, Main was the frazzled-haired, raspy-voiced swaggering farm wife who maintains a sense of humor despite poverty, 13 kids, and an indolent husband. Her role has been described as that of "a hardboiled egg who hasn't cracked yet," with Kilbride as her hen-pecked husband. *The Egg and I* set the boisterous tone for the forthcoming series.

One of the amazing aspects of the nine black and white *Kettle* films made between 1949–1956, was that each entry cost only between $200,000 and $400,000 to make, and usually grossed about $3 million each, making the top ten earning film list of each year. Most of the series was top-billed on double-feature programs at cinemas. For eight of the nine *Kettle* films, Miss Main was on loan from MGM to Universal, and thus did not share in the wealth her work engendered. Although initially she had turned down the idea of doing a *Kettle*

series (the idea was prompted by the vast fan mail from the Kettles' appearance in *The Egg and I*) MGM told her to do them. In time, she came to say: "I loved that role. I always thought of Ma Kettle as a real person—someone I could drive out into the country and see. . . . Ma Kettle was a grand woman." Miss Main wrote most of her own dialogue, selected her costumes and makeup, and did much to publicize the quickly turned out programmers, all filmed with little fanfare on the studio's backlot.

Marjorie Main was born Mary Tomlinson on February 24, 1890, in Acton, Indiana; her father was a Church of Christ minister. She attended the Hamilton School of Dramatic Expression in Lexington, Kentucky, and after completing its three year course, she went on the Chatauqua lecture circuit giving Shakespearian readings. After playing stock in Fargo, North Dakota she went into vaudeville, and at that time adopted the name of Marjorie Main. One of her frequent co-stars on the Palace Theatre bill in New York was W. C. Fields. In 1921, she married psychologist-lecturer Dr. Stanley L. Krebs and retired from the theatre for three years. She returned to the stage in the late 1920s, appearing in *Burlesque, The Wicked Age,* and others. She made her film debut in Universal's *A House Divided* (1932).

When her husband died in 1935, she found it therapeutic to return to the New York stage, and played Mrs. Martin in Sidney Kingsley's *Dead End*. Main repeated her role in the Samuel Goldwyn film version. Thereafter, she played a host of slum mothers, repeated her stage role in MGM's *The Women* (1939) and signed a seven-year contract with Metro, which was renewed for another seven years at its expiration. She often co-starred with gruff Wallace Beery in such features as *Barnacle Bill* (1941) and *Rationing* (1944) as well as appearing in such musicals as *Meet Me in St. Louis* (1945) and *Summer Stock* (1950). Then came *The Egg and I*, which earned her a nomination for an Academy Award. *Mrs. O'Malley and Mr. Malone* (1950) was MGM's attempt to create a new screen team with Main and James Whitmore, but it failed to duplicate the Main-Beery success. Besides the "Kettle" films in the 1950s, Miss Main appeared in such films as *Rose Marie* (1954), *The Long, Long Trailer* (1954) and *Friendly Persuasion* (1956). Her 82nd and final film to date is ... *On Old MacDonald's Farm* (1957). Miss Main has no children; she has three homes: Los Angeles, Palm Springs, and Idyllwild.

In *Ma and Pa Kettle*, Miss Main's co-star for seven of the films was veteran character actor Percy Kilbride. He bowed out of the series after ... *At Waikiki* (he died December 11, 1964) forcing Universal to seek a new replacement. The previous year, the studio had teamed Main and Chill Wills in *Ricochet Romance* which created no screen magic, so ... *In the Ozarks* found Main soloing; in the final entry ... *On Old MacDonald's Farm* Parker Fennelly (noted in recent years for Pepperidge Farm bread television commercials) essayed the Pa Kettle role, but the chemistry was wrong; and the *Kettle* films had run their course. With the novelty worn off the property, and television's competition curtailing the making of programmer's, Universal dropped the Kettle. Only the dwindling rural cinema audiences seemed to mind, and not strongly enough to cause the studio to revive the rambunctious pair.

Supporting Main and Kilbride in the series were Richard Long as Tom, their eldest son; Meg Randall as Tom's wife, Kim; Ray Collins and Barbara Brown as the snobbish Parkers, the Bostonian in-laws; Lori Nelson as daughter Rosie; and Brett Halsey as son Elwin. Other eccentric characters populating the locale around the Kettle ranch were Indians Crowbar (played by Vic Potel, Chief Yowlachie, Teddy Hart, Zachary Charles), Geoduck (John Berkes, Lester Allen, or Oliver Blake), and busybody neighbor Mrs. Hicks (Esther Dale).

In *Ma and Pa Kettle,* Mr. Kettle wins a national contest, is given a modern house to occupy, and later has to prove his innocence on a phony charge of cheating. ... *Go to Town* has the befuddled country couple loose in Manhattan (having won a letter-writing contest) and being pursued by bank robbers whose loot the Kettles are accidentally in possession of—there is a mild, wild finale at a square dance. ... *Back on the Farm* has the Kettles unwillingly welcoming their rich and disapproving Boston in-laws for a visit, with the latter planning to take the Kettles' grandson with them back to Massachusetts for a proper upbringing. Tied up with this is a subplot involving a mistaken belief that there is uranium on the Kettles' property. ... *At the Fair* revolves around Ma's hopes of winning prize money at the fair to send daughter Rosie to college. With her half of the projected prize money, Pa buys a horse, forcing the Kettles to become participants in the horse racing sweepstakes.

... *On Vacation* sees the Kettles on a Parisian trip, where they become entangled with an international spy ring. They agree to help American authorities expose the gang. One sequence in this film has Ma tangling with Apache dancers, allowing for a slight change from the usual Kettle formula of rural slapstick. ... *At Home* focuses on the farm couple returning to their old homestead with their brood, trying to spruce up the run-down place, so eldest son Elwin may win a scholarship to the state agricultural college. ... *At Waikiki* has the couple traveling to Hawaii, where Pa is asked to take over the management of a fruit processing plant when his cousin has a heart attack. Business rivals kidnap Pa, and resourceful Ma must come to the rescue. The Kettles' typical social *faux pas* provide much of the comic results for their Island romp.

... *In the Ozarks* finds Ma off to visit her lazy brother-in-law Sedge (Arthur Hunnicutt) on his Ozark farm. Ma busies herself with engineering his marriage to his fiancee of twenty years, Bedelia Baines (Una Merkel), and brings to justice three local bootleggers who have set up illegal stills in Sedge's barn.

... *On Old MacDonald's Farm* concerns Ma and Pa's efforts to help Sally Flemming (Gloria Talbot), the debutante daughter of a rich acquaintance, to live on their old farm with her fiancee, Brad Johnson (John Smith)—the Kettles being the ever present chaperones for this experiment in roughing-it living. Before lethargic Pa can undo his misplaced helpful efforts, the young couple are inadvertently caught up in a logging company scheme and all the hassle of the annual lumberman's rodeo.

In retrospect, the *Kettle* films relied largely on the dynamic personality of Marjorie Main, countered by the easy going manner of Percy Kilbride, to carry the series' vehicles. With run of the mill scripts, lacklustre settings, and only an occasional sparkling guest performer (such as the arrogant blustering of Alan Mowbray as Mannering in . . . *At Home*), there was little distraction from the basic premise of the hick farm couple caught up in the modern, sophisticated world. That rural adult audiences and matinee-going children would accept *Ma and Pa Kettle* films was a sociological quirk of post-World War II America, when viewer innocence still existed in the theatrical film market (today such farmyard, bucolic comedy is seen on television with *The Beverly Hillbillies, Green Acres* and *Petticoat Junction*).

Marjorie Main, Claudette Colbert. (The Egg and I)

Marjorie Main, Fred MacMurray, Claudette Colbert.
(The Egg and I)

Marjorie Main. (Ma and Pa Kettle)

Collins, Marjorie Main, Kilbride. (. . . Back on the Farm)

Marjorie Main in publicity pose.

Kilbride, Emory Parnell. (. . . at the Fair)

Percy Kilbride, Marjorie Main, Barbara Brown,
Major Sam Harris, Ray Collins. (. . . On Vacation)

Kilbride and Marjorie Main. (. . . at Waikiki)

Marjorie Main and Arthur Hunnicutt. (The Kettles in the Ozarks)

Parker Fennelly and Marjorie Main. (The Kettles on Old MacDonald's Farm)

MA and PA KETTLE

THE EGG AND I (Univ., 1947) 108 M.

Producer-director, Chester Erskine; screenplay, Chester Erskine, Fred Finklehoff; music director, Frank Skinner; camera, Milton Krasner; editor, Russell Schoengarth.

Betty MacDonald	Claudette Colbert
Bob MacDonald	Fred MacMurray
Ma Kettle	Marjorie Main
Harriet Putnam	Louise Allbritton
Pa Kettle	Percy Kilbride
Tom Kettle	Richard Long
Billy Reed	Billy House
Old Lady	Ida Moore
Mr. Henty	Donald MacBride
Sheriff	Samuel S. Hinds
Mrs. Hicks	Esther Dale
Betty's Mother	Elisabeth Risdon
Geoduck	John Berkes
Crowbar	Vic Potel
Cab Driver	Fuzzy Knight

MA AND PA KETTLE (Univ., 1949) 75 M.

Producer, Leonard Goldstein; director, Charles Lamont; screenplay, Herbert Margolis, Louis Morheim, Al Lewis; music, Milton Schwarzwald; art director, Bernard Herzbrun, Emrich Nicholson; camera, Maury Gertsman; editor, Russell Schoengarth.

Ma Kettle	Marjorie Main
Pa Kettle	Percy Kilbride
Tom Kettle	Richard Long
Kim Parker	Meg Randall
Secretary	Patricia Alphin
Mrs. Birdie Hicks	Esther Dale
Mr. Tomkins	Barry Kelley
Mayor Swiggins	Harry Antrim
Mrs. Hicks' Mother	Isabel O'Madigan
Emily	Ida Moore
Billy Reed	Emory Parnell
Mr. Simpson	Boyd Davis
Mr. Billings	O. Z. Whitehead
Sam Rogers	Ray Bennett
Alvin	Alvin Hammer
Geoduck	Lester Allen
Crowbar	Chief Yowlachie

MA AND PA KETTLE GO TO TOWN (Univ., 1950) 79 M.

Producer, Leonard Goldstein; director, Charles Lamont; author-screenplay, Martin Ragaway, Leonard Stern; art director, Bernard Herzbrun, Charles Van Enger; music director, Milton Schwarzwald; editor, Russell Schoengarth.

Ma Kettle	Marjorie Main
Pa Kettle	Percy Kilbride
Tom Kettle	Richard Long
Kim Kettle	Meg Randall
Jonathan Parker	Ray Collins
Elizabeth Parker	Barbara Brown
Birdie Hicks	Esther Dale
Emily	Ellen Corby
Crowbar	Teddy Hart
Billy Reed	Emory Parnell
Geoduck	Oliver Blake
Manson	Peter Leeds
Burley	Jerry Hausner
Danny Kettle	Dale Belding
Benjamin Kettle	Teddy Infuhr

MA AND PA KETTLE BACK ON THE FARM (Univ., 1951) 81 M.

Producer, Leonard Goldstein; director, Edward Sedgwick; story-screenplay, Jack Henley; art director, Bernard Herzbrun, Emrich Nicholson; music director, Joseph Gershenson; camera, Charles Van Enger; editor, Russell Schoengarth.

Ma Kettle	Marjorie Main
Pa Kettle	Percy Kilbride
Tom Kettle	Richard Long
Kim Kettle	Meg Randall
Jonathan Parker	Ray Collins
Elizabeth Parker	Barbara Brown
Billy Reed	Emory Parnell
Manson	Peter Leeds
Crowbar	Teddy Hart
Geoduck	Oliver Blake

MA AND PA KETTLE AT THE FAIR (Univ., 1952) 78 M.

Producer, Leonard Goldstein; director, Charles Barton; author, Martin Ragaway, Leonard Stern, Jack Henley; screenplay, Richard Morris, John Grant; art director, Bernard Herzbrun, Eric Orbom; music director, Joseph Gershenson; camera, Charles Van Enger; editor, Ted J. Kent.

Ma Kettle	Marjorie Main
Pa Kettle	Percy Kilbride
Rosie Kettle	Lori Nelson
Marvin Johnson	James Best
Birdie Hicks	Esther Dale
Clem Johnson	Russell Simpson
Billy Reed	Emory Parnell
Geoduck	Oliver Blake
Mrs. Hicks' Mother	Hallene Hill
Medicine Man	James Griffith
Sheriff	Rex Lease
Crowbar	Zachary Charles
Benjamin Kettle	Teddy Infuhr
Willie Kettle	George Arglen
Danny Kettle	Ronald R. Rondell

MA AND PA KETTLE ON VACATION (Univ., 1953) 75 M.

Producer, Leonard Goldstein; director, Charles Barton;

author-screenplay, Jack Henley; art director, Bernard Herzbrun, Robert Boyle; camera, George Robinson; editor, Leonard Weiner.

Ma Kettle	Marjorie Main
Pa Kettle	Percy Kilbride
Jonathan Parker	Ray Collins
Inez Kraft	Bodil Miller
Cyrus Kraft	Sig Ruman
Elizabeth Parker	Barbara Brown
Henri	Ivan Triesault
Geoduck	Oliver Blake
Crowbar	Teddy Hart
Mr. Wade	Peter Brocco
Andre	Jay Novello
Chef Chantilly	Jean De Briac
Farrell	Larry Dobkin
Harriman	Harold Goodwin
Jacques	Jack Kruschen
Soubrette	Rita Moreno

MA AND PA KETTLE AT HOME (Univ., 1954) 81 M.

Producer, Richard Wilson; director, Charles Barton; author-screenplay, Kay Lenard; art director, Bernard Herzbrun, Robert Boyle; camera, Carl Guthrie; editor, Leonard Weiner.

Ma Kettle	Marjorie Main
Pa Kettle	Percy Kilbride
Mannering	Alan Mowbray
Pete Crosby	Ross Elliott
Sally Maddocks	Alice Kelley
Elwin Kettle	Brett Halsey
Miss Wetter	Mary Wickes
Mr. Maddocks	Irving Bacon
Billy Reed	Emory Parnell
Mrs. Maddocks	Virginia Brissac
Crowbar	Stan Ross
Geoduck	Oliver Blake
Jones	Guy Wilkerson
Jefferson	Edmund Cobb
Danny Kettle	Tony Epper

MA AND PA KETTLE AT WAIKIKI (Univ., 1955) 79 M.

Producer, Leonard Goldstein; director, Lee Sholem; screenplay, Harry Clark, Elwood Ullman; art director, Bernard Herzbrun, Eric Orbom; camera, Cliff Stine; editor, Leonard Weiner.

Ma Kettle	Marjorie Main
Pa Kettle	Percy Kilbride
Rosie Kettle	Lori Nelson
Bob Baxter	Byron Palmer
Rodney Kettle	Loring Smith

Robert Coates	Lowell Gilmore
Mrs. Andrews	Mabel Albertson
Fulton Andrews	Fay Roope
Geoduck	Oliver Blake
Crowbar	Teddy Hart
Birdie Hicks	Esther Dale
Eddie Nelson	Russell Johnson
Marty	Myron Healey
Chuck Collins	Rick Roman

THE KETTLES IN THE OZARKS (Univ., 1956) 81 M.

Producer, Richard Wilson; director, Charles Lamont; author-screenplay, Kay Lenard; art director, Alexander Golitzen, Alfred Sweeney; music director, Joseph Gerschenson; camera, George Robinson; editor, Edward Curtiss.

Ma Kettle	Marjorie Main
Professor	Ted de Corsia
Sedge Kettle	Arthur Hunnicutt
Miss Bedelia Baines	Una Merkel
Billy	Richard Eyer
Conductor	David O'Brien
Bancroft Baines	Joe Sawyer
Cod Head	Richard Deacon
Benny	Sid Tomack
Small Fry	Pat Goldin
Joe	Harry Hines
Jack Dexter	Jim Hayward
Nancy	Olive Sturgess
Freddie	George Arglen
Sammy	Eddie Pagett
Man	Roscoe Ates

THE KETTLES ON OLD MACDONALD'S FARM (Univ., 1957) 81 M.

Producer, Howard Christie; director, Virgil Vogel; screenplay, William Raynor, Herbert Margolis; art director, Alexander Golitzen, Philip Barber; music director, Joseph Gershenson; camera, Alfred E. Arling; editor, Edward Curtiss.

Ma Kettle	Marjorie Main
Pa Kettle	Parker Fennelly
Sally Flemming	Gloria Talbott
Brad Johnson	John Smith
George	George Dunn
Pete Logan	Claude Akins
J. P. Flemming	Roy Barcroft
Bertha	Pat Morrow
Henry	George Arglen
Elmer	Ricky Kelman
Abner	Donald Baker
Agnes Logan	Polly Burson

MAISIE

In 1939, MGM released *Maisie,* a respectable B film in black and white based on Wilson Collison's novel *Dark Dame* (1935). It starred blonde Ann Sothern as a brassy showgirl from Brooklyn who wins her battles with a flashy smile and a quick wit. Mounted in typical glossy Metro style, the pleasant but unambitious film received extensive audience and exhibitor approval, and harkened the beginning of another film series that was to last through eight additional entries before its finale in 1946. The *Maisie* films used a battery of MGM leading men and competent players who formed the background for the vivacious personality of its lovely star, whose fine sense of comedy matched her ability to wring pathos from the most nondescript stock situation. On radio, "honky-tonk Maisie with a heart of spun sugar" was heard on CBS (1945–47) and on MGM stations (1949–52) with Miss Sothern in the lead role. A projected television series based on *Maisie,* with Ann Sothern, was slated for the mid-1950s, but never materialized.

Ann Sothern (nee Harriette Lake) was born in Valley City, North Dakota, January 22, 1909, the eldest of three daughters; her mother was a concert singer. After schooling in Waterloo, Iowa, and Minneapolis, she won several awards for musical composition. She started at the University of Washington, but left to join her mother in Hollywood, where the latter taught singing and diction. After unsuccessful term contracts at Christie Comedies and MGM, she obtained roles in such Broadway musicals as *Smiles* (1930), *America's Sweetheart* (1931), and *Everybody's Welcome* (1931). Miss Sothern gained popular acclaim in a touring version of *Of Thee I Sing* and returned to Hollywood

with a Columbia Pictures contract. Among her films as a singing ingenue were *Let's Fall in Love* (1934), *Hooray for Love* (1935). Her first typical brash role was as a secretary in *Trade Winds* (1938). Besides the *Maisie* films, she sang in *Panama Hattie* (1942) and *April Showers* (1948), had dramatic roles in *Cry Havoc* (1943) and *The Blue Gardenia* (1953) and showed her comic flair in *Lady Be Good* (1941) and *Nancy Goes to Reno* (1950). Recurrent bouts of hepatitis interrupted her career in the 1940s and early 1950s. She debuted in her television series *Private Secretary* in 1953, and in *The Ann Sothern Show* in 1958. Since then, she has made occasional television and film appearances, in strong character roles such as *Lady in a Cage* (1964), *Sylvia* (1965), and *Chubasco* (1968). She married band leader-actor Roger Pryor (1936), divorced him in 1942, married actor Robert Sterling (1943), and they were divorced in 1949. Their daughter Tisha is now an actress.

All the *Maisie* films began with the established situation of luckless Maisie, a not so successful chorine, losing her job and being stranded, forced to fend for herself. Most of the entries gave saucy, scatterbrained Maisie the chance to sing a song, before coming into conflict and eventual harmony with the film's hero.

In *Maisie,* optimistic Maisie Ravier is a small time actress who lands in a tank town in Wyoming with a job in view, only to discover that her prospects have vanished. She accepts a job in the shooting gallery at the local rodeo. Ranch manager Slim Martin (Robert Young) accuses Maisie of stealing his wallet, and she is hauled off to jail, where she proves her innocence. Stowing away in Martin's car, she goes to Martin's ranch where she wangles a post as personal maid to the owner's wife. When the owner kills himself because of his wife's many infidelities, he leaves the ranch to good-natured, helpful Maisie.

Congo . . . (a loose remake of *Red Dust* [1932] which later became *Mogambo* [1953]) has the South Brooklyn performer stranded in Africa near Kamada. She stows away on a river boat where she meets Doctor Michael Shane (John Carroll) who has given up medicine to become a rubber planter. They go ashore at the medical station, run by Doctor McWade (Sheppard Strudwick) and his wife Kay (Rita Johnson). Maisie helps to patch up their shaky marriage, Shane operates on McWade's inflamed appendicitis, and Maisie later saves the day by quelling a native uprising with her demonstration of magic tricks, an art she acquired as a magician's stooge on the vaudeville circuit.

Gold Rush . . . finds her again an out-of-work singer-dancer, who ends up in a broken-down car at the edge of a derelict mining camp. Joining up with a poverty-stricken family living there, they all set out on a gold rush. They find no gold, but win over the surly, bad-tempered local rancher (Lee Bowman) who offers the family land to farm on a cooperative basis.

In . . . *Was a Lady* Bob Bigelow (Lew Ayres), celebrating at the Fun Fair amusement show, causes Maisie (playing in the Headless Woman Sideshow) to lose her job. To make amends, Bigelow arranges for her to become the personal maid to his sister Abby (Maureen O'Sullivan). Abby takes a near-fatal dose of poison when her engagement is called off, and it is for Maisie to instill in the girl's brother and father a new sense of proper family life. Maisie leaves the Bigelow home, but is wooed back by Bob. Once again, Maisie who is far from being a blue-blood, proves she has her own dignity. An interesting contrast is offered between brash Maisie and the Bigelow's proper old English butler Walpole (C. Aubrey Smith).

Ringside . . . revolves around Maisie's wandering into a prizefighting camp, located in the mountains outside of New York City. Maisie at first falls in love with the on-the-rise boxer Terry Dolan (Robert Sterling) but later discovers she really cares for the fight manager Skeets Maguire (George Murphy). In the course of the maudlin story, Dolan is temporarily blinded in a fight, and only an emergency operation saves his eyesight. One of the more sprited moments in the film has

Maisie Lindy-hopping as the hostess in a taxi dance hall.

. . . *Gets Her Man* shows the chorine as the target in a knife thrower's act. When he gets furious with his unfaithful wife and takes his aggressions out on Maisie, she deserts the show, and is stranded in Chicago. She takes a job in a theatrical office building, where she encounters Hap Hixby (Red Skelton). She and the hick ex-druggist form a stage act, which proves an artistic bust. Later, Hap becomes innocently entangled with a con artist, and it is his girlfriend Maisie who saves the day. Maisie and Hap go their separate ways; later when she is touring with a USO camp show, she meets Hap, now a member of the Army.

Swing Shift . . . finds the Brooklyn performer suddenly at liberty from her touring dog act, so she takes a job at an airplane factory. Donned in overalls and still filled with her Good Samaritan ways, she becomes the hit of the plant. Out of misplaced altruism, she introduces Iris Reed (Jean Rogers), a new girl at the factory, to her flyer-boyfriend Breezy McLaughlin (James Craig). Not only does the two-timing Iris steal Maisie's boyfriend—temporarily—but she accuses Maisie of trying to sabotage the plant.

In . . . *Goes to Reno* the "hep" Irish gal decides to spend a two-week vacation from the riveting job at the plant by taking a trip to Reno, where she has a singing engagement. Before departing for the west, Maisie promises soldier Bill Fullerton (Tom Drake) that she will try to intervene and keep his wife Gloria (Ava Gardner) from divorcing him. Maisie discovers that wealthy Gloria is being hoodwinked by her unscrupulous business manager Pelham (Paul Cavanagh) and his dishonest social secretary Winifred Ashbourne (Marta Linden). Maisie nearly ruins her romance with casino employee Flip Hannahan (John Hodiak) and almost ends up in the lunatic asylum before she restores order to the situation. Maisie gets to sing "Panhandle Pete" and "This Little Bond Went To Battle" in the course of the madcap production.

Up Goes . . . reflects the post-World War II flavor of America. Maisie is seeking a new type position, so she dons horn-rimmed glasses and a prudish hat, to get a secretarial position with helicopter inventor Joseph Morton (George Murphy). She discovers that he is being victimized by his own financial backer who wants to fleece him of his unpatented invention. Maisie comes to the rescue again, this time piloting the helicopter away from rival plane manufacturers who have stolen the experimental aircraft.

Besides displaying Ann Sothern's fine acting talents, the *Maisie* series offers an interesting study of the changing role of the American woman between 1939–46, during which time the war changed social values. While critics constantly berated MGM for wasting Miss Sothern's abilities in a series that became increasingly formula-laden, audiences were generally delighted with her portrayal of an emancipated gal who took no nonsense from men, and who could stand on her own feet in any given situation. That the production values of the series were low-budgeted, and certainly non-innovative, bothered few viewers. And exhibitors were pleased to have a non-controversial entry to utilize on their double-bill program, a forgettable but entertaining product.

Rita Johnson, Ann Sothern. (Congo . . .)

John Hubbard, Marty Faust, Ann Sothern. (Maisie)

John Carroll, Ann Sothern. (Congo Maisie)

Virginia Weidler, Baby Quintanilla, Ann Sothern, Mary Nash. (Gold Rush . . .)

Ann Sothern. (. . . Was a Lady)

Ann Sothern, Maureen O'Sullivan. (. . . Was a Lady)

Ann Sothern, Robert Sterling. (Ringside . . .)

Red Skelton, Ann Sothern. (. . . Gets Her Man)

Dick Rich, Ann Sothern, Tom Drake. (. . . Goes to Reno)

George Murphy, Ann Sothern, Stephen McNally. (Up Goes . . .)

MAISIE

MAISIE (MGM, 1939) 74 M.

Producer, J. Walter Ruben; director, Edwin L. Marin; author, Wilson Collinson; screenplay, Mary C. McCall, Jr.; art director, Cedric Gibbons; camera, Leonard Smith, editor, Frederick Y. Smith.

Slim Martin	Robert Young
Maisie Ravier	Ann Sothern
Clifford Ames	Ian Hunter
Sybil Ames	Ruth Hussey
Dick Raymond	Anthony Allan
Shorty	Cliff Edwards
Rico	George Tobias
Roger Bannerman	Richard Carle
Prosecuting Attorney	Minor Watson
Sheriff	Harlan Briggs
Judge	Paul Everton
Wilcox	Joseph Crehan
Red	Art Mix

CONGO MAISIE (MGM, 1940) 70 M.

Producer, J. Walter Ruben; director, Henry Potter; author, Wilson Collison; screenplay, Mary C. McCall, Jr.; camera, Charles Lawton; art director, Cedric Gibbons; music, Edward Ward; editor, Frederick Y. Smith.

Maisie Ravier	Ann Sothern
Michael Shane	John Carroll
Dr. John McQuade	Shepperd Strudwick
Kay McQuade	Rita Johnson
Captain Finch	J. M. Karrigan
Horace Snell	E. E. Clive
Zia	Martin Wilkins
Varnai	Ernest Whitman
Jallah	Everett Brown
Dr. Farley	Leonard Mudie
Nelson	Tom Fadden

GOLD RUSH MAISIE (MGM, 1940) 82 M.

Producer, J. Walter Ruben; director, Edwin L. Marin; author, Wilson Collinson; screenplay, Betty Reinhardt, Mary C. McCall, Jr.; camera, Charles Lawton; editor, Frederick Y. Smith.

Maisie Ravier	Ann Sothern
Bill Anders	Lee Bowman
Jubie Davis	Virginia Weidler
Bert Davis	John F. Hamilton
Sarah Davis	Mary Nash
Fred Gubbine	Slim Summerville
Harold Davis	Scotty Beckett
Harry	Irving Bacon
Elmo Beecher	Louis Mason
Ned Sullivan	Victor Kilian, Jr.
Matt Sullivan	Wallace Reid, Jr.
Graybeard	Clem Bevans
Drunk	John Sheehan

Greek	Charles Judels
Harry's Wife	Virginia Sale

MAISIE WAS A LADY (MGM, 1941) 79 M.

Producer, J. Walter Ruben; director, Edwin L. Marin; author-screenplay, Betty Reinhardt, Mary C. McCall, Jr.; camera, Charles Lawton; editor, Frederick Y. Smith.

Maisie Ravier	Ann Sothern
Bob Bigelow	Lew Ayres
Abigail Bigelow	Maureen O'Sullivan
Walpole	C. Aubrey Smith
Link Phillips	Edward Ashley
Diana Winters	Joan Perry
"Cap" Bigelow	Paul Cavanagh
Judge	William Wright
Cop	Edgar Dearing
Doctor	Charles D. Brown
Barker	Joe Yule
Guest	Hans Conried
Guest	Hillary Brooke

RINGSIDE MAISIE (MGM, 1941) 96 M.

Producer, J. Walter Ruben; director, Edwin L. Marin; screenplay, Mary McCall, Jr.; camera, Charles Lawton; editor, Frederick Y. Smith.

Maisie Ravier	Ann Sothern
Skeets Maguire	George Murphy
Terry Dolan	Robert Sterling
Cecelia Reardon	Natalie Thompson
Chotsie	Maxie Rosenbloom
Mrs. Dolan	Margaret Moffat
Peaches	John Indrisano
Virginia O'Brien	Virginia O'Brien
Billy-Boy Duffy	Eddie Simms
Rickey DuPrez	Jack LaRue
Dr. Taylor	Purnell Pratt
Day Nurse	May McAvoy
Checker	Tom Dugan

MAISIE GETS HER MAN (MGM, 1942) 86 M.

Producer, J. Walter Ruben; director, Roy Del Ruth; screenplay, Betty Reinhardt, Mary McCall, Jr.; art director, Cedric Gibbons; music, Lennie Hayton; camera, Harry Stradling; editor, Frederick Y. Smith.

Maisie Ravier	Ann Sothern
"Hap" Mitchell	"Red" Skelton
Pappy Goodring	Allen Jenkins
Mr. Stickwell	Donald Meek
Mr. Denningham	Lloyd Corrigan
Orco	Fritz Feld
Jasper	Walter Catlett
Cecil	Leo Gorcey
Louis Tappe	Ben Weldon
"Ears" Kofflin	Rags Ragland
Art	Frank Jenks
Mrs. Taylor	Florence Shirley

250 THE GREAT MOVIE SERIES

Theatre Manager .... Frank Faylen

SWING SHIFT MAISIE (MGM, 1943) 87 M.

Producer, George Haight; director, Norman McLeod; screenplay, Mary McCall, Jr., Robert Halff; music, Lennie Hayton; art director, Cedric Gibbons; camera, Harry Stradling; editor, Elmo Vernon.

Maisie Ravier .... Ann Sothern
Breezy McLaughlin .... James Craig
Iris Reid .... Jean Rogers
Maw Lustvogels .... Connie Gilchrist
Curley .... John Qualen
Judd Evans .... Fred Brady
Emmy Lou Grogan .... Marta Linden
Joe Peterson .... Donald Curtis
Helen Johnson .... Celia Travers
Judge .... Pierre Watkin
Myrtle Lea .... Lillian Yarbo
Schmitt Brothers .... Wiere Brothers
Billie .... Pamela Blake
Grace .... Jacqueline White
Ruth .... Betty Jaynes
Ann .... Kay Medford
Louise .... Katharine Booth
Clerk .... John Hodiak
Lead Woman .... Rose Hobart
Doctor .... Jack Mulhall
Flyer .... William Bishop
Detective .... James Davis

MAISIE GOES TO RENO (MGM, 1944) 90 M.

Producer, George Haight; director, Harry Beaumont; author, Harry Ruby, James O'Hanlon; screenplay, Mary McCall, Jr.; music, David Snell; art director, Cedric Gibbons, Howard Campbell; camera, Robert Planck; editor, Frank E. Hull.

Maisie Ravier .... Ann Sothern
"Flip" Hannahan .... John Hodiak

Bill Fullerton .... Tom Drake
Winifred Ashbourne .... Marta Linden
Pelham .... Paul Cavanagh
Gloria Fullerton .... Ava Gardner
J. E. Clave .... Bernard Nedall
Jerry .... Roland Dupree
Tommy Cutter .... Chick Chandler
Elaine .... Bunny Waters
Parsons .... Donald Meek
Dr. Hanley Fleeson .... James Warren
Master of Ceremonies .... Douglas Morrow
Lead Man .... William Tannen
Clerk .... Edward Earle
Dr. Cummings .... Byron Foulger
Boy .... Leon Tyler
Girl At Party .... Katharine Booth

UP GOES MAISIE (MGM, 1946) 90 M.

Producer, George Haight; director, Harry Beaumont; screenplay, Thelma Robinson; music, David Snell; art director, Cedric Gibbons, Richard Luce; special effects, A. Arnold Gillespie; camera, Robert Planck; editor, Irvine Warburton.

Maisie Ravier .... Ann Sothern
Joseph Morton .... George Murphy
Barbara Nuboult .... Hillary Brooke
Tim Kingby .... Horace McNally
Mr. Hendrickson .... Ray Collins
Elmer Saunders .... Jeff York
Mr. J. G. Nuboult .... Paul Harvey
"Mitch" .... Murray Alper
Bill Stuart .... Lewis Howard
Jonathan Marbey .... Jack Davis
Miss Wolfe .... Gloria Grafton
Benson .... John Eldredge
1st Cop .... Lee Phelps
2nd Cop .... Glen Strange
Business Man .... James Davis

MATT HELM

The mid 1960s saw the fabulous financial success of the Ian Fleming-James Bond novels and films, giving a new twist to the waning tongue-in-cheek format of super spy thrillers. Cashing in on the popularity of the trend were such carbon copy film entries as *The Man From U.N.C.L.E., Our Man Flint, The Spy With the Cold Nose* and *The Third Best Spy in the World.* And then veteran producer Irving Allen rightly saw the potential goldmine in translating Donald Hamilton's series of Matt Helm novels into a new motion picture series, adjusting the demands of the lead role to fit the image of Columbia contract star Dean Martin. Between 1966 and 1968, four highly profitable *Matt Helm* productions were churned out, all glossy in color, filled with pretty girls (including the gimmicky appearance of the Slay Girls), gadgets and gimmicks provided by the special effects department, and enough romantic clinches and unsubtle double entendres to keep the action-hungry audiences contented. If critics carped that the *Matt Helm* films contained blatant improbabilities, gross non-acting, and a camouflage of technological fantasy, viewers seemed unmindful.

Commandeered to portray the successful girlie-photographer-turned-American-agent for ICE (Organization for Intelligence and Counter-Espionage) was Dean Martin, the singing half of the former Martin and Lewis comedy team. Since splitting with Lewis in 1957, Martin has created a tremendously successful solo career as singer-film actor-television performer, with the carefully controlled public image of an easy-going girl-chasing boozer who perpetually gambles (the antithesis of

the real, hard-working Martin). Born June 7, 1917, in Steubenville, Ohio, Dino Paul Crocetti grew up there where his father operated a barber shop. He left high school without graduating, turning to prize fighting for a spell. After less successful tries as a gas station attendant and a blackjack dealer in a gambling house he turned to singing. During a booking in 1946 in Atlantic City, he met comedian Jerry Lewis who was also on the bill. They soon joined together as a team, performing in nightclubs, theaters, and on television. Their film career began with a featured role in Hal Wallis's *My Friend Irma* (1949). Eight years and 16 Paramount boxoffice successes later, the team split apart. Martin renewed his nightclub career and expanded his cinema career with non-singing roles in such films as *The Young Lions* (1958) and *Some Came Running* (1958). Later came such comedies as *Oceans Eleven* (1960), *Kiss Me Stupid* (1964), and *How to Save a Marriage* (1968), westerns like *Sergeants 3* (1968) and *Bandolero!* (1968) and dramatic appearances in *Toys in the Attic* (1963) and *Airport* (1970). Martin has been twice married and has seven children, many of whom have appeared on his weekly television shows and in his films.

The *Matt Helm* movies are all based on the premise that its super-hero, a happy-go-lucky cheesecake photographer, would much rather girl chase that follow up his orders as a reserve member of ICE. ICE's chief, MacDonald (played with ascorbic straightness in the first three productions by James Gregory) would never think of calling on Helm's service, but an unfortuitous reliance on the wisdom of the computer-selector always seems to come up with Helm's name whenever a special agent is required . . . thus putting the plot into gear. In each film, Helm is very reluctant to leave his lush pad (more inventive than a Playboy penthouse, with its push-button bed and poolside bath, and with secretary Lovey Kravezit [Beverly Adams] usually in attendance) . However, some curvacious female involved in the crisis at hand usually falls into Helm's arms, giving him enough incentive to carry on in the name of freedom-fighting.

In *The Silencers,* Tung-Tze (Victor Buono), nominal boss of Big O, is merrily instigating another world war by fomenting plans for a testing mishap involving an American atomic rocket. Helm becomes involved with the gal friend of a Big O agent (Stella Stevens) and works along with confederate Wigman (Arthur O'Connell) . A perennial gag in the series is a gun that fires backward, saving Helm's life on numerous occasions. There are the expected jacket buttons that become hand grenades, car crashes, and an impressive underground headquarters for Big O operations. And for nonchalant fun there are gags about Martin's professional and personal friend Frank Sinatra, and assorted throwaway lines in keeping with the lackadaisical personality of Martin. Besides the flamboyant Slaygirls, each film has an assortment of guest villainesses and victims, such as Sarita (Cyd Charisse) who performs an athletic nightclub dance before being killed in *The Silencers.*

In *Murderers' Row* arch villain Julian Wall (Karl Malden) of the Big O organization has kidnapped Dr. Norman Solaris (Richard Eastham), inventor of the Helio-Beam, a device whcih by harnessing the sun's rays can wreak instant havoc (the villains here want to wipe out Washington, D.C.) . Unknown to Wall, who thinks he has eliminated all of the United States' top secret agents, Helm zooms off to the Riviera to investigate the case. There he meets Suzie (Ann-Margret), Solaris's daughter. Wall, thinking Helm to be a freelance gunman, hires him, leading to the climax at Wall's island fortress. The film contains two lengthy discotheque sequences, allowing Suzie to demonstrate her dancing prowess. Gags herein are variations of those tried out in *The Silencers,* from the delayed-action gun to Helm's continual shaking of his head with a mild "darn it" when things go wrong. An inventive piece of characterization has Ironhead (Tom Reese), a variation of

Oddjob from *Goldfinger,* fitted with a steel plate skullcap, which eventually leads to his magnetic doom.

The Ambushers finds pilot Sheila Sommers (Janice Rule) wandering out of the Mexican jungle in a state of amnesiac shock, after the mysterious disappearance of an experimental flying disc on a special government test flight. Helm's investigations lead him to Acapulco and beer-manufacturer Quintana (Kurt Kasznar) . Helm links up with the enigmatic Francesca Madeiros (Senta Berger) who is after Quintana and the flying disc. After a series of crosses and double-crosses, the climax occurs at co-villain Ortego's (Albert Salmi) jungle hideout. One of the more amusing (if not new) gimmicks of this entry is a man-killing bra, containing miniature pistols.

The Wrecking Crew is set into motion when $1 billion in U.S. gold meant to bolster the British economy is hijacked from a Danish train, and Helm is sent to Denmark to prevent an international economic crisis. His confrere on the caper is Freya Carlson (Sharon Tate), a bungling escort assigned to him by the Danish tourist bureau (she turns out to be a British agent). The villain of the piece is Count Massimo Contini (Nigel Green) who besides having a seemingly impenetrable headquarters, has his own private railroad, leading to a smashing helicopter-train chase and climax. Among the gimmicks of this production are handy incendiary bombs, collapsible helicopters, and sub-basement torture chambers.

The Ravagers was scheduled to get underway as the fifth *Matt Helm* adventure in the fall of 1969, with Sharon Tate as Martin's leading lady. Her grisly murder (August 9, 1969) postponed production and when no suitable replacement could be found and Martin went on to other projects, the *Matt Helm* series was shelved, along with a projected *Matt Helm Meets Tony Rome* (to co-star pal Frank Sinatra) .

Critical reaction to the Helm series never improved, but even in reissue, the quartet of *Matt Helm* films do well. Reviewers objected to the perfunctory acting, the tired wisecracks, the mechanical double entendres, and the improbable gimmicks and gadgets. Stella Stevens was consistently lauded for her sparkle in *The Silencers.* Her presence was sorely missed in the follow-ups, and even a surprisingly effective performance from Sharon Tate in *The Wrecking Crew* could not equal the often-underrated Miss Shevens. Nigel

Green as Count Contini in *The Wrecking Crew* was considered the most overly stereotyped, ultra-sauve villain, while Karl Malden as Julian Wall in *Murderers' Row* was criticized for his uninspired mastermind portrayal, relying on hamming rather than grandiose gestures. Highest praise for each entry went to the lavish set decorations which made even the trite set-ups seem fresher, and the pacing of director Phil Karlson (*The Silencers, Wrecking Crew*) hid many of the series' obvious flaws. As with the *James Bond* series, at the end of each film, the next adventure was announced.

While more location shooting was utilized in the *Matt Helm* series, large studio sets with the integration of process rear projector shots were nevertheless used to give a pseudo international flavor to the proceedings.

Another reason for concluding the Helm series was decreasing box-office revenue and increasing of production cost (*The Silencers* earned $7,350,000 in domestic rentals, while *The Wrecking Crew* earned only $2,400,000—showing that the novelty had worn off the property).

Dean Martin. (The Silencers)

Daliah Lavi, Martin. (The Silencers)

Daliah Lavi, Martin. (The Silencers)

Martin, Stella Stevens. (The Silencers)

"Slay Girls" and Martin. (The Ambushers)

Ann-Margret, Martin. (Murderer's Row)

Martin, Sharon Tate. (The Wrecking Crew)

John Larch, Martin. (The Wrecking Crew)

MATT HELM

THE SILENCERS (Col., 1966) 105 M.

Producer, Irving Allen; director, Phil Karlson; screenplay, Oscar Saul; author, Donald Hamilton; camera, Burnett Guffey; music, Jerry Goldsmith; art director, Joe Wright; editor, Charles Nelson.

Matt Helm	Dean Martin
Big O's Girl	Stella Stevens
Tina	Daliah Lavi
Tung-Tze	Victor Buono
Wigman	Arthur O'Connell
Sam Gunther	Robert Webber
MacDonald	James Gregory
Barbara	Nancy Kovack
Andreyev	Roger C. Carmel
Sarita	Cyd Charisse
Lovey Kravezit	Beverly Adams
Domino	Richard Devon
Dr. Naldi	David Bond
Traynor	John Reach
1st Armed Man	Robert Phillips
M. C.	John Willis
Frazer	Frank Gerstle
Radio Man	Grant Wood

MURDERERS' ROW (Col., 1966) 108 M.

Producer, Irving Allen; director, Henry Levin; author, Donald Hamilton; scenario, Herbert Baker; camera, Sam Leavitt; assistant director, Ray Gosnell; music, Lalo Schifrin; special effects, Danny Lee; editor, Walter Thompson.

Matt Helm	Dean Martin
Suzie	Ann-Margret
Julian Wall	Karl Malden
Coco Duquette	Camilla Sparv
MacDonald	James Gregory
Lovey Kravezit	Beverly Adams
Dr. Norman Solaris	Richard Eastham
Ironhead	Tom Reese
Billy Orcutt	Duke Howard
Singer at Wake	Jacqueline Fontaine
Guard	Ted Hartley

Captain Devereaux	Marcel Hillaire
Miss January	Corinne Cole
Dr. Rogas	Robert Terry
Dino, Desi, Billy	Themselves

THE AMBUSHERS (Col., 1967) 102 M.

Producer, Irving Allen; director, Henry Levin; author, Donald Hamilton; scenario, Herbert Baker; camera, Barnett Guffey, Edward Colman; music-music director, Hugo Montenegro; special effects, Danny Lee; editor, Harold F. Kress.

Matt Helm	Dean Martin
Francesca Madeiros	Senta Berger
Sheila Sommers	Janice Rule
MacDonald	James Gregory
Jose Ortega	Albert Salmi
Quintana	Kurt Kasznar
Lovey Kravezit	Beverly Adams
Nassim	David Mauro
Karl	Roy Jenson
Rocco	John Brascia
Linda	Linda Foster

THE WRECKING CREW (Col., 1968) 105 M.

Producer, Irving Allen; director, Phil Karlson; author, Donald Hamilton; scenario, William McGivern; camera, Sam Leavitt; assistant director, Jerome Siegel; music-music director, Hugo Montenegro; set decorator, Frank Tuttle; editor, Maury Winetrobe.

Matt Helm	Dean Martin
Linka Karensky	Elke Sommer
Freya Carlson	Sharon Tate
Yu-Rang	Nancy Kwan
Count Massimo Contini	Nigel Green
Lola Medina	Tina Louise
McDonald	John Larch
Karl	John Brascia
Kim	Weaver Levy
Gregor	Wilhelm Von Homburg
Ching	Bill Saito
Toki	Fuji
Frankie	Pepper Martin

MR. MOTO

Having found a successful formula with its oriental detective series *Charlie Chan,* Twentieth Century-Fox activated a new low-budget series in 1937, based on John P. Marquand's novels about the ubiquitous Far Eastern master sleuth, *Mr. Moto.* Within a period of two years, Fox produced eight popular black and white assembly line programmers starring Peter Lorre in the title role. Then with Lorre busy elsewhere and the building pre-World War II tensions of East versus West, the property lay dormant for 26 years. In 1965, Warner Bros. reactivated the Marquand creation in a dehydrated version to cash in on the *James Bond* super secret agent cycle. Their interest lasted for one labored entry with Caucasian Henry Silva as the not so quizzical Moto.

It is said that Hungarian-born actor Peter Lorre utilized little more than a pair of spectacles to capture the essence of the undersized almost insignificant looking Japanese detective. The enigmatic Mr. Moto was characterized in the series as an extremely perceptive gentleman, posing as the mildest, soft spoken and most inoffensive of Orientals. In the atmospheric Fox productions, Moto is always seen melting into the busy background, soaking up needed information from those around him. In contrast to the expressive faces on the other characters, Moto wore an imperturbable blank mask. With his background and motivation a mystery, Moto's personality magically acquired a suspenseful, unreal air. Once having sorted out the clues in the case and deduced the conclusions, the quick thinking Moto was fast to act. With his expertise at ju-jitsu and his ability to handle a gun, he was always well prepared to meet any enemy's challenge and always ended victorious in his confrontations. That his "crimes" are always in the interest of law and order, made him a hero rather than a villain. As with Charlie Chan, Moto in the films found little time for romancing the gallery of women that pass through his active life.

Peter Lorre was born June 26, 1904, in Rosenberg, Hungary. The family moved to Vienna in 1910, where Lorre grew up. In 1921, Lorre left home to explore a career in the theatre, living a day to day existence. In 1924, he joined a small stock company in Breslau, later going to Zurich and then back to Vienna to perform in shows. He eventually was hired by the *Volksbuehne,* the People's Theatre in Berlin. He made his film debut in 1930 in Fritz Lang's *M,* a German-made masterpiece about a child-killing psychopath. Then followed a series of films for Ufa Studios. Due to the Nazi upsurge, Lorre left Berlin for Austria and then moved on to Paris. He wangled the role of the anarchist in Alfred Hitchcock's *The Man Who Knew Too Much* (1934), which led to his going to Hollywood. *Mad Love* (1935) for MGM was his first American film. After an up-again-down-again cinema career, came the *Mr. Moto* films. In 1940, John Huston fortuitously paired Lorre with Sydney Greenstreet in *The Maltese Falcon* and a new screen team was born. Then followed roles in *Arsenic and Old Lace* (1944), *The Mask of Dimitrios* (1944) (in which he played a good guy), *Three Strangers* (1945), *Quicksand* (1950), *Beat the Devil* (1953), *20,000 Leagues Under the Sea* (1954) and *The Big Circus* (1959). In the 1960s, he appeared in such American International horror spoofs as *Tales of Terror* (1962),

259

The Raven (1963) and *The Comedy of Terrors* (1963). His last film role was a guest appearance in *Muscle Beach Party* (1964). Lorre died of a heart attack on March 23, 1965. He had married Anna Brenning in 1952; they had a child Kathryn.

Think Fast . . . has Moto picking up the trail of a band of diamond smugglers in San Francisco's Chinatown, and following it across the Pacific to Shanghai's underworld. During his investigations, he saves the son of a ship line owner Bob Hitchings (Thomas Beck) who has become involved with the international crime gang. One sequence shows Moto's typical resourcefulness in wearing a bulletproof vest, which saves his life.

Thank You . . . is an elaborate story concerning the sole remaining members of an impoverished Chinese royal family, Madame Chung (Pauline Frederick) and her son, Prince Chung (Philip Ahn). They possess six of the seven scrolls that are the key to the fabulous hidden treasures of Genghis Kahn. Moto comes into ownership of the seventh scroll, which he smuggles into Peiping. Before the gun shooting climax, competing villains Colonel Tchernov (Sig Rumann) and Schneider (William Von Brincken) cause the Chungs to be kidnapped and later tortured to death; Tchernov is knifed in his library, an antique dealer is murdered by machine gun fire, and a legation deputy is found dead on an abandoned junk. Here again, Moto is seen disguised, this time as a Mongolian camel driver sneaking into Peiping.

. . .'s Gamble finds the little detective embroiled in the alleged killing of a boxer by ringmate Bill Steele (Dick Baldwin) when poison is found on Steele's boxing gloves. Moto discovers the crooked maneuverings of a big betting syndicate that led to the fighter's murder. He cagily draws the criminals out by packing an oversized bet on the championship fight. (This vehicle was designed as a *Charlie Chan* film, and when star Warner Oland died during the filming, it was transformed into a *Moto* entry; thus the appearance of Keye Luke as Lee Chan in the story.)

. . . Takes a Chance is set near the ruins of Ankor Wat in the Indo-Chinese jungle, where Moto is employed as a Japanese archaeologist. In reality, he is a spy for his country's secret service, who discovers that the local temple is being utilized to store munitions. Controlling the artillery depot is Boker (George Regas), a fanatical native who wants all whites out of Asia, and promises a bloody day of deliverance. Complicating Moto's investi-

gation are Victoria Mason (Rochelle Hudson), a spy employed by the British Intelligence Force, and her American photographer husband Marty (Robert Kent) and his bumbling cohort Chick (Chick Chandler). A highlight of the film is Moto's inventive disguise as a Tibetan Guru, who employs magic tricks to get native help, just before a large-scale explosion wrecks the arms depot.

Mysterious . . . has the Japanese sleuth tracing the ringleaders of the League of Assassins to London where their chief victim is to be Anton Darvak (Henry Wilcoxon), a man holding an important steel formula. Moto's involvement leads him into a Limehouse brawl, a wild chase through London streets, with the climax occurring at a private showing of a painting exhibition.

In *. . .'s Last Warning*, he foils a plot to blow up the French fleet at the entrance to the Suez Canal, which would disrupt Franco-British diplomatic relations. Moto saves the day after the most sinister happenings occur and several murders take place. Among the colorful characters populating this production are Fabian (Ricardo Cortez) as a suave villain and Port Said Connie (Virginia Field), a girl with a shady past. One gruesome scene details the suffocation of a victim in an abandoned diving bell.

. . . In Danger Island sees Moto being summoned to Puerto Rico (Danger Island) to investigate diamond smuggling there. He feigns an appendicitis attack as a cover to get himself ashore. Dangers are encountered almost hourly: he is dodging death traps, his helper is electrocuted in his place, he penetrates a deadly swamp to uncover the smugglers' hideout, and in the climactic chase in a police speedboat, he emerges victorious. In the well-jumbled plot—which has the benefit of Warren Hymer as Twister McGurk, a well-meaning goon who invites himself to assist Moto on the case—the valuable gems are found to be hidden in coconut shells.

. . . Takes a Vacation concerns the excavation of the priceless Queen of Sheba's crown by a young American archaeologist, Howard Stevens (John King). It is destined for the San Francisco museum, and Moto is on hand, allegedly for a vacation, but in reality to guard the treasure. Moto is sure a supposedly dead notorious jewel thief is alive and will attempt to steal the crown. In the complicated unraveling of the tale, the gem snatcher's identity is well hidden till the finale, since the crook is only shown in a variety of disguises.

Included in the story is a fast-moving rooftop chase and a free-for-all fight on the streets of San Francisco.

In *The Return of . . .* , Moto (Henry Silva) appears as a member of Interpol assigned to protect McAllister (Gordon Tanner), an executive with the Beta Oil Company. McAllister is killed in London by Dargo (Martin Wyldeck), a sadistic ex-Nazi involved in a plot to wean away the Middle East oil concessions from the Shadirdar of Wadi Shamar (Marne Maitland). Before the finish, Moto has trapped and exposed the syndicate involved in the world domination plot. Silva appears as a hip contemporary Moto (without makeup) who only dons the disguise of a Japanese businessman in the latter portion of the film.

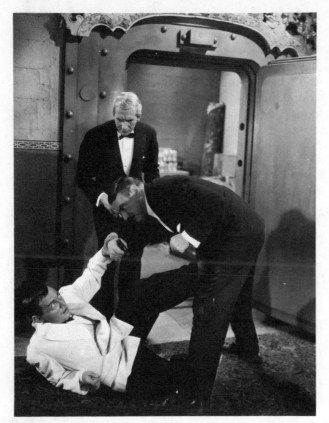

Peter Lorre, Murray Kinnell, Sig Rumann. (Think Fast, Mr. Moto)

Lorre, Keye Luke, Harold Huber. (. . .'s Gamble)

Lorre, John Carradine. (Thank You . . .)

Luke, Harold Huber, Lorre. (. . .'s Gamble)

Lorre, Rochelle Hudson. (. . . Takes a Chance)

Mary Maguire, Lorre. (Mysterious . . .)

Lorre, Paul McVey (with moustache). (Mysterious . . .)

John Carradine, Lorre. (. . .'s Last Warning)

Lorre, Rochelle Hudson. (. . . Takes a Vacation)

Robert Coote, Lorre. (. . .'s Last Warning)

Henry Silva, Terence Longdon. (The Return of . . .)

MR. MOTO

THINK FAST, MR. MOTO (20th, 1937) 66 M.

Producer, Sol M. Wurtzel; director, Norman Foster; author, J. P. Marquand; screenplay, Howard Ellis Smith, Norman Foster; art director, Lewis Creber; music director, Samuel Kaylin; camera, Harry Jackson; editor, Alex Troffey.

Mr. Moto	Peter Lorre
Gloria Danton	Virginia Field
Bob Hitchings	Thomas Beck
Nicholas Marloff	Sig Rumann
Mr. Wilkie	Murray Kinnell
Lela	Lotus Long
Carson	John Rogers
Muggs Blake	George Cooper
Adram	J. Carrol Naish
Mr. Hitchings	George Hassell
Doorman	Dick Alexander

THANK YOU, MR. MOTO (20th, 1937) 66 M.

Producer, Sol M. Wurtzel; director, Norman Foster; author, John P. Marquand; screenplay, Norman Foster, Willis Cooper; camera, Virgil Miller; editor, Irene Morra, Nick DiMaggio.

Mr. Moto	Peter Lorre
Tom Nelson	Thomas Beck
Madam Chung	Pauline Frederick
Eleanor Joyce	Jayne Regan
Eric Koerger	Sidney Blackmer
Colonel Tchernov	Sig Rumann
Pereira	John Carradine
Schneider	William Von Brincken
Madame Tchernov	Nedda Harrigan
Prince Chung	Philip Ahn
Ivan	John Bleifer
Officer	James Leong

MR. MOTO'S GAMBLE (20th, 1938) 71 M.

Producer, Sol M. Wurtzel; director, James Tinling; author, John P. Marquand; screenplay, Charles Belden, Jerry Cady; camera, Lucien Andriot.

Mr. Moto	Peter Lorre
Lee Chan	Keye Luke
Bill Steele	Dick Baldwin
Penny Kandall	Lynn Bari
Nick Crowder	Douglas Fowley
Linda Benton	Jayne Regan
Lieutenant Riggs	Harold Huber
Knock-out Wellington	Maxie Rosenbloom
Philip Benton	John Hamilton
Connors	George E. Stone
Biff Moran	Ward Bond
Joey	Lon Chaney, Jr.
Gangster	Paul Fix

MR. MOTO TAKES A CHANCE (20th, 1938) 63 M.

Producer, Sol M. Wurtzel; director, Norman Foster; author, William Cooper, Norman Foster; screenplay, Lou Breslow, John Patrick; camera, Virgil Miller.

Mr. Moto	Peter Lorre
Vicki	Rochelle Hudson
Marty Weston	Robert Kent
Rajah Ali	J. Edward Bromberg
Chick Davis	Chick Chandler
Boker	George Regas
Zimmerman	Fredrik Vogeding
Yao	Al Kikume
Wife	Gloria Roy
Bit Man	James B. Leong

MYSTERIOUS MR. MOTO (20th, 1938) 62 M.

Producer, Sol Wurtzel; director, Norman Foster; author, John P. Marquard; screenplay, Philip MacDonald, Norman Foster; camera, Lewis Creber.

Mr. Moto	Peter Lorre
Anton Darvak	Henry Wilcoxon
Ann Richman	Mary Maguire
David Scott-Frensham	Erik Rhodes
Ernst Litmar	Harold Huber
Paul Brissac	Leon Ames
George Higgins	Forrester Harvey
Gottfried Brujo	Fredrik Vogeding
Sir Charles Murchison	Lester Matthews
Sniffy	John Rogers
Lotus Liu	Karen Sorrell

MR. MOTO'S LAST WARNING (20th, 1939) 71 M.

Producer, Sol M. Wurtzel; director, Norman Foster; author, John P. Marquand; screenplay, Philip Macdonald, Norman Foster; camera, Virgil Miller; editor, Norman Colbert.

Mr. Moto	Peter Lorre
Fabian	Ricardo Cortez
Connie	Virginia Field
Donforth	John Carradine
Eric Norvel	George Sanders
Mary Delacour	Joan Carol
Rollo	Robert Coote
Madame Delacour	Margaret Irving
Hawkins	Leyland Hodgson
Hakim	John Davidson
Fake Mr. Moto	Teru Shimada
Admiral Delacour	Georges Renavent
Commandant	E. E. Clive
Bentham	Holmes Herbert
First Lord of Admiralty	C. Montague Shaw

MR. MOTO IN DANGER ISLAND (20th, 1939) 69 M.

Producer, John Stone; director, Herbert I. Leeds; author, John P. Marquand, John Vandercook, John Reinhardt,

George Bricker; screenplay, Peter Milne; camera, Lucien Andriot; editor, Harry Reynolds.

Mr. Moto .... Peter Lorre
Sutter .... Jean Hersholt
Joan Castle .... Amanda Duff
Twister McGurk .... Warren Hymer
Commissioner Gordon .... Richard Lane
Commissioner Madero .... Leon Ames
Commander La Costa .... Douglass Dumbrille
Col. Tom Castle .... Charles D. Brown
Gov. John Bentley .... Paul Harvey
Lieut. George Bentley .... Robert Lowery
Petty Officer .... Don Douglas
Wrestler — Sailor Sam .... Ward Bond

MR. MOTO TAKES A VACATION (20th, 1939) 68 M.

Producer, Sol M. Wurtzel; director, Norman Foster; author, John P. Marquand; screenplay, Philip MacDonald, Norman Foster; camera, Charles Clarke; editor, Norman Colbert.

Mr. Moto .... Peter Lorre
Bayard Manderson .... Joseph Schildkraut
Professor Hildebrand .... Lionel Atwill
Eleanor Kirke .... Virginia Field
Howard Stevens .... John King
Susan French .... Iva Stewart
Rollo .... George P. Huntley, Jr.
Paul .... Victor Varconi

Wendling .... John Bleifer
Wong .... Honorable Wu
Perez .... Morgan Wallace
Rubla .... Anthony Warde
O'Hara .... Harry Strang
Prince Suleid .... John Davidson
Colored Driver .... Willie Best

THE RETURN OF MR. MOTO (20th, 1965) 71 M.

Producer, Robert L. Lippert; director, Ernest Morris; scenario, Fred Eggers; camera, Basil Emmott; music, Douglas Gamley; editor, Robert Winter.

Mr. Moto .... Henry Silva
Dargo .... Martin Wyldeck
Jonathan Westering .... Terence Longdon
Maxine Powell .... Suzanne Lloyd
Wasir Hussein .... Marne Maitland
Shahrdar of Wadi .... Harold Kasket
David Lennox .... Henry Gilbert
Magda .... Brian Coburn
Inspector Halliday .... Stanley Morgan
Ginelli .... Peter Zander
Hovath .... Anthony Booth
McAllister .... Gordon Tanner
Chief Inspector Marlow .... Richard Evans
Chapel .... Dennis Holmes
Rogers .... Ian Fleming
Arab .... Tracy Connell
The Belly Dancer .... Sonyia Benjamin
Maitre d'Hotel .... Alister Williamson

PHILO VANCE

Philo Vance is generally considered the classic modern fictional detective; the essence of the aristocratic, stuffy, gentleman private investigator. First introduced to the reading public in *The Benson Murder Mystery* (1926) the learned sleuth was the creation of scholar Willard Huntington Wright (1888–1939), writing under the pseudonym of S. S. Van Dine. Paramount Pictures purchased the film rights to the initial three *Philo Vance* novels and began production in 1929, with William Powell, an ex-heavy, as the suave lead. In 1930, MGM had its *The Bishop Murder Case* with Basil Rathbone in the top part; then after an additional entry and a cameo in *Paramount On Parade*, Vance showed up at Warner Bros. with Powell repeating his polished characterization in *The Kennel Murder Case*. Warren William was Warner's next Philo, and MGM utilized Paul Lukas for *The Casino Murder Case* in 1935, and Edmund Lowe the following year in *The Garden Murder Case*. Back at Paramount, Grant Richards appeared as a more down-to-earth Philo in *Night of Mystery* (1937). Van Dine wrote *The Gracie Allen Murder Case* for the Paramount comedienne with William repeating his detective part. In 1940, Warners had bland James Stephenson in *Calling Philo Vance*. The low budget Producers Releasing Corp. made a trio of *Philo Vance* entries in 1947, the first with William Wright, and the two remaining episodes with Alan Curtis as the much altered gumshoe private investigator. (On radio, Jackson Beck and later Jose Ferrer were heard as Philo Vance, with George Petrie as District Attorney Markham, Humphrey Davis as Sergeant Heath, and Joan Alexander and Frances Farrar as Vance's secretary.)

The premise of the *Philo Vance* stories had Vance, an independently wealthy New Yorker, as an amateur detective. Usually District Attorney John F. X. Margham (played to pragmatic perfection in the early films by E. H. Calvert) would call Vance into the case, forcing the detective to work along with—often leading by the nose—burly affable but dumb Sergeant Heath (Eugene Pallette). Also around was matter-of-fact Dr. Emanuel Doremus (Etienne Girardot usually), a most prosaic police coroner.

The Canary Murder Case—filmed in both silent and sound versions—has Broadway performer Margaret Odell (Louise Brooks) strangled, which leads to the demise of petty burglar Tony Skeel (Ned Sparks). Vance utilizes a card game as the focal point upon which to sort out the suspects and solve the case. Jimmie Spotswoode (James Hall) and Alice LaFosse (Jean Arthur) appeared as the love interest, with Dr. Ambrose Lindquist (Gustav Von Seyffertitz) as a leading suspect. This production, slow moving by today's standards, is noteworthy for its élan and first-rate production values.

The Greene Murder Case is situated at the palatial Greene Mansion, overlooking the Manhattan side of the East River. With Mrs. Tobias Greene (Gertrude Norman) as the parsimonious matriarch of a grasping wealthy family, the greedy relatives include Sibella Greene (Florence Eldredge), Ada Greene (Jean Arthur), Chester Greene (Lowell Drew), Rex Greene (Morgan Farley). Among the gimmicks effectively used were mysterious foot tracks, a disappearing revolver, a fatal plunge over the roof garden into the icy water, a locked room, and ever present lurking shadows.

The Bishop Murder Case pitted Vance (Rathbone) against a berserk killer known as The Bishop, who ingeniously maneuvered his murders to follow Mother Goose rhymes. Tied into the case are elderly Mrs. Drukker (Zelda Sears), the terrified heroine Belle Dillard (Leila Hyams), the hunchbacked cripple Adolph Drukker (George Marion). The potent production had most inventive camerawork which subjectively followed the creative excursions of the Bishop on his homicide sprees.

The Benson Murder Case is set in a plush hunting lodge on a stormy night. When Anthony Benson (Richard Tucker) falls down a flight of stairs, shot through the heart, the adventure is underway with Vance (Powell) applying his most skilled deductive methods to ferret out which one of the suspects gathered at the country house is the culprit. Among the most colorful people involved are: gigolo Adolph Mohler (Paul Lukas) and as the self-sufficient mistress Fanny Del Roy (Natalie Moorhead).

In *Paramount on Parade*, an all-star variety film, there is a sketch with Vance (Powell) emerging from an Egyptian sarcophagus into a bizarre setting, where he and Sherlock Holmes (Clive Brook) are shot to death by Dr. Fu Manchu (Warner Oland). An amazed Sergeant Heath (Eugene Pallette) looks on in amazement as Fu Manchu flies away.

The Kennel Murder Case is situated at the blue nose Long Island Kennel Club on a rainy night; a murdered dog in an alleyway sets off the action. Later the dog's killer, Archer Coe (Robert Barrat), is found bludgeoned and shot in his room, his dead brother Brisbane (Frank Conroy) stuffed into a closet, and Sir Thomas MacDonald (Paul Cavanaugh) lying dead with a knife in his back. An unusual aspect of the crime solving had an elaborate flashback narrated by Vance. Hilda Lake (Mary Astor) was a particularly effective heroine, and there were such newcomers to the series as Robert McWade as Markham, Spencer Charters as homicide detective Snitkin, and Charles Wilson as Detective Hennessey. Etienne Girardot was his usual antiseptic self as the coroner, Dr. Doremus, and Henry O'Neill was on hand as Captain Dubois of the fingerprint department.

The Dragon Murder Case centers on a party at the Stamm estate, a household ruled over by deranged elderly Matilda Stamm (Helen Lowell), who believes a legendary dragon has caused the strange disappearance of Montague Stamm (George Meeker) from the swimming pool. The expansive mansion setting and the murky pool locale combined with the artistic camera work to build the necessary tension, distracting from the leisurely paced story. McWade, Pallette, Girardot repeated their policemen roles.

The Casino Murder Case found scholarly Vance (Paul Lukas) pushed into the sphere of an eccentric household via an anonymous letter. Of course, there are unexplained deaths stalking the Llewellyn premises. Vance romances secretary Doris Reed (Rosalind Russell), with his valet Currie (Eric Blore) supplying comic relief. Scientific testing played a prominent part in determining the manner of one victim's strange death. Alison Skipworth was most effective as the overbearing Mrs. Llewellyn.

In *The Garden Murder Case* Vance (Edmund Lowe) must solve the murders of Floyd Garden (Douglas Walton), killed when he plunges from his horse during a steeplechase; Lowe Hammle (Gene Lockhart), shot to death; and Mrs. Fenwicke-Ralston (Frieda Inescort), pushed from a double decker bus. Philo is surrounded by Grant Mitchell as Markham, Nat Pendleton as Heath, and Girardot as Dr. Doremus.

Night of Mystery was a weak remake of *The Greene Murder Case* with Grant Richards as Vance and Roscoe Karns in the pivotal role as Heath, and Purnell Pratt as Markham and Barlowe Borland as the medical examiner. The inexpensive programmer lacked the flavor or rationale of the original.

The Gracie Allen Murder Case was a tailor-made novel by Van Dine suited to the scatterbrain personality of comedienne Gracie Allen. Vance (Warren William), called "Fido" by Gracie throughout the film, takes a backseat role to the wacky blonde who becomes implicated in the sordid death of escaped convict Benny "The Buzzard" Nelson (Lee Moore). One of the minor highlights of this mystery comedy has Gracie a reckless passenger on the back seat of a motorcycle being chased by four police motorcycles. Among the chief suspects in the adventure are Daniel Murche (Jerome Cowan) and Richard Lawrence (H. B. Warner).

Calling . . . is a remaking of *The Kennel Murder Case* updated with World War II espionage overtones. James Stephenson played Vance, a federal agent, investigating the peculiar death of plane manufacturer Archer Coe (Richard Kipling). As the female lead, Margot Stevenson played Hilda Lake, with Henry O'Neill as Markham, James Conlon as Dr. Doremus, and Edward Brophy as Ryan (a replacement for the Sergeant Heath part).

. . . *Returns*—as with the other two Producers Releasing Corp. entries—are set in Los Angeles, with the less than suave and subtle Vance (William Wright) on the prowl to solve the murder of a playboy and several of his girlfriends. The weak gimmicks used included: a poisoned bubble bath, a stabbing, and assorted shootings. Vance was reduced to asking very obvious deductive questions, and relying most heavily on the police's assistance. (Markham and Heath were not present in these concluding entries.)

. . .'s *Gamble* had tough guy Vance (Alan Curtis) involved with an underworld syndicate, stolen gems, and a trio of homicides, with Laurian March (Terry Austin) the pert quasi-heroine.

The final *Philo Vance* film to date, . . .'s *Secret Mission*, gave Vance a secretary, Mona Bannister (Sheila Ryan), to aid him in his crime solving. This original screenplay had Vance serving as a technical adviser on crime stories for a publishing company, with the publisher bent on solving a seven-year-old mystery of his own.

Of all those who played Philo Vance on the screen, William Powell was undoubtedly best suited for the sophisticated, high society role, although he gained greater fame playing another amateur detective in *The Thin Man* series. Basil Rathbone, usually associated with costume dramas as the oily heavy, was a prosaic Vance, but this one-time part was overshadowed by expert—albeit hammy—characterization in later years as the resourceful Sherlock Holmes. Warren William was serviceable as Vance, but lacked the needed pep and tongue-in-cheek quality to enhance the role. He found more audience acceptance in the 1940s in the less demanding series role of The Lone Wolf.

The continental acting style of Paul Lukas gave a different twist to the personality of Vance. He was born Paul Lugacs in Budapest, May 26, 1894. He received his stage training at the Actor's Academy of Hungary and made his theatrical debut in *Lilom* (1916). He entered the cinema in 1917 in *Sphinx,* and after a career in European films came to America where he made his first Holly-

wood motion picture in 1928—*Two Lovers,* co-starring Vilma Banky. He played suave hero-villains throughout the 1930s in such movies as *Half Way to Heaven* (1929), *Little Women* (1933), *I Found Stella Parish* (1935), *The Lady Vanishes* (1938). In 1943, he won the best actor's Oscar for repeating his stage role in *Watch on the Rhine.* Subsequently, he has been seen in films like *Deadline at Dawn* (1946), *20,000 Leagues Under the Sea* (1954), *The Four Horsemen of the Apocalypse* (1962), *Sol Madrid* (1968), and *The Challenge* (1970).

Edmund Lowe, born March 3, 1892, in San Jose, California, was an overearnest Vance, who failed to project the proper suave qualities. A stage actor who made his film debut in *The Silent Command* (1923), he became a leading man in such films as *What Price Glory?* (1926) and appeared in a variety of decreasingly important roles in minor films throughout the 1930s–1950s; *Heller in Pink Tights* (1960) was his last screen role to date.

Grant Richards, a second-string leading man, was born in New York City in 1916, and educated at William and Mary College and the University of Miami. He was on stage in *Half Way to Hell, Too Much Party,* and others. After scoring in *Hopalong Cassidy Returns* (1936) he later turned up in such films as *Under the Big Top* (1938), *Isle of Destiny* (1940), and *Just Off Broadway* (1942). He died July 4, 1963.

James Stephenson, a minor Warner Brothers leading man, was born in Yorkshire, England, in 1903, and gravitated to a film career, with parts in *The Perfect Crime* (1938) and *Dark Stairway* (1938); he appeared in such Hollywood films as *Boy Meets Girl* (1938), *Beau Geste* (1939), *The Letter* (1940) and *International Squadron* (1941). He died July 29, 1941.

William Wright was born in Ogden, Utah, January 5, 1913, played in stock in upstate New York, worked at the Pasadena Playhouse, and obtained a Columbia Pictures contract before being drafted in World War II. He appeared after his army years in such films as *Lover Come Back* (1946), *Down Missouri Way* (1946) and *The Beginning or the End* (1947). He was little heard of professionally after his brief stab at the Philo Vance role.

Alan Curtis—born Harry Ueberroth in Chicago in 1910—made his film debut in *Winterset* (1936) and had such film credits as *Mannequin* (1938),

Follow the Boys (1944), *See My Lawyer* (1945), and *The Pirates of Capri* (1949). At the end of his career, he received much publicity when his heart stopped beating during surgery and he was revived from death. He died February 1, 1953. He had married three times: Priscilla Lawson, Ilona Massey and Betty Doders.

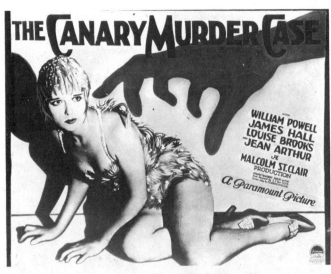

Louise Brooks.

Mary Astor, Powell.

Eugene Pallette, William Powell, E. H. Calvert.
(The Benson Murder Case)

Charles C. Wilson, James Durkin (?), Powell, Robert McWade. **(The Kennel Murder Case)**

Warren William, Eugene Pallette, Robert McWade, Lyle Talbot, George E. Stone, Dorothy Tree, Margaret Lindsay. **(The Dragon Murder Case)**

Powell and Mary Astor. **(The Kennel Murder Case)**

Rosalind Russell, Paul Lukas. **(Casino Murder Case)**

Art Pendleton, Grant Mitchell, Edmund Lowe, Gene Lockhart. (The Garden Murder Case)

Grant Richards, Roscoe Karns, Purnell Pratt, Ruth Coleman (?). (Night of Mystery)

Henry O'Neill, Ed Brophy, James Stephenson, Martin
Kosleck, Don Douglas. (Calling . . .)

William Demarest, Gracie Allen, Judith Barrett.
(Gracie Allen Murder Case)

Cliff Clark, Charles Mitchell, Alan Curtis, Francis
Pierlot, James Burke. (. . .'s Gamble)

Frank Fenton, Alan Curtis, Toni Todd, David
Leonard, Paul Maxey, Tala Birell (in chair), Sheila
Ryan (in portrait). (. . .'s Secret Mission)

PHILO VANCE

CANARY MURDER CASE (Par., 1929) 82 M.

Director, Malcolm St. Clair; author, S. S. Van Dine; screenplay, Florence Ryerson, Albert S. LeVino; dialoguer, S. S. Van Dine; camera, Harry Fishbeck; editor, William Shea.

Philo Vance	William Powell
Margaret O'Dell	Louise Brooks
Jimmie Spotswoode	James Hall
Alice LaFosse	Jean Arthur
Dr. Ambrose Lindquist	Gustav Von Seyffertitz
Charles Spotswoode	Charles Lane
Ernest Heath	Eugene Pallette
John Cleaver	Lawrence Grant
Tony Skeel	Ned Sparks
Louis Mannix	Louis John Bartels
District Attorney John F. X. Markham	E. H. Calvert
Stuttering Hallboy	Oscar Smith
George Y. Harvey	Tim Adair

THE GREENE MURDER CASE (Par., 1929) 71 M.

Director, Frank Tuttle; author, S. S. Van Dine; screenplay, Louise Long, Bartlett Cormack; dialoguer, Bartlett Cormack; camera, Henry Gerrard; editor, Verna Willis.

Philo Vance	William Powell
Sibella Greene	Florence Eldredge
Dr. Arthur Von Blon	Ullrich Haupt
Ada Greene	Jean Arthur
Sergeant Heath	Eugene Pallette
District Attorney John F. X. Markham	E. H. Calvert
Mrs. Tobias Greene	Gertrude Norman
Chester Greene	Lowell Drew
Rex Greene	Morgan Farley
Sproot	Brandon Hurst
Gertrude Mannheim	Augusta Burmeister
Hemming	Marcia Harriss

BISHOP MURDER CASE (MGM, 1930) 80 M.

Director, Nick Grinde, David Burton; author, S. S. Van Dine; screenplay-dialoguer, Lenore J. Coffee; camera, Roy Overbaugh; editor, William Le Vanway.

Philo Vance	Basil Rathbone
Belle Dillard	Leila Hyams
Arnesson	Roland Young
Adolph Drukker	George Marion
Prof. Bertrand Dillard	Alec B. Francis
Miss Drukker	Zelda Sears
Grete Menzel	Bodil Rosing
John E. Sprigg	Carroll Nye
John Pardee	Charles Quartermaine
Sgt. Ernest Heath	James Donlan
Pyne	Sidney Bracey
District Attorney Markham	Clarence Geldert
Raymond Sperling	Delmar Daves
Beedle	Nellie Bly Baker

BENSON MURDER CASE (Par., 1930) 65 M.

Director, Frank Tuttle; author, S. S. Van Dine; screenplay-dialoguer, Bartlett Cormack; camera, A. J. Stout; editor, Doris Drought.

Philo Vance	William Powell
Fanny Del Roy	Natalie Moorhead
Sergeant Heath	Eugene Pallette
Adolph Mohler	Paul Lukas
Harry Gray	William Boyd
District Attorney Markham	E. H. Calvert
Paula Banning	May Beatty
Albert	Mischa Auer
Sam	Otto Yamaoka
Burke	Charles McMurphy
Welch	Dick Rush
Anthony Benson	Richard Tucker
Dealer	Perry Ivins

THE KENNEL MURDER CASE (WB, 1933) 73 M.

Director, Michael Curtiz; author, S. S. Van Dine; adaptation-dialogue, Robert N. Lee, Peter Milne; camera, William Reese; editor, Ed. M. McLarnin.

Philo Vance	William Powell
Hilda Lake	Mary Astor
Sergeant Heath	Eugene Pallette
Raymond Wrede	Ralph Morgan
Doris Delafield	Helen Vinson
Edvardo Grassi	Jack LaRue
Sir Bruce MacDonald	Paul Cavanaugh
Archer Coe	Robert Barrat
Gamble	Arthur Hohl
Dubois	Henry O'Neill
Markham	Robert McWade
Brisbane Coe	Frank Conroy
Dr. Doremus	Etienne Girardot
Snitkin	Spencer Charters
Hennessey	Charles Wilson

THE DRAGON MURDER CASE (WB, 1934) 68 M.

Director, H. Bruce Humberstone; author, S. S. Van Dine; screenplay, F. Hugh Herbert, Robert N. Lee; camera, Tony Gaudio; editor, Terry Morse.

Philo Vance	Warren William
Bernice	Margaret Lindsay
Leland	Lyle Talbot
Sgt. Heath	Eugene Pallette
Mrs. Stamm	Helen Lowell
Ruby	Dorothy Tree
Markham	Robert McWade
Stamm	Robert Barrat
Tatum	George E. Stone
Greeff	William B. Davidson
Montague	George Meeker
Doremus	Etienne Girardot
Hennessey (Snitkin)	Charles Wilson
Dr. Holliday	Robert Warwick

CASINO MURDER CASE (MGM, 1935) 85 M.

Producer, Lucien Hubbard; director, Edwin L. Marin; author, S. S. Van Dine; screenplay, Florence Ryerson, Edgar Allan Woolf; camera, Charles Clarke; editor, Conrad A. Nervig.

Philo Vance .... Paul Lukas
Doris .... Rosalind Russell
Mrs. Llewellyn .... Alison Skipworth
Lynn .... Donald Cook
Kincaid .... Arthur Byron
Sergeant Heath .... Ted Healy
Currie .... Eric Blore
Amelia .... Isabel Jewell
Becky .... Louise Fazenda
Dr. Kane .... Leslie Fenton
Virginia .... Louise Henry
Markham .... Purnell Pratt
Smith .... Leo Carroll
Dr. Doremus .... Charles Sellon
Auctioneer .... William Demarest

THE GARDEN MURDER CASE (MGM, 1936) 62 M.

Producer, Lucien Hubbard, Ned Marin; director, Edwin L. Marin; author, S. S. Van Dine; screenplay, Bertram Milhauser; camera, Charles Clarke; editor, Ben Lewis.

Philo Vance .... Edmund Lowe
Zalia Graem .... Virginia Bruce
Lowe Hammle .... Gene Lockhart
Nurse Beeton .... Benita Hume
Sergeant Heath .... Nat Pendleton
Major Ralston .... H. B. Warner
Woode Swift .... Kent Smith
Markham .... Grant Mitchell
Mrs. Ralston .... Frieda Inescort
Floyd Garden .... Douglas Walton
Dr. Garden .... Henry B. Walthall
Mrs. Hammle .... Jessie Ralph
Inspector Colby .... Charles Trowbridge
Doremus .... Etienne Girardot
Sneed .... William Austin
Japson .... Rosalind Ivan

NIGHT OF MYSTERY (Par., 1937) 75 M.

Director, E. A. Dupont; author, S. S. Van Dine; screenplay, Frank Partos, Gladys Unger; camera, Harry Fischbeck.

Philo Vance .... Grant Richards
Sergeant Heath .... Roscoe Karns
Ada Greene .... Helen Burgess
Sibella Greene .... Ruth Coleman
Mrs. Tobias Greene .... Elizabeth Patterson
Dr. Von Blon .... Harvey Stephens
Barton .... June Martel
Secretary .... Terry Ray (Ellen Drew)
John F. X. Markham .... Purnell Pratt
Chester Greene .... Colin Tapley

Rex Greene .... James H. Bush
Sproot .... Ivan F. Simpson
Mrs. Mannheim .... Greta Meyer
Lister .... Leonard Carey
Hemming .... Nora Cecil
Detective Snitkin .... George Anderson
Medical Examiner .... Barlowe Borland
Police Nurse .... Myra Marsh

THE GRACIE ALLEN MURDER CASE (Par., 1939) 74 M.

Producer, George Arthur; director, Al Greene; author, S. S. Van Dine; screenplay, Nat Perrin; camera, Charles Lang; art director, Hans Dreier, Earl Hedrick; editor, Paul Weatherwax.

Philo Vance .... Warren William
Ann Wilson .... Ellen Drew
Bill Brown .... Kent Taylor
Uncle Ambrose .... Jed Prouty
Daniel Mirche .... Jerome Cowan
Dist. Atty. Markham .... Donald MacBride
Richard Lawrence .... H. B. Warner
Sergeant Heath .... William Demarest
Dixie Del Marr .... Judith Barrett
Gus, the Waiter .... Horace MacMahon
Two Thugs .... Al Shaw and Sam Lee
Fred .... Richard Denning
Clerk .... Irving Bacon
Gracie Allen .... Herself

CALLING PHILO VANCE (WB, 1940) 62 M.

Producer, Bryan Foy; director, William Clemens; author, S. S. Van Dine; screenplay, Tom Reed; camera, Lou O'Connell; editor, Benjamin Liss.

Philo Vance .... James Stephenson
Hilda Lake .... Margot Stevenson
Markham .... Henry O'Neill
Ryan .... Ed Brophy
Tom MacDonald .... Ralph Forbes
Philip Wrede .... Donald Douglas
Gamble .... Martin Kosleck
Dr. Doremus .... James Conlin
Grassi .... Edward Raquello
Du Bois .... Creighton Hale
Hennessey .... Harry Strang
Avery .... George Irving
Archer Coe .... Richard Kipling
Brisbane Coe .... Wedgwood Nowell
Ling Toy .... Bo Ling
Hotel Clerk .... De Wolfe Hopper
Steamship Clerk .... George Reeves

PHILO VANCE RETURNS (PRC, 1947) 64 M.

Producer, Howard Welsch; director, William Beaudine; author, S. S. Van Dine; screenplay, Robert E. Kent; art director, Perry Smith; camera, Jackson Rose; editor, Gene Fowler, Jr.

Philo Vance	William Wright
Lorena Simms	Terry Austin
Alexis	Leon Belasco
Stella Blendon	Clara Blandick
Virginia	Ramsey Ames
Larry Blendon	Damian O'Flynn
George Hullman	Frank Wilcox
Choo-Choo Divine	Iris Adrian
Helen	Ann Staunton
Policeman	Tim Murdock
Maid	Mary Scott

PHILO VANCE'S GAMBLE (PRC, 1947) 62 M.

Producer, Howard Welsch; director, Basil Wrangell; author, S. S. Van Dine; original story, Lawrence Edmund Taylor; screenplay, Eugene Conrad, Arthur St. Claire: music director, Irving Friedman; camera, Jackson Rose; editor, W. Donn Hayes.

Philo Vance	Alan Curtis
Laurian March	Terry Austin
Ernie Clark	Frank Jenks
Tina Cromwell	Tala Birell
Oliver Tennant	Gavin Gordon
Inspector	Cliff Clark
Geegee Desmond	Toni Todd

Lieutenant Burke	James Burke
Robert	Francis Pierlot
District Attorney	Joseph Crehan
Charles O'Mara	Garnett Marks
Mr. Willets	Grady Sutton
Guy Harkness	Charles Mitchell
Norma Harkness	Joanne Frank
Jeff	Dan Seymour

PHILO VANCE'S SECRET MISSION (PRC, 1947) 58 M.

Producer, Howard Welsch; author, S. S. Van Dine; director, Reginald Le Borg; original screenplay, Lawrence Edmund Taylor; art director, Perry Smith; camera, Jackson Rose; editor, W. Donn Hayes.

Philo Vance	Alan Curtis
Mona Bannister	Sheila Ryan
Mrs. Philips	Tala Birell
Ernie Clark	Frank Jenks
Harry Madison	James Bell
Paul Morgan	Frank Fenton
Martin Jamison	Paul Maxey
Louise Roberts	Toni Todd
Carl Wilson	David Leonard

THE SAINT

One of the most mixed bags among cinema detective series was "The Saint" which over a fifteen-year period saw three different actors portray the lead in nine undistinguished black and white programmers. Leslie Charteris's sophisticated sleuth, Simon Templar, first appeared in print in the late 1920s, but did not attract film interest until 1938 when RKO produced . . . *In New York,* starring Louis Hayward, considered to be the best of the cinema Templars. Then George Sanders, prior to his undertaking the Falcon role, played The Saint in five additional minor RKO entries. Just as RKO lost interest in the property, the British became interested in the crime fighter, and filmed two entries with Hugh Sinclair in the title role, one of which RKO released and the other which Republic Pictures picked up for distribution. In 1954, RKO released a final entry in the series, starring Louis Hayward again, in another British-produced Saint package. Ironically, The Saint had little going for it as an original cinema property; at its best it was merely serviceable. With the gallant Simon Templar, half crook, half detective, the interweaving of comedy and drama was thin strung, and suffered in comparison to the similar but superior The Falcon and The Lone Wolf entries. But a sturdy reputation has built up around the property, based on the solid writings of Charteris and helpers. On radio, Simon Templar was played by Edgar Barrier, Brian Aherne, Tom Conway, and Vincent Price; the Inspector by John Brown; Larry Dobkin as Louie, Louise Arthur as Patricia Holmes, and Ken Christy as Happy. On television Roger Moore stars in the hour-long, British-made color series as a worldly traveler seeking adventure, which began production in 1965.

The few distinguishing characteristics of *The Saint* series had Simon Templar as a debonair Britisher, who spends most of his time roaming around the Continent and America, chasing lovely ladies and trying to avoid the responsibility of marriage or any stable job. While The Saint was a hardened killer in . . . *In New York,* in the later entries he is just a reformed crook. As his semi-serious comic foil, there were in the British-set films Inspector Teal (Gordon McLeod, later Charles Victor) of Scotland Yard, and in the American-locale productions, Chief Inspector Fernack (Jonathan Hale) of the New York homicide squad. Both these policemen usually needed the Saint's help, but were more than reluctant to ask for his aid. Both would usually assume that the highly illegal but vastly ethical Saint was more involved in the caper at hand than he should be.

Characteristically, the Saint (as most other rogue sleuths) would aid the police and handle his enemies as he saw fit. He was a smooth worker, not adverse to loose pilfering from those with too much money; in short, a modern Robin Hood.

In the George Sanders films, Templar would generally leave his calling card to those involved in the caper, and at some point in the film would jauntily stroll along whistling his theme song, oblivious to the cares of the world. To give further contrast to the upper crust bachelor sleuth, the RKO entries incorporated a rather flavorful character, generally a reformed crook, who offers to help The Saint for one reason or another. Paul Guilfoyle was Pearly Gates in two productions,

Barry Fitzgerald, David Burns, and Wylie Watson appeared in other episodes as the do-gooder ex-underworld figure. The production-line programmer policy demanded economy, and the fact that such players as Wendy Barrie appeared as a different female lead in three *Saint* films seemingly bothered no one.

. . . *In New York* has Simon Templar enlisted by William Valcross (Frederick Burton), head of a businessmen's committee to rid New York of six gangsters. One by one, the Saint stalks his prey and kills them. He is helped by Fay Edwards (Kay Sutton), the mistress of the "Big Fellow" who is number seven on the Saint's extermination list. Before the finale, the Saint is off traveling again to South America, his job well done.

. . . *Strikes Back* is set in San Francisco, where Val Travers (Wendy Barrie), the daughter of a former police detective who died in disgrace, has organized an underworld gang to revenge her father's death. Inspector Fernack, a friend of the late detective, shows up in San Francisco, to poke into the case. For comedy relief, there is Zipper Dyson (Barry Fitzgerald), a prosaic safecracker, with a touch of goodness in his old heart. . . . *In London* has Templar, after a sojourn in the United States, arriving in England and becoming entangled with the counterfeiting gang of Kusella (Ralph Truman), Stengler (Carl Jaffe), and Lang (Henry Oscar). The gang had robbed a Balkan count and stolen £1 million, which he was taking to the Embassy. The Saint takes over from the murdered nobleman. He is assisted by Dugan (David Burns), a reformed crook who used to be the cook at San Quentin, Penny Parker (Sally Gray), a fluttery social butterfly, and gloomy Inspector Teal (Gordon McLeod), who spends most of his time following Templar. This entry consisted more of humorous moments and a quantity of incidents, than any quality of mystery or suspense.

. . .'s *Double Trouble* is set in Philadelphia, where the Saint has gone for a visit, after having been to Cairo on the track of diamond smugglers bringing gems into the United States, encased in a mummy's tomb. Coincidentally, Inspector Fernack arrives on the scene in Philadelphia, and finds himself involved in the case. The Saint gallantly tries to extricate Professor Bitts (Thomas W. Ross) and his daughter Anne (Helene Whitney) who are implicated in several murders instigated by the international jewel thieves prowling about town.

One of the film's gimmicks has Sanders in the dual role of the Saint and Duke Piato, the gangland boss, after the jewels.

. . . *Takes Over* has the reverse gambit of the Saint being asked to help Inspector Fernack. Fernack has been framed on a bribery charge by a slick gang of racetrack fixers. The Saint has sailed back to Manhattan from London where he met Ruth (Wendy Barrie), who is also part of the case. A nitwit stool pigeon, Pearly Gates (Paul Guilfoyle), joins forces with the Saint to help wrap up the $50,000 bribe case. Once again, the elegant Saint handles the problems with uncommon unconcern and methodical precision.

. . . *In Palm Springs* finds Simon Templar being asked by Inspector Fernack to go to California where Elna Johnson (Wendy Barrie), a tennis instructor, is heir to $200,000 in stamps smuggled from England. Elna's uncle, who is to accompany Templar, is killed in New York, and Templar takes the stamps himself to the resort where Elna is, being trailed by a gang after the valuable goods. Once in Palm Springs, the Saint reluctantly accepts the cooperation of Pearly Gates, now the house detective at the Twin Palm Hotel. After two additional murders, the case is neatly cleared up by the Saint. Seemingly he cannot lose; being a spectator with little to do but sit back and wait for an easy chance to unravel the crime and then exit the scene gracefully.

. . .'s *Vacation* has the sleuth on holiday in Switzerland but becoming enbroiled with an Axis vs. Allies espionage scheme in the Alpine country. A little metal music box is the key to a much-sought-after secret code. Among those in the caper are Rudolph (Cecil Parker), a foreign agent dealing in military secrets; Mary Langdon (Sally Gray), the heroine-newspaper gal; Valerie (Leueen MacGrath), the British secret service agent; and Monty Hayward (Arthur Macrae), the Saint's comic sidekick.

In . . . *Meets the Tiger* the story opens with a murder on the Saint's doorstep, and Templar is thereafter in hot pursuit of gold thieves who are burying their stolen loot in an abandoned ore mine, intending to "discover" later a rich gold vein and sell bogus stock. Seen in this caper are the ever-present Inspector Teal (Gordon McLeod), the sinister gangster Tiger (Clifford Evans), and the Saint's funny valet Horace (Wylie Watson).

. . .'s *Girl Friday* is again set in London, where

the Saint has come at the request of a girl now dead. Templar believes she was heavily involved with a gambling syndicate, which runs a luxurious casino on a barge in the Thames River. The siren-heroine Carol Denby (Naomi Chance) is paying off her gambling debts by luring suckers to the casino. Teal (Charles Victor), now Chief Inspector at Scotland Yard, is more pompous and less astute than usual, with Max Lennar (Sidney Tafler) an above-average chief villain.

The five *Saint* films did much to raise George Sanders's prestige in Hollywood, giving him a new image as an urbane leading man instead of the epic heel whose greatest asset to that date had been his famous sneer. Sanders was born in what was then St. Petersburg, Russia, July 3, 1906, the son of a British rope manufacturer; his mother was a horticulturist. During the Russian Revolution, the family escaped to Scandinavia and then to England. After prep school, he attended Brighton College, and later went to the Manchester Technical School, to specialize in textiles. He then went into the tobacco business in South America. By the early 1930s, the versatile performer (he sang baritone, played the piano, guitar and saxophone) was appearing in such London productions as *Ballyhoo*. His film debut was in *Strange Cargo* (1929), then *The Man Who Could Work Miracles* (1935). After playing in a succession of stinker roles, he appeared in *The Lodger* (1944), *The Picture of Dorian Gray* (1946) and *The Strange Affair of Uncle Harry* (1946). He won a best support-Oscar for the theatrical critic role in *All About Eve* (1950). He sang opposite Ethel Merman in *Call Me Madam* (1953). Since then his assorted film roles have included *Death of a Scoundrel* (1956), *Village of the Damned* (1960), *The Amorous Adventures of Moll Flanders* (1966) and *The Kremlin Letter* (1970). Sanders, who resides in California, has been married to Elise Poole (who acted under the stage name of Susan Larson), Zsa Zsa Gabor, Benita Hume and Magda Gabor. In 1960, he wrote his autobiography, *Memoirs of a Cad*.

Sanders's replacement in *The Saint* series was Hugh Sinclair (1903–62), a London-born actor, who made his stage debut in 1922. He was featured in such films as *Escape Me Never* (1935), *Tomorrow We Live* (1942), *Don't Ever Leave Me* (1948) and *Mantrap* (1952).

Louis Hayward, the first and last cinema Saint to date, was born in Johannesburg, South Africa, March 19, 1909. After appearing on the English stage in such productions as *Dracula* and *Another Language* he made his film debut in *Self Made Lady* (1932). Then followed roles in *Duke of West Point* (1938), *My Son, My Son* (1940), *The Son of Monte Cristo* (1940), *Ruthless, The Search for Bridie Murphy* (1956), *Chuka* (1967) and others. On television, he has most recently been seen in a recurring role in *The Survivors*. Hayward has been married to Ida Lupino, Peggy Morrow, and June Blanchard.

Jonathan Hale, Louis Hayward. (. . . In New York)

Hayward, Kay Sutton, Cliff Bragdon. (. . . in New York)

George Sanders, Wendy Barrie, Neil Hamilton,
Russell Hopton, Ed Gargan.

Sanders, Peggy Carroll. (. . . Strikes Back)

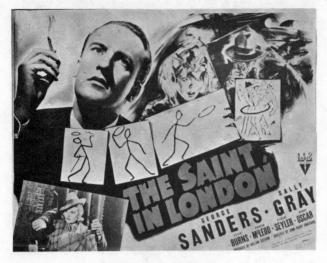

Sanders, Sally Gray.

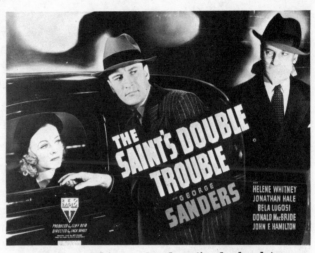

Helene Whitney, Sanders (in dual role).

Sally Gray, Sanders. (. . . in London)

Wendy Barrie, Sanders, Jonathan Hale. Insert: Jonathan Hale, Robert Emmett Keane, Paul Guilfoyle, Sanders.

Cecil Parker, Sinclair, Sally Gray.

Eddie Dunn, Paul Guilfoyle, Sanders, Harry Shannon.
(. . . in Palm Springs)

Sanders, Wendy Barrie. (. . . in Palm Springs)

Hugh Sinclair, Jean Gillie.

288 THE GREAT MOVIE SERIES

Hayward, Fred Johnson. (. . .'s Girl Friday)

THE SAINT

THE SAINT IN NEW YORK (RKO, 1938) 72 M.

Producer, William Sistrom; director, Ben Holmes; author, Leslie Charteris; screenplay, Charles Kaufman, Mortimer Offner; art director, Van Nest Polglese; camera, Joseph August, Frank Redman; editor, Harry Marker.

The Saint	Louis Hayward
Fay Edwards	Kay Sutton
Hutch Rellin	Sig Rumann
Inspector Fernack	Jonathan Hale
Red Jenks	Jack Carson
Hymie Fanro	Paul Guilfoyle
William Valcross	Frederick Burton
Papinoff	Ben Welden
Vincent Nather	Charles Halton
Sebastian	Cliff Bragdon

THE SAINT STRIKES BACK (RKO, 1939) 64 M.

Producer, Robert Sisk; director, John Farrow; author, Leslie Charteris; screenplay, John Twist; camera, Frank Redman; editor, Jack Hively.

Simon Templar (The Saint)	George Sanders
Val Travers	Wendy Barrie
Inspector Fernack	Jonathan Hale
Cullis	Jerome Cowan
Allan Breck	Neil Hamilton
Zipper Dyson	Barry Fitzgerald
Webster	Robert Elliott
Harry Donnell	Russell Hopton
Pinky Budd	Edward Gargan
Commissioner	Robert Strange
Martin Eastman	Gilbert Emery
Secretary	James Burke
Mrs. Fernack	Nella Walker

THE SAINT IN LONDON (RKO, 1939) 72 M.

Producer, William Sistrom; director, John Paddy Carstairs; author, Leslie Charteris; screenplay, Lynn Root, Frank Fenton, camera, Claude Friese-Greene.

Simon Templar (The Saint)	George Sanders
Penny Parker	Sally Gray
Dugan	David Burns
Inspector Teal	Gordon McLeod
Lang	Henry Oscar
Kusella	Ralph Truman
Stengler	Carl Jaffe
Mrs. Brighton	Norah Howard
Blake	Ballard Berkeley

THE SAINT'S DOUBLE TROUBLE (RKO, 1940) 68 M.

Producer, Cliff Reid; director, Jack Hively; author, Leslie Charteris; screenplay, Ben Holmes; camera, J. Roy Hunt; editor, Theron Warth.

Simon Templar (The Saint) Duke Piato	George Sanders
Anne Bitts	Helene Whitney
Inspector Fernack	Jonathan Hale
Partner	Bela Lugosi
Bohlen	Donald MacBride
Limpy	John F. Hamilton
Professor Bitts	Thomas W. Ross
Monk	Elliott Sullivan
Express man	Pat O'Malley
Card player	Donald Kerr

THE SAINT TAKES OVER (RKO, 1940) 69 M.

Producer, Howard Benedict; director, Jack Hively; author, Leslie Charteris; screenplay, Lynn Root, Frank Fenton; camera, Fred Redman; editor, Desmond Marquette.

Simon Templar (The Saint)	George Sanders
Ruth	Wendy Barrie
Inspector Fernack	Jonathan Hale
Pearly Gates	Paul Guilfoyle
Sam Reese	Morgan Conway
Leo Sloan	Robert Emmett Keane
Max Bremer	Cyrus W. Kendall
Mike	James Burke
Captain Wade	Robert Middlemass
Weldon	Roland Drew
Lucy Fernack	Nella Walker
Egan	Pierre Watkin

THE SAINT IN PALM SPRINGS (RKO, 1941) 66 M.

Producer, Howard Benedict; director, Jack Hively; author, Leslie Charteris; screenplay, Jerry Cady; camera, Harry Wild; editor, George Hively.

Simon Templar (The Saint)	George Sanders
Elna Johnson	Wendy Barrie
Pearly Gates	Paul Guilfoyle
Inspector Fernack	Jonathan Hale
Margaret Forbes	Linda Hayes
Mr. Evans	Ferris Taylor
Chief Graves	Harry Shannon
Detective Barker	Eddie Dunn
Whitey	Richard Crane
Mr. Fletcher	Charles Quigley

THE SAINT'S VACATION (RKO, 1941) 78 M.

Producer, William Sistrom; director, Leslie Fenton; author, Leslie Charteris; screenplay, Jeffry Dell, Leslie Charteris; art director, Paul Sheriff; music director, Bretton Byrd; camera, Bernard Knowles; editor, Al Barnes, R. Kemplin.

Simon Templar (The Saint)	Hugh Sinclair
Mary Langdon	Sally Gray
Monty Hayward	Arthur Macrae
Rudolph	Cecil Parker
Valerie	Leueen MacGrath

Inspector Teal	Gordon McLeod
Gregory	John Warwick
Emil	Ivor Barnard
Marko	Manning Whiley
Leighton	Felix Aylmer

THE SAINT MEETS THE TIGER (Rep., 1943) 70 M.

Producer, William Sistrom; director, Paul Stein; author, Leslie Charteris; screenplay, Leslie Arliss, James Seymour, Wolfgang Wilhelm; art director, Paul Sheriff; camera, Bob Krasker; editor, Ralph Kemplen.

Simon Templar (The Saint)	Hugh Sinclair
Pat Holmes	Jean Gillie
Inspector Teal	Gordon McLeod
Sidmarsh	Clifford Evans
Horace	Wylie Watson
Bently	Dennis Arundell
Bittle	Charles Victor
Aunt Agatha	Louise Hampton
Merridon	John Salew
Police Constable	Arthur Humbling

Mrs. Jones	Amy Veiness
Mr. Jones	Claude Bailey
Burton	Noel Dainton
Frankie	Eric Clavering
Joe	Ben Williams
Paddy	Tony Quinn

THE SAINT'S GIRL FRIDAY (RKO, 1954) 70 M.

Producer, Julian Lesser, Anthony Hinds; director, Seymour Friedman; story-screenplay, Allan MacKennon; camera, Walter Harvey; editor, James Needs; music, Ivoy Slanley.

Simon Templar	Louis Hayward
Carol Denby	Naomi Chance
Max Lennar	Sidney Tafler
Chief Inspector Teal	Charles Victor
Katie French	Jane Carr
Jarvis	Harold Lang
Keith Merton	Russell Enoch
Margie	Diana Dors
Irish Cassidy	Fred Johnson
Hoppy Uniaty	Thomas Gallagher

SHERLOCK HOLMES

A continually popular film series has been Sherlock Holmes, the prototype of all twentieth century detective characters. Arthur Conan Doyle (1859–1930) was a practicing physician in 1887 when he wrote his first Sherlock Holmes novel, *A Study In Scarlet,* and since then his batch of Holmes novels and stories have been in constant reprint. Sherlock Holmes reached the movie screen in 1903 in an American Mutual and Biograph Company one-reel subject, and since then he has been the subject of countless films in a variety of countries, with such personalities as William Gillette, John Barrymore and Eille Norward enacting the scholarly sleuth. The first Holmes to talk on the screen was Clive Brooks in *Return of Sherlock Holmes* (1929). Other actors appearing as the sleuth of 221-B Baker Street were Arthur Wontner, Raymond Massey, and Reginald Owen (who had also played Dr. Watson in the 1932 Sherlock Holmes film). Then Twentieth Century-Fox filmed *The Hound of the Baskervilles,* starring Richard Greene as the hero, with a cape and capped Basil Rathbone and pipe smoking Nigel Bruce, as Holmes and Watson. The casting in this lush costumer proved so ideal that Fox made another Holmes film later that year. In 1942, Universal picked up the Holmes property and signed Rathbone and Bruce for a series. Over the next four years, 12 *Sherlock Holmes* entries appeared (as well as a guest appearance in the studio's potpourri, *Crazy House*). Then film interest in Holmes died till the late 1950s, when Hammer Films' *The Hound of the Baskervilles,* starring Britisher Peter Cushing, appeared. Then came Christopher Lee in a German-made Holmes production, John Neville in *A Study In Terror,* and most recently, Ronald Stephens in Billy Wilder's elaborate but unsuccessful serious satire, *The Private Life of . . .* (1970). (On radio, *Sherlock Holmes* was a long running series, with Basil Rathbone, Louis Hector, Richard Gordon, Tom Conway, Ben Wright and John Stanley among those heard as Holmes; Leigh Lovel, Nigel Bruce, Eric Snowden, Alfred Shirley, and Ian Martin were at various times Dr. Watson; Louis Hector played Moriarty. Joseph Bell was on the show as a character named Mr. Bell, who [when George Washington Coffee was the sponsor] always encountered Holmes and Watson and suggested they stop for a good cup of coffee. A 39-episode, half-hour British-made television series of 1955, starred Ronald Howard as Holmes and M. Marion Crawford as Dr. Watson.)

The first two Rathbone-Bruce *Sherlock Holmes* films were done in true late Victorian style, and were generally serious attempts at re-creating the Conan Doyle flavor. The dozen Universal *Sherlock Holmes* entries were all updated in setting to the 1940s, and the first grouping of them were strong anti-Axis World War II propaganda. The Universal productions were considerably lower in quality than the Fox features, what with the Doyle stories considerably altered, the utilization of (confusing) prologues spoken by Holmes, and the encouragement of a hammy performance by Rathbone in the increasingly incredible pompous part of Holmes, who was given to lengthy soliloquies, absurdly intuitive deductive reasoning, and a less than charitable attitude toward the intellectual capacity of his fellow man. It was good old hale-and-hearty Watson who gave the needed common-man touch to the series, besides offering a generally acceptable comic foil to his cultured comrade in arms.

The Hound of the Baskervilles closely followed the original novel, with its scenes of desolate moors and the ancient Baskerville mansion—complete with the atmospheric howlings in the night. Establishing the successful mold that was to continue thereafter, Nigel Bruce shared screen time with Rathbone, bumbling along as well-meaning Dr. John H. Watson, and Mary Gordon made much of her token appearance as the housekeeper, Mrs. Hudson. In contrast to heroine Beryl (Wendy Barrie) there were such arch villains as Dr. Mortimer (Lionel Atwill) and Barryman (John Carradine).

Fox's follow-up film *The Adventures of . . .* was largely based on the William Gillette play, delving into Holmes's age-old conflict with scoundrel Professor Moriarty (George Zucco); there was also a heroine in distress, Ann Brandon (Ida Lupino), and such atmospheric sequences as Ann being chased through a fog-laden park by the club footed killer. The best remembered sequence is the suspenseful Holmes-Moriarty death struggle atop the Tower of London. Seen as stuffy Scotland Yard Inspector Bristol was E. E. Clive, who served to accentuate the supermental powers of Holmes's omnipresent nature.

Voice of Terror (based on *His Last Bow*) is set in World War II London, with Holmes being implored to stop Nazi saboteurs working in England. The Axis enemy has masterminded a "Voice of Terror" campaign on the radio predicting all sorts of dire events. Among the several evildoers are Sir Evan Barham (Reginald Denny) and General Jerome Lawford (Montagu Love). Unfortunately the villain of the piece is obvious to even the most unsophisticated filmgoer.

Secret Weapon (utilizing *The Adventure of the Dancing Men*) concerns an amazing invention Dr. Franz Tobel (William Post, Jr.) has engineered—a new bomb sight for the Allied cause! Holmes is requested to guard Tobel's safety, and with Professor Moriarty (Lionel Atwill) at hand, there is much to be concerned about. At one point, a much discomforted Holmes is under Moriarty's control, having his blood drained from his body. Appearing as the affable but slow-witted Inspector Lestrade of Scotland Yard was Dennis Huey, who repeated the role in later Universal chapters. Roy William Neill

directed this entry and all others in the studio's series.

. . . In Washington is an original screenplay delving into the whereabouts of a microfilm of an important document, hidden in a matchbook cover. Among the chief criminals are Stanley (George Zucco), and William Raster (Henry Daniell). The denouement as always, contained an incredible piece of deductive (almost mystical) reasoning on Holmes's part, which fit together all the divergent clues and solved the puzzling case. The setting in the nation's capital allowed for some (il)logical and patronizing hands-across-the-Atlantic brotherly love anti-Axis propaganda, spouted with élan by Holmes.

. . . Faces Death (from *The Musgrave Ritual*), centers around eerie Musgrave Manor and the bizarre neighboring town filled with a conglomeration of suspects to an assortment of strange crimes. Among the flavorful set pieces utilized are a lofty tower clock, which strikes thirteen just before a murder; a chessboard with living players; a subterranean crypt, and a seemingly invisible murderer. Dr. Sexton (Hillary Brooke) was the focal point of interest in this chapter. One of Holmes's gambits to force the denouement involved a self-inflicted pseudo-death.

In *Crazy House* (1943), a slam-bang variety show film featuring the vaudeville comedy team of Olsen and Johnson, Holmes and Watson made a brief cameo appearance on the Universal backlot.

The Spider Woman (combining elements from *The Sign of the Four* and *The Final Problem*) deals with a vicious murder syndicate headed by exotic villainess Andrea Spedding (Gale Sondergaard). Disguised as a Hindu (among other dodges), Holmes investigates the series of pajama murders, in which the victims, once bitten by oversized spiders, go mad and kill themselves in a frenzy. Among the physical trials Holmes suffers are two death attempts, where his persecutors leave him to die in a most gruesome way. One especially effective moment has Holmes tied behind a life size drawing of Adolph Hitler, at a carnival shooting gallery, with patrons (Watson included) unknowingly using Holmes for target practice.

The Scarlet Claw, an original screenplay, is laid in the fog drenched village of La Morte Rouge, Canada, where Holmes and Watson endeavor to unmask the fiendish murderer who attacks not only the town people but animals as well. The gloomy background of the marshes, the old church where one of the victims is found dead, and the abiding superstitions of the villagers all add up to an exciting entry, exceedingly well photographed. Once again, before the killer—who stalks the moors in luminous clothing—is caught, Holmes must adopt a new disguise to try and outwit the clever villain. Among the victims are young Marie Journet (Kay Harding), invalid Judge Brisson (Miles Mander), and Lord Penrose's wife Nora (Victoria Horne).

The Pearl of Death (from *The Adventures of Six Napoleons*) concerns the fabulous Borgia pearl stolen by Naomi Drake (Evelyn Ankers) and secreted in one of six newly made busts of Napoleon. When the busts are sold to assorted Londoners, the new owners are soon found with their backs broken. Among the offbeat villains running loose in this story are Giles Conover (Miles Mander), an expert jewel thief, and his unpleasant assistant "The Creeper" (Rondo Hatton). As expected, the formula calls for Holmes to don another disguise to aid his deductive reasoning in trapping the culprit.

The House of Fear (from *The Five Orange Pips*) centers on an eccentric group of men, known as "The Good Comrades," residing in a Scottish mansion. Besides their preoccupation with the facets of death, the club is heavily self-insured to protect their declining years. A la ten little Indians, one by one, the members are murdered in ghastly fashion, with Holmes—and for an amusing change, especially Watson—ferreting out the necessary bits of evidence to wrap up the case.

The Woman in Green (loosely adapted from *The Adventure of the Empty House*) has Holmes delving into the "Finger Murders" in which women are found murdered, all with their right forefinger missing. Besides the sinister Professor Moriarty (Henry Daniell) there is nefarious, hysterical Lydia (Hillary Brooke).

Pursuit to Algiers (from *The Return of Sherlock Holmes*) is set almost exclusively on a transatlantic ocean liner, in which Holmes and Watson are escorting Nikolas (Leslie Vincent), heir to a far Eastern throne, on an official diplomatic visit. Also on board the vessel are a group of homeland assassins headed by Mirko (Martin Kosleck) who are on the prowl attempting to kill their sovereign. Holmes here has to use an ultra-witty gambit to confound the intelligent Mirko; the denouement reveals that Holmes is not the only one who knows how to use an effective disguise.

Terror By Night, an original screenplay, is situated on a fast-moving train traveling from London to Edinburgh, with Holmes aboard to protect the priceless Star of Rhodesia diamond. Among the many fascinating passengers on the streamliner are Major Duncan Bleek (Alan Mowbray), a scholarly friend of Watson, and Sands (Skelton Knaggs) who for ulterior motives hides in a secret compartment of a coffin during the journey. Holmes parries with his adversary in the caper, again using a decoy, and fortuitously discerning the villains' disguises in the nick of time.

Dressed To Kill, another original screenplay, pits Holmes against the vile Hilda Courtney (Patricia Morison), who has set her sights on obtaining engraving plates recently stolen from the Bank of England. The needed clue to their hiding place is secreted in code in the melody of a music box made at Dartmoor Prison. Trick for trick, disguise for disguise, Miss Courtney matches wits with Holmes, proving a most worthy adversary. Also in the story is the vicious Hamid (Harry Cording), a murderous underworld henchman.

According to informed sources, Universal would have continued the popular *Sherlock Holmes* series, but Rathbone had tired of the typecast role and wanted other challenges. Nevertheless, although the films are so outrageously overacted on all scores, they have attracted a legion of followers, who marvel at the oversized performance of Rathbone, and the assorted guest villains. The straightforward acting of such supporting players as Nigel Bruce (who could be overly precious at times), Mary Gordon, and Dennis Huey, gave the series the needed backbone to proceed with assurance of competence, bolstering the storyline.

Basil Rathbone was born in 1892 in Johannesburg, South Africa, the son of a British mining engineer. Schooled in England, he went to work as an insurance agent, but forsook that profession for the stage. He came to America in 1912 with his cousin's repertory group. After serving in World War I, he returned to the London stage, debuting in films in *The Fruitful Vine* (1921). By 1924 he had moved back to the United States; his first American made film was *The Masked Bride* (1925). Among his most noted roles, usually as the suave villain, were in *David Copperfield* (1935), *Anna Karenina* (1935), *A Tale of Two Cities* (1935), and a series of swashbucklers opposite stars like Errol Flynn in *Captain Blood* (1935), Gary Cooper in *The Adventures of Marco Polo* (1938), and Tyrone Power in *The Mark of Zorro* (1940). After the Holmes films, he returned to stage work. In the 1950s, he was in such Hollywood films as *Casanova's Big Night* (1954), *The*

Court Jester (1956) and *The Last Hurrah* (1958). In the 1960s, he, along with Karloff, Lorre, and Vincent Price appeared in several horror film spoofs like *Tales of Terror* (1962) and *A Comedy of Terror* (1963). Rathbone died July 21, 1967, survived by his second wife, Ouida Fitzmaurice.

Nigel Bruce was born February 4, 1895, in Ensenada, Mexico, where his British parents were traveling at the time. Educated in England, he fought in World War I, sustained a leg injury, and was forced into a wheelchair for three years. He made his theatrical debut in 1920 in *The Creaking Chair,* which starred C. Aubrey Smith. After de-

buting in silent films in 1928, he returned to the stage, coming to America in the early 1930s to appear in such Broadway vehicles as *Springtime for Henry.* Once in Hollywood, he usually was featured as the comedy relief in period pictures, including *The Scarlet Pimpernel* (1935), *Kidnapped* (1938), *Rebecca* (1940), *Forever and a Day* (1943) and *The Corn Is Green* (1945). His last film appearance was in the 3-D jungle story *Bwani Devil* (1953). Bruce married actress Violet Shelton (Campbell) in 1922; they had two daughters. He died of a heart attack on October 8, 1953.

Nigel Bruce, Basil Rathbone. (The Hound of the Baskervilles)

Rathbone, Eily Malyon, John Carradine, Richard Greene. (The Hound of the Baskervilles)

Rathbone, Evelyn Ankers. (. . . and the Voice of
Terror)

George Zucco, Rathbone, Thurston Hall. (. . . In Washington)

Rathbone, Gale Sondergaard. (. . . and the Spider Woman)

Rathbone, Gale Sondergaard, Bruce. (. . . and the Spider Woman)

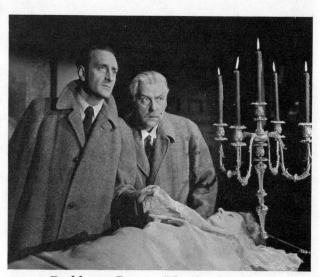

Rathbone, Bruce. (The Scarlet Claw)

Rathbone, Bruce. (Pearl of Death)

Rathbone, Bruce. (The Woman in Green)

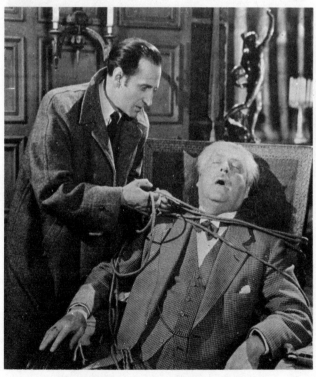

Rathbone, Bruce. (House of Fear)

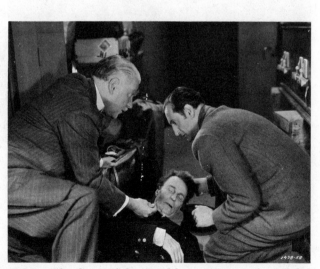

Bruce, Charles Knight, Rathbone. (Terror by Night)

Rathbone, Patricia Morison. (Dressed to Kill)

SHERLOCK HOLMES

THE HOUND OF THE BASKERVILLES (20th, 1939) 80 M.

Producer, Gene Markey; director, Sidney Lanfield; author, Sir Arthur Conan Doyle; screenplay, Ernest Pascal; camera, Reverell Marley; editor, Robert Simpson.

Sir Henry	Richard Greene
Sherlock Holmes	Basil Rathbone
Beryl	Wendy Barrie
Dr. Watson	Nigel Bruce
Dr. Mortimer	Lionel Atwill
Barryman	John Carradine
Frankland	Barlowe Borland
Mrs. Mortimer	Beryl Mercer
Stapleton	Morton Lowry
Sir Hugo	Ralph Forbes
Gabby	E. E. Clive
Mrs. Barryman	Eily Malyon
Convict	Nigel De Brulier
Mrs. Hudson	Mary Gordon
Roderick	Peter Willes
Sir Charles	Ian Maclaren

THE ADVENTURES OF SHERLOCK HOLMES 20th, 1939) 82 M.

Producer, Gene Markey; director, Alfred Werker; based on a play by William Gillette; screenplay, Edwin Blum, William Drake; music director, Cyril J. Mockridge; camera, Leon Shamroy; editor, Robert Bischoff.

Sherlock Holmes	Basil Rathbone
Dr. Watson	Nigel Bruce
Ann Brandon	Ida Lupino
Jerrold Hunter	Alan Marshal
Billy	Terry Kilburn
Prof. Moriarty	George Zueco
Sir Ronald Ramsgate	Henry Stephanson
Inspector Bristol	E. E. Clive
Mrs. Jamison	May Beatty
Lloyd Brandon	Peter Willes
Mrs. Hudson	Mary Gordon
Justice	Holmes Herbert
Mateo	George Regas
Lady Conyngham	Mary Forbes
Dawes (Butler)	Frank Dawson
Bassick	Arthur Hohl

SHERLOCK HOLMES AND THE VOICE OF TERROR (Univ., 1942) 65 M.

Associate producer, Howard Benedict; director, Jack Rawlins; author, Sir Arthur Conan Doyle; screenplay, Lynn Riggs, Robert D. Andrews; art director, Jack Otterson; music director, Charles Previn; camera, Woody Bredell.

Sherlock Holmes	Basil Rathbone
Dr. Watson	Nigel Bruce
Kitty	Evelyn Ankers

Sir Evan Barham	Reginald Denny
General Jerome Lawford	Montagu Love
Anthony Lloyd	Henry Daniell
Meade	Thomas Gomez
Fabian Prentiss	Olaf Hytten
Captain Ronald Shore	Leyland Hodgson
Crosbie	Arthur Blake
Taxi Driver	Harry Stubbs
Mrs. Hudson	Mary Gordon
Jill Grandis	Hillary Brooke

SHERLOCK HOLMES AND THE SECRET WEAPON (Univ., 1942) 68 M.

Associate producer, Howard Benedict; director, Roy Neill; author, Sir Arthur Conan Doyle; adaptation-screenplay, Edward T. Lowe, W. Scott Darling, Edmund L. Hartmann; camera, Lester White; art director, Jack Otterson; music director, Charles Previn.

Sherlock Holmes	Basil Rathbone
Dr. Watson	Nigel Bruce
Charlotte Eberli	Kaaren Verne
Moriarty	Lionel Atwill
Dr. Franz Tobel	William Post, Jr.
Lestrade	Dennis Hoey
Kurt	Harry Woods
Gottfried	George Burr MacAnnan
Mueller	Paul Fix
Sir Reginald	Holmes Herbert
Mrs. Hudson	Mary Gordon
Hoffner	Henry Victor
Peg Leg	Harold de Becker

SHERLOCK HOLMES IN WASHINGTON (Univ., 1943) 71 M.

Associate producer, Howard Benedict; director, Roy Neill; story, Bertram Millhauser; screenplay, Bertram Millhauser, Lynn Riggs; camera, Lester White; music director, Charles Previn; editor, Otto Ludwig.

Sherlock Holmes	Basil Rathbone
Dr. Watson	Nigel Bruce
Nancy Partridge	Marjorie Lord
William Raster	Henry Daniell
Stanley	George Zucco
Lt. Peter Merriam	John Archer
Bart Lang	Gavin Muir
Detective Lt. Grogan	Edmund MacDonald
Howe	Don Terry
Cady	Bradley Page
Mr. Ahrens	Holmes Herbert
Senator Henry Babcock	Thurston Hall
Sir Henry Marchmont	Gilbert Emery

SHERLOCK HOLMES FACES DEATH (Univ., (1943) 68 M.

Associate producer-director, William Roy Neill; author, Sir Arthur Conan Doyle; screenplay, Bertram Millhauser; camera, Charles Van Enger; art director, John Goodman; music director, H. J. Satter; editor, Fred Feitchans.

Sherlock Holmes	Basil Rathbone
Dr. Watson	Nigel Bruce
Lestrade	Dennis Hoey
Dr. Sexton	Arthur Margetson
Sally Musgrave	Hillary Brooke
Brunton	Halliwell Hobbes
Mrs. Howells	Minna Phillips
Captain Vickery	Milburn Stone
Phillip Musgrave	Gavin Muir
Langford	Gerald Hamer
Clavering	Vernon Downing
Captain MacIntosh	Olaf Hytten
Jenny	Heather Wilde
Geoffrey Musgrave	Frederick Worlock
2nd Sailor	Peter Lawford
Pub Proprietor	Harold de Becker

SHERLOCK HOLMES AND THE SPIDER WOMAN (Univ., 1944) 63 M.

Producer-Director, Roy William Neill; author, Sir Arthur Conan Doyle; screenplay, Bertram Millhauser; camera, Charles Van Enger; art director, John B. Goodman; editor, James Gibbon.

Sherlock Holmes	Basil Rathbone
Doctor Watson	Nigel Bruce
Adrea Spedding	Gale Sondergaard
Lestrade	Dennis Hoey
Norman Locke	Vernon Downing
Radlik	Alec Craig
Gilflower	Arthur Hohl
Colonel	Stanley Logan
Artie	Donald Stuart
Croupier	John Roche
Mrs. Hudson	Mary Gordon
Announcer	John Burton
Colonel's Wife	Lydia Bilbrook
Fortune Teller	Belle Mitchell
Fred Garvin	Harry Cording
Clerk	John Rogers
Boy	Teddy Infuhr
Charwoman	Marie de Becker

THE SCARLET CLAW (Univ., 1944) 74 M.

Producer-director, Roy William Neill; story, Paul Gangelin, Brenda Weisberg; screenplay, Edmund L. Hartman, Roy W. Neill; camera, George Robinson; art director, John B. Goodman, Ralph M. DeLacy; editor, Paul Landres.

Sherlock Holmes	Basil Rathbone
Doctor Watson	Nigel Bruce
Potts, Tanner, Ramson	Gerald Hamer
Lord Penrose	Paul Cavanagh
Emile Journet	Arthur Hohl
Judge Brisson	Miles Mander
Marie Journet	Kay Harding
Sergeant Thompson	David Clyde
Drake	Ian Wolfe
Nora	Victoria Horne
Father Pierre	George Kirby

Cab Driver	Frank O'Connor
Storekeeper	Harry Allen

THE PEARL OF DEATH (Univ., 1944) 69 M.

Producer-director, Roy William Neill; author, Sir Arthur Conan Doyle; screenplay, Bertram Millhauser; camera, Virgil Miller; art director, John B. Goodman, Martin Obzine; editor, Ray Snyder.

Sherlock Holmes	Basil Rathbone
Doctor Watson	Nigel Bruce
Lestrade	Dennis Hoey
Naomi Drake	Evelyn Ankers
Giles Conover	Miles Mander
Amos Hodder	Ian Wolfe
Digby	Charles Francis
James Goodram	Holmes Herbert
Bates	Richard Nugent
Mrs. Hudson	Mary Gordon
The Creeper	Rondo Hatton
Teacher	Audrey Manners
Boss	Harold de Becker
Customs Officer	Leland Hodgson

THE HOUSE OF FEAR (Univ., 1945) 69 M.

Producer-director, Roy William Neill; author, Sir Arthur Conan Doyle; screenplay, Roy Chanslor; music director, Paul Sawtell; art director, John B. Goodman, Eugene Lowrie; camera, Virgil Miller; editor, Saul Goodkind.

Sherlock Holmes	Basil Rathbone
Doctor Watson	Nigel Bruce
Alastair	Aubrey Mather
Lestrade	Dennis Hoey
Simon Merrivale	Paul Cavanagh
Alan Cosgrave	Holmes Herbert
John Simpson	Harry Cording
Mrs. Monteith	Sally Shepherd
Chalmers	Gavin Muir
Alison MacGregor	Florette Hillier
Alex MacGregor	David Clyde
Guy Davies	Wilson Benge
Sergeant Bleeker	Leslie Denison
Angus	Alec Craig
King	Dick Alexander

THE WOMAN IN GREEN (Univ., 1945) 68 M.

Producer-Director, Roy William Neill; screenplay, Bertram Millhauser; music director, Mark Levant; art director, John B. Goodman, Martin Obzine; camera, Virgil Miller; editor, Edward Curtiss.

Sherlock Holmes	Basil Rathbone
Watson	Nigel Bruce
Lydia	Hillary Brooke
Moriarity	Henry Daniell
Fenwick	Paul Cavanagh
Inspector Gregson	Matthew Boulton
Maude	Eve Amber

Onslow	Frederick Worlock
Williams	Tom Bryson
Crandon	Sally Shepherd
Mrs. Hudson	Mary Gordon
Dr. Simnell	Percival Vivian
Norris	Olaf Hytten
Shabby Man	Harold De Becker
Newsman	Tommy Hughes

PURSUIT TO ALGIERS (Univ., 1945) 65 M.

Producer-director, Roy William Neill; author, Sir Arthur Conan Doyle; screenplay, Leonard Lee; camera, Paul Ivano; music director, Edgar Fairchild; art director, John B. Goodman, Martin Obzine; editor, Saul Goodkind.

Sherlock Holmes	Basil Rathbone
Dr. Watson	Nigel Bruce
Sheila	Marjorie Riordan
Agatha Dunham	Rosalind Ivan
Mirko	Martin Kosleck
Jodri	John Abbott
Prime Minister	Frederick Worlock
Sanford	Morton Lowry
Nikolas	Leslie Vincent
Kingston	Gerald Hamer
Gregor	Rex Evans
Restaurant Proprietor	Tom Dillon
Johansson	Sven Hugo Borg
Gubec	Wee Willie Davis
Clergyman	Wilson Benge
Ravez	Gregory Gay
Fuzzy Looking Woman	Dorothy Kellogg

TERROR BY NIGHT (Univ., 1946) 60 M.

Producer-director, Roy William Neill; author, Sir Arthur Conan Doyle; screenplay, Frank Gruber; camera, Maury Gertsman; music director, Mark Levant; art director; John B. Goodman; editor, Saul A. Goodkind.

Sherlock Holmes	Basil Rathbone
Dr. Watson	Nigel Bruce
Major Duncan Bleek	Alan Mowbray
Inspector Lestrade	Dennis Hoey
Vivian Wedder	Renee Godfrey
Lady Margaret	Mary Forbes
Trail Attendant	Billy Bevan
Prof. Kilbane	Frederick Worlock
Conductor	Leyland Hodgson
Ronald Carstairs	Geoffrey Steele
McDonald	Boyd Davis
Mrs. Shallcross	Janet Murdoch
Sands	Skelton Knaggs
Mr. Shallcross	Gerald Hamer
Mock	Harry Gording
Guard	Charles Knight
Mock, Jr.	Bobby Wissler

DRESSED TO KILL (Univ., 1946) 72 M.

Producer-director, Roy William Neill; author, Sir Arthur Conan Doyle; screenplay, Leonard Lee; music director, Milton Rosen; art director, Jack Otterson, Marvin Obzine; camera, Maury Gertsman; editor, Saul A. Goodkind.

Sherlock Holmes	Basil Rathbone
Doctor Watson	Nigel Bruce
Hilda Courtney	Patricia Morison
Gilbert Emery	Edmond Breon
Colonel Cavanaugh	Frederick Worlock
Inspector Hopkins	Carl Harbord
Evelyn Clifford	Patricia Cameron
Detective Thompson	Tom P. Dillon
Hamid	Harry Cording
Kilgour Child	Topsy Glyn
Housekeeper	Mary Gordon

TARZAN

The multi-media history of Tarzan is a long and profitable one. Edgar Rice Burroughs (1875–1950), an ex-miner and businessman-turned-writer, wrote his first Tarzan story in 1912. It appeared in the October issue of *All-Story Magazine*. The story was novelized in 1914 and published by A. C. McClurg. Altogether Burroughs wrote 26 *Tarzan* books, which are still in constant paperback republication. In 1918, the first *Tarzan* feature film was made, . . . *of the Apes,* starring Elmo Lincoln and Enid Markey. *Tarzan* came to radio in 1932 in a series of 364 pre-recorded fifteen-minute episodes starring Joan Burroughs Pierce (Burroughs's daughter) and husband, former *Tarzan* actor Jim Pierce. A new half-hour radio series began in 1951 with Carlton Kardell as the voice of the jungle man. In 1932, United Features Syndicate began its comic strip of *Tarzan,* originally drawn by Hal Foster. On September 8, 1966, the NBC-TV Network debuted the hour-long color *Tarzan* series with Ron Ely in the lead role and a host of guest stars ranging from Ethel Merman, Helen Hayes, and Julie Harris to Diana Ross and the Supremes. The show, which lasted two seasons, is now spawning theatrical feature films, which are being edited from the video episodes. To date, there have been 36 *Tarzan* feature films, four serials, and three combination feature-serials.

Although 15 actors have portrayed Tarzan in American-made motion pictures, the most enduring performance of the Ape Man has been that of former Olympic champion Johnny Weissmuller who swung, swam, and trumpeted his jungle call through fourteen productions of the series. Among those who played Tarzan before Weissmuller were Elmo Lincoln, Gene Pollar, P. Dempsey Tabler, Jim Pierce and Frank Merrill. Competing with Weissmuller for the jungle kingship in the early 1930s was Larry "Buster" Crabbe, who appeared in Principal's *Tarzan the Fearless,* released both as a serial and a 71-minute feature film. In 1935, *New Adventures of . . .* was issued as a serial and a 75-minute feature, and later reedited as . . . *and The Green Goddess.* It starred Herman Brix (later Bruce Bennett), another Olympic champion who was seeking the Tarzan crown. The film found the right mood.

Glenn Morris, the 1936 Olympic decathlon champion, played the lead part in Principal's . . .*'s Revenge,* giving a most static performance. Former playboy Lex Barker took over for Weissmuller in 1949 in . . .*'s Magic Fountain* and held the part for five entries. The eleventh Tarzan was an ex-Las Vegas lifeguard, Gordon Scott, who starred in . . .*'s Hidden Jungle*—the last RKO *Tarzan* film. Between Scott's fourth and fifth *Tarzan* vehicles, Denny Miller, former UCLA basketball star, gave a dismal performance in *Tarzan the Apeman* for a rival film studio. Jock Mahoney, ex-stuntman and former screen villain in . . . *the Magnificent,* performed his athletics in *Tarzan Goes to India* and . . .*'s Three Challenges.* Next came Mike Henry, previously a star linebacker for the Los Angeles Rams football team, who made a trio of *Tarzan* productions before bowing out of the genre. Texas born actor Ron Ely was the fifteenth Tarzan to appear in the American film media, having graduated from minor screen roles and a short-lived video series, *Malibu Run*.

To add a feminine and romantic touch to the *Tarzan* entries, the films at first utilized the Burroughs' character, Jane Porter. Most memorable of Tarzan's mates was Maureen O'Sullivan—who smiled, swam, cooked, cleaned and remained patient through six of the Weissmuller efforts. Never very happy with the lacklustre role, Miss O'Sullivan was most content to bow out of the treetop adventure yarns, when Sol Lesser moved the property from MGM to RKO in 1942. (In fact, through several of her Jane outings, she was pregnant and had to be placed behind high tables and food baskets to hide her bulging stomach.) RKO then utilized a rash of contract actresses to fill in for Tarzan's love interest: there was Frances Gifford as Zancra, white princess of a lost civilization, in . . . *Triumphs;* Nancy Kelly was a lost American magician carrying a vital message for the Allies in . . .'s *Desert Mystery* (Jane's absence was explained away by the statement that she was in England visiting relatives and nursing British soldiers). Then came Brenda Joyce as a blonde Jane, beginning with . . . *and the Amazons* and lasting for five chapters (lending additional color to these entries were such supporting second leads as Evelyn Ankers, Acquanetta, and Patricia Morison).

RKO replaced Joyce with Vanessa Brown in . . . *and the Slave Girl*, but Denise Darcel as Lola the half breed nurse who lusts after men—Tarzan in particular—stole the show. The next three Janes were competent portrayals at best of one-dimensional characterizations: Virginia Huston, Dorothy Hart, and Joyce MacKenzie (in the latter's entry . . . *and the She-Devil* Monique Van Vooren shone as Lyra a sinister temptress involved in illegal ivory trading. . . .'s *Hidden Jungle* omitted the Jane role, utilizing Vera Miles as nurse Jill Hardy. In . . . *and the Lost Safari* Yolande Donlan was Gamage Dean and Betta St. John was Diana Penrod, two of five passengers rescued from an air crash by Tarzan; Eva Brent was a desultory blonde Jane in . . .'s *Fight for Life*. Sara Shane was pert aviatrix Angie in . . .'s *Greatest Adventure,* and an oversensible Joanna Barnes as Jane lolled through . . . *the Ape Man,* a paltry remake of the 1932 epic. Betta St. John was Lionel Jeffries' wife on a police safari through the underbrush in . . . *the Magnificent.* Simi played Princess Kamara in . . . *Goes to India,* begging the jungle lord to help save a herd of 300 elephants. Tsuruko Kobayashi was Cho San, nursemaid to Kashi (Ricky Der), the prince of an oriental country, in . . .'s *Three Challenges.*

For the final trio of *Tarzan* features to date, Jane has also been missing: Nancy Kovack was the heroine Sophia in . . . *and the Valley of Gold;* Diana Millay was Dr. Ann Phillips, who accompanies Tarzan on a water trek to help a native village in peril, in . . . *and the Great River;* and Alicia Gure was Myrna Claudel, the heroine in despair in . . . *and the Jungle Boy.*

Although MGM scripters decided to give Tarzan and Jane a son in the fourth Weissmuller-O'Sullivan *Tarzan* motion picture, they felt it more decorous to have Boy (Johnny Sheffield) be the lone survivor of a plane crash, which killed his parents, Mr. and Mrs. Richard Lancing (Morton Lowry and Laraine Day). Sheffield romped through eight installments as the miniature Tarzan, agile as his new-found father in all athletic pursuits. By the time . . . *and the Mermaids* made its appearance Sheffield was fully grown. His absence was explained by the fact that he had gone to school in England. Not until . . .'s *Savage Fury* did another Boy substitute appear, Joey Tommy Carlton), whose presence on the Tarzan homefront was never adequately explained. . . .'s *Fight For Life* introduced a new son, Tartu (Rickie Sorenson). . . . *Goes to India* focuses on Jai as the young elephant boy, and Ricky Der was a fledgling oriental potentate in . . .'s *Three Challenges.*

Manuel Padilla, Jr.—who was to play Jai in the teleseries—appeared as Ramel, Tarzan's small companion in . . . *and the Valley of Gold,* and Pepe in . . . *and the Great River.*

The sound *Tarzan* feature films got off to a prestigious start in 1932, when Irving Thalberg, head of plush MGM, decided to activate the property on a grand scale. Unlike some later *Tarzan* films, this entry was shot entirely on the MGM backlot, soundstages, and Valley locations, utilizing leftover footage from the studio's *Trader Horn* (1930), which had been shot on location in Africa. The rather sensuous yet pure romance of Weissmuller's Tarzan and O'Sullivan's Jane set the tone that other directors after W. S. Van Dyke II would try to duplicate. The fact that in pre-Code 1932 Jane was allowed to wear a most flimsy jungle attire was remedied when more conservative elements took control in Hollywood. The highlights of the subsequent Tarzan films were always the idyllic swimming sequences with the king of the jungle, his mate, and later Boy. One of the campier elements (by later standards anyway) of the series was the monosyllabic dialogue given to Tarzan, largely of the *"Me Tarzan, you Jane, him Boy"* variety. Thus most of Weissmuller's emoting was saved for his shattering jungle yell, or his vine-swinging escapades.

The second MGM *Tarzan* entry was considered the best of the lot and a top notch adventure picture by any standards, with corrupt hunters invading the elephant grounds to carry on an illegal ivory trade. Involved in the fast paced plot were the expected native tribes on the warpath, a gorilla herd hurling boulders at the invading natives, and Tarzan battling a rhinoceros and a crocodile. The climax utilized a massive elephant stampede engineered by Tarzan to save Jane from being thrown to the lions.

Milestones of later *Tarzan* productions include: . . . *Escapes* which was filmed twice. The first unreleased version had been filmed as *The Capture of* . . . but it had too many gruesome scenes including barbaric native ritual murder, and marsh sequence filled with killer pygmies, devil bats, and oversized lizards. The film was reedited and additional scenes were added by Richard Thorpe, making it suitable for juvenile audiences. This . . . *Escapes* marked the beginning of the treehouse setting for future chapters and emphasized the comic relief role of the pet chimp Cheetah, whose precocious behavior supplied much footage for later entries. . . . *Finds a Son* introduced the orphan child Boy (Johnny Sheffield). The film was also noted for its reuse of the crocodile fight from . . . *and his Mate.* (Previously it had been utilized in . . . *Escapes.*) . . .'s *New York Adventure* brought the ape man to Manhattan and had him wear dress clothes for the first time in the series. The same crocodile combat scene appeared again in this film.

The first two RKO *Tarzan* films, both released in 1943, omitted Jane. These two chapters also introduced the then-timely element of Nazi enemies afoot in Africa fomenting trouble. Perhaps the low ebb of RKO *Tarzan* motion pictures was the second of these films . . .'s *Desert Mystery,* almost entirely filmed on soundstages, with hardly any expansive outdoor relief. The budget-conscious studio also utilized stock shots from *One Million B.C.* to show Tarzan battling prehistoric monsters.

. . .'s *Savage Fury* had Lex Barker, the new Tarzan, playing the jungle kind. His face was also used on a photograph used in the film of Lord Greystoke, Tarzan's father. This entry was also noted for the extensive dialogue given to Tarzan, and for the poor boxoffice returns.

. . . *and the Lost Safari* was the first entry to be filmed in color, and . . .'s *Fight for Life* was the last production helmed by the series's long-standing producer, Sol Lesser. The worst of the *Tarzan* pictures was MGM's remake of its . . . *The Ape Man* which utilized much tinted footage from the original masterpiece, and tossed in sequences from the studio's earlier *King Solomon's Mines* (1950).

. . . *and the Lost Safari* was filmed entirely on location in Africa. . . .'s *Greatest Adventure* was Sy Weintraub's first credit as producer of the series, and he altered the format by deleting Jane, intensifying the maturity of the dialogue, and increasing the already over-reliance on endless safaris to shape the plots. Cheetah's role diminished in the Weintraub films and sex was given a much lighter rein.

. . . *Goes to India* was shot in color and cinemascope on location in that country, a distinct departure from the African backdrop of all the earlier efforts. . . .'s *Three Challenges* had the new-breed Tarzan (played for the second time by Jock Mahoney) go to Thailand. The film boasted Hungry, a baby elephant, in a bid to find a new "cute" jungle companion for the ape man.

. . . *and the Valley of Gold* made a completely new style Tarzan come alive on the screen—almost a super agent who returns to the jungle only when necessary. His loincloth turned into a mini-garment, in the hopes of adding more sex appeal, and the hip Tarzan could use a gun as well as swing from tree to tree. In . . . *and the Valley of Gold* the chimp Dinky was much in evidence, helping Tarzan along with a pet lion and jaguar. This entry was shot on location in Mexico; . . . *and the Great River* was shot in Brazil, as well as the next adventure, . . . *and the Jungle Boy.*

The television Tarzan series was shot in Brazil and Mexico—to insure a curdling yell from new star Ron Ely, Johnny Weissmuller's original yell was dubbed into the opening credits.

Buster Crabbe. (Tarzan the Fearless)

Johnny Weissmuller, Maureen O'Sullivan, Paul Cavanagh, Neil Hamilton. (. . . and His Mate)

Ula Holt and Herman Brix (Bruce Bennett). (New Adventures of . . .)

Weissmuller, Johnny Sheffield, Maureen O'Sullivan. (. . . Finds a Son)

Weissmuller, Maureen O'Sullivan. (. . .'s Secret **Treasure**)

Weissmuller, Maureen O'Sullivan.

Russell Hicks, Eddy Chandler, Maureen O'Sullivan, Weissmuller, Howard Hickman, John Dilson, Paul Kelly, Philip Morris, Virginia Grey. (. . .'s New York Adventure)

Frances Gifford, Weissmuller, Johnny Sheffield. (. . . Triumphs)

Joe Sawyer, Weissmuller. (. . .'s Desert Mystery)

Weissmuller, Maria Ouspenskaya. (Shirley O'Hara on steps.) (. . . and the Amazons)

Sheffield, Brenda Joyce, Weissmuller. (. . . and the Huntress)

Charles Drake, Albert Dekker, Barker. (. . .'s Magic Fountain)

Lex Barker. (. . .'s Peril)

Gordon Scott, Vera Miles, Peter Van Eyck. (. . .'s Hidden Jungle)

Barker. (. . . and the She Devil)

Mahoney. (. . . Goes to India)

Scott, Gary Cockrell. (. . . the Magnificent)

Lionel Jeffries, Scott, Charles Tingwell. (. . . the Magnificent)

Woody Strode, Jock Mahoney. (. . .'s **Three Challenges**)

Barker, Tommy Carlton. (. . .'s **Savage Fury**)

Mike Henry. (. . . and the Great River)

Mike Henry. (. . . and the Great River)

Manuel Padilla Jr., Henry. (. . . and the Valley of Gold)

Henry, Ed Johnson, Alizia Gur, Steven Bond. (. . . and the Jungle Boy)

Ron Ely. (. . .'s Jungle Rebellion)

TARZAN

TARZAN, THE APE MAN (MGM, 1932) 99 M.

Director, W. S. Van Dyke; author, Edgar Rice Burroughs; screenplay, Cyril Hume; dialogue, Ivor Novello; camera, Harold Rosson, Clyde DeVinna; editor, Ben Lewis, Tom Held.

Tarzan	Johnny Weissmuller
Harry Holt	Neil Hamilton
Jane Parker	Maureen O'Sullivan
James Parker	C. Aubrey Smith
Mrs. Cutten	Doris Lloyd
Beamish	Forrester Harvey
Riano	Ivory Williams

TARZAN THE FEARLESS (Principal, 1933) M.

Producer, Sol Lesser; director, Robert Hill; adaptation, Basil Dickey, George Plympton, Walter Anthony.

Tarzan	Buster Crabbe
Mary Brooks	Jacqueline Wells
Dr. Brooks	E. Alyn Warren
Bob Hall	Edward Woods
Jeff	Philo McCollough
Nick	Matthew Betz
Abdul	Frank Lackteen
High Priest	Mischa Auer

TARZAN AND HIS MATE (MGM, 1934) 105 M.

Producer, Bernard H. Hyman; director, Cedric Gibbons; author, Edgar Rice Burroughs; screenplay, Howard Emmett Rogers, Leon Gordon; camera, Charles Clarke, Clyde De Vinna; editor, Tom Held.

Tarzan	Johnny Weissmuller
Jane Parker	Maureen O'Sullivan
Harry Holt	Neil Hamilton
Martin Arlington	Paul Cavanagh
Beamish	Forrester Harvey
Pierce	William Stack
Van Ness	Desmond Roberts
Saidi	Nathan Curry
Monsieur Gironde	Paul Porcasi

NEW ADVENTURES OF TARZAN (Burroughs Tarzan, 1935) 75 M.

Director, Edward Kull, W. F. McGaugh; adaptation, Charles F. Royal, Edwin H. Blum; scenario, Charles F. Royal; camera, Ernest F. Smith, Edward Kull.

Tarzan	Herman Brix
Ula Vale	Ula Holt
Major Martling	Frank Baker
Alice Martling	Dale Walsh
Gordon Hamilton	Harry Ernest
Raglan	Don Castello
George	Lewis Sergent

Bouchart	Merrill McCormick
Jiggs the Monkey	Herself

TARZAN ESCAPES (MGM, 1936) 95 M.

Associated producer, Sam Zimbalist; director, Richard Thorpe; screenplay, Cyril Hume; camera, Leonard Smith; editor, W. Donn Hayes.

Tarzan	Johnny Weissmuller
Jane	Maureen O'Sullivan
Captain Fry	John Buckler
Rita Parker	Benita Hume
Eric Parker	William Henry
Herbert Henry Rawlins	Herbert Mundin
Masters—the Resident	E. E. Clive
Bomba	Darby Jones
Cheetah	Herself

TARZAN'S REVENGE (20th, 1938) 70 M.

Producer, Sol Lesser; director, D. Ross Leterman; author, Edgar Rice Burroughs; screenplay, Robert Lee Johnston, Jay Vann; camera, George Meehan; editor, Gene Milford.

Tarzan	Glenn Morris
Eleanor	Eleanor Holm
Roger	C. Henry Gordon
Penny	Hedda Hopper
Nevin	George Meeker
Jigger	Corbet Morris
Olaf	Joe Sawyer
Koko	John Lester Johnson

TARZAN AND THE GREEN GODDESS (Principal, 1938) 72 M.

Director, Edward Kull; author, Edgar Rice Burroughs; adaptation, Charles F. Royal, Edwin H. Blum; scenario, Charles F. Royal; camera, Ernest F. Smith, Edward Kull.

Tarzan	Herman Brix
Ula Vale	Ula Holt
Major Martling	Frank Baker
Alice Martling	Dale Walsh
Gordon Hamilton	Harry Ernest
Raglan	Don Castello
George	Lewis Sergent
Bouchart	Merrill McCormick
Jiggs the Monkey	Herself

TARZAN FINDS A SON! (MGM, 1939) 90 M.

Producer, Sam Zimbalist; director, Richard Thorpe; screenplay, Cyril Hume; camera, Leonard Smith; editor, Frank Sullivan, Gene Ruggiero.

Tarzan	Johnny Weissmuller
Jane	Maureen O'Sullivan
Boy	John Sheffield

Austin Lancing	Ian Hunter
Sir Thomas Lancing	Henry Stephenson
Mrs. Lancing	Frieda Inescort
Mr. Sande	Henry Wilcoxon
Mrs. Richard Lancing	Laraine Day
Richard Lancing	Morton Lowry
Pilot	Gavin Muir

Sergeant	Sig Rumann
Patriarch	Pedro de Cordoba
Bausch	Philip Van Zandt
Archmet	Stanley Brown
Schmidt	Rex Williams
Cheta	Herself
German Soldier	Otto Reichow
German Soldier	Sven Hugo Borg

TARZAN'S SECRET TREASURE (MGM, 1941) 81 M.

Producer, B. P. Fineman; director, Richard Thorpe; screenplay, Myles Connolly, Paul Gangelin; art director, Cedric Gibbons; camera, Clyde De Vinna; editor, Gene Ruggiero.

Tarzan	Johnny Weissmuller
Jane	Maureen O'Sullivan
Boy	John Sheffield
Professor Elliott	Reginald Owen
O'Doul	Barry Fitzgerald
Medford	Tom Conway
Vandermeer	Philip Dorn
Tumbo	Cordell Hickman

TARZAN'S NEW YORK ADVENTURE (MGM, 1942) 71 M.

Producer, Frederick Stephani; director, Richard Thorpe; author, Myles Connolly; screenplay, Myles Connolly, William R. Lipman; music director, David Snell; art director, Cedric Gibbons; camera, Sidney Wagner; editor, Gene Ruggiero.

Tarzan	Johnny Weissmuller
Jane	Maureen O'Sullivan
Boy	John Sheffield
Connie Beach	Virginia Grey
Buck Rand	Charles Bickford
Jimmy Sheilds	Paul Kelly
Manchester Mountford	Chill Wills
Col. Sergeant	Cyrus W. Kendall
Judge Abbotson	Russell Hicks
Blake Norton	Howard Hickman
Gould Beaton	Charles Lane
Portmaster	Matthew Boulton
Doorman	Milton Kibbee
Sam	Mantan Moreland
Girl	Anne Jeffreys
Roustabout	Elmo Lincoln

TARZAN TRIUMPHS (RKO, 1943) 78 M.

Producer, Sol Lesser; director, William Thiele; author, Carroll Young; screenplay, Roy Chanslor, Carroll Young; art director, Hans Peters; music director, Paul Sawtell, C. Bakaleinikoff; camera, Harry Wild; editor, Hal Kern.

Tarzan	Johnny Weissmuller
Boy	Johnny Sheffield
Zandra	Frances Gifford
Col. Von Reichart	Stanley Ridges

TARZAN'S DESERT MYSTERY (RKO, 1943) 70 M.

Producer, Sol Lesser; associate producer, Kurt Neumann; director, William Thiele; author, Carroll Young; screenplay, Edward T. Lowe; art director, Hans Peters, Ralph Berger; music director, C. Bakaleinikoff; music, Paul Sawtell; camera, Harry Wild; Russ Harlan; editor, Ray Lockert.

Tarzan	Johnny Weissmuller
Boy	Johnny Sheffield
Connie Bryce	Nancy Kelly
Hendrix	Otto Kruger
Karl	Joe Sawyer
Prince Selim	Robert Lowery

TARZAN AND THE AMAZONS (RKO, 1945) 76 M.

Producer, Sol Lesser; associate producer, Kurt Neumann; director, Kurt Neumann; screenplay, Hans Jacoby, Marjorie L. Pfaelzer; art director, Walter Koessler; music director, Paul Sawtell; camera, Archie Stout; editor, Robert O. Crandall.

Tarzan	Johnny Weissmuller
Jane	Brenda Joyce
Boy	Johnny Sheffield
Henderson	Henry Stephenson
Amazon Queen	Maria Ouspenskaya
Ballister	Barton MacLane
Andres	Don Douglas
Splivers	J. M. Kerrigan
Athena	Shirley O'Hara
Brenner	Steven Geray

TARZAN AND THE LEOPARD WOMAN (RKO, 1946) 72 M.

Producer, Sol Lesser; associate producer, Kurt Neumann; director, Kurt Neumann; screenplay, Carroll Young; art director, Lewis Greber; music director, Paul Sawtell; camera, Karl Struss; editor, Robert O. Crandall.

Tarzan	Johnny Weissmuller
Jane	Brenda Joyce
Boy	Johnny Sheffield
Lea	Acquanetta
Lazar	Edgar Barrier
Kimba	Tommy Cook
Commissioner	Dennis Hoey
Mongo	Anthony Caruso
Corporal	George J. Lewis
Zambesi Maiden	Iris Flores

Zambesi Maiden	Lillian Molieri
Zambesi Maiden	Helen Gerald
Zambesi Maiden	Kay Solinas

TARZAN AND THE HUNTRESS (RKO, 1947) 72 M.

Producer, Sol Lesser; director, Kurt Neumann; author-screenplay, Jerry Gruskin, Rowland Leigh; music director, Paul Sawtell; art director, McClure Capps; camera, Archie Stout; editor, Merrill White.

Tarzan	Johnny Weissmuller
Jane	Brenda Joyce
Boy	Johnny Sheffield
Tanya	Patricia Morison
Weir	Barton MacLane
Marley	John Warburton
Smithers	Walter Scott
King Farrod	Charles Trowbridge
Prince Suli	Maurice Tauzen
Prince Ozira	Ted Hecht
Monak	Mickey Simpson
Cheta the Monkey	Herself

TARZAN AND THE MERMAIDS (RKO, 1948) 68 M.

Producer, Sol Lesser; director, Robert Florey; author-screenplay, Carroll Young; art director, McClure Capps; music director, Dimitri Tiomkin; camera, Jack Drapper; editor, Merrill White.

Tarzan	Johnny Weissmuller
Jane	Brenda Joyce
Mara	Linda Christian
Benji	John Lanenz
Varga	Fernando Wagner
Commissioner	Edward Ashley
Palanth	George Zucco
Luana	Andrea Palma
Tike	Gustavo Rojo
British Inspector General	Matthew Bolton

TARZAN'S MAGIC FOUNTAIN (RKO, 1949) 73 M.

Producer, Sol Lesser; director, Lee Sholem; screenplay, Curt Siodmak, Harry Chandlee; art director, McClure Capps; camera, Karl Struss; editor, Merrill White.

Tarzan	Lex Barker
Jane	Brenda Joyce
Gloria James	Evelyn Ankers
Trask	Albert Dekker
Dodd	Charles Drake
Jessup	Alan Napier
Vredak	Henry Kulky

TARZAN AND THE SLAVE GIRL (RKO, 1950) 74 M.

Producer, Sol Lesser; director, Lee Sholem; screenplay,

Hans Jacoby, Arnold Belgard; music director, Paul Sawtell; camera, Russell Harlan; editor, Christian Nyby.

Tarzan	Lex Barker
Jane	Vanessa Brown
Neil	Robert Alda
Prince	Hurd Hatfield
Doctor	Arthur Shields
Sengo	Tony Caruso
Lola	Denise Darcel
High Priest	Robert Warwick

TARZAN'S PERIL (RKO, 1951) 79 M.

Producer, Sol Lesser; director, Byron Haskin; screenplay, Samuel Newman, Francis Swann; art director, John Meehan; camera, Karl Struss; editor, John Murray.

Tarzan	Lex Barker
Jane	Virginia Huston
Radijeck	George Macready
Trask	Douglas Fowley
Andrews	Glenn Anders
Bulam	Frederick O'Neal
Melmendi	Dorothy Dandridge
Peters	Alan Napier
Connors	Edward Ashley
Nessi	James Moultrie
Barney	Walter Kingsford

TARZAN'S SAVAGE FURY (RKO, 1952) 80 M.

Producer, Sol Lesser; director, Cyril Endfield; associate director, Mack V. Wright; screenplay, Cyril Hume, Hans Jacoby, Shirley White; music director, Paul Sawtell; art director, Walter Keller; editor, Frank Sullivan.

Tarzan	Lex Barker
Jane	Dorothy Hart
Edwards	Patric Knowles
Rokov	Charles Korvin
Joey	Tommy Carlton

TARZAN AND THE SHE-DEVIL (RKO, 1953) 76 M.

Producer, Sol Lesser; director, Kurt Neumann; screenplay, Karl Lamb, Carroll Young; art director, Carroll Clark; music director, Paul Sawtell; editor, Leon Barsha.

Tarzan	Lex Barker
Jane	Joyce MacKenzie
Lyra	Monique Van Vooren
Vargo	Raymond Burr
Fidel	Tom Conway
Maka	Robert Bice
Selim	Mike Ross
M'Tara	Henry Brandon
Lavar	Michael Grainger
Cheta	Herself

TARZAN'S HIDDEN JUNGLE (RKO, 1955) 73 M.

Producer, Sol Lesser; director, Harold Schuster; screenplay, William Lively; art director, William Flannery; camera, William Whitley; editor, Leon Barsha.

Tarzan	Gordon Scott
Jill Hardy	Vera Miles
Dr. Celliers	Peter Van Eyck
Johnson	Don Beddoe
Witch Doctor	Jester Hairston
Sukulu Makumwa	Rex Ingram
Burger	Jack Elam
DeGroot	Charles Fredericks
Reeves	Richard Reeves
Malenki	Ike Jones
Suma	Madie Norman
Cheta	Herself
Lucky	Herself

TARZAN AND THE LOST SAFARI (MGM, 1957) 84 M.

Executive producer, Sol Lesser; producer, N. Peter Rathvon; director, Bruce Humberstone; screenplay, Montgomery Pittman, Lillie Hayward; art director, Geoffrey Drake; music, Clifton Parker; camera, C. R. Pennington-Richards.

Tarzan	Gordon Scott
"Tusker" Hawkins	Robert Beatty
Gamage Dean	Yolande Donlan
Diana Penrod	Betta St. John
"Doodles" Fletcher	Wilfrid Hyde White
Carl Kraski	George Coulouris
Dick Penrod	Peter Arne
Chief Ogonooro	Orlando Martins
Cheta	Herself

TARZAN'S FIGHT FOR LIFE (MGM, 1958) 86 M.

Producer, Sol Lesser; director, Bruce Humberstone; screenplay, Thomas Hal Phillips; music, Ernest Gold; assistant director, William Forsyth.

Tarzan	Gordon Scott
Jane	Eva Brent
Tantu	Rickie Sorensen
Anne Sturdy	Jill Jarmyn
Futa	James Edwards
Dr. Sturdy	Carl Benton Reid
Dr. Ken Warwick	Harry Lauter
Ramo	Woody Strode
High Counselor	Roy Glenn
Cheta	Herself

TARZAN'S GREATEST ADVENTURE (Par., 1959) 90 M.

Producer, Sy Weintraub, Harvey Hayuting; director, John Guillermin; author, Les Crutchfield; screenplay, John Guillermin, Bernie Giler.

Tarzan	Gordon Scott

Slade	Anthony Quayle
Angie	Sara Shane
Kruger	Niall McGinnis
O'Bannion	Sean Connery
Dino	Al Mulock

TARZAN, THE APE MAN (MGM, 1959) 82 M.

Producer, Al Zimbalist; director, Joseph Newman; screenplay, Robert Hill; art director, Hans Peters, Malcolm Brown; music, S. Rogers; camera, Paul C. Vogel; editor, Gene Ruggiero; (Remake of the 1932 film, with scenes from it).

Tarzan	Dennis Miller
Jane Parker	Joanna Barnes
Holt	Cesare Danova
Colonel Parker	Robert Douglas
Riano	Thomas Yangha

TARZAN THE MAGNIFICENT (Par., 1960) 88 M.

Producer, Sy Weintraub; director, Robert Day; screenplay, Berne Giler, Robert Day; music, Ken Jones; art director, Ray Simm; camera, Ted Scaife.

Tarzan	Gordon Scott
Coy Banton	Jock Mahoney
Fay Ames	Betta St. John
Abel Banton	John Carradine
Ames	Lionel Jeffries
Lori	Alexandra Stewart
Tate	Carl Cameron
Conway	Charles Tingwell
Martin Banton	Al Mulock
Johnny Banton	Gary Cockrell
Ethan Banton	Ron MacDonnell
Warrior Leader	Harry Baird
Native Chief	Christopher Carlos
Winters	John Sullivan

TARZAN GOES TO INDIA (MGM, 1962) 86 M.

Producer, Sy Weintraub; director, John Guillermin; screenplay, Robert Hardy Andrews, John Guillermin; music, Shankar, Jaikishhan.

Tarzan	Jock Mahoney
O'Hara	Mark Dana
Princess Kamara	Simi
Bryce	Leo Gordon
Rama	Feroz Khan
Maharajah	Murad
Elephant Boy	Jai

TARZAN'S THREE CHALLENGES (MGM, 1963) 92 M.

Producer, Sy Weintraub; director, Robert Day; screenplay, Bernie Giler, Robert Day.

Tarzan	Jock Mahoney

Tarim Khan	Woody Strode
Kashi	Ricky Der
Cho San	Tsuruko Kobayashi
Baby Elephant	Hungry

Myrna Claudel	Alizia Gur
Eric Brunik/Jukaro	Ronald Gans
Nagambi	Rafer Johnson
Ken Matson	Ed Johnson
Buharu	Steven Bond

TARZAN AND THE VALLEY OF GOLD (American International, 1966) 90 M.

Producer, Sy Weintraub; director, Robert Day; screenplay, Clair Huffaker; music Val Alexander; camera, Irving Lippman.

Tarzan	Mike Henry
Vinaro	David Opatoshu
Ramel	Manuel Padilla, Jr.
Sophia	Nancy Kovack
Mr. Train	Don Megowan
Rutz	Frank Bandstetter
Talmadge	Eduardo Noriega
Perez	Enrique Lucero
Manco	Francisco Riquerio
Romululo	Carlos Rivas
Rodriguez	Jorge Beirute
Antonio	Oswald Olvera

TARZAN AND THE GREAT RIVER (Par., 1967) 88 M.

Producer, Sy Weintraub; director, Robert Day; author, Bob Barbash, Lewis Reed; screenplay, Bob Barbash; art director, Herbert Smith; music, William Loose, Edward Marm, James Nelson; camera, Irving Lippman; editor, Anthony Carras.

Tarzan	Mike Henry
Captain Sam Bishop	Jan Murray
Pepe	Manuel Padilla, Jr.
Dr. Ann Phillips	Diana Millay
Barcuna	Rafer Johnson
Professor	Paulo Grazindo

TARZAN AND THE JUNGLE BOY (Par., 1968) 90 M.

Executive producer, Sy Weintraub; producer, Robert Day; director, Robert Gordon; screenplay, Stephen Lord; music, William Loose; camera, Ozen Sermet.

Tarzan	Mike Henry

TARZAN'S JUNGLE REBELLION (National General, 1970) 92 M.

Executive producer, Sy Weintraub; associate producer, Vernon E. Clark; production executive, Steve Shagan; director, William Witney; screenplay, Jack Gillis; camera, Abraham Vialla; editor, Gabriel Torres.

Tarzan	Ron Ely
Jai	Manuel Padilla, Jr.
Mary	Ulla Stromstedt
Singleton	Sam Jaffe
Tatakombi	William Marshall
Miller	Harry Lauter
Ramon	Jason Evers
Matto	Lloyd Haynes
Sargeant	Chuck Wood

TARZAN'S DEADLY SILENCE (National General, 1970) 88½ M.

Executive producer, Sy Weintraub; producer, Leon Benson; associate producer, Vernon E. Clark; production executive, Steve Shagan; director, Robert L. Friend, Lawrence Dobkin; screenplay, Lee Erwin, Jack A. Robinson, John Considine, Tim Considine; music, Walter Greene; camera, Abraham Vialla; editor, Gabriel Torres.

Tarzan	Ron Ely
Jai	Manuel Padilla, Jr.
The Colonel	Jock Mahoney
Marshak	Woodrow Strode
Chico	Gregorio Acosta
Officer	Rudolph Charles
Ruana	Michelle Nicols
Metusa	Robert Do Qui
Akaba	Kenneth Wm. Washington
Boru	Lupe Garnica
Okala	Jose Chaves
Tabor	Virgil Richardson

THE THIN MAN

Perhaps no other film series caught the mood of American ideology in the 1930s and 1940s as well as *The Thin Man* entries, produced by MGM between 1934 and 1946. The six grade A films starred William Powell and Myrna Loy as the screen's perfectly matched couple; who proved marriage could be just the beginning of an exciting relationship together. The series engagingly blended domestic comedy with fast paced detective melodrama. Powell was the invariably inebriated Nick Charles who practiced inductive sleuthing as a finely honed art, and Myrna Loy as Nora, who was smart enough for her husband and could be insultingly polite amidst her chitchat repartee in the drawing room or helping-hindering Nick in solving a case. Unlike the bulk of film series, *The Thin Man* films were top-quality productions, turned out at a leisurely rate, and always were top billed on major booking circuits of the theatres. (On radio, Nick Charles was played by Lester Damon, Les Tremayne, Joseph Curtin, and David Gothard, with Claudia Morgan as Nora, and Parker Fennelly as Ebenezer Williams, Sheriff of Crabtree County. On television, *The Thin Man* debuted on NBC September 20, 1957, with Peter Lawford and Phyllis Kirk as the stars for 72 half-hour episodes, and a new Asta as the wire haired terrier.)

William Powell, the epitome of screen suavity, was born July 29, 1892, in Pittsburgh, the son of a public accountant. He grew up in Kansas City and in 1911 entered the University of Kansas, only to withdraw after a few weeks. He attended the American Academy of Dramatic Arts and by 1912 was obtaining small roles in Broadway productions. In 1922, he made his cinema debut in John Barrymore's version of *Sherlock Holmes,* and was seen in *Beau Geste* (1926), *The Last Command* (1928), and others. After his talking film debut in *Interference* (1929), he appeared as detective Philo Vance in *The Canary Murder Case* (1929), which started him on a new career as a leading man. Powell moved to Warner Bros. where he frequently costarred with Kay Francis in romantic melodramas such as *One Way Passage* (1933). At MGM, his second film there was *The Thin Man,* for which he received an Oscar nomination. He appeared as *The Great Ziegfeld* (1934) *My Man Godfrey,* and *Crossroads* (1942) among others. For his portrayal of Clarence Day in *Life With Father* (1947), he received another Oscar nomination. By 1953, he was playing featured roles in *How to Marry a Millionaire;* in 1955 he made his 95th and last film to date, *Mister Roberts.* Powell has been twice married: to Eileen Wilson and Diana Lewis; he lives in retirement in southern California.

Myrna Loy (nee Williams) the chic screen wife, was born August 2, 1905, in Raidersburg, Montana, the daughter of a rancher. She grew up in Helena, Montana; in 1918 she moved to California. After graduating from Venice High School in 1923, she took a job in the chorus at Grauman's Chinese Theatre, making her motion picture debut in *Pretty Dadies* (1925). She then obtained a five-year contract at Warner Bros., playing a succession of oriental villainesses and vamps. She had top featured billing in *Fancy Baggage* (1929), a part talking comedy. After roles in *Emma* (1932), *The Animal Kingdom* (1932) and others, she played in a string of romantic tales such as *Test*

Pilot (1938) with Clark Gable, with sporadic returns to *The Thin Man* films. During World War II, she devoted herself to Red Cross Work, her only screen appearance being ". . . *Goes Home.* After the war came *The Best Years of Our Life* (1946), *The Bachelor and the Bobby Soxer* (1947) and such 1950s films as *Cheaper By the Dozen* (1950), *The Ambassador's Daughter* (1956) and *Lonelyhearts* (1958). In the 1960s she returned to stage work, with occasional film work: *From The Terrace, Midnight Lace* (1960) and *April Fools* (1969). Loy has been married to: Arthur Hornblower, Jr.; John Hertz, Jr.; Gene Markey, and Howard Sargeant. She currently resides in New York.

Based on Dashiell Hammett's 1934 detective novel, *The Thin Man* series followed its own special format, steeped in the author's exciting, unreal world. Nick Charles, a retired detective, is ostensibly business manager for his wealthy wife Nora. They reside in a plush San Francisco home. He spends most days at the race track or at home drinking scotch and soda. Inevitably, at the beginning of a *Thin Man* film, Nick has sworn off becoming involved in any more crime solving capers, but a pretty gal or a persuasive acquaintance implores his expert aid, and he relents. Then with Nora (and later Nick, Jr.) in tow and Asta the dog chewing up essential clues, Nick sets out on his deductive course. Before the climax, about three murders occur, and to wrap up the case, Nick and Nora usually invite the suspects to their apartment for a confrontation get together. The dull witted detective Lt. Abrams (played by Nat Pendleton, then by Sam Levine) appears off and on to lend his unskillful aid.

The initial *Thin Man* film was turned out in 14 days and earned over $2 million. W. S. Van Dyke directed the first five films, instilling them with a professional, if increasingly leisurely paced tempo. Dashiell Hammett wrote some of the screenplays for the series, giving vigor to the plot-line. While critics carped that the series and its leading characters were all too predictable and the routine of the Charles's life all too repetitious, the public flocked to the *Thin Man* productions; only *Song of the Thin Man* lost out at the boxoffice. Few people realized that the actual *Thin Man* character appeared only in the initial film, and that Edward Ellis had the supporting title role.

In *The Thin Man* a noted inventor is divorced because of an affair with his secretary. His ex-wife has remarried. The inventor learns that his girl friend has stolen $50,000 as well as carrying on with several other men. When she is found dead, the inventor's daughter, Dorothy Wynant (Maureen O'Sullivan), goes to Nick Charles for help. Nick and Nora, who are in New York, at Christmastime, on their honeymoon, investigate the case, and at a formal dinner expose the culprit. One episode in the film that took audiences aback occurred when Nick is being held at gunpoint by a hoodlum. To insure that Nora will be out of gun range, he clips her on the chin and she is knocked unconscious.

After . . ." finds the Charles duo back in San Francisco, midst the rich life of Nob Hill. Nora's cousin's husband disappears and the relative Selma (Elissa Landi) appeals to Nick to help out, informing the sleuth that her husband had been blackmailing her to finance his love affairs. Nick trails the missing man, Robert Landis (Alan Marshall), to Chinatown, where the latter is involved with songstress Polly Burnes (Penny Singleton)). Before the case is closed, there are two additional murders, and a total of seven suspects. In the by now typical denouement, the suspects are gathered together, and the criminal routed out and captured. A small sidelight of the film has Asta's loved one having pups.

In *Another . . .* Nick and Nora are parents of eight-month-old Nick, Jr. Nick, who is more domestic now, calls Nora "Moms," but he still is a wisecracker. The trio arrive in New York, where they spend a weekend on the Victorian estate of Colonel MacFay (C. Aubrey Smith). Their host is an explosives manufacturer, who believes his life is threatened by an ex-business associate, (Sheldon Leonard), whom he once had sent to prison for ten years. While still invulnerable to the effects of scotch and soda, Nick is not as astute as usual, and takes longer to sort out the red herrings and confront the suspect at the conclave meeting at his apartment.

In *Shadow of . . .* Nick agrees to help unravel a murder case involving race track manipulators. Among the suspects are: Link Stephens (Loring Smith) a big shot gambler; his associates Fred Macy (Joseph Anthony), and "Rainbow" Benny Loomis (Lou Lubin); and Link's blonde girl friend Claire Porter (Stella Adler). Fighting the crime ring are newspaper reporters "Whitey Barrow" (Alan Baxter), and Paul Clarke (Barry Nelson); Major Jason I. Sculley (Henry O'Neill), the head of the state athletic commission; and Lt. Abrams (Sam Levine). Another apartment confrontation climaxes the film.

... *Goes Home* shows Nick, Nora, and the baby going to Sycamore Springs. Nick's parents (Harry Davenport, Lucile Watson) are still disappointed that their son did not become a physician like the father. When the local painter is shot dead on the Charles's doorstep, Nick and Nora become entangled in sabotaging and spying incidents occurring in a local war plant. Nora is still the ever loving zany spouse, although Nick remains sober most of the film—since there is nothing but cider at Dr. Charles' home. As a result of Nick's amateur sleuthing, the suspects include: Laura Ronson (Gloria DeHaven) a rich society girl; Brogan (Edward Brophy) a traveling salesman; Bruce Clayworth (Lloyd Corrigan), a young doctor; and Edgar Draque (Leon Ames) a well-heeled crook.

Among the more bizarre murder victims is Crazy Mary (Anne Revere). One domestic highlight of the film has Nora bent over Nick's knee, receiving a thrashing for her misbehavior.

Song of ... concerns Nick's efforts to clear up a mysterious slaying on a big gambling ship. Keenan Wynn is "Clinker" Clarence Krause, a verbose, hip clarinetist who steers Nick to the many hangouts of after-hour musicians in trying to locate a missing bandsman, who holds the clue to the case. There are a trio of lovely bad dames to complicate the proceedings: Phyllis Talbin (Patricia Morison), Fran Page (Gloria Grahame), and Jayne Meadows as Janet Thayer, in love with a crafty gambler. Nick, Jr. (much grown up and portrayed this time by Dean Stockwell) becomes the object of the mobsters trying to stop Nick's snooping, but all the pieces fit together and the climax occurs.

William Powell, Myrna Loy. (The Thin Man)

Standing: Pat Flaherty, Charlie Williams. Myrna Loy,
Huey White, Powell, Ben Taggart, Harry Tenbrook.
(The Thin Man)

Elissa Landi, Powell, Myrna Loy. (After . . .)

Nat Pendleton, Powell, Myrna Loy, Otto Kruger. (An-other . . .)

Powell, Inez Cooper. (Shadow of the . . .)

Powell, William Anthony Poulsen, Myrna Loy. (Another . . .)

Myrna Loy, Powell, Dickie Hall, Asta. (Shadow of . . .)

Powell, Asta, Myrna Loy. (. . . Goes Home)

Myrna Loy, Powell. (. . . Goes Home)

Powell, Myrna Loy. (. . . Goes Home)

Powell, Myrna Loy. (Song of . . .)

Helen Vinson, Myrna Loy, Thomas Dillon, Powell, Anita Sharp-Bolster, Donald MacBride, Gloria De-Haven, Bill Hunter. (. . . Goes Home)

Keenan Wynn, Patricia Morison, Leon Ames, Myrna Loy, Powell. (Song of . . .)

THIN MAN

THE THIN MAN (MGM, 1934) 93 M.

Director, W. S. Van Dyke, II; author, Dashiell Hammett; screenplay, Albert Hackett, Frances Goodrich; camera, James Wong Howe; editor, Robert J. Kern.

Nick Charles .... William Powell
Nora Charles .... Myrna Loy
Dorothy Wynant .... Maureen O'Sullivan
Lt. John Guild .... Nat Pendleton
Mimi Wynant .... Minna Gombell
McCauley .... Porter Hall
Tommy .... Henry Wadsworth
Gilbert Wynant .... William Henry
Nunheim .... Harold Huber
Chris Jorgenson .... Cesar Romero
Julia Wolf .... Natalie Moorhead
Joe Morelli .... Edward Brophy
First Reporter .... Thomas Jackson
Mrs. Jorgenson .... Ruth Channing
Clyde Wynant .... Edward Ellis
Marion .... Gertrude Short
Stutsy Burke .... Walter Long
Reporter .... Creighton Hale

AFTER THE THIN MAN (MGM, 1936) 110 M.

Producer, Hunt Stromberg; director, W. S. Van Dyke, II; author, Dashiell Hammett; screenplay, Frances Goodrich and Albert Hackett; camera, Oliver T. Marsh; editor, Robert J. Kern.

Nora Charles .... Myrna Loy
Nick Charles .... William Powell
David Graham .... James Stewart
Dancer .... Joseph Calleia
Selma Landis .... Elissa Landi
Aunt Katherine Forrest .... Jessie Ralph
Robert Landis .... Alan Marshall
Lt. Abrams .... Sam Levene
Polly Byrnes .... Dorothy McNulty
                                (Penny Singleton)
Charlotte .... Dorothy Vaughn
Helen .... Maude Turner Gordon
Floyd Casper .... Teddy Hart
Lum Kee .... William Law
General .... William Burress
William .... Thomas Pogue
Dr. Adolph Kammer .... George Zucco
Henry (the butler .... Tom Ricketts
Phil Byrnes .... Paul Fix

ANOTHER THIN MAN (MGM, 1939) 102 M.

Producer, Hunt Stromberg; director, W. S. Van Dyke, II; author, Dashiell Hammett; screenplay, Frances Goodrich, Albert Hackett; art director, Cedric Gibbons; music, Edward Ward; camera, Oliver T. Marsh, William Daniels; editor, Frederick Y. Smith.

Nick Charles .... William Powell

Nora Charles .... Myrna Loy
Col. Burr MacFay .... C. Aubrey Smith
Van Slack .... Otto Kruger
Lieut. Guild .... Nat Pendleton
Lois MacFay .... Virginia Grey
Freddie Coleman .... Tom Neal
Smitty .... Muriel Hutchison
Dorothy Waters .... Ruth Hussey
Phil. Church .... Sheldon Leonard
Mrs. Bellam .... Phyllis Gordon
"Diamond Back" Vogel .... Don Costello
Dudley Horn .... Patric Knowles
"Creeps" Binder .... Harry Bellaver
Dum-Dum .... Abner Biberman
Mrs. Dolley (landlady) .... Marjorie Main
Asta .... Himself

SHADOW OF THE THIN MAN (MGM, 1941) 97 M.

Producer, Hunt Stromberg; director, W. S. Van Dyke, II; author, Harry Kurnitz; screenplay, Irving Brecher, Harry Kurnitz; camera, William Daniels; editor, Robert J. Kern.

Nick Charles .... William Powell
Nora Charles .... Myrna Loy
Paul Clarke .... Barry Nelson
Molly Ford .... Donna Reed
Lieutenant Abrams .... Sam Levene
Whitey Barrow .... Alan Baxter
Nick Charles, Jr. .... Dickie Hall
Link Stephens .... Loring Smith
Fred Macy .... Joseph Anthony
Major Jason I. Sculley .... Henry O'Neill
Claire Porter .... Stella Adler
"Rainbow" Benny Loomis .... Lou Lubin
Stella .... Louise Beavers
Maguire .... Will Wright
Policeman .... Robert Kellard

THE THIN MAN GOES HOME (MGM, 1944) 100 M.

Producer, Everett Riskin; director, Richard Thorpe; author, Robert Riskin; screenplay, Robert Riskin, Dwight Taylor; music director, David Snell; art director, Cedric Gibbons, Edward Carfagno; camera, Karl Freund; editor, Ralph E. Winters.

Nick Charles .... William Powell
Nora Charles .... Myrna Loy
Mrs. Charles .... Lucile Watson
Laura Ronson .... Gloria DeHaven
Crazy Mary .... Anne Revere
Dr. Charles .... Harry Davenport
Helena Draque .... Helen Vinson
Bruce Clayworth .... Lloyd Corrigan
Willie Crump .... Donald Meek
Brogan .... Edward Brophy
Edgar Draque .... Leon Ames
Tom Clayworth .... Paul Langton
Chief MacGregor .... Donald MacBride

Sam Ronson	Minor Watson	Nora Charles	Myrna Loy
Fat Man	Rex Evans	Clarence Krause (Clinker)	Keenan Wynn
Woman With Baby	Connie Gilchrist	Nick Charles, Jr.	Dean Stockwell
Tom—Proprietor	Irving Bacon	Tommy Drake	Philip Reed
First Man	Mike Mazurki	Phyllis Talbin	Patricia Morison
		Fran Page	Gloria Grahame
		Janet Thayar	Jayne Meadows
		Buddy Hollis	Don Taylor

SONG OF THE THIN MAN (MGM, 1947) 86 M.

Mitchell Talbin	Leon Ames
David I. Thayer	Ralph Morgan
Bertha	Connie Gilchrist
Helen Amboy	Marie Windsor
Asta	Asta, Jr.
Headwaiter	George Sorel
Dr. Monolaw	Warner Anderson
Al Amboy	William Bishop

Producer, Nat Perrin; director, Eddie Buzzell; author, Stanley Roberts; screenplay, Steve Fisher, Nat Perrin; art director, Cedric Gibbons, Randall Duell; music director, David Snell; camera, Charles Rosher; editor, Gene Ruggiero.

Nick Charles	William Powell